A HISTORY
OF POWER
IN EUROPE

Wim Blockmans

A HISTORY OF POWER IN EUROPE

Peoples
Markets
States

Preface Jacques Santer, *President of the European Commission*
Epilogue Marcelino Oreja Aguirre, *Member of the European Commission*

Fonds Mercator Paribas
distibuted by Harry N. Abrams, Inc., Publishers

Picture research and captions: An Delva

Translation: Alastair Weir
in association with First Edition Translations Ltd, Cambridge, UK

© 1997 Fonds Mercator, Antwerp

D/1997/703/6
ISBN 90 6153 383 x

Distributed in North America in 1997
by Harry N. Abrams, Incorporated, New York
ISBN 0-8109-6347-7

Frontispiece:
**Ceremonial opening of the English Parliament
in April 1523 in the presence of King Henry VIII.
The judges sit in scarlet robes on large woolsacks
in the middle of the chamber.
Windsor Castle, Royal Collection**

Contents

Preface

History is, in many respects, a matter of the balance of power, of force and counterforce. And underlying this concept is the notion of strength. This work, by Professor Wim Blockmans, is a skilful analysis of the interplay of power in Europe during the last thousand years, focusing on three key aspects: State, nation and the marketplace. It is an examination of the interaction between these three factors – the political (the States), the cultural (the nations) and the economic (the marketplace). And, judging by the interesting results it has produced, it is a rewarding approach to take.

From historical works published over the last decade it has become increasingly clear that Europe as an entity is a very old concept, older than the States that comprise it. It dates back to an encounter between the Roman Empire – and its romanic peoples – and the Germanic and Slavonic nations. However, this was not all. The encounter between these groups was further enriched by the contributions made to European civilisation by the Arab world – of particular importance during the Middle Ages – and by such peoples as the Magyars and the Finns who, though initially isolated, found their place within Europe.

From these numerous encounters there soon emerged a series of kingdoms: France and Germany – in the form of *Francia occidentalis* and *orientalis* – England, Spain (Castile and Aragon), Portugal, but also Poland, Hungary, Serbia, Bulgaria and others. From these kingdoms States of a more permanent nature developed, the majority of which, in the form of nation-states, now constitute contemporary Europe, though not necessarily within the same borders they occupied in the past.

In the second half of the twentieth century, a period dominated by the concept of European integration, this is a fact of importance to politicians. The European community was built – and continues to be built – on the foundation of its States. Contrary to certain expectations in the immediate post-war period, the aim of the Community was not to put an end to these States. However the nature of history is, by definition, one of evolution and even revolution. Nothing escapes the ravages of time – a nation no more than a State. During the course of this second millennium States have changed a great deal – from feudal monarchies to absolute monarchies, from 'enlightened despotism' to nation-states. The totalitarian, communist and fascist States produced by the twentieth century can be seen as both a culmination and also an aberration of this long ascent towards power.

In fact, since then, we have seen a reversal which might well signal a complete change of trend. Although Western European States now have the financial resources and the means at their disposal that their eighteenth- and nineteenth-century predecessors could only dream of, their power has actually diminished. For the first time in the history of Europe States have voluntarily given up a share of their sovereignty in favour of an organisation on a higher level – the European Community. This has meant that, thanks to the bold concepts of Jean Monnet, the European Community has, from the outset, gone beyond the framework of a traditional confederation. The strength of the nation-state has, however, prevented the Community from developing into a federal body.

In 1882, Ernest Renan, speaking at the Sorbonne stated that 'Nations are not eternal. They began and they will come to an end. The European confederation will probably replace them. But this is not within the compass of the century in which we are living'.

The nineteenth century has gone down in history as the century of nations, but the twentieth century has proved itself to be equally so. What Renan was, however, unable to foresee was that the unifying process would begin with the economy. A work such as this demonstrates clearly the power of the marketplace in European history. Is it perhaps possible that the market will dominate other forces of a political and cultural nature? Will we see the values of the market economy triumph? On a purely national level States and nations would not be in a sufficiently strong position to take up such a challenge. Only a united Europe is capable of defending the values it has established over the course of the centuries.

To gain a true understanding of Europe we need to view it from two different angles: the retrospective view of the historian and the forward-looking approach taken in general by men of action, and by politicians in particular. This work provides an excellent analysis of the dynamics of power in Europe. It now falls to the politicians to provide a prospect for the future based on projects to be achieved through our mutual cooperation.

Jacques Santer
President of the European Commission

FOREWORD

It is, of course, presumptuous to want to write a book about such a fundamental aspect of European history as power, and that over a period of a thousand years. Nobody nowadays can still profess to be able to command a first-hand knowledge of the immense quantity of academic literature about so wide a subject. Any dwarf who wants to attempt it must hoist himself onto the shoulders of giants.

So did this author. He was inspired by the work of the American sociologists Charles Tilly and Michael Mann, who propounded fundamental and innovative insights into the long-term development of European states. He also enjoyed the inspiration of a large-scale research programme by the European Science Foundation, in which some hundred scholars from twenty countries took part. They examined aspect by aspect the Origin of the Modern State in Europe from 1300 to 1800. This book is heavily indebted to discussions with these many colleagues, and to perusal of their publications. It was particularly important that this collaboration made it possible to break through the barriers of national frontiers, which still constrict so much academic work.

Originally this book was conceived as an analysis of the development of state power in Europe. During the 1980s there was animated discussion about the tasks and functions of the state. Many people thought that these needed to be 'slimmed down' because the state had assumed too much power to itself. Large-scale waves of privatization were set in hand in which even institutions which everyone had previously thought to be of 'public utility' and not necessarily needing to

be profit-making, such as museums and record offices, were dragged along. Research into the origin of this functional shift might increase understanding of the proper role of states and public authorities in general. At the same time it must, however, be said that by now states have for some time not been exercising as much power as was claimed. The state is part of a specific stage of historical development, which is already coming to an end. There have always been other active nuclei of power, and now some of these even appear to be becoming more influential than the much maligned states. The focus of this book therefore shifted from the state to the diversity of configurations of power, in particular to those in the economic and cultural areas, in the hope that this might clarify the current discussion about the role of the state.

In the light of its scale and ambition, this book cannot offer any complete factual account. Indeed, such manuals already exist. It aims to concentrate on the interaction of power configurations in the areas of politics, economics and cultures over a thousand years. If rulers strive to maximize their potentialities, they will have to develop them in these three fundamental areas of human activity. The option of covering the period from about AD 1000 until the present day has been chosen in the conviction that this defines a continuous historical process. Any later starting point would disregard the fundamental roots of this development. To trace the continuity through to today justifies the role of the historian in present-day society.

The vicissitudes of fate.
Moralists warned the great of the earth that they, too,
cannot escape the wheel of Dame Fortune. Miniature (1503)
from a French translation of Petrarch's
De remediis utriusque fortunae.
Paris, Bibliothèque nationale de France

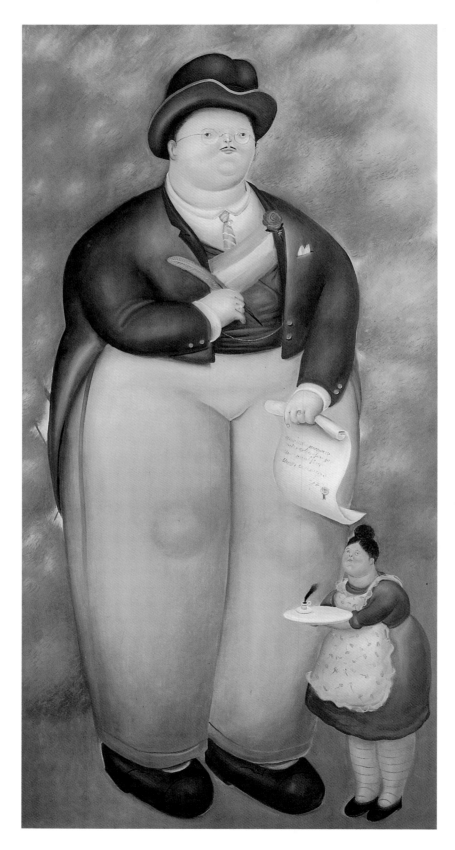

Fernando Botero, *The president*, 1969. Munich, Bayerische Staatsgemäldesammlungen, Neue Pinakothek

Alfred Kubin, *Power,* 1903. Pen drawing.

Munich, Städtische Galerie im Lehnbachhaus

King Louis XII of France (1498–1515) sits enthroned under a baldaquin;
his head is in profile just like the nine illustrious Roman emperors in the border.   Paris, Bibliothèque nationale de France

INTRODUCTION
General principles and a wide scope

Two opposite movements

Just when the rich and self-satisfied Europe of the Twelve was preparing itself to celebrate the unification of the internal market on 31 December 1992, it was unexpectedly confronted with that other Europe, which for forty-five years had been so inextricably shackled behind the Iron Curtain. Before the amazed eyes of observers and of those involved, a series of events unprecedented in history occurred at high speed: the voluntary withdrawal of the Soviet imperium from Afghanistan and from the countries it had occupied since the end of the Second World War, and the internal disintegration of the Soviet Union itself. Scarcely ten years earlier the USSR had still looked like a menacing world power, surrounded by a broad *cordon sanitaire*, whose arms and, above all, whose ideology used to inspire the Third World to wars of liberation.

In the presence of such radical, fast and especially unexpected changes, people are asking how and why. How is it conceivable that in western Europe unification constantly gains strength, while at the same moment the Soviet empire disintegrates, and the former Yugoslavia, too, reverts to an atavistic civil war? Why is it that two such opposite movements occur at the same time in the same continent? How is it possible that nationalism and religion, which in western Europe are rallying cries of decreasing power, appear in eastern Europe to be precisely the uniting forces for which people are prepared to fight to the last and even commit genocide? What then underpins the unity of the various peoples and states in the west, while in the Soviet Union seventy years of political unity and linguistic

and ideological harmonization have apparently only given a new lease of life to the old values of God and the mother country? Is there, in the light of all these contradictions, indeed a 'common European house', or does this continent really consist of two incompatible spheres?

All these questions point to the bonds holding people together. The developments in the former Soviet Union and Yugoslavia – and to a considerably lesser degree also those in Czechoslovakia and relating to the reunification of Germany – show that national consciousness and religious faith are still very much live forces there, with a formidable power to mobilize the masses, unaffected by many decades of power exercised by a state with very different ideas. State, religion and people therefore seem to be three different uniting forces, often working independently of each other. They developed at different points in time from their own dynamic, answering to different needs. The way in which political, religious and national entities influenced each other produced a variety of forms of society.

Over the centuries Europe has always shown a tendency towards the formation of empires, extensive political unions made up of many peoples and cultures. The memory of the Roman empire ran through the mind of every ruler who had substantially expanded his territory. The emperors of Byzantium quite rightly saw themselves as the direct inheritors of the imperial crown. They handed on this ambition both to their Turkish conquerors and to the Russian tsars. In the west, Charlemagne was the first to see himself awarded a new imperial crown,

The great imperial stride of Catherine the Great (Catherine II), empress of Russia (1762–1796).

This French satirical print warns against Russian expansion towards the Mediterranean. Paris, Bibliothèque nationale de France, Estampes

Napoleon was inspired by many aspects of the symbolism of Roman power, as he demonstrated in his consecration as emperor in 1804.

In contrast to the kings of France, he took the coronation ritual out of the hands of the clergy. Detail from the painting by J.L. David.

Paris, Musée du Louvre

in 800 – in Rome, and not by chance in that particular city. In doing so he moved imperial ambition away from the area around the Mediterranean to the much less developed region between the Meuse and the Rhine. The Holy Roman Empire lasted in name until 1806 – after which there were still to be the Second (in 1872) and Third (in 1933) *Reich* – but an effectively centralized state power was never created in those thousand years. In central and eastern Europe, however, empires were more significant. In the sixteenth century the Ottoman empire expanded into the Balkans and even laid its hands on Hungary. From the middle of the seventeenth century both Austria and Russia grew into empires which first opposed the Ottoman empire and then each other. The First World War sealed the fate of all three. Their inheritance was a mishmash of peoples and small states which had been thoroughly shuffled up among each other by centuries of wars, but had acquired sharply defined identities from the numerous confrontations with the dominant imperial power. The Second World War offered the Soviet Union the opportunity to take up again the Russian imperial tradition, beginning with the seizure of eastern Poland in 1939 and the Baltic States in 1940. The year 1989 brought an end to this hegemony.

Imperial ambitions were not exclusive to central and eastern Europe. The Napoleonic empire overran large parts of Europe for several years, and linked up with Roman tradition in its symbolism. The classical designs of triumphal arches, quadrigas, columns, laurel wreaths and fasces were adopted by the imperial regimes who in the nineteenth century needed to lend some extra substance to their various authoritative states: France from 1852 to 1870, Germany from 1872 to 1918, Britain – in title only – in India from 1876 to 1947. Italian fascism and German nazism both revealed themselves as imperial powers, but stopped just short of calling their leaders emperors. All these western empires were, however, only able to maintain substantial territorial expansion in Europe for a few years. Britain, too, had to abandon its sovereignty over most of Ireland in 1921, and is still in trouble in the remainder. The difference with eastern Europe is striking: in the east the territorial expanse was immense, almost unlimited, whereas in the west each expansion was immediately checked by the opposition of the surrounding powers. Each empire, however, was vulnerable from the great diversity of peoples within its unmeasurable frontiers. In the field of religion there was greater homogeneity: the Catholic Church supported the Austrian empire which in its

turn served the Church, just as the Ottoman and the Russian empires leaned respectively on Islam and on the established Orthodox Church.

It is certainly no accident that far-flung empires could thrive in eastern, but not in western Europe. For many centuries the forms of their societies have, after all, displayed fundamental differences. The long-lasting empires in central, south-east and eastern Europe could maintain themselves because they were supported by archaic societies. Their populations, spread very thinly over extended territories, had few contacts with the outside world, and therefore retained an absolute faith in the unchanging values of their ancestral traditions. It was precisely the lack of mutual contacts between peoples which made the domination of an imperial power supported by great landowners possible. Apart from that, these empires lacked both the power and the will to bring western culture to their subjects. In exchange for their support the central authorities granted the great landowners extensive power to keep the peasants in their domains under the knout. The exceptionally large-scale bureaucracies of these empires are therefore characterized by their extremely limited power to communicate with their own subjects. In fact, control of the interior was left to the great landowners, who exercised it at their own discretion and above all in their own interests. Peasant revolts offered only some occasional and never enduring resistance to this exploitation.

In the west, on the other hand, societies were more diversified in status, rank and class. The market economy introduced commercialization and diversification of crops into agriculture. In the vicinity of the towns intensive methods of cultivation gained ground, making the emergence of a class of independent farmers possible. In the towns themselves lived citizens whose legal charters had been divorced from the structures of feudal power since the Middle Ages. Various social groups were formed for the protection of professional interests. Urban life was certainly rich in dissension, but this taught them to develop mechanisms to resolve conflicts of interest with proper regard for everyone's rights. The towns were the cradle of public forms of government supported by the participation of differing segments of the population. The economic, demographic and cultural weight of the towns determined the balance of power in western European societies. In heavily urbanized areas the aristocracy could not maintain its dominance as it was still able to do in the east until the late nineteenth century. Various checks and balances arose, in which the

Later European emperors employed not only symbols
but also authentic Roman artefacts to display their imperial grandeur.
Charles VI had two Roman columns put on either side of the Karlskirche in Vienna (1716–1737).
Watercolour of *c.* 1790 by Lorenz Janscha. Vienna, Graphische Sammlung Albertina

proximity of many rival power centres became an ever present factor in the power equation. No single player in the west was successful in exercising total dominance over other social groups for long: the opportunity for alternative coalitions with opponents, inside or outside the system, was too real. Thus in the west a pattern of society developed in which many players in similar or different social positions held each other in balance, and were therefore forced to work out peaceful procedures for consultation. Parliamentary democracy is a creation of western Europe based on these multilateral divisions of power.

In 1991, with the crumbling of the Soviet Union, the last remnants of the imperial form of state seemed to have disappeared from Europe. In view of the oppressive nature of every empire such an evolution can be interpreted as a delayed emancipation and modernization. At the same time the west is again much further ahead, in the construction, *from the bottom up*, of a federal union of states which allows all participants equal partnership. In this way a new stage is reached in the relationship between states and their peoples, as the states transfer authority and resources to supranational institutions.

In the long term, and discounting the many vicissitudes of history, there seems to be a continuous tendency towards the expansion of the range of at least certain types of power apparatus. The exercise of power always shows various facets which in the past have often been expressed by separate organizations, such as churches, states or national traditions. Increases in scale and the expansion of authority of state institutions inevitably increased their contacts with their subjects. Was the expansion of the power of the state accompanied by an equivalent loss of power by the churches and by the representatives of older national traditions? What happens to the influence of these entities when there is a further increase in scale of the power of the state towards supranational organizations? At the moment that the split development of western and eastern Europe draws attention to the different paths of development displayed for centuries by the old continent, I want to examine in this book the significance of the various configurations of power in European history. Among them states are the most striking, but certainly never the only ones. Why have new states arisen during the last thousand years and up to today at such different points of time? Why do

The tree as the principle of hierarchic order, in this case representing the three Estates of medieval society: the priesthood, the knights and the burghers. The positioning of the pope above King Charles VII and the Dauphin of France is as significant here as the dedication of this manuscript by the Constable of Brittany, Arthur of Richmond (1393–1458), who played an important role in driving out the English, but was at least temporarily able to keep Brittany independent.

Paris, Bibliothèque de l'Arsenal

The labour movement hoped to achieve an improvement in the lot of the workers
by gaining political power in general elections.
The French socialist leader Jean Jaurès paid for his principles by his death in 1914.
Paris, Musée Carnavalet

they have the peculiar shapes shown on the maps? Why were they always acquiring ever more sweeping powers, while they lost others? Was the role of the states really so beneficial for their subjects as the schoolbooks would have us think? Were there any alternatives? And finally, why is it that in the west the power of the state appears to be moving on to levels of an even greater scale, while in the east a contrary evolution appears to be occurring?

Three integrative forces

In distinguishing three kinds of social systems – states, religions and peoples – the question is whether we take account of enough factors to understand all the aspects of the process of power formation in Europe. Until now one factor has been left out of consideration, which at least in the former Soviet Union and the countries of the eastern bloc seems to be of crucial importance. Was it not in the end the bankruptcy of the socialist economy

which forced the political regimes to start reforms? Did they not everywhere move in the direction of openings for the free market economy? Do not economic circumstances therefore form an essential factor in the explanation of the fall of the socialist regimes in central and eastern Europe? Let us therefore examine whether this factor, too, in a general sense should be involved in our consideration. This would then mean that we would in practice concentrate the very general concept of power on the control of the means of satisfying material needs (means of subsistence and wealth), as well as of the means of compulsion mentioned earlier and those of persuasion (collective values and identities or, in other words, cultures).

A state exercises power from a decision centre within a finite territory. To do this at all effectively, it must have a superiority in the instruments of power over all separate concentrations of power within its territory. At the start of this chapter we established that in the very recent developments nationality and religion are to be identified as forces creating and

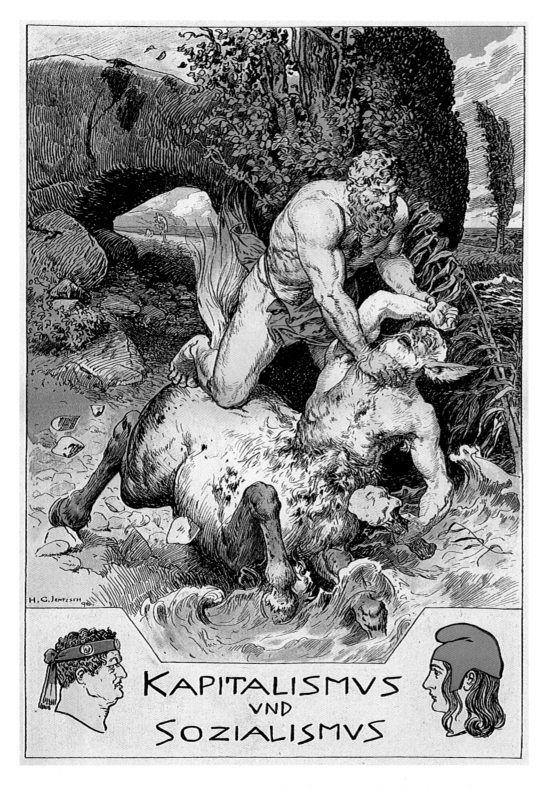

The battle between capitalism and socialism. Coloured pen drawing of 1896 by H.C. Jentzsch.

In this satirical print Hercules, the symbol of socialism, defeats the centaur Nessus, symbol of capitalism.

The conflict is reflected again below, by a grim-looking Roman emperor

and Marianne, symbol of the French revolution.

Amsterdam, International Institute for Social History

The characters of Gunnlöð and Þokk from the Prose Edda are part of Iceland's cultural heritage.
The image of a famous common past forms the basis of every national consciousness.
Illustrations from a late seventeenth-century manuscript.
Reykjavik, The Arnamagnaean Institute

dissolving states. In so far as a people is convinced that the satisfaction of its legitimate desires depends on a state of its own, the self-consciousness of the subjects plays a great role in the breaking-up of empires and the founding of new political units, usually smaller states. Here, therefore, the integrating force of the national consciousness, whether or not reinforced by a specific religious denomination, appears to compete with the efforts that states also display in this respect. The claim to exercise power – that is to say, to arrange the distribution of the means of subsistence in a society in a regulated way – can therefore be disputed to states on the grounds of their assumed failure in the protection of what is legitimately felt to be the cultural interests of some of their subjects.

In the development of Europe, religious denominations are in most cases the oldest models of institutionalization. In most parts of the continent Christianity was established as an organization during the first millennium of our era, though in the peripheral areas there was still to be a delay of some centuries. For instance, in southern Spain

Islam was only gradually forced back and only entirely driven out in the decades after the fall of Granada in 1492. The conversion of Scandinavia and East Prussia was only completed in the late Middle Ages. On the other hand, the Reformation and the wars of religion in the late sixteenth and seventeenth centuries in many parts of the continent also brought about numerous state-imposed adjustments to the religious map of Europe. The structure and operations of the churches are therefore undoubtedly factors which influenced the configurations of power in a variety of ways.

The bases for ethnic and linguistic identities, too, were mostly already laid down before AD 1000. Here, however, migrations and processes of assimilation have also by now brought about substantial changes, making the link between people and territory a very tenuous one. Which culture can justify an exclusive right to a piece of land: the first occupant or whatever group later becomes dominant? How far back in time should one go to determine whose rights are the oldest? And why should the oldest rights be unalterable?

Breton society retained its cultural traditions until around 1900.

Paul Gauguin shows the piety of peasant women in his *Yellow Christ* (1889).

Buffalo, NY, Albright Art Gallery

Both religion and language profoundly determine the nature of individuals and communities, because from the first thoughts, words or actions they impress their stamp on an individual, so that he can be integrated into the group. They are therefore seen by those concerned as unassailable. Governments which do not show enough attention and respect for them trample on the souls of their subjects and can expect resistance sooner or later. As political powers – which expanded into ever larger and more powerful states – consolidated themselves in most parts of Europe *after* the religious structures had already become embedded there and the identity of its peoples had already taken shape, they had to take account of these earlier realities. The tensions between people, religion and the state have become basic facts of European history. The more the power of the state spread over more extensive territories, and within them began to interfere in more aspects of life, the more it also met opposing forces grouped round the primary identities of people and religion. The past thousand years of European history clearly show an abundance of integration processes, which by their nature never displayed a linear development. Many have been interrupted, forced into reverse, or delayed. Efforts towards integration were in no sense limited to the political field; they were, for example, also manifested in the universalism of the Catholic Church. Trade networks can also be seen as an integrative force. It is clear that since AD 1000 political units have become larger, more comprehensive, and therefore less numerous. A multitude of seigneuries grew into more integrated counties and duchies, and from these emerged larger kingdoms which, in turn, absorbed further border principalities. The process of expansion in size was by no means either uniform or simultaneous: in 1800 the Holy Roman Empire still consisted of some three hundred almost autonomous territories, and even now mini-states such as Liechtenstein, Andorra, San Marino and Monaco still exist. Until 1989, however, the general tendency was unmistakably towards the creation of larger units. On the basis of the west European experience one could venture the hypothesis that, once the nations which since 1989 have freed themselves from the dominance of empires and larger neighbouring peoples have consolidated themselves into new states, larger combinations will again grow out of these, though probably on a voluntary basis.

It is not only on the political plane that the tendency towards steady expansion can be observed; it is probably even more clearly visible in the economy, where in a millennium the extent of markets has grown from a half-day's journey on foot to cover the whole world. The world economy runs on an all-embracing system of division of labour and integrated markets which ensures that the products we buy are a construct of entrepreneurial spirit, labour, capital and raw materials from every continent. To the extent that cultural goods are equally subject to market mechanisms, their dissemination takes place in accordance with the same integrated principles.

Inevitably, political increases in scale and integration encountered entities formed by the earlier processes of economic and cultural integration. Language and religion are two very strong determining factors for a nation's identity, although certainly not the only ones; it is obvious that the spread of both in some areas is the result of centuries-old and centuries-long processes of penetration and assimilation. Other cultural aspects of a people, such as the way they dress, live and eat, and their ritual celebrations, go back to very old traditions. In modern societies these aspects are somewhat depreciatingly seen by other nations as traditional folklore. But even the strong levelling effects of the international market economy still allow clearly different patterns of daily life to appear even in the most modern areas of Europe: the preference for beer, wine or gin, for the *baguette* and the French stick or the large round two-pound loaf, for deerstalker or beret, for leaving shutters or curtains open or closed, for the Protestant ethic or the Catholic... these are all examples of cultural patterns stabilized in the course of centuries into the infinite variety that is Europe's wealth and its attraction.

Cultural characteristics and common experiences have in the course of many centuries given different nations their identity. Community life and the maintenance of mutual contacts within a limited area are the most effective breeding-ground for this. Language and religion are essential for the process: language is pre-eminently the means of communication, religion offers an image of the world as a common point of reference. The same customs, rituals, beliefs, convictions, prejudices and forms of expression have actually been derived from them, and continually reinforce the identity of a nation. During the phase of so-called

The crusades in the twelfth century signified a high point in the Church's struggle for power. Pinturicchio's fresco of around 1500 immortalized the pope blessing the departure of the crusaders' galleys from the port of Ancona.
Siena, Duomo, Libreria Piccolomini

The deification of the emperor is demonstrated here quite plainly.
Hans Reinhart the Elder has portrayed God the Father
with the features of Charles v in this 1544 medal of the Trinity.
Budapest, Magyar Nemzeti Muzeum

'cultural nationalism' – which in Germany, for instance, was already flourishing in the first decades of the nineteenth century, and which in its turn provoked the pan-Slavic movement – the protagonists of nationalist aims exploited these often already neglected traditions. They were rekindled, historical events were extolled and revised out of all proportion, sometimes even completely invented. Community consciousness was in part recreated, in the view of some researchers even 'dreamt up'. None the less it had real political consequences.

It will, on the other hand, be clear that during the past two thousand years Christianity, the largest of the European religions, was primarily universally oriented, striving to embrace the population of the entire world. As such the formal religion offered less definition of identity to the various individual peoples. The churches, however, not only manifest themselves as a hierarchy, but have also put down local roots throughout the centuries. The parish church was pre-eminently the centre of the community; it was where many of the local customs and rituals were blended into the official religious framework. These local churches contributed considerably to keeping the various cultural identities alive.

Should religion then be discounted as a separate integrating factor, beside the market, the political system and the people? Christianity is many centuries older – in its organization too – than the states, peoples and market systems of Europe. In its Greek Orthodox version, just as in its Roman Catholic one, it is organized on the remains of the Roman empire, but it is aimed at everyone. In the eleventh and twelfth centuries the papal claims to universal power provided the material for conflicts with the patriarchs of Constantinople, with emperors and with kings. The autonomous integrative power of the Catholic Church was evident in the crusades of the twelfth and thirteenth centuries; however, they showed mainly how limited its grasp was. The Church was only able to operate with real autonomy in the earliest phase of the formation of states, which was largely over in the west in the thirteenth century. From the fourteenth century it was clear that the popes had lost out, not least because they did not have their own military resources to counterbalance those of temporal rulers. Besides,

This thirteenth-century miniature of a Muslim and a Christian musician
illustrates the peaceful co-existence and blending of cultures in southern Spain.
Madrid, Biblioteca del Escorial

its self-imposed celibacy placed the Church in a continual position of dependency *vis-à-vis* the secular elites when it came to recruitment of its officials. The result was that religion was more and more absorbed into the structure of the states. The Reformation reinforced this process of confessionalizing the states: rulers imposed their own religious choice on their subjects and the state Church acquired a free hand to accomplish its mission within the state territory; at the same time it was also considered to confer a divine right upon the state power. This status applied to the Orthodox Church in the Russian empire too. In this situation the integrating role of religion is a derivative of the power of the state, and so can no longer be considered as a separate integrating factor.

I have concentrated first on the cultural identity of a society; that is, after all, a general basic fact. Whether in addition economic or political bonds can also circumscribe a nation depends upon how it is embedded into its wider environment. At this stage of the argument I will only state that the specific path followed by European history, with all its diversity and ceaseless conflicts, can be understood in a new light by looking at the continuous interaction between the three basic components which bring people together – and which therefore also separate them from others, and even turn them against each other: the unity of the cultural, economic and political systems. Compatibility of these three integrative systems brings homogeneity and stability. However, European history, in comparison with those of other continents, is characterized by the continual *in*compatibility of cultural, economic and political units. This has always caused great diversity, tensions, competition, conflicts and wars. From this stems the restlessness of the European, inspiring him to those special achievements which people in other parts of the world did not accomplish so consistently – if they ever attempted them.

Around the year AD 1000, chosen as the start of this investigation, only the southern edge of the European continent was highly developed: Muslim Spain, Sicily, southern Italy, the coast along the Adriatic and Aegean Seas and the Sea of Marmara, at that time the core of the Byzantine empire. In comparison with the cultural, economic and political level in these areas, the rest of Europe was in a

Florentine street scene with fortified palazzo and imposing private houses.
Detail from the fresco painted c. 1426 by Masaccio and Masolino in the Capella Brancacci in Florence.

pitiful state of underdevelopment. There was nothing then to suggest that western Europe, from central Italy to Lübeck, would develop a culture which would conquer the rest of the world. Even in 1500 there was still no clear preponderance over, for instance, the Chinese or Ottoman empires. On the contrary, the fragmentation of Europe made the various states, and even Charles v's empire, vulnerable to the military advance of the Turks.

Even so, the foundations had already been laid for a European model of society at variance with anything that had by then come to maturity elsewhere. Its specific characteristic is in fact diversity. In the other empires referred to, a single centre of power dominated the population in all respects: religious, economic and political. In Europe similar totalitarian claims to power have never lasted long, and where they did – as in Russia – it only increased the relative backwardness of that area in relation to the west. Certainly, from its origins in the late Roman empire the Catholic Church had aspirations of universal power, but at an early stage it ran into the resistance of the secular princes, who in fact reduced its influence to the level of that of the states. From the time of the Reformation this situation was even elevated to a principle, so that Anglican, Catholic and Protestant states emerged. But because there were hundreds of large and small states in competition with each other, it was never difficult for dissentients to escape to a territory where they could breathe freely again. In this way new ideas always had their chance somewhere.

There was therefore an abundance of mutually competing powers in the fields of politics and religion, creating a situation in which personal opinions could be developed with relative freedom. Looking at the world as a whole, academic thinking has therefore had more opportunities in Europe than in the great empires – even if here and there narrow-minded conservatism stood in the way of experiments and innovations. An analogous assumption is valid for the economy. Although the Ottoman empire might try – in vain, as it happened – to control markets everywhere and to impose regular deliveries to the state warehouses at controlled prices, in the west the diversity of small pockets of power prevented such a thing happening. Even more: economic development occurred principally in radically autonomous towns, governed by merchants. If the state interfered too pointedly in business – by exaggerated taxation, by waging war, by imposing religious or administrative conditions which impeded the freedom of trade – there would be a flight of capital which would seek refuge elsewhere. Economic development, too, escaped the suffocating clutches of a single centre of power until the eve of industrialization. The diversity could cause damage locally, without, however, allowing the commercial system itself to be destroyed. In fact the competition between the various areas and trading centres led to a keen calculation of the chances of profit, with a constant eye out for the most favourable circumstances. Like parliamentary democracy, capitalism is a typically European system particularly capable of development in this richly varied environment. The variety of cultural and power centres found here was also the breeding-ground for the rational, empirically deductive logic without which neither the scientific, technological and industrial revolutions, nor the concept of the sovereignty of peoples, would have been possible.

Great power systems over a thousand years

In this book the choice has been made for a broad and very ambitious approach. This has advantages and disadvantages. To deal with the latter first: a single author could hardly command all the relevant knowledge; he is forced to make a rigorous selection of the factual material on offer, and the representativeness of that material can rarely be demonstrated statistically. There is enormous risk of an all too abstract argument, poised far above practical reality. Why then make the attempt? Apart from concrete factual descriptions more comprehensive analyses deserve attention, because they draw attention to general tendencies and continuities. Consideration of a broad frame in time and space offers the possibility of explaining individual events from their position in the whole and in the long-term development.

The choice of a development over some thousand years was not made because it is a convenient round number, but just because at the end of the tenth century all kinds of new tendencies began to be manifest in the Mediterranean and western Europe which were to be decisive in the long term. At that moment the main linguistic frontiers had stabilized, the ecclesiastical structures were consolidated and were acquiring a new drive, some growth had started in agricultural production, from which in due course more intensive trade and the growth of towns would follow. The power of princes was gradually acquiring a more enduring character, less dependent upon the personality of the office-holder. The Holy Roman Emperor, and some decades later also the kings of France, England, León and Castile – as well as numerous territorial rulers of lower degree – had begun to expand the apparatus of control which would eventually form the nucleus of states. The developments which were getting into their stride during the eleventh century have given Europe a new face and set in place a dynamic which was never interrupted and is still maintained on a global scale.

This does not mean that evolution since about the year 1000 has only been in one and the same direction – the actual course of events is too complex for that, and often contrary. What is clear is that the continuous growth of production and of population, together with the formation of states and the development of a capitalist market economy, started in that period. In some areas these developments took place earlier than in others, but the trend was established. Centres of gravity and development areas shifted in the course of centuries, here and there there was stagnation and regression, but the dynamic of the system continued to be operative over the long term, and still is. To obtain a view of such long-term processes demands a high level of abstract thought in the analysis.

It is unusual to make a study covering the last thousand years, though there have recently been some brilliant examples. Industrialization is usually chosen as the starting or finishing point, or the great revolutions of the eighteenth and nineteenth centuries. This book, too, acknowledges the structural changes of that transitional period, and they will have their place in its structure. On the other hand it must be said that the revolutions were phases of acceleration in the long-drawn-out process of the formation of states, and that just because of their changes they contributed to the strengthening of the power of the state. In the nineteenth century states were no novelty, any more than markets. It therefore makes sense to give some attention to the continuities, the more so because all sorts of obstacles and contrary movements – such as regionalism – were in fact inspired by earlier situations. In the course of the centuries there has been continual rebuilding on old foundations.

As well as the long term, there is also the wide spatial frame – the whole of Europe – an ambitious, risky, but defensible choice. Let me begin by accepting that this, too, in its turn implies limitations: I shall hardly touch on the colonies, although these were politically part of their home countries. Equally little attention will be paid to the influence which neighbouring cultural areas, such as Islam, have exerted on developments within Europe. It should be acknowledged that in the course of time human societies function less and less as closed systems. For the sake of clarity, I nevertheless assume that, with the exception of the effects of Arabic science in southern Spain and Sicily during the Middle Ages, influences from outside Europe only became decisive in the twentieth century.

On the other hand I think that the research into the formation of power systems should certainly not choose too small a territorial definition as a starting point. First, because the frontiers themselves are continually shifting, and therefore with a small area the selected field of study will change in size in the course of time or might well remain vague and therefore fail in an essential characteristic, that of being a defined area. Secondly, because both the territory and the internal and external functioning of political power systems are to a large extent determined by their mutual interactions. Thirdly, I consider it essential to introduce variation into the observations by means of the large size of the area, which can help to avoid conclusions biased by the selection of a sample. Fourthly, a core element of my vision is to be found in the multiplicity of systems of power which have never entirely overlapped each other. Precisely because some of these systems, for example the empires and the Catholic Church, aimed at having a very comprehensive reach, a dividing line between them at any one moment would easily be artificial.

A multiplicity of systems of power: we have already come back to this several times in the preceding pages. The idea seems so simple and obvious that it arouses surprise when one establishes that it has almost never been applied. By far most studies limit themselves to a single domain, for example politics, or combine at most two, state and economy, or Church and state. I start from the assumption that the exercise of power over groups of people can by definition be referred to three main heads: the first that of coercion, which in the last resort is associated with physical violence, acquiring its legitimacy from serving the apparatus of power; the second that of the appropriation of scarce material goods; the third that of culture, under which I mean both an orientation towards specific values and norms, society's image of the world and of itself, and the expression of this image. All other forms of the exercise of power seem to me to bring us back to these three main areas. My proposition is therefore that it is necessary to devote attention simultaneously

The Anglo-Saxon kings were at the top of a well-organized state apparatus for its time.

They governed, published laws, and administered justice through the Witan, a council of high ecclesiastics and laymen.

The king and the Witan administering justice and an execution, eleventh-century miniature. London, British Library

Thomas à Becket, archbishop of Canterbury after being chancellor to Henry II of England,

paid for the tension between Church and crown

by his martyrdom. London, British Library

to each of these three main areas if the exercise of power in a society is to be understood. The more they overlap in practice, the more total is the power; if on the other hand they operate autonomously or even in mutual conflict, then there is more freedom of action for their subjects. The fascination of European history is that the three ranges of power were generally located in clearly separate institutions, in spite of strenuous efforts by various rulers to acquire complete power – what the popes in the eleventh century in their struggle for authority with the Holy Roman Emperors called the *plenitudo potestatis* – the fullness of power. These institutions often worked very closely together, but each also stood upon its rights. It is not my intention to seek for the primacy among these systems. What concerns me is the examination of their mutual configuration in every situation, and in how far this throws light on the specific course of events.

Two examples from fictional literature may illustrate this point of view. The situation in which a small Italian town in the 1950s had to serve two competing masters – Peppone, the communist mayor, and the doughty priest Don Camillo – illustrates the limits of a position of power confined to a single area. On the other hand the continuity in the position of power of a large French nineteenth-century landowner, who in collusion with the priest keeps the peasants poor and ignorant, but is none the less always re-elected by them, is typical of the plenitude of power in a relatively closed society.

Some further explanation may still be needed of the concept of culture I have adopted. As mentioned earlier, it includes a great deal, and a great deal of diversity: whole assumptions about the world and the hereafter, what is valuable and what should be rejected, who belongs and who is a stranger, and how you should show it all. Previously there has been mention of religions, which propounded opinions about all of these things, and also of the self-awareness of peoples. The comment has already been made that the universalism of Christianity did not simply enable it to function everywhere as the guardian of popular tradition, even though the parish priests might try to be integrated locally. Besides the religious image of the world other interpretations of reality were also at work, such as historical tales and myths about the origins of their own people and their leaders. During the Romantic period the national awareness of peoples acquired a new impetus, so that it became an independent force. In more recent times the mass media have acquired a new and very intrusive influence both on the material culture and on the

Three examples of both bad and good government are shown opposite each other in Nicolas Oresme's fourteenth-century French translation of Aristotle's *Politics*.

On the left the bad: tyranny, oligarchy and democracy;

on the right the good: monarchy, aristocracy and timocracy.

Brussels, Bibliothèque royale de Belgique

image of the world and of oneself. Dependent upon time and place, the cultural dimension will therefore acquire different interpretations which justify themselves by their functional analogy.

This book does not therefore concentrate on a specific form of the exercise of power such as, for example, the state, but on the exercise of power *as such*. It has no fixed model in view, for instance the creation of the centralized nation state, but just the question why in these ten centuries great changes have steadily occurred in the timing and nature of configurations of power, in spite of all the interactions and increases of scale in all kinds of areas. The cultural dimension of the problem posed will in this book be given particular attention in its visual aspects, which for the majority of contemporary people were the most important way in which the rulers could try to convince the rulers lower down the scale of their superior objectives.

With its analysis of systems of power in Europe during the past millennium, this book will also attempt to answer the question of how in the course of time certain tasks, competences and functions have been acquired or lost by institutions. To put it in practical terms: the loss of their function by the churches, particularly over the last two centuries, has been associated with an appreciable expansion in the package of tasks undertaken by the state. This phenomenon has since the 1980s been strongly opposed by conservative and neo-liberal politicians who were of the opinion that the state had taken far too many tasks upon itself, and they set in motion a radical wave of privatization. In this debate it makes sense to ask how, in what circumstances, and under the pressure of what needs, the growth and loss of functions occurs, and how any gaps arising are filled. Moreover, in present-day discussion surprisingly little attention is paid to the growth of the range of power of commercial organizations, not least in the area of culture, where in previous centuries Church and state directed their efforts for a monopoly. It is precisely the perspective of the whole continent of Europe, and the length of the period covered, which will, hopefully, make it possible to throw light on several new aspects of the problem of the development and loss of power in different areas.

CHAPTER I
The Conquest of Space

Distance and communication

In about AD 300 the emperor Diocletian reorganized the Roman empire. He created some hundred provinces out of the forty-two of the second century; they were in turn subdivided into *civitates*. Towns were designated as the administrative centres of the areas delineated, and they were linked with each other and to Rome by an efficient network of straight roads. In each town the layout reflected the planned and systematic nature of the design: a square town plan with streets in a chequer pattern; axes which led from the gates to a central square, the *forum*, where a *basilica* and several temples gave expression to the established values of public order.

This kind of grand-scale and methodical planning, carried out down to the smallest units, has often inspired later authorities, most strongly perhaps the innovators of the French revolution and the Napoleonic empire. However, such a concept of an imperial state has never again been achieved in practice in Europe. It was an ideal image, often imitated fragmentarily, but never equalled in the grandeur of its scale. Imitations involved separate elements such as the Roman architectural vocabulary and symbolism of power, titles (Caesar – Kaiser – tsar, pontifex, consul, prefect, diocese, civitas and so on) and, particularly from the twelfth century onwards, also the legal system. This is the more surprising since the technical possibilities, certainly from the seventeenth century on, exceeded those of the Roman period. The problem therefore lay not in technology, but in organization, more specifically in the ability to exercise power over people. Just because their technical lead was at that time not very great, the Romans continually had the greatest difficulty in resisting the pressure of the surrounding peoples, an effort which the empire was eventually unable to sustain. The standing armies which had to defend the long frontiers along the Rhine and the Danube numbered from 300,000 to 400,000 men. These strengths were not reached again in Europe until around 1635 in Spain (300,000) and in France around 1705 (400,000). The 80,000 kilometres of the road network, with its milestones, posthouses and inns, formed the backbone of the organization of the Roman state, a tangible expression of its integration and centralization. Only in the eighteenth century did the states of Europe begin to construct similar communication systems within their frontiers – and always on a much more modest scale.

The needs of the Roman state determined its economic organization. There was, of course, free private enterprise, but above all the supply of grain for Rome and the garrison towns had to be assured. Large tracts of land were distributed by the state to discharged soldiers. Thanks to the power of the state the labour market could be regulated by a steady supply of slaves. It was the state and its officers who initiated great public works. Private entrepreneurs occupied a less prominent position in society. The Romans had an established religion, in

Map of Britannia of *c.*1240, clearly showing Hadrian's Wall,
built between AD 122 and 128
as a frontier between England and Scotland.
Illustration in Matthew Paris, *Chronica Majora*.
London, British Library

which the emperors, thanks to their deification, held a place of honour. The recognition of Christianity by the emperor Constantine in 325 and its elevation into the state religion in 391 achieved the incorporation of a liberation movement, which might possibly, as an alternative ideology, have undermined the empire from within.

Bearing in mind that this general description is susceptible to many qualifications, it can be said of the Roman empire that the power of the state displayed so much of an intermixture with religious observance and with other cultural expressions (such as the role of the theatre, physical culture and the games), and exercised such a great influence on economic life, that the three areas of power were to a large extent combined. Political power made use of the economy and of culture to achieve its ends.

The wide coverage of the Roman state apparatus is only apparent in its full grandeur when it is compared with later attempts to establish great empires. The Holy Roman Empire of the German Nation – in name the first to inherit the empire, tracing its history back to the coronation of Charlemagne in AD 800, and lasting until its abolition in 1806 as a consequence of Napoleon's conquest of large parts of it – never extended so far, but above all was never so solidly integrated administratively or as centralized. It always remained a rather artificial conglomerate of essentially independent principalities and other territories. Only in exceptional circumstances did it seem possible to apply for a short time an imperial policy with specific imperial resources. In fact it owed its long survival to its own extremely limited power.

One great age of the Holy Roman Empire, perhaps in this context better described as 'emperorship', was that of the Hohenstaufen dynasty, with as its most prominent figures Frederick I Barbarossa (1152–1190) and his grandson Frederick II (1211–1250). Both were also king of Sicily, and there not only became fascinated by the rich cultural traditions of the Mediterranean region, but increasingly oriented towards Italy and the Levant, where they took an active part in the crusades. In theory their authority extended over a north–south axis of some three thousand kilometres. From west to east the greatest distance was some thousand kilometres, only a fragment of the area of the Roman empire. Yet both powerful emperors had the greatest difficulty in maintaining their authority over their German empire as well as Lombardy and Sicily. Rivals mobilized rebellions by barons and towns, which continually had to be settled with concessions by

the emperor. Their succession was disputed; in the Holy Roman Empire a long interregnum followed after 1250, which seriously affected the imperial power, and Sicily was lost to the Hohenstaufens after a few years of conflict.

This episode demonstrates some fundamental differences between the structure of the Roman empire and that of later expansive powers. First, the empire arose from the conquest of areas of which a large proportion, particularly the European regions, displayed a lower level of development; because of this they had less effective weapons and their political (and therefore also military) organization was smaller and less stable. From a military point of view they were therefore weaker. Secondly, it would seem essential to underline that the Roman conquests were achieved over some three centuries, which made systematic integration of the new provinces possible. Thirdly, in their early stages the conquests were the work of generals in the service of the Republic. A state which was already consolidated let its servants conquer territory which was then added to the state, would produce taxes, and whose population could acquire rights as citizens. The Republic, *res publica*, the public weal, was the legal person taking the action, and the empire perpetuated this role. A successful general could count on a triumph, personal fame and wealth, possibly a triumphal arch, and possibly, too, an honourable office, but the conquered country belonged to the state. Rome was successful in maintaining its dominance for a long time through its rational system of exploiting human and material resources in all the subject territories.

On all these points the situation was quite different in the later Europe. First of all the massive population movements between the fifth and the tenth centuries reduced the differences in development, so that the sides became more equal, at least in the west. Rival rulers in medieval and early modern Europe generally fought with more or less equal weaponry. Secondly, many conquests were soon lost again to the conqueror or his descendants, so that there was no question of consolidation. Thirdly, rulers regarded territory primarily as the heritage of their own dynasty, which they could personally acquire and control without this making any difference to the status of the areas under their authority. This heritage could be passed down, possibly divided among different heirs, or lacking heirs could be appropriated more or less legitimately by others. The abstract concept of a republic, which the Romans had thought out constitutionally long before

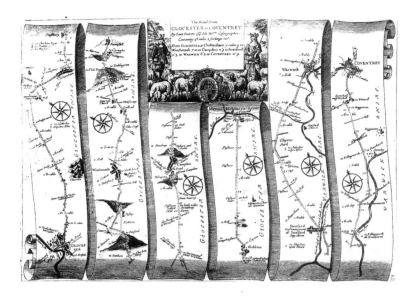

Convenient route maps of 1675–1698 by John Ogilby for the road from Gloucester to Coventry.

Under the *ancien régime* by far and away the best and most extensive road network of all the western countries was in the Low Countries.

From the late Middle Ages it became fashionable to adopt splendid ceremonies from classical Rome, such as this Roman general's triumph.

Limoges dish executed in enamel on copper by Jean de Court, second half of the sixteenth century. Berlin, Kunstgewerbemuseum

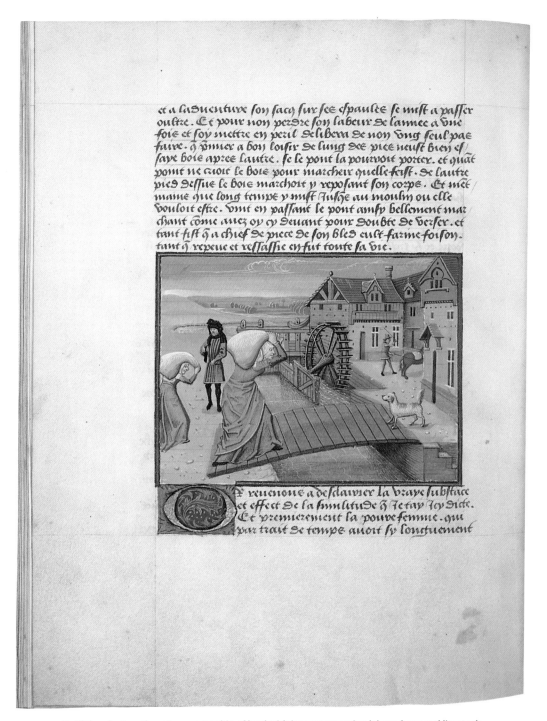

et a lasuenture son sacq sur ses espaulte se mist a passer
oultre. Et pour non perdre son labeur de lannee a vne
fois et soy mettre en peril delibera de non vng seul pas
fuire. q pmier a bon loisir de lung de pie neust bien es
saye bois apres lautre. se le pont la pouuoit porter. et quat
pomt ne croit le bois pour marcheir quelle fist. de lautre
pied dessue le bois marchoit y reposant son corps. Et met
mame que long temps y mist Iusqe au moulin ou elle
vouloit estre. vint en passant le pont ainsy bellement mar
chant come auez oy cy deuant pour doubte de verser. et
tant fist q a chief de piece de son bles eust farine foison.
tant q repeue et ressassie en fut toute sa vie.

P reuenions a desclairier la vraye substace
et effect de la similitude q Ie vay Icy dicte.
Et premierement la pouure femme. qui
par trait de temps auoit sy longuement

Until the nineteenth century ownership of land with its accompanying labour force and livestock
was the most important form of wealth in the interior of Europe. Estate with manorial mill and women working (c. 1470–1480).
Cambridge, The Fitzwilliam Museum

The legitimization of princely power through exalted ancestry was traced back in time as far as possible.
An illustrious family tree was essential for a dynasty. Part of the family tree of the kings of Aragon.
Miniature by Simon Bening (1530–1534).
London, British Library

From the thirteenth century the increase in international trade made an international network for information and communication essential.
Merchants often organized their own courier services. Franciabigio, *Portrait of a young man at his writing desk*, sixteenth century.
Berlin, Gemäldegalerie

the beginning of the Christian era, would only with difficulty find acceptance in the later Europe, and was very much against the wishes of the ruling dynasties, as can be understood.

The formation of territories happened in such a capricious way because conquests resulted not from the efforts of an impersonal organization such as the Holy Roman Empire, but of flesh-and-blood rulers, striving not for the public good but for their dynasty, even when they, like the Hohenstaufens, were Holy Roman Emperors. They fought for *Hausmacht*, the heritage of their dynasty, on which their consequence and power rested. The high-risk course of a ruler's life and the unpredictability of his successors made the inherited assumption of authority a factor of discontinuity and division. Later in this chapter an attempt will be made to acquire further insight into the circumstances which determined whether territories did or did not form durable combinations.

From the above it may be plain that after the fragmentation and eventual collapse of the Roman empire during the fifth century, control of territory was much more difficult to achieve. Power became direct and personal. A ruler had to be physically present to be respected, which obliged him to make continuous tours. The German concept of *Reisekönigtum*, literally the touring kingship, indicates the need for early medieval rulers to keep continually moving to the centres of their territorial power. In this period the economy declined to a high degree of self-sufficiency because the roads were dangerous, means of transport scarce and markets uncertain. Little survived of the Roman system of centralized taxation. Gold coins were melted down and reworked into jewellery and objects for religious worship because they had lost their function as a universal medium of exchange. There was, after all, no longer any state to guarantee the value of money, and trade was restricted from now on to luxury items and barter. The ownership of land, with its accompanying labour force and livestock, became the most important form of wealth. Rulers therefore had to resort to showing themselves regularly in their domains with their armed supporters and to take advantage on site of the supplies available there. The nuclei of the power of the Carolingian kings, which they called 'palaces', derived from the Latin *palatium*, were hardly more than a spacious hall and a fortification, both in stone, with an extensive home farm.

At the high point of the Empire, during the rule of the emperor Charles V (1519–1555) the very sensitive question of the link between Church and state shows the extent to which the emperor was powerless to impose his ideas on the princes of the Empire. Very much against his will he had to accept that a number of them actively supported Protestantism in their territories. The much more short-lived imperial dream of Napoleon only proved by its speedy disintegration the impossibility of repeating the imperial ethos in Europe. A system of solidly paved roads provided with signposts showing distances, relays of horses every ten miles (15 kilometres) and inns for travellers every twenty miles, along which a state postal service carried messages with an average speed of forty miles a day; this, the situation in the Roman empire, would only be achieved again on a much smaller scale after the sixteenth century. As governments were so late in seeing the importance of an efficient communications system, journeys were precarious and above all slow ventures. To cross the Holy Roman Empire demanded a month in any direction. As late as 1765 it took news from Paris twelve days to reach Marseilles, fourteen to Bordeaux, and sixteen to Toulouse. Rennes required eight days of travel, Strasbourg ten. To cross the kingdom from Lille to the Pyrenees or from Strasburg to Brittany at least three weeks had to be allowed. The establishment of the State Stagecoach Service (the *Régie des diligences et messageries*) in 1775 by Turgot, the minister, reduced travelling time appreciably: Marseilles and Toulouse could then be reached in eight days, Rennes in three, and Strasbourg in five.[1] This was accomplished at the time that James Watt was already hard at work on his steam engine, but it still depended entirely on techniques which had not substantially changed from those used by the Romans. That seventeen centuries were needed to recreate a smaller replica of their system of communications says much about the ability to organize human performance on a grand scale.

Notes: see p. 73

In the fourteenth century commercial organizations had already worked out systems for the rapid dispatch of news across Europe. About 1400 letters of credit and commercial correspondence already circulated speedily and often between the trading towns, from Konigsberg via Bruges and Genoa to the Black Sea. As a standard the maximum duration of a journey was set at six days from Genoa to Milan, ten to Rome, twenty to Barcelona, and thirty to Valencia and Montpellier; for Bruges two months, and for London three were acceptable travelling times. In this period the courier service developed into a commercial activity of which rulers also made use. The dukes of Milan called on these services at great expense in times of tension or war. About 1450 they themselves developed a system of relays (posts) every thirteen to twenty-four kilometres, and services which also ran at night, so that they were successful in bridging the distance from Milan to Rome in about eighty-four hours. The best commercial courier then took at least seven days over it, the pope's personal couriers five to six days, and the ordinary services ten to eleven. This involved, however, expensive and exceptional situations which only applied on well-defined communication routes. The Tassis family from the Bergamo region supplied the papal postmasters for generations. In 1490 they started a regular courier service between Malines, Innsbruck and Italy, to which Maximilian, the king of the Romans, granted a monopoly in 1500. Yet overland travelling times hardly altered between 1500 and 1750. From Venice the distance to the south coast of England, or to Hamburg, always took three weeks, to Lisbon or Moscow six. The more natural or man-made obstacles there were to overcome or circumvent, or the lower the density of population and therefore the frequency of travel, the longer everything took. It is clear that the problem of communication was a much more serious one in the thinly populated central, northern and eastern regions of Europe than in the more commercialized areas.

All in all there were only tentative and partial solutions to what was a basic problem for every ruler. The lack of an overall transport and communications system appreciably slowed down the ability to take decisions. A world-wide kingdom such as that of Philip II of Spain (1555–1598) appeared to be wrestling continually with the problem of slow and uncertain communications. The fact that his territories in Spain and Italy on the one hand, and the Netherlands on the other, were separated by an often hostile France, only made the problem worse. The troops he sent to the Netherlands from Lombardy took on average forty-eight days for the 1,100 kilometres, and in some cases two months.[2] He could therefore only react very tardily to information from the revolting Netherlands, with the consequence that his interventions took place in a situation which had meanwhile developed further, and hence went awry.

The comparison of the communications system of the Roman empire with that evolving later in Europe demonstrates the enormous importance of the classical

The Holy Roman Emperor Frederick III (1452–1493), accompanied by his son Maximilian, is handed a letter by Frans de Tassis, who then held the imperial monopoly for carrying mail. Fragment of a tapestry woven to a design by Bernard van Orley (1516). Brussels, Municipal Museum

state's ability to mobilize. For its own purposes of control, supply and the movement of troops the empire had been able to develop a very extensive and intensive system. To do this required abstract geographical and political concepts and the organizational ability to apply them and make them operative. It was, however, to be eleven centuries before western Europe could improve on the knowledge of the Roman map of the world in the fourth century, which extended from Britain to India. Until far into the eighteenth century anything like this was lacking in the later Europe. The fundamental explanation for this seems to lie in the conditions of the process of development of power itself: the Roman state conquered new provinces gradually as a result of a lead in development compared with many of them. This enabled it to raise tribute, including that in the form of slave labour. Christianity set its face against this with reasonably effective results: at least among Christians slavery disappeared during the early Middle Ages. This meant that the labour factor became appreciably scarcer. Moreover, the general lowering of the level of development as a consequence of the mass movements of people and the resulting levelling out of the opportunities for small potentates is also important. The high Middle Ages demonstrate a laborious reconstruction of stable forms of power, from the bottom up, after a free-for-all battle of elimination. This resulted not in a monopoly, but in some large and many smaller power complexes, not one of which was stabilized by the eleventh century. This pluralism was dominated by continual competition, in which there was obviously a lack of the peace in which large-scale systems might have been devised, and particularly the opportunity of realizing them.

Until the sixteenth century therefore the rulers only had meagre geographical knowledge. Administrative surveys of a complete territory were rare, and only in the 1560s did geographers begin to record whole provinces on the basis of scientific measurements. Some princes, such as the Elector of Saxony, regarded this knowledge as a state secret, which above all should not be allowed to fall into the hands of potential enemies. The development of cartography, however, proceeded unstoppably because of two interest groups: the seafarers, for whom the description of sea transport routes, distances and landing places was of vital importance; and the

The construction of the Devil's Bridge over a deep ravine dates from *c.* 1235.

The bridge made it possible to take a short cut through the Alps

from Zürich to Milan along the north side of the St Gothard.

Local farming communities looked after the maintenance of the road and hired out vehicles and draught animals.

Painting of *c.* 1833 by Carl Blechen.

Munich, Bayerische Staatsgemäldesammlungen, Neue Pinakothek

generals, for whom precise knowledge of the country meant an important competitive edge. As in so many cases, the traders and seafarers were earlier with the development of realistic maps than the country's leaders. Arab geographers built on the knowledge of the ancient Greeks. From 1138 to *c.* 1165 Al Idrisi produced in Palermo seventy-one maps of countries and one map of the world for the Norman kings of Sicily. Several Greek manuscripts also ended up at their court and were translated there, including Ptolemy's *Almagest* of AD 140 which remained the basic manual of astronomy until the sixteenth century. With the death of the emperor Frederick II (1250) the cultural leadership of this melting pot received no further stimulation.[3] Jewish cartographers in the kingdom of Majorca made

an important contribution to the portolan charts which originally described routes for seafarers from port to port with a detailed drawing of coast lines and caravan routes. In 1375 the king of Aragon presented a unique example of an unfolding one to the French king Charles V, which as well as the Mediterranean Sea also offered views of the rest of the world, from the Atlantic Ocean to China and from the Baltic Sea to the Niger. Based on Ptolemy's *Cosmographia*, translated into Latin for the pope in 1410 – specimens of which were soon distributed across Europe – Master Guillaume Hobit, in the service of the duke of Burgundy, made between 1440 and 1444 a map of the world 'in the round', three-dimensional, *i.e.* in the form of a globe.[4] In the sixteenth century maps of the then known world were

Increasing road and courier traffic forced the French government to carry out drastic improvements
to the road network in the eighteenth century. Jacques-François-Joseph Sweebach, *The Mail,* early nineteenth century.
Paris, Musée Nissim de Camondo

painted as frescos in the Palazzo Vecchio in Florence, evidently because they contributed to the renown of the ruling Medicis.

In the second half of the sixteenth century private engravers, instrument makers, surveyors and cartographers made a breakthrough with the publication of printed atlases. In Antwerp, and later in Amsterdam, there was a ready market among merchants and particularly seafarers for the increasingly more accurately produced maps. In 1570 Abraham Ortelius published his first atlas with fifty-three maps. In 1585 and 1589 Gerard Mercator published two series of maps, using a much more accurate projection, with respectively fifty-one and twenty-three maps of France, Switzerland, the Netherlands, Germany, Italy and the Balkans. This scholarly geographer had already worked for Charles V, constructing astronomical instruments. From 1560 he was in the service of the duke of Julich, Cleves

and Berg, who as ruler of a frontier territory was early to recognize the significance of this knowledge. During the seventeenth century private printer – publisher – cartographers working in Holland, such as the famous Willem and Joan Blaeu, published important atlases, first of the coasts, later of the Netherlands and of the whole world. The political importance of cartography was so much appreciated in the west during the seventeenth century that the king of France took several geographers into his service. The city government of Amsterdam thought it added to their splendour to have maps of the world designed into the floor of the majestic civic hall of their town hall built in 1650, so that every visitor would be impressed with their mastery of the oceans of the world. For them, as for their Mediterranean predecessors, this knowledge had a commercial value.

Natural frontiers?

After outlining the post-Roman situation in Europe in its internal competitiveness, the next question should be: what determined the chances of success? Why were some kingdoms already able to achieve a reasonable stability during the eleventh century, while others only took shape in the last two centuries? The answer to this question can here be only a superficial one, because it naturally depends on what is meant by stability and by an effective power apparatus. This will be discussed later in this book. We now limit ourselves to the question, which others have posed before us, of whether in the European arena there were at some times protected geographical locations which encouraged an early consolidation and held off later threats.[5]

First it must be made clear that no single geographical situation was obviously equally protective at all times. Italy, which after its own unification in the third century BC was for five centuries the core of a world empire, appears – as a peninsula well protected behind the Alps – destined to be a unity. Yet after the fifth century it was not until 1860–1870 that it reached this stage again, and certainly not because of underdevelopment. The Alps did not offer sufficient protection, for they were frequently crossed by massive armies, such as that of Hannibal in 218 BC, of the Germanic peoples in the fifth and sixth centuries, of the French in 1494 and of the Habsburgs and others many times after that.

It is difficult to suggest a really protected situation. The most stable frontier in European history is that between Portugal and the rest of the Iberian peninsula; in spite of the lack of clear geographical obstacles it has been in existence since 1250. Also the political frontier between England and Scotland, defined between 122 and 128 AD by the emperor Hadrian's Wall, lasted until 1707; since then its significance has not disappeared. Both Portugal and Scotland can be considered as fringe areas of land masses already to some extent isolated as islands or peninsulas. They were each united under one crown with their larger neighbour in 1580 and 1603 respectively as a result of quite deliberate marriage policies, but Portugal only until 1640. In Scandinavia, Sweden could be suggested as being in a comparable protected position. However, after repeatedly being overrun by the Norwegians and the Danes, it was incorporated in the Union of Kalmar which united the three Scandinavian crowns in 1397. Sweden itself ruled Finland for centuries, and for a time part of central Norway; that country

was ruled for centuries by Denmark. Distant Russia was spared for a long time, because at first there was still a power vacuum there. Lithuania expanded strongly to the east and south in the late Middle Ages, and until the seventeenth century also included Severia, Little Russia and the western Ukraine. But even after the Russian empire had conquered all these areas and many more in all directions, it was not shielded from Napoleon's destructive invasions and the two World Wars. A peripheral situation in the west offered no more protection, even to islands; Scotland, Ireland and the islands of the kingdom of Man were all taken by England, and the island groups further north by the Danes and Norwegians. Despite its off-centre position and the obstacle of the Pyrenees, the Iberian peninsula appears to have been troubled by a series of invasions: that of the Carthaginians in the third century BC, those of the Romans, the Vandals and Visigoths, the longest-lasting of all – that of the Arabs and Berbers in AD 711–719, and finally that of Napoleon in 1807. The Balkans, peripheral and mountainous, were from the fifteenth to the early twentieth century subjected to the oppression of Ottoman rule, and before that of Byzantine. So a situation can only be called relatively remote or protected, particularly in relation to an expansive nucleus.

Islands were in general the least protected of all, as is shown by the conquest of England in the eighth and ninth centuries by the Vikings, in the tenth by the Danes, and in 1066 by the Normans. Sicily, too, became a typical target for successive invasions by Byzantines, Muslims, Normans, Germans, French and southern Italians. In general the transport of large numbers was easier by sea than overland, so that Sweden was successful in conquering the Finns, but did not overcome the south-western flank of their peninsula, the fertile region of Skania, until 1658. Other long-lasting aggregates of overseas territories were the possessions of the English crown in France – from Normandy to Aquitaine – from the twelfth to the mid-fifteenth century, and the possessions of the royal house of Aragon, which included the Balearics, Sardinia, Sicily and the kingdom of Naples; this led to the last two coming under Spanish rule, again for many centuries. Maritime empires were also important, particularly Venice and Genoa in the Mediterranean. From the twelfth until the late eighteenth century Venice occupied Istria and a large part of the Dalmatian coast, and until the sixteenth century held countless islands, the largest being Corfu, Euboea, Crete and Cyprus.

Mountainous districts such as the Peloponnese,

In 1699 Joseph Parrocel recorded for posterity Louis XIV's army crossing the Rhine in 1672.
The Rhine was then assumed to be the natural frontier between France and Germany.
Paris, Musée du Louvre

Albert II of Mecklenburg symbolically hands over the flag with the three Swedish crowns to his son Albert III at his enthronement in 1364.

Miniature from Ernst von Kirchberg's *Chronicle in rhyme* (c. 1378).

Schwerin, Staatarchiv

In Copenhagen the royal town, the administrative centre,

was situated on an island that could be completely closed off.

Print by Frans Hogenberg, *Hafnia vulgo Kopenhagen urbs Daniae* (1587), from G. Braun, *Civitates Orbis Terrarum*,

of which the first edition appeared in 1572 and the last in 1622.

Thessaly, Serbia and Bosnia were conquered by various armies and were occupied by the Ottomans for centuries. On the other hand, the Mongols, a typical equestrian horde, seized the Bulgarian and Hungarian plains in the course of the thirteenth century, but avoided mountainous Serbia. This lay appreciably better protected than the neighbouring regions of Bosnia, Croatia, and Slovenia, which were regularly overrun by their neighbours; Slovenia by Carinthia, Croatia and Bosnia during the eleventh and twelfth centuries by Hungary, and both the last two after 1180 by Serbia. The highlands of the Alps, the Pyrenees and the Tatra, and the thickly forested areas of Sweden, southern Germany and southern Poland, are natural niches which could not become a theatre of war, because large troop movements were impossible there and ran too much risk of ambush. In this way many different political formations could achieve stabilization in the same environment.

In the Alps, for instance, the shelter of the high peaks and the isolation of the valleys made it possible for the three original cantons, Schwyz, Uri and Unterwalden, to forge a union in 1291 against the claims to power of the Habsburgs. In the course of the next two centuries another ten regions and towns voluntarily joined this confederation, and others were made subject by it. The infantry of the cantons showed that they were able to withstand the army of the Habsburg chivalry in three pitched battles. During the following centuries the mountain cantons placed their surplus population as mercenaries at the disposition of warring powers, who came to respect Swiss neutrality for this and other reasons. From this process of development sprang a wholly individual republican configuration of power, allowing extensive autonomy to the districts forming the confederation, and retaining the direct participation of the men in the farming districts. In stark contrast to this the Habsburgs were able not only to maintain themselves in neighbouring Tyrol, Carinthia, Krajina, Steiermark and the archduchy of Austria, but were even able to expand their dynastic base appreciably. By a carefully planned marriage policy the dynasty came into possession of the hereditary Burgundian lands in 1477, expanded in 1506 with the vast Spanish empire, and in 1526 with the kingdom of Bohemia, Moravia, Silesia and Lausitz, forming an enormous contiguous block of land on the Empire's south-eastern flank. From 1438 to 1740 the emperors were chosen from the house of Habsburg without interruption. It is hard to imagine a greater contrast than that between the republican Swiss cantons and their monarchic rivals, both formed in the same Alpine region. All geographic determinism seems to miss the point.

The Franco-Spanish frontier treaty of 1659 stated about the Pyrenees that they 'from of old had separated the Gauls from the Spaniards, and from henceforth should form the frontier between the two kingdoms'.[6] To establish this frontier, a bilateral commission had to start work putting frontier posts on the ground. They divided Cerdaña, a valley inhabited by a Catalan community acknowledging no relationship to either kingdom, down the middle. On the other hand, in 1276 neighbouring Andorra was given a typically feudal solution, the joint exercise of authority by the bishops of Urgel and the count of Foix. The latter's successor, the president of France, exercises these rights up to the present day. At the Atlantic end the kingdom of Navarre extended across the mountains, and the Basques still live on both sides. At the Mediterranean end the kingdom of Aragon included the county of Roussillon, to the north of the Pyrenees. It is not the mountains which have divided people, it is states, and those really only since the nineteenth century.

With this qualification it can none the less be established that if the Pyrenees do not form a highly delineated frontier, they have provided a strikingly stable frontier region – which is also true of the Alps, as well as the Sudeten mountains and the Carpathians which have always separated Poland from Bohemia, Moravia and Hungary. Away from these geographical obstacles, frontiers in the course of time have been much more changeable. It is striking that the east–west orientation of the Pyrenees, Alps, Sudeten mountains and Carpathians has prevented potential mass movements particularly of nomadic hordes from north to south or south to north, but not from east to west or west to east. The great plains to the north of these mountains were therefore a corridor area with no natural frontiers. The Oder already served as a dividing line between Poland and the Holy Roman Empire in the eleventh century, but it was no real obstacle to colonization of the east. The territories of Poland, Lithuania and the Baltic sea coast shifted very dramatically. Up to 1683 the Ottoman empire penetrated to the gates of Vienna, but after that systematically lost territory to the expanding Austrian and Russian empires.

One curious shift in frontiers is that between France and Germany. Since Carolingian days the rough division was formed by the Scheldt, the Meuse, the Saone and the Rhone. Up until the twentieth century France has been doing its best to

Mountain cantons in Switzerland with surplus populations put mercenaries at the disposal of warring powers, which helped to guarantee Swiss neutrality. *The recruitment of soldiers near Berne.* Coloured drawing by Franz Niklaus König, eighteenth century. Berne, Kunstmuseum

move this eastwards, in which it has bit by bit been largely successful, except that in the north, in the Low Countries, it had itself to give up territory – as had the Empire, for that matter, to a greater degree. The fragmentation started in the south: in 1246 the French house of Anjou acquired Provence, Lyons became French in 1307, the Dauphiné in 1349. The free county of Burgundy, Franche Comté, came into Valois-Burgundian hands in 1369 and was conquered by France in 1678; Alsace became French in 1648, Lorraine followed in 1766. The Empire lost still more territory on its southern frontier in central Italy. It had already been apparent in the twelfth century how theoretical the imperial authority was; even after his sack of Rome in 1527 Charles v could only exercise influence there indirectly. On its eastern frontier the Empire incurred no territorial losses in the seventeenth or eighteenth centuries, but on the other hand was able to consolidate and expand some of its components: Austria, Bohemia, Brandenburg-Prussia. The balance of power which had characterized the Empire for a thousand years

Thickly wooded areas hindered major troop movements. Ultimately they determined the formation of specific political units in these areas. *Nuremberg in the Reichswald,* 1516. Nuremberg, Germanisches Nationalmuseum

was threatened by this, and this was to lead to its break-up in the nineteenth century.

The colossal land mass which the Empire had held together for so long with an extremely loose rein had undoubtedly been able to maintain itself so long because no single hostile power had been able to threaten the core itself. The strongest, France, had conquered fringe regions in a period of five centuries. Northern and central Italy had become independent quite early. The Netherlands did so between the fourteenth and the sixteenth centuries. Disputes with the king of Denmark about Schleswig and Holstein gradually evolved in his favour, but this was marginal. The threat of the Turks, for which the Empire imposed a general tax for the first time in the sixteenth century, came no further than Hungary. The Swedish invasion of 1630–1634, which advanced from Pomerania through Saxony, Thuringia and Franconia, meant a very serious, but short-lived, threat. Swedish territorial gains were confined to Hither Pomerania, which was already reconquered by Brandenburg-Prussia in 1675. Looked at in the long

The Ottoman empire penetrated as far as Vienna until 1683; the Turks then steadily lost ground to Austria and Russia.
Johannes Stradanus, *The departure of the Turks after the siege of Vienna.* Leiden, Universiteitsbibliotheek, Prentenkabinet

In the seventeenth century frontier incidents between France and Spain were legion. Generally speaking, however,
the Pyrenees formed one of the most stable frontier regions of western Europe.
Peter van der Meulen, *The exchange of French and Spanish princesses on the Bidasoa in 1615.* Madrid, Museo Convento de la Encarnacion

Port activities beside the Main at Frankfurt in the eighteenth century.

Frankfurt am Main, Städtische Galerie

term, the Swedish expansion in the seventeenth century had a much more enduring effect in activating the resistance to it in Brandenburg-Prussia than in the actual expansion of Sweden's territory.

During the thousand years of the Holy Roman Empire no single power could entertain the ambition of controlling that enormous territory. Fringe areas, over which there was in practice hardly any control, were ceded without the central position of the Empire coming under pressure in any way. The Empire as a whole was in any case hardly capable of developing its power, or of aggression. In the disastrous Thirty Years War, which was entirely fought out on imperial territory, the emperor was in no way capable of collecting together forces, so that in the long run the centrifugal tendencies were further strengthened. In the peace of 1648 even the right of the Estates of the Empire – and therefore also of the individual principalities – of forming associations with foreign countries was established, provided they were not directed against the emperor or the Empire. The play of coalitions meant that every increase of power in one territory invited countermovements, so that for a long time the balance of power between the principalities was maintained.

These conclusions about the Empire can actually be a model for the whole of Europe. They can perhaps be summarized in two deductions. First of all, before 1800 very extensive land masses appear not to have been directly controllable, which again ties up with the earlier considerations about the slowness and limited level of organization of communications. Secondly, it is striking that the coastal regions displayed a totally different orientation from that of the inland regions. All along the coasts of Europe towns and narrow strips of land enjoyed extensive autonomy. The seaward orientation of the coastal areas along the Baltic, the North Sea and the Mediterranean gave them mutual links, made seagoing traffic possible, made them richer than the average hinterland, and made it difficult for them to be controlled by dynasties based on the possession of land. A few great rivers, such as the Rhine, the Vistula and the Po, fit in with this. Less emphasis should preferably be laid on geopolitical location and natural frontiers than on the twofold nature of Europe: the communicative coastal areas and great river valleys versus the 'slow' land masses. From the shape of the continent this also indicates a contrast between west and east, as central and eastern Europe again are more continental.

The Empire reborn

The most important areas of authority in Europe were demarcated during the tenth and eleventh centuries, and since then they have kept not only their names but also the outlines of their territories, even though for some of them at times this was more wishful thinking than reality. Claims on areas and the hierarchy of rights of authority, however vaguely they were defined, became established and recognized, and it was on these that a political programme could be based in times of conflict. The vague memory of ancient privileges and situations could in later periods be inflated into the justification for territorial demands.

Kingship was a title from the Germanic world. Kings were the elected war leaders of a tribe or people. As the Roman historian Tacitus described them around AD 100, they acquired fame from their heroic achievements and their generosity in distributing plunder among their band of trusted followers. The more victories a leader could bring home, the more warriors attached themselves to him. He could even assume the leadership of several tribes and nations. If success was not forthcoming, then the *Gefolgschaft* disappeared and with it the position of king. The Germanic peoples who overflowed into western and southern Europe in the fourth and fifth centuries spread the concept of this strongly personal form of exercising authority. Clovis (*c.* 481–511) was one of the most successful kings of the Franks, who for a time brought the area between the Rhine and Aquitaine under his rule. The personal character of his leadership meant not only that his conversion to Christianity determined at the same time the religious faith of his people, but also the distribution of the conquered territory among various leaders after his death.

This Germanic kingship was therefore based on a very direct bond between a people and its leader, whose role was strictly defined by his personal abilities. There was no question of a fixed territory, as conquests were regarded as the most important activity and source of income. This concept of power was fundamentally different from the Roman one, in which there were strictly defined notions about the hierarchy of functions and offices. Nevertheless, everything that was Roman still retained the glitter of ancient civilization and imperial grandeur, and for that reason exercised an irresistible attraction on the Germanic kings, who wanted nothing more than to imitate the Caesars.

The Franks seem to have been the most martial

The conversion to Christianity of Clovis determined the religious faith of his people.

This was the logical consequence of the personal nature of his government and the magical dimension of Frankish kingship.

Late-medieval picture of his baptism.

Wolfenbüttel, Herzogliche Bibliothek

Coloured drawing of a cavalry battle,
inspired by the destructive raids of the Hungarians in southern Germany and Switzerland in 925.
Leiden, Universiteitsbibliotheek

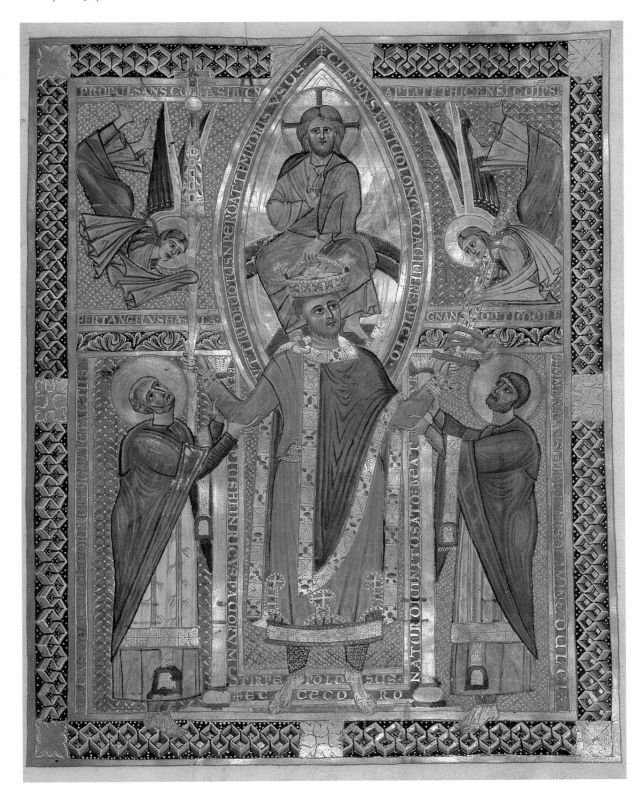

God with his own hands crowning the Emperor Henry II, who on both sides is offered the tokens of his investiture,
the sword and the holy lance, by an angel. St Ulrich of Augsburg and St Emmerga of Regensburg help him to carry these imperial insignia.
Miniature dating between 1002 and 1014.
Munich, Bayerische Staatsbibliothek

of the Germanic peoples in western Europe – though the Saxons, too, had shown their strength along the coasts of the North Sea and in eastern Britain. The effective Frankish war leaders superseded the Merovingian kings from the days of Charles Martel, whose fame was based on the battle of Poitiers where he held the Muslims in 732. Frankish support for the pope, whose position became constantly more threatened by the invading Lombards, brought the title of king to Charles Martel's son Pepin. Although both Charles Martel and his successors applied the principle of distributing the inheritance of the kingdom among their sons, their territory still remained a single whole because again and again it occurred that a son withdrew, retiring into a monastery, or died young. For more than a century, between 732 and 840, the Frankish leadership stayed not only undivided, but in the hands of strong personalities. Charlemagne waged campaigns of conquest against the Saxons, the Bavarians, in Catalonia, and also against the Lombards, whose kingship he assumed in 774. He was always able to appeal for the propagation of the Christian faith or the protection of the papacy. This role of defender of the Church won him his coronation as emperor on Christmas Day 800.

These events are described so factually here because in the long term they had far-reaching consequences both materially and ideologically. The restoration of the imperial title in the west meant an affront for the only successors, until then, of the Roman empire in Byzantium. In days to come the popes would with increasing emphasis claim their privilege of crowning the emperors of the west. Because of their defence of the Church in this world, the popes awarded to the emperors supremacy over the Germanic kings. In 1054 the claims of the bishops of Rome were to lead to the Great Schism with the eastern (Greek Orthodox) Church. The Frankish kings gained a double advantage over their rivals, and so elevated themselves at least in theory above the worldly hurly-burly of the struggle for power; their imperial title was a reference to the universal power of late antiquity, and their papal anointing made them pre-eminently the defenders of the Christian faith. This position would ultimately lead to a struggle for precedence with the popes, an issue which Gregory VII and Urban II would take up against the emperor Henry IV between 1076 and 1093. In addition – and in the long term perhaps more importantly – what was

called the 'doctrine of the two swords', which distinguished between the worldly authority of princes and the spiritual authority of the Church, meant a kind of division of power which would make its gradual secularization possible. At the territorial level Charlemagne's titles of emperor and king of the Lombards continued to involve the Holy Roman Emperors in Italy for centuries, which contributed in no small measure to its political fragmentation. On the other hand the imperial orientation towards the south – which in the time of Frederick II (1211–1250) was even localized in Sicily – strengthened the centrifugal forces in the Empire: it was no accident that his reign was succeeded by the Great Interregnum.

The elevation of Charlemagne to emperor also produced fresh paradoxes. The first is that this highest dignity in no way prevented his dynasty – he himself had only one surviving son – from proceeding to split the heritage again after 843, so that the title of emperor was soon restricted to one part of the old Frankish kingdom, and at some times could no longer be granted. That part was the eastern part, the least Frankish and the least Romanized, so that the ancient torch had to be taken up by peoples of whom only a small minority south of the Danube had experienced the blessings of Roman civilization. The concept of *translatio Imperii*, the transfer of the empire of the Romans to other peoples, had to take a step backward from this course of events.

What is the explanation for the immense Frankish empire of Charlemagne ultimately finding its continuation in its least developed and least Christianized eastern parts? Ultimately German kings were successful in calling a halt to the centrifugal forces after the Carolingian expansion sooner than their West-Frankish rivals. First of all there was the dynastic factor: King Henry I (919–936) first broke the tradition of dividing the inheritance. He was succeeded by the Ottonian and Salic dynasties of emperors, who ensured a long continuity.

On the other hand the West-Frankish Carolingians lacked a firm power base during the tenth century. They were faced with both territorial princes and feudal lords who, secure in their fortresses and surrounding land, made alliances with anyone who could offer any prospect of expanding their power. The feudal fragmentation of power was nowhere else, nor ever, as total as it was there. Even after the archbishop of Rheims, Adalbero, had been able to persuade the barons to remove the last weak Carolingian from the

Otto I, his wife Adelaide, and his young son, the later Otto II, kneel at the feet of Christ, St Maurice and the Virgin. Relief in ivory of c. 963. Milan, Castello Sforzesco, Museo de Arte Antica

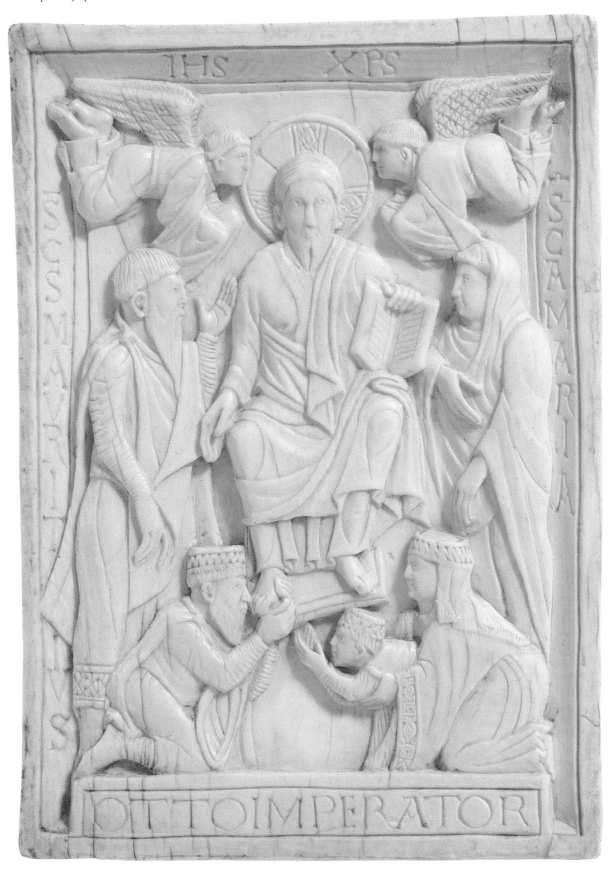

The royal crown of Hungary goes back to the magnificent past of the Byzantine empire.
It is made up of two separate crowns; a dome-shaped Greek one, as once worn by the Byzantine emperors, and a circular Latin crown,
made about 1160. The combined crown probably dates from before 1290, when Andreas III was crowned with it.
Budapest, Magyar Nemzeti Muzeum

Coronation robe with dedicatory inscriptions of King Steven (997–1038) and Queen Gisela of Hungary.
Byzantine silk with gold border.
Budapest, Magyar Nemzeti Muzeum

throne, and had brought about the election of Hugh Capet in 987, little changed except that the title of king was retained. Only in the twelfth century would this dynasty show itself capable of a slow reconstruction of some central power. The first generations of Capetian kings remained completely dependent upon the co-operation of territorial princes such as the dukes of Normandy, who possessed substantially more land than they did. Their influence was limited to the Ile-de-France, where they, with the assent of the local potentates, could apply some degree of superiority.

A second factor which explains the predominance of the East-Frankish empire is concealed in the fact that the emperors based their power on that of the Church, which they linked very closely to their empire. At the imperial court they surrounded themselves with scholarly priests who were entrusted with the control of the chancellery and other central functions. From there, at the instigation of the emperor, they were appointed to ecclesiastical dignities as bishops, archbishops or abbots, so that they could fulfil their services to the empire at the expense of their ecclesiastical properties, and contribute to the integration of the region. Priestly celibacy meant that the ecclesiastical authorities presented no direct problem of the build-up of a dynastic heritage of their own, as lay vassals were wont to do. This established Church could exist in the service of an emperor who was after all the supreme defender of Christianity and also actively supported its dissemination. For instance, the archiepiscopal seat of Magdeburg served as an advanced German mission station against the heathen Slavs in the north (between the Elbe and the Oder) and particularly in the east. The very real confrontation with the Slav and Magyar peoples strengthened both co-operation between Church and Empire in the fight against the heathen, and the mutual solidarity of the peoples within the Empire. The definitive defeat inflicted by the Emperor Otto I on the Magyars at Lechfeld in 955 was achieved through the joint efforts of Saxons, Franks, Alemanns, Bavarians and Lotharingians, who without this challenge would have been more inclined to fight among themselves.[7] From their solid *Hausmacht* in Saxony the Ottonian emperors were able in the tenth century to gather in the remains of Lotharingia, once thought of in 843 as a buffer state to which the imperial title would remain linked, at the expense of the totally weakened West-Frankish kings.

The East-Frankish kingdom had, just like all the other large regions of Europe in the tenth and eleventh centuries, a richly variegated population which as well as the German tribes mentioned above also included Romansch speakers (the Burgundians, who inhabited the Moselle region and the Lower Rhone valley), Latins in Italy, and West Slavs in the region between the Elbe and the Oder. The north-Italian region was able to maintain its identity against German domination, the area round Treves was gradually assimilated into Germany, and the links with the other Romansch areas remained very loose, as did those with the Low Countries. In the German language area the difference between north and south actually posed just as great a problem of communication as that with other western languages. This made the confrontation with the Magyars and Slavs, who spoke completely different languages, clearly sharper. The Empire developed a frontier belt along the Danube, where reinforced 'marches' (Krajina, Carinthia, Steiermark, and the Ostmark) had to drive back the Slavs and Magyars, and also the outposts of Byzantium.

The new Kingdoms

The foundation – by the Holy Roman Empire and the papacy – of Christian kingdoms on the open east flank of Christianity may also be understood from two points of view, that of conversion, and that of pacification. St Stephen (997–1038), crowned as king of Hungary by Pope Silvester II in 1001, and the Arpad dynasty had – originally under vassalage to the Empire – to subdue the Magyars in the extensive low-lying plains protected to north and east by the Carpathians. From this position Croatia was incorporated in about 1100, and from 1120 to 1150 Bosnia, too, brought under Hungarian protection. In this way the new kingdom acquired an outlet to the Adriatic which it would continue to hold for centuries.

In Poland emperor and pope applied the same strategy: the name Polonia and the title of king date from the same period as does the kingdom of Hungary, but internal rivalries and conflict over the rule of Bohemia incited new interventions by the Empire. The dioceses founded under papal protection in Gniezno and Esztergom had a central significance in both new kingdoms. Also of importance was the massive movement of migration, in which people from the Low Countries and western Germany, because of relative overpopulation, set off eastwards to exploit new lands there with favourable conditions for development. In this way, in countless villages and towns to the east of the Elbe,

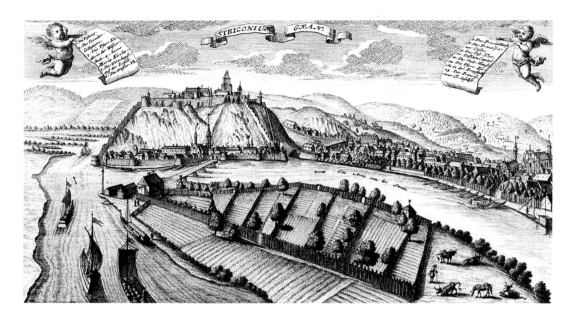

Under papal protection various bishoprics were established in the new kingdoms of Poland and Hungary.
The principal one in Hungary was Esztergom on the Danube. Sixteenth-century engraving by F.B. Wener and J.C. Leopold.
Budapest, Magyar Nemzeti Muzeum

colonies were formed of Christians coming from the west, who brought with them their own traditions, including their language and their customary laws. The traces of this migration are still clearly recognizable in place names and the local culture. It should be mentioned here that these settlements of people in the Slav areas accelerated their submission and assimilation. In the period of rising tension between emperor and pope, Henry IV in 1085 granted kingly authority over Bohemia, with the status of imperial vassal, to the Premyslid dynasty, while the bishop of Prague was placed under the supervision of the archbishop of Mainz.

Although it would be naive to equate the establishment of these offices with conversion on the one hand, and territorial control on the other, the co-ordinated – even if sometimes also rival – development of three Christian kingdoms in the frontier region between Slavs and Germans, heathens and Christians was undoubtedly of enormous significance for the patterns of the future. The names and status of these kingdoms have through all the vicissitudes of history until today remained points of reference for the political activities of states.

The internal consolidation of these kingdoms remained an immense task, the more so because the Slavs and Magyars at that time were still equestrian hordes, disinclined to take up a sedentary lifestyle on a defined piece of territory. The same

observation is largely valid, though with different vehicles, for the Danes. About the year 1000 they had by no means discarded the expansionary drive of the Vikings. In 1029 the Normans established their first overlordship in southern Italy, and a year earlier the Danish King Canute (1019–1035) had conquered Norway and Sweden. In 950 and 980 the Danes and Norwegians had begun to raid England again, which in 1014 gave Sweyn the crown of England, a dignity which his son Canute combined with his rule over Scandinavia. This episode again illustrates the impressive mobility of peoples across seas.

The Scandinavian excursions to Britain came to an abrupt end in 1066, when the newly elected King Harold defeated his Danish rival Harald Hardrada. However, when Harold in his turn was defeated at Hastings by the Norman claimant William the Conqueror, English history took a new turn. He consolidated his victory on the battlefield by a drastic elimination of the native aristocracy, rewarding his continental supporters with their possessions. He also built castles on the Norman model in London, York and also, together with cathedrals, in Rochester and Durham. The Frankish feudal system, not previously known in England, was introduced to provide a material basis of power for the new foreign rulers, most of whom anyhow combined their holdings with others in the Frankish kingdoms. Because as foreign conquerors their position was vulnerable, it

The expansion of the Vikings came as a shock to western Europe.
This shows Danish Vikings landing on the east coast of England, where they made permanent settlements. Miniature of c. 1130.
New York, The Pierpont Morgan Library

was essential for the Normans to enforce a firm administrative system. For this they were able to base themselves on Anglo-Saxon tradition. The counties, which still largely exist within the same boundaries, dated from Anglo-Saxon times; they were subdivided into 'hundreds'. The king appointed sheriffs at the head of each shire, with fiscal, military and judicial duties. In contrast to the Frankish empire, neither the sheriffs nor other notables such as bishops and abbots were vassals of the king, and they were not rewarded in the form of lands given in fief. Through this hierarchically constructed system of communities which decided on certain matters by holding meetings – the *gemot* of the county and the hundred – England was able to create a central royal civil service much sooner than the continent, with at the same time an effective system of representation, without having to go through the long-drawn-out process of fragmentation characteristic of the Frankish feudal system.

Now that England had escaped the toils of Scandinavian invasions, the Norman dynasty brought a new bond with the continent, which as said above extended further than just one man being both king and duke. In 1154 the course of hereditary succession brought the Plantagenet Henry II to the English throne, while he was simultaneously duke of Normandy, count of Anjou and, through his wife, Eleanor of Aquitaine, also duke of Aquitaine. This power complex was in France alone larger than the crown demesnes of the king of France. Fifty years later King Philip Augustus was strong enough to conquer Normandy and Anjou, but Aquitaine remained English, though held as a fief of the king of France. Here lay the basic elements of the long-lasting personal union of England and Aquitaine, and the much more dramatic English claims to the crown of France, which from 1337 were to be fought out – mainly on French soil – in the Hundred Years War.

During the thirteenth century, however, the

William the Conqueror often built castles and cathedrals near each other on the frontiers of his new territory.
Durham is a fine example of this. *Durham cathedral and bridge from the River Wear,* 1799, watercolour by Thomas Girtin.
Manchester, The Whitworth Art Gallery

English expansionary drive went further. In the direction of Ireland they had already undertaken a first conquest in 1171–1172, with papal support for the missionary offensive as their justification. In 1341 the Pale was demarcated, to the east of which English authority was recognized. In 1541 King Henry VIII took the title of king of Ireland, and began a large-scale policy of annexation. The conquest and incorporation of Wales into the kingdom occurred in 1282 under the energetic King Edward I (1272–1307). Although the Normans built castles throughout the land originally inhabited by Celtic people, it retained many of its ancient traditions and rebelled in 1400. King Edward's attack on Scotland was less successful: in 1296 this evoked such vigorous resistance that after the famous battle of Bannockburn in 1314 – still commemorated by the Scots – the English had to acknowledge Scottish independence.

Among the earliest expansive kingdoms in Europe we must include the Iberian ones. It must be remembered first of all that in the tenth century the caliphate of Cordoba, with Byzantium, was the most highly civilized region in Europe. The Berber dynasty of the Almoravids succeeded from 1086 to 1114 in reoccupying Saragossa and Barcelona. Despite the losses of territory suffered afterwards by the Muslims, their area remained during subsequent centuries the cradle for a transfer of culture for which Christian Europe is extremely in its debt. Europeans, however, are inclined to look at these matters from the opposite point of view and to label every small piece of land regained from Islam as a mark of progress. From this point of view it is striking that the southerly expansion of the Christian kingdoms under the pretext of the crusades proclaimed by the popes in 1063 proceeded along three

The Court of Chancery, c. 1450. This English court was empowered to decide disputes about the ownership of property, inheritance and contracts. Its influence increased noticeably in the course of the fifteenth century with the growing number of disputes. London, The Honourable Society of the Inner Temple

After the incorporation of Wales into England in 1282, Edward I had many imposing castles built there. One of these was Carnarvon. Watercolour by J.M.W. Turner, c. 1883. London, British Museum, Prints and Drawings

parallel axes. After military successes the count of Portugal in 1137 proclaimed himself king, a title in which the popes later confirmed him by virtue of the role of his region in the *reconquista*. It is also striking that the king of León had earlier claimed the title of emperor of Spain, a claim which attempted to emphasize the unity of the Christians compared with the fragmentation then ruling among the Muslims. In 1147 Lisbon fell into Christian hands. Further conquests proceeded by stages, with occasional set-backs, with crusaders from north-west Europe and particularly Provence sometimes providing reinforcements. The areas of the Alentejo and the Algarve mostly came into the hands of the orders of religious knights, who thereafter assured both their conquest and their exploitation. Faro was reached in 1249.

In the neighbouring kingdoms of León and Castile, which in 1230 came under a single rule and of which the county of Portugal was originally a dependency, the successes on the west coast were followed with some suspicion, for fear of excessive strengthening of their neighbour's position. The advance of Castile also took place in stages: Toledo was conquered in 1085, but it was not until 1236 that Cordoba fell. It was followed by Seville in 1247, after which two centuries of stagnation again intervened. One of the problems of expansion southwards was that of the scarcity of peasants to work the conquered land. Attractive liberties had to be granted to communities in villages and towns, which in the long term substantially restricted the power of the kings over the countryside. Along the east coast the centuries-long conflict against the Muslims brought about the union of the individual regions, the county of Barcelona, the kingdom of Aragon, Majorca, Valencia, Murcia, with various overseas settlements of the Barcelona merchants as well. Integration of the Christian Iberian peninsula therefore proceeded from north to south, but allowed the kingdoms of Portugal, Castile-León and Aragon to advance side by side, and not infrequently also against each other. From the linguistic point of view these still appear to be the main dividing lines in the region, clearly as a result of this particular process of expansion. The comment made earlier needs to be repeated here, that the theory of coastal areas organizing themselves differently from extensive land masses such as the Castilian plateau is clearly demonstrated in Iberia.

This survey of the formation of new expansionary kingdoms may here perhaps permit a small chronological excursion to have a quick look at the Balkans. The Slav population there were converted to Christianity by the Greek Orthodox Church, starting with Methodius and Cyril, who led a mission to the Bulgars in 861/862. For that purpose they provided a Slav translation of the Holy Scriptures; to do this they had first to invent a Slav script. The result was that the Great Schism in 1054 also divided the Slavs between a Roman and an Orthodox Slav liturgy. The occupation of the Balkans by the Byzantine empire obviously passed through strong and weak phases. In the last decades of the twelfth century the Bulgarians were able to fight themselves fairly free, and were ruled by their own tsar. The Mongol invasion of 1242 brought an end to that. The conquest of Byzantium by the Latin emperors in 1204 then weakened their control of the remains of the Greek empire. The rivalry between the western and eastern churches played into the hands of the local rulers. Thus the pope recognized the kingship over Serbia of the Bulgarian tsar in 1204, and of the Serbian Stephen in 1218. In this power vacuum, and spared the Mongol invasions, the Serbians were able to expand their territory substantially into Macedonia, Bosnia and Slavonia. Their King Milutin (1282-1321) was a Roman Catholic.

Europe's monarchic foundations

In the previous paragraphs the circumstances giving rise to the emergence of the great European monarchies have been examined. In doing so it was striking that in the tenth and eleventh centuries the foundations were actually laid for a whole list of monarchies which have since continued to exist under more or less the same names to the present day, in the same core territories. This finding is important because, once established, a large organization does not disappear so easily. It acquires a life, interests become bound up in it, people accept it as an established framework. The first large kingdoms determined to a high degree the future fate of Europe, because they were important agents which gathered forces together and fought out conflicts with each other. If some of the kingdoms mentioned above were in later centuries taken up into larger

Allegorical illustration by P.P. Rubens of the dynastic union of England and Scotland which came into being in 1603. Both countries are represented by female figures crowning Prince Charles. Sketch in oils as design for part of a large painted ceiling in London in the Banqueting House in Whitehall. Rotterdam, Museum Boymans-van Beuningen

political unions – consider, for example, the royal marriage which in 1469 permanently united the kingdoms of Castile-León and Aragon; the union of England with Wales, Scotland and Ireland; or the unification of the Balkans – the older entities have come up once again in more recent times as the frameworks within which populations wish to be recognized.

The early formation of these monarchies distinguished them from areas whose structures in that period had either not been stabilized, for example the Balkans and Russia, or else had been condensed on a smaller scale, as in Italy or the Low Countries. The creation of a kingdom or of an empire must not be interpreted as the end or the completion of an evolution; on the contrary, all these constructs for centuries appeared to be internally unstable and to have experienced internal conflicts, which have put their very survival at risk. Their internal organizations will have to be examined further. However, it can already be established, with the knowledge available at the end of the twentieth century, that greater Germany, France, England, Poland, Hungary, the Czech republic (Bohemia), Denmark, Portugal, Spain (with a Catalan region), Serbia and Bulgaria now exist within frontiers which do not depart so very substantially from those formed between the tenth to the thirteenth centuries. From this thousand years of survival, in spite of phases in which every country except England has been taken over or disappeared, one must at least conclude that their early establishment worked to perpetuate their existence. Unlike the early Germanic kingdoms, they formed in the long run tightly institutionalized states. Latecomers found life more difficult in a landscape that was already largely parcelled out.

In the circumstances surrounding the establishment of the earliest monarchies some general characteristics can be distinguished. The first and most common is that of the close coincidence of the formation of the early monarchies and conversion to Christianity, particularly to Roman Catholicism, but also to Greek Orthodoxy. Only the Scandinavian and Norman expansions do not seem to have been linked in the first place to a drive for conversion. The Empire initially, and later all the kingdoms, were given an expressly missionary task with their recognition by the Church. Three circumstances explain this link. First was the fact that the process of conversion of Europe to Christianity had not by the year 1000 proceeded very far, and large areas of heathens or followers of other religions lay open to the universal Church. In western Europe

there was certainly still much to do, but it was principally against the massive presence of whole nations of Muslims, Slavs and Scandinavian heathens that it made a strong appeal on valiant warriors to devote themselves to the propagation of the true faith. Secondly, it should be remembered that during the early and high Middle Ages the Church was the only institution keeping the cultural standard of the Roman empire flying on a continental scale. In the midst of the chaos of feudal competition and movements of peoples the Church formed the only institution which stood above parties, legal systems, languages and values. In the third place, ambitious warlords adorned themselves all too readily with the sacramental dignity which the Church could offer them in return for their proven services. This enabled them to elevate themselves above their competitors and to make their position of power unassailable by their neighbours – except, of course, by the ecclesiastics themselves.

A second general characteristic of the early monarchies is that they can be divided into two categories, a primary and a secondary one, or in other words, an autonomous development and a derived one. Of course, no single development in large human communities can be called entirely autonomous, because it is always built to some extent on earlier foundations. By the primary category is meant here the establishment of a kingship as the result of a development within the society involved itself. The Frankish expansion appeared to originate primarily from that people, and consequently so did the formation of the West-Frankish and East-Frankish realms, to become the Empire and the kingdom of France. The English expansion – admittedly itself a secondary one from the point of view of the Danes and the Normans – is primary in respect of western France, Wales, Scotland and Ireland. Although the *reconquista* was instigated by the popes, and crusades also attracted warriors from more northern countries, the core of this southward expansion movement can still be said to have originated in the north Iberian Christian societies. Finally the Serbian expansion in the thirteenth century can also be labelled autonomous.

By a derived formation is here meant the creation of a kingdom by another, as Poland, Bohemia and Hungary were created by the Empire and the papacy. Analogous developments can be observed in England under the Danes and the Normans, in Norway and Sweden, in the south-easterly marches of the Empire, in Sicily, and possibly in Bulgaria. From the start this distinction demonstrates a differ-

The formation of the early monarchies usually went together with their conversion to Christianity.
Baptism of King Grimbaut and his daughter. Flemish miniature made between 1460 and 1467.
Brussels, Bibliothèque royale de Belgique

ence in dynamism: the monarchies formed autonomously obviously disposed of more human and material resources by which they in particular were capable of bringing about developments elsewhere.

A third general characteristic is limited to the autonomous formation processes. Particularly in the development of the Empire, France and England, it is established that the extent, the concentrated location, and the productive capacity of the crown demesnes were essential trump cards in the growth of the power of the monarchy. The Carolingians had at their disposition a very substantial and productive crown demesne, which formed the basis of their operations. For the Ottonians one can point to their *Hausmacht* in Saxony, while the laborious rise of the Capets is rightly connected with the sparseness and limited extent of their holdings. William the Conqueror on the other hand took care that the lands of his greatest vassals were located in the distant corners of his newly conquered country. In this way he retained control over both the territory and his human resources. Because of the need to hold suffi-

cient farmland, pasture and forest, the cores of the early kingdoms lay in plains or gently sloping plateaux, with fertile land which could be exploited in a variety of ways. South-east England, the Paris basin, the area between the Meuse and the Rhine, and the plain of Saxony are obvious examples.

The fourth general characteristic of the early monarchies is that they essentially involve territorial developments. Kings had plenty of fertile land and could therefore conquer yet more land. Again the Danish and Norman expansions must be considered separately; though they moved across the seas in the Viking tradition they too had in the period under discussion – the tenth and eleventh centuries – finally turned towards the long-term possession of land for sedentary exploitation. When the demarcation lines between the kingdoms were provisionally and roughly established in the year 1200, some marginal areas were left over. These were small-scale regions, but already in some cases with an intensively developed structure, situated along the coasts and where the spheres of influence of the great powers

The wave of English expansion was not only into Wales, Scotland and Ireland, but also into western France.

The Black Prince paying homage to King Edward III for the duchy of Aquitaine, July 1362.

London, British Library

Dynastic vicissitudes not uncommonly brought usurpers with dubious legal title to power. In a system of hereditary succession, the legitimacy of the ancestry and the prestige of the ruling family were decisive. The earlier famous ancestors could be traced back, the more illustrious was the dynasty. Thirteenth-century genealogy of the kings of England, going back to the Trojan Brutus, the legendary grandson of Aeneas. Of interest is the description in the circles of the territories comprising the seven Anglo-Saxon kingdoms of the heptarchy: Essex, Kent, Sussex (Wiltshire and Yorkshire), Gloucester, Winchester and Warwick, Northumbria, Suffolk and Norfolk. The circle in the centre gives the dimensions of the whole territory of the English. The Hague, Koninklijke Bibliotheek

In yards of embroidery the Bayeux tapestry tells the story of the Norman seizure of power in England in 1066;
it was made soon after William the Conqueror's victory, and here he is shown enthroned and holding his sword upright.
Bayeux, Musée de la Tapisserie de Bayeux

met. Italy satisfied both criteria: emperor and pope, Byzantium, Muslims and Normans all contributed to keep that highly developed and maritime-oriented land divided. On a more limited scale the same applied to the areas of the Catalan coast with their maritime expansion zone; the Low Countries, squashed between the Empire, France and England, and also oriented towards the sea, the areas along the south coast of the Baltic; and the Balkans. For these regions a logic must be sought along two lines: the threat but also the relative autonomy presented by their position on the frontiers of the great powers, and on the other hand the explanation of their heterogeneous structures. Monarchs could influence much, but not everything.

Finally it must be noted that in the formative stages of the kingdoms the various components of power were very tightly interwoven. As has been said, they arose out of the drive for expansion of the lords ruling the largest territories, and their success remained largely dependent on the effective control of fertile land, its cultivators and its produce. Feudal landlords directed all their attention and their efforts on the maintenance – and where possible the expansion – of their inherited lands. With that as

their object families followed carefully thought-out strategies of contracting marriages and passing on inheritances. These were the 'soft' instruments for the expansion of possessions and hence power, which in case of argument were unhesitatingly supported by the instruments of physical force. The masters of the demesne economy commanded the essential wealth with which they could wage their battles for power: the sparse surpluses from agriculture and animal husbandry, barely sufficient to give the warrior class the opportunity of acquiring their expensive horses and military equipment, to train themselves in the arts of war, and to assure themselves of sufficient followers on horse or on foot. The rising territorial rulers, the kings and emperors of the tenth to the thirteenth century, were in essence nothing more than the winners in the free-for-all for control over the sparse surpluses of a still relatively unproductive agricultural economy. Once a position of supremacy was acquired, they still remained to a high degree reliant upon the good management of their extensive crown lands.[8]

If the basis of the power of the monarchy was obviously in the economy of the crown lands, it was also clear that it was in every way in the interest of

Allegory of the order of succession to the Swedish throne, from which women were not excluded.
Painting of 1693 by the court painter D.K. Ehrenstrahl.
Stockholm, National Museet

the champions in the competition to add splendour and persuasive power to their position by assuring themselves of the support of the priests. The sacring of their offices as emperors and kings helped to underpin their often shaky position. An intensive call on the competences of the clergy, the only literate members of a society of peasants and warriors, was absolutely essential. In their turn they not only provided the kings with their ideological justification, but also conferred a strong impetus to the policy pursued of disseminating the faith. From the late tenth century the clergy were also successful in laboriously and gradually imposing some Christian principles on the behaviour of the princes and feudal lords. From 989 a series of regional synods proclaimed the Peace of God, a movement starting in the south of France, which set limits to feudal acts of violence against the property of the Church, and against humble peasants and traders. In the mid-eleventh century they published a ban against acts of violence during liturgically significant days and periods: Sundays, Thursdays, Advent and Lent, the 'Truce of God'. Also with regard to marriages the Church imposed its authority by formulating strict rules for this contract, now

elevated to a sacrament. Bishop Ivo of Chartres forced King Philip I of France to abjure his bigamy publicly in 1105. Marriages within the fourth grade of relationship, and the repudiation of wives, often on the grounds of barrenness, were forbidden. In this way the Church cautiously imposed its rules, setting limits to some extent to the unbridled lust for power of the feudal lords. Power which was legitimized, thanks to the Church, was less and less able to escape its regulation. Until about 1300 both Church and kings still controlled the agricultural economy which then produced by far the greatest wealth. Mutual competition between the Church and the secular power increased, in which the original superiority of the clergy was reduced just because the warriors were successful in subjecting greater areas to their control.

1   Braudel 1966–1972, 355–379; 1979, 3
2   Parker 1972, 280
3   Haverkamp 1993, 89
4   Paviot 1991
5   Tilly 1975, 41
6   Sahlins 1989, 17–22, 299–300
7   Prinz 1993, 223–243
8   Dhondt 1948, Barthélémy 19s

CHAPTER II

Men and Resources

Concentrations of population

The geographical location of a region was not only important for the scope it gave its rulers to develop power. Quite apart from their actions, the lie of the land and soil conditions were major factors in creating opportunities for societies to develop a particular style of living. The likelihood that agriculture would become more intensive, or products be commercialized, depended to a high degree on geographical factors such as the fertility of the land, the presence of minerals and the proximity of navigable rivers and coasts with harbour facilities. The differences can be seen very clearly in the density of population and the existence of large towns associated with it. It is evident that only an area of high agricultural productivity can allow a significant part of its population to exist in what we call the secondary and tertiary sectors of the economy. Only when enough food is produced or imported can a large part of the population devote itself to tasks in skilled trades, industry or services. The density of population depends therefore in the first place on the opportunities in the natural environment that make high levels of production possible. Only in the second place can a high density of population be supported by constructive co-operation between regions compensating for each other's deficiencies. This implies transport, trade, technical expansion – in short, development. The density of habitation may in the first phase have been determined by fa-

vourable environmental conditions, but later it can only be maintained by a society which has achieved an effective mastery over nature in the form of sufficient agricultural productivity, regulating the supply of clean water for town and country, and the development of a reliable transport system and tools.

Until the middle of the nineteenth century great concentrations of population were only viable along easily navigable rivers and on the coast, because ships could ensure the transport of mass-produced goods considerably more easily than carts. Later the railway opened up a new network of communications, making the transport of mass-produced goods also possible in the interior of the country. This explains why before industrialization the large towns and thickly populated hinterlands were always found along coasts with accessible harbours and in the proximity of great rivers. Thus about 1600 the Netherlands reached an average population density of forty-eight per square kilometre and Italy one of forty-four; the great land-based countries showed significantly lower scores: France thirty-four, Germany twenty-eight, the Iberian peninsula seventeen, Poland and Prussia fourteen; in those days Scandinavia had fewer than two inhabitants per square kilometre. Naturally such averages conceal exceptions, as for instance along the south coast of Sweden. But in Italy, too, and even in the tiny Netherlands, there was great regional variation. In 1795, 166

Only in regions with a plentiful production of food could a large proportion of the population engage in industry and services, which in their turn stimulated trade.
Detail from the *Port of Seville*, located in the fertile plain of the Guadalquivir.
Sixteenth-century painting by Alonso S. Coello.
Madrid, Museo de America

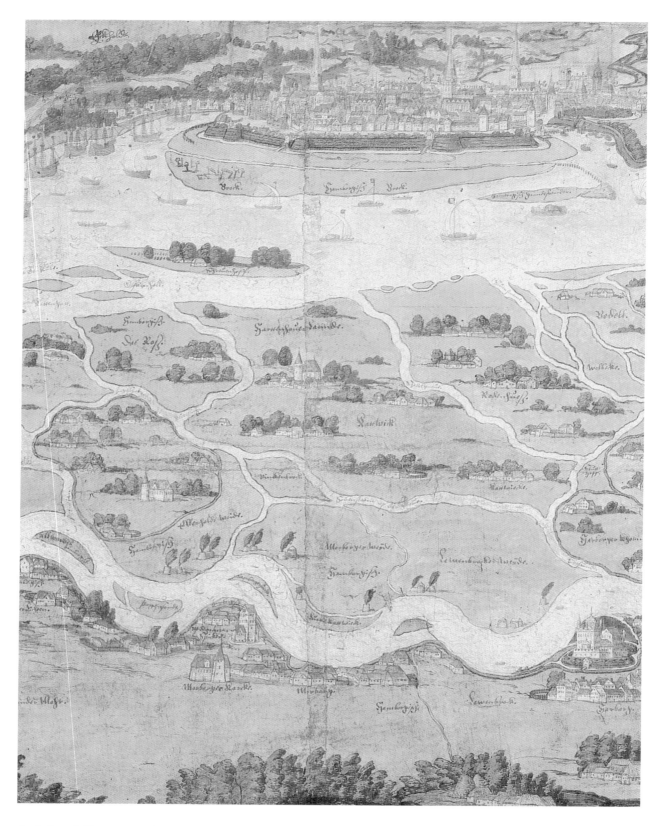

In the late Middle Ages great densities of population were concentrated in the coastal regions from the mouth of the Seine to that of the Elbe.
Hamburg on the Elbe, detail of a geographical map of 1568, drawn by Melchior Lorich.
Hamburg, Staatsarchiv

people lived in every square kilometre of North Holland and scarcely fifteen in the eastern province of Drente; the country's average score of sixty-four was also comparatively very high.

Taken as a whole the figures show a sharp difference in order of size. About 1600 the immeasurable expanse of Russia numbered as many subjects as the Holy Roman Empire, and fewer than France which then had some 18.5 million. To the east of the Vistula the only towns with more than 40,000 inhabitants were Moscow, Novgorod, Sofia, Smolensk and Kiev. Constantinople, Naples and Paris then had more than 200,000, while there were nine other western towns with more than 100,000. Of the total 105 million population of Europe at that time, about 12 per cent lived in towns; in Russia the figure was only 5 per cent. The great concentrations of population were on the coast of the North Sea from the mouth of the Seine to that of the Elbe, and along the north coast of the Mediterranean.

For many centuries the interior of the continent was much more thinly populated than the areas near the coasts and along the great rivers. The harsher climate also generally made the interior rather less suitable for agriculture. Vast steppes which could barely support a very thin nomadic population existed in central and eastern Europe into this century. The enormous distances reduced traffic between these peoples to occasional contacts, which did not give rise to profound mutual influences. Here, too, the railway brought fundamental changes. Before, the speed of travel was determined by the stamina of a horse; at the most a system of relays on a few important routes could extend the length of that capability but not its speed. But the pattern of towns which had developed since the high Middle Ages determined in its turn the layout of the railway system: where there were no towns, and where few people lived, the trains did not go either.

In the ages before industrialization the size of most European towns remained rather modest, largely as a result of the difficulties of supplying them. About 1500 there were at most five towns with around 100,000 inhabitants: Venice, Genoa, Naples, possibly by then Milan, and Paris. Rome, Cordoba and Constantinople, as the capitals of great empires, had in former centuries had comparable or even greater populations, but since then had contracted. The Mediterranean situation of all these metropolises, except Paris, is striking. The reasons for this are plain: the fertility of the region and its ancient traditions and good maritime links made economic development possible on a scale that would only be equalled on the North Sea in the seventeenth century. By about 1500 no more than fifty towns had at least 20,000 inhabitants, and some hundred had between 10,000 and 20,000. The thousands of other towns, particularly in the interior, were therefore quite small, containing only a few thousand people each. This was the case until the middle of the eighteenth century. About 1800 the picture had already changed radically. In 1500 5.6 per cent of Europeans lived in towns of at least 10,000 inhabitants; three centuries later this was 10 per cent. Of the towns with a population of 100,000 or more – of which there were now seventeen – only eight were on the Mediterranean.

If one looks not just at individual towns, but at the density of the whole network of large towns, then Lombardy and the Po valley – with Milan, Genoa and Venice at its extremities – was about 1500 the most urbanized region in Europe. The Bay of Naples and the southern Netherlands reached 80 per cent of that level. Appreciably lower, the Paris basin and the valleys of the Rhine and Rhone scored 50 per cent of the urbanization level of the Po valley. Outside these zones of intensity the level of urbanization of the interior of France, Spain and Germany was very low, while – apart from the coasts – towns were really very thinly scattered in Scandinavia, the north and west of the British Isles, and central Europe. This pattern fundamentally maintained its validity till about 1750, although the total population in towns of over 10,000 inhabitants more than doubled from 3.4 to 7.5 million, and their share of the total population rose from 5.6 per cent to 10 per cent. The most important difference was that from the sixteenth century the highest urban density was located in the countries around the North Sea, with south-east England, the Low Countries and northern France as its nuclei. In this region the importance of London about 1800 already far outweighed that of all the other highly urbanized regions.[1]

Notes: see p. 103

This brings us to the overall evolution of population density throughout the period under discussion. Roughly four phases can be distinguished. From the tenth to the end of the thirteenth century the population increased strongly in the whole of Europe, from an estimated 38.5 million around AD 1000 to nearly twice this, about 75 million, about 1300. During the fourteenth and fifteenth centuries the population of Europe declined by a third to 50 million. The sixteenth century showed renewed growth, followed by stagnation, so that about 1750 the total reached about 120 million. During the subsequent

The region around Naples was already thickly populated
in classical times, because of its convenient location
and the fertility of the volcanic soil.

period of demographic explosion the resident population of Europe climbed to 210 million about 1850 and to 393 million in 1950. For our current argument it is important to underline that the earliest expansion and consolidation of kingdoms coincided with the first period of sustained population growth. Moreover, it is fundamental that each phase of overall growth is associated with a more than proportional growth in the urban population, so that the degree of urbanization also kept increasing.

What then was the significance of these concentrations – and the shifts in them – for the configurations of power? Because of their dependence on navigable waterways the metropolises and their satellite towns were situated close to coasts and large rivers. The great majority of them therefore found themselves in the frontier regions of the earliest consolidated and expanding monarchies, which had, after all, developed from fertile areas in

the continental interior. London, always by far the largest town in the British Isles, was located off-centre in England, and still more so in Great Britain as a whole. Urbanized regions in the Holy Roman Empire lay along the Rhine and Danube basins or along the northern coasts, all eccentrically sited *vis-à-vis* the main land mass. Thanks to their size and concentrated location the towns of Lombardy were in the twelfth century already uncontrollable by the otherwise powerful emperor Frederick Barbarossa. Apart from Paris, the waterhead that sucked up the surplus population of the whole of the Ile-de-France, the urbanized regions of France lay on the periphery: Gascony, the Rhone

About 1500 the town had a population of about 100,000.

Detail of the *View of the port of Naples*, painted by a Florentine master before 1487. Naples, Museo Nazionale di Capodimonte

valley, Alsace and the north-west. In Iberia the problem was partly overcome by moving the capitals further south (from Coimbra to Lisbon, from León and Valladolid to Toledo and Madrid), or left unsolved, later to become a source of regionalism (Barcelona, Valencia). A shift to the centre also occurred in Poland, from Cracow to Warsaw, when Prussia was incorporated in that kingdom in the fifteenth and sixteenth centuries. Until then Danzig, with its urbanized hinterland in the valley of the Vistula, had formed a typically eccentric centre of gravity. In the heavily urbanized coastal areas of the Low Countries no extensive monarchic state had been consolidated before 1600.

The large towns – pre-eminently oriented towards international, often overseas, trade – were clearly located eccentrically in relation to the monarchies which had after all grown out of large territorial units. This made it difficult for these monarchies to govern them. Nevertheless rulers tried to bring these concentrations of people and wealth under their control, but because of the resources available in the towns, they came up against strong resistance. In the best cases a kind of condominion emerged, in which the citizens of the town acquired a high degree of say in the administration of their territory. An example of this is the right of access – and in the case of seagoing trade even extensive autonomy – of Barcelona to its count, and to the later king of Aragon. The most commercially oriented urban societies had in any case often developed in the period when the territorial principalities and kingdoms could not yet exercise any

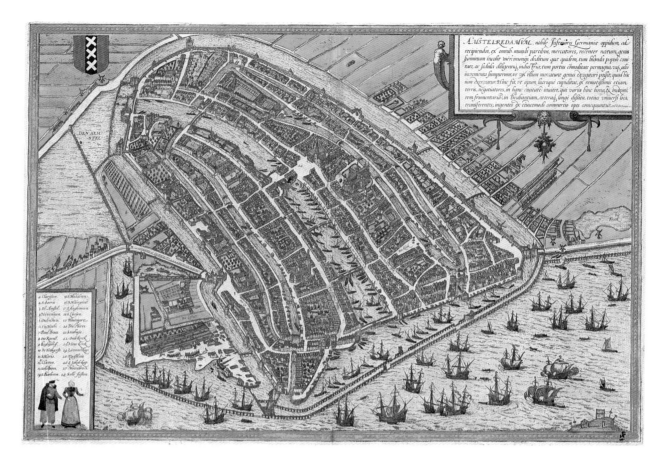

From the sixteenth century the regions round the North Sea were the most urbanized in Europe.
The Low Countries formed the heart of this region. Map of Amsterdam by Frans Hogenberg after a woodcut by Cornelis Anthonisz., 1544.
Amsterdam, Gemeentearchief

A strong monarchy would choose a central town for its capital, as did Castile, first in Toledo, and after the sixteenth century Madrid,
which was artificially expanded. *View and town plan of Toledo, c.* 1600, by El Greco. The Spanish king's Alcazar is clearly visible on the left.
Toledo, Museo del Greco

authority in the outlying corners of the continent, which offered the most strategic locations for harbours. This had given them the scope to develop systems themselves by which they could secure the protection of their essential interests in provisions and trade.

Concentrations of capital

For princes there were various advantages attached to the growth of towns within their territory, a dynamism which started in the tenth century in parallel to the formation and consolidation of the kingdoms. They could hope with some justification that their incomes from minting coinage, levying tolls, and the administration of justice would rise as the population, and particularly urban activity, grew. When petitioned they granted the right of self-government to the young municipalities, but in doing so they also reserved specific revenues to themselves. As the towns became more important, they began to carry more weight in the political power relationships of a region. It would suit a prince quite well to receive some support from them against his most important rivals, who were feudal lords and sometimes also great ecclesiastics, who after all were also great landowners. From the thirteenth century a very concrete form of support was added to this, which will be discussed below: the opportunity for the prince to request special subsidies from the towns beyond those he received regularly as the customary dues of a territorial lord.

In regions where large commercial centres developed, the princes had one more great opportunity open to them, that of applying to the wealthy traders and to the towns with a request for credit. Towns were after all where the skilled crafts and commercial activities generating the new riches were concentrated. Since the tenth century yields from traditional land revenues had certainly grown as a consequence of the increasing demand for agricultural land and the rise in its productivity, though in the thirteenth century inflation led to the erosion of all fixed levies. The increase in revenue, however, was in no way proportional to the fabulous fortunes piled up by the rich merchants.

In the twelfth century in some regions long-distance traders already made use of their surplus liquidity to satisfy the urgent demands of princes and feudal lords for short-term credit for their military expeditions. When King Louis ix of France was taken prisoner in Limassol while on a crusade

in 1249, the Sienese trading and banking house of the Scotti paid his ransom, against repayment a year later at the annual trade fair at Provins in Champagne. They regularly financed papal enterprises and in 1282 lent King Edward i of England the sums he needed for his conquest of Wales. He was not to repay them until 1287 in Paris. This prince had already in 1275 handed over the farming of his customs revenues to Tuscan merchant bankers. As large purchasers of English wool they had a direct interest in the orderly collection of these taxes, but they knew also how to make a profit from it. Good relations with the pope gave them the task of collecting the taxes of the Apostolic Chancery. With the money collected in England they paid there for their wool purchases so that they did not have to finance these themselves. Rome received her taxes a few months later from the yield of the sale of the finished cloth in Italy.

This ingenious system of combining their trade in goods and in money also offered them the opportunity to make further profits from their surplus liquidity in England in the form of credits to the king. Ever larger amounts were advanced to him, with the customs revenues as collateral. From a purely economic point of view the risk was covered, but political factors also played a role in the close links between high finance and the monarchy. By moving constantly in royal circles, the merchant-bankers could keep themselves adequately informed about planned military operations, and this foreknowledge did them no harm in their financial and commercial transactions. However, by the increasing complications of their interests the Italians worked themselves into a dilemma. Their claims against the crown became steadily larger and so, too, did the need to continue to assure themselves of good relations. Reluctance on their part might give the king the idea of interfering with their trade by confiscations or increased levies, or of approaching their competitors. For example, until 1299 the Riccardi from Lucca enjoyed the king's confidence, but after that date the Frescobaldi from Florence were mainly in favour. The benefits to the king were obvious: he succeeded – thanks to the flow of credit – not only in bringing his armies into the field for a specific campaign, as was normal under the system of feudal service, but also in being able to pay them afterwards. Moreover, he was able to fill Wales with castles built to keep the conquered region firmly under his authority. The credit not only provided him with money at short notice, independently of the slow revenues he could obtain

In the late Middle Ages there were already extensive demesnes in the region to the east of the Elbe
where mainly rye was cultivated for export to the west.
View of the castle of Marienburg beside the Vistula.
With Königsberg, more to the north-east, this was the headquarters of the Teutonic knights,
who in the fourteenth and fifteenth centuries had a substantial share of the grain trade to western Europe.

from his traditional demesne, but in the long term also gave him much more than his normal income. In this way he built up a public debt which was not repaid on his death. When the Frescobaldi became more reluctant to provide the cash, they were expelled from the country in 1311. They had to declare themselves bankrupt soon afterwards.

North Italian merchant-bankers were certainly not the only ones to provide credit to princes, but they undoubtedly controlled the largest capital resources and had the widest connections, so that they were the most sought-after partners. It was the Bonsignori of Siena who lent Charles of Anjou, the brother of Louis IX, the money with which in 1266 he was able to achieve his conquest of the kingdom of Sicily. The same Sienesi were also not afraid to talk openly about the interest they charged on their loans and about the size of the penalties for failing to meet the agreed repayment date. In 1275 they even

made the countess of Flanders declare in writing that none of the prohibitions of canon law against loans on interest and usury would apply to the consolidation of their debts, which involved a penalty of 0.97 per cent per week (equivalent to 50.5 per cent per year).

Nevertheless it was the accusation of charging usurious interest that disgraced the Templars in France. Since the twelfth century they had, with the pious aim of financing the crusades, collected money in the west and accepted it on deposit, arranged transfers to the Mediterranean area, and made loans on interest. Since 1146 the Templars had functioned as bankers and the most important financial backers to the French crown. King Philip IV (1285-1314), however, disposed of their services and went on to prosecute them, demanding the confiscation of their not inconsiderable property. The Avignon pope condemned the Order and abolished it.

Capital from merchant bankers like the Medici made it possible for princes
to finance wars without being dependent on their own revenues.
About 1440 Domenico Veneziano painted portraits of members of the Medici family in the retinue of his *Adoration of the Magi*.
Piero, with a hawk on his wrist, is behind the kneeling king, with Cosimo and Giovanni more towards the centre.
Berlin, Gemäldegalerie

In spite of all the evidence of the risks threatening relations between princes and bankers, the great Florentine houses also forked out enormous sums to Edward III, giving him a decisive advantage in the first stages of the Hundred Years War. The king, however, had to declare himself bankrupt by 1339, which meant that the Florentines could not recover their capital. This made the bankruptcy of the Peruzzi bank unavoidable in 1342, and in 1346 that of the Bardi. Similarly, the industrialist and wholesale merchant from Bourges, Jacques Cœur, worked his way up in the service of King Charles VII. He became Master of the Mint, and controlled the king's finances, using his extensive

St Eloy, patron saint of silversmiths, is a seventeenth-century Lombard work
which until the nineteenth century adorned the wall of the Milan mint or *Zecca.*
It shows various stages of the minting process in fine detail.
Milan, Castello Sforzesco, Civica Pinacoteca

commercial network in the Mediterranean for this purpose. In 1449 he financed the king's conquest of Normandy. Two years later he had to flee the country under accusations of embezzlement.[2]

Two conclusions about the period up to the fifteenth century emerge. First, that in regions where distance trade was an important factor in the economy, there was an appreciable flow of capital in circulation which brought unprecedented opportunities for expansion within the reach of those holding political power. The assignment of customs levies as security for credit was not a burden on a prince's own subjects, but on international trade. To the

During the seventeenth and eighteenth centuries credit was extremely cheap in the commercially advanced Republic of the United Provinces, enabling this small state to play the role of a great power. An impression of the Exchange in Amsterdam, painted after 1668 by J. Berckheyde.
Rotterdam, Museum Boymans-van Beuningen

extent that debts were not repaid, it was the affluent purchasers of the goods distributed by the merchant-bankers who paid the price of an expansionary policy. Secondly, it will be plain that the concentrations of capital, which made it possible for princes to finance wars costing more than their traditional demesne revenues, only occurred in a few regions of Europe. In this way the heavily commercialized regions acquired an advantage over the zones which had remained more agricultural.

The more both foreign traders with large capital resources operated in a region and also substantial trading and industrial capital was concentrated in the

towns, the more this offered extra reserves and guarantees for the credit-hungry princes. During the period under discussion this is evidenced by the military successes of France during the thirteenth century, of England after 1268, of Aragon, and of course of the north Italian city states. The central European kingdoms, Castile, Scotland, and even to a large extent France, remained on the other hand mainly dependent on the traditional feudal incomes which were much more modest, and above all much more difficult to mobilize. For instance, the kings of Denmark in the fourteenth and fifteenth centuries still had to mortgage castles and fiefs to solve their liquidity problems. Because commercial credit was scarcer in central and northern Europe than in the regions where the Italian merchants had settled, it was more expensive there and so less accessible to princes. In the west and south the public debt was already such a familiar phenomenon around 1500 that when there were problems repaying it, it was regularly converted into consolidated debt in the form of long-term bonds.

The acceleration and expansion experienced by commercial capitalism during the sixteenth century inevitably found its reaction in the volume and systemization of public credit. The shift of the economic centre of gravity to the Atlantic coasts, the flow of American silver into Spain, and the boom in the economy of southern Germany had their effects on the financial resources of princes. Genoese bankers became the most important financiers of various states, particularly Spain and France. The Fuggers, wholesale merchants and bankers in Augsburg, managed financial transactions in Germany, Austria, Poland and Hungary for the popes. Jacob Fugger had led the consortium of banks which assembled the capital promised by Charles v to the Electors who had elected him emperor in 1519, and from this the Fuggers derived their dominance of the Antwerp capital market. There they sold bearer letters of credit, so that the increasing circulation of money was again drawn off in the form of short-term credit. During the sixteenth century the great south German and Genoese bankers bought ever more *asientos* – claims on a share in the American silver fleet on its arrival in Seville – from the Spanish government, in exchange for making capital available to that government on the exchanges in Spain, Italy, Germany and the Low Countries. The costs charged for this by the banks increased from an average of 18 per cent in the 1520s to 49 per cent between 1552 and 1556. Originally the bankers were satisfied with guarantees on the yield of the American silver, of the royal demesnes, or of silver mines. The hunger of the Habsburgs for credit, and particularly the urgency with which the money was needed for their wars, especially against France and later against the revolt in the Netherlands, drove the price of government credit up to a crazy height. The debt of the Habsburg state in the Low Countries climbed from 500,000 pounds in 1535 to 1.4 million after 1538 and 7 million in 1555.

The great leaps in this deficit were always made during periods of warfare. Logically the same problems presented themselves to the great rivals of the Habsburgs, the kings of France. Their mutual competition ruined both states; after this period they repeatedly had to declare a moratorium on the repayment of their obligations so as to reach an agreement with their creditors for a consolidation of the floating debt at a lower rate of interest. The Spanish empire imposed such a moratorium nine times between 1557 and 1662, always because of the insolvency of the crown as a result of urgent military expenditure. The French crown had recourse to this method in 1559, 1598 and 1648.[3]

It is striking that the states where citizens of the towns had a strong representation in the government had a more careful financial policy. A unique case is that of the Swiss cantons, led by Geneva and Basle, who were prominent in granting credit and from 1650 were successful in ridding themselves of their government debt. The public town exchange at Basle had ever since 1506 concentrated on the issue by public subscription of the government loans of other states. For this they charged less than 2 per cent commission. The financial orthodoxy of the Swiss was very publicly demonstrated in 1555 when the Assembly of the Confederation expropriated the territory of the insolvent count of Gruyère and divided it between the cantons of Berne and Fribourg, who took on the count's debts.

In the Republic of the United Provinces, the commercial leader of the time, the accumulation of capital during the seventeenth and eighteenth centuries made credit extremely cheap, with an interest rate of 3 per cent, whereas in England it was normally 6 per cent and in times of crisis rose to 10 or 15 per cent, as it did in France. In Poland, which was only marginally penetrated by the money economy, 12 or even 18 per cent was normal. With such differences in the price of money it is understandable that a small but very wealthy state such as the United Provinces could play the role of a great power. In England the parliamentary revolution of 1688 also led to a sharp scrutiny of the government finances.

The first state bank, the Bank of England, was established in England in 1694. It not only acted as banker to the government, but also as a bank of issue, since its banknotes were guaranteed by the state. *The great hall of the Bank of England in London, a watercolour of 1808 by Thomas Rowlandson. Paris, Bibliothèque des Arts décoratifs*

Parliament would in future guarantee the government borrowings on which it took decisions in its budget. The establishment in 1694 of the Bank of England, the first state bank, followed a year later by the Bank of Scotland, combined the functions of government paymaster with those of a commercially sound issue of bank notes. These circulated quickly as paper credit, which opened the way for London's role as a financial centre in the eighteenth and nineteenth centuries. In the course of the eighteenth century many states created central banks with the function of controlling the public debt and the issue of money by convertible bank notes. The first on the continent was the *Wiener Stadtbank* in 1703, followed by the central banks of Denmark, Sweden, Prussia, Russia and Spain. The attempt launched in 1716 by the Scot John Law for a *Banque Générale* in France to issue paper money ran

into trouble after a few years, because of the discrepancy between its issues and their coverage by precious metals. This could be ascribed to the public's lack of confidence because of the enormous state debt and doubt about the commercial validity of the experiment. Paris was not to try it again until 1776.

Meanwhile the paper of various states found a very international purchasing public. When in 1794–1796 Prussia was in acute need of cash as a result of its war against France, the Amsterdam money market provided a third of the capital needed. State debts had become an established phenomenon. Princes, without any sense of economic reality, have always thrust their countries into renewed megalomaniac adventures, made possible by financiers who by doing so could make exorbitant short-term profits. The princely state of Prussia, which during the first half of the eighteenth century

LAW, als een tweede Don-Quichot, op Sanches Graauwtje zit ten spot.

Dulcinia en 't Actie R…,   In't groot betoovert Actie-huis.   Hy kruipt zyn baas na als een pad.
Verzoekt den Lauwen Don-Quichot,   En Sanche, tot zyn droevig kruis   En Heintjemaat te drommels plat
Op Sanches Eseltje gezeeten,   Moet voor Bombario hier speelen;   Weet vast een ider te bespotten,
(Wyl Rosinant wat hooy gaat vreeten)   Het kan den bloed zo zeer verveelen;   Daar een Zot maakt veel duizent Zotten

The attempt by J. Law in 1716 to rescue France from its financial morass ended in fiasco.
In 1720 Bernard Picard satirized these events in a series of prints. *Law, the second Don Quixote* is one of them.
Amsterdam, Rijksmuseum, Rijksprentenkabinet

by a draconian administrative system achieved a well-filled treasury and a sound balance sheet, was quite exceptional; elsewhere this was not then to be encountered outside the small Swiss republics.[4]

The development of commercial capitalism was undoubtedly one of the most fundamental turning points in the history of Europe. From the description just given it may be clear that the great merchant-bankers entered into specific ties with political and ecclesiastical rulers, but were never entirely controlled by them. The most strategic sections of the agricultural economy lay firmly in the hands of the princes and other large ecclesiastical and feudal landowners. However, capital was in the nature of things less controllable: it consisted of goods which had to be transported and processed, of ships, of tools, money itself, and also the results of entrepreneurial activity. Capitalists are by definition con-

tinually searching for the most favourable combination of factors from which they can make the greatest profit. These factors are constantly subject to change, so that Max Weber's 'rational restlessness' is typical of the system. If a prince imposed too many restrictions and levies on free trade – in the form of tolls, customs duties, devaluations of currency, legal harassment, or a failure to repay his debts, so that the cost of transactions rose extravagantly – individual traders might suffer damage, but their colleagues avoided that prince's territory and tried their luck elsewhere. The system as such was dynamic and therefore intangible for the rulers of well-defined territories. Certainly, whenever raw materials from a specific region had a strategic importance – such as salt, wool from the British Isles, or alum that could only be mined in Phocaea or Tolfa but was essential for the textile industry –

The Fugger family, the Augsburg merchant bankers who financed the emperors Maximilian and Charles v,
acquired princely status. The Fugger coat of arms, a print from 1618 by Wolfgang Kilian.
Augsburg, Stadtarchiv

the ruler of its country of origin could drive its price up high, as the kings of England in fact did from the thirteenth to the sixteenth centuries. By doing so they actually encouraged the search for more profitable alternatives.

Commercial capital did not require vast fixed investments and tried to spread its risks as widely as possible and to pass them on to others. Major bankruptcies, such as the notorious ones of the Florentine bankers Peruzzi and Bardi in 1342 and 1346, were followed by the establishment of new consortia based on what was left of the original capital. The Fuggers suffered great losses from the rearrangement of the Habsburgs' debts, but meanwhile they had earned and invested new fortunes. The bank of the Fugger family, who have themselves been elevated to the ranks of the nobility, exists to this day. Mutual competition meant that

the regular passing on of the role of pioneer was inherent in capitalism, because dynamism in continually changing circumstances could not be retained in a single family or business for more than three to four generations. Changes of people, methods, products and locations were characteristic of commercial capitalism so that as a system it remained extremely flexible and dynamic.

The relative distance from the Church kept by the merchant-bankers is no less remarkable than their relationship with the secular rulers. The old ecclesiastical structures were closely interwoven with the feudal world: bishops, chapters and monasteries were large landowners who exploited their estates and their populations in the same way as did the aristocracy. For several centuries the emerging towns formed a strange world which aroused mistrust—and often disapproval and opposition—

quelle enuariſt touo ceulx aqui elle ſe baille · Conſeſ
ſion fait pluo blanc que ſait ce que pechie fait noir
et obſcur · Item confeſſion embeliſt tant lôme q̃
lennemy ne le recongnoiſt · Confeſſion ayme et
mettra encore mant hôme en paradie · Cellui
doncques ſe murtriſt tue aſſole et dampne ſans
redemption qui nayme point le ſacrement de cô
feſſion · car ſi nectoye et eſpurge le corpe quant
elle eſt pure vraye nette et entiere

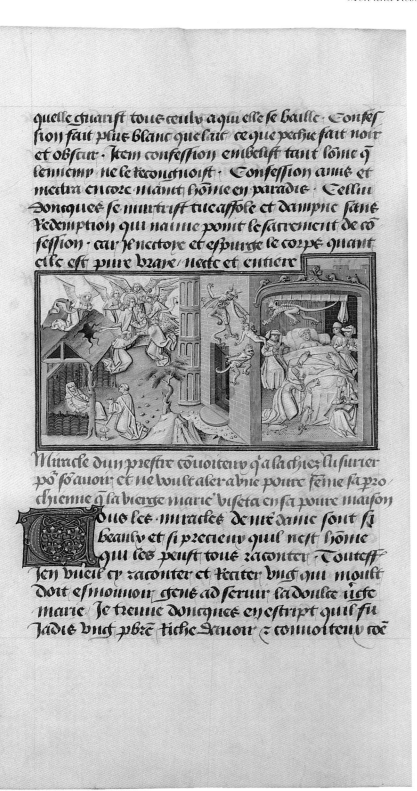

Miracle dun preſtre conuoiteur q̃ a la chier lu ſurier
po ſ ſauoir et ne voulſt aler abne poure ſeme ſa pro
chienne q̃ la vierge marie viſeta en ſa poure maiſon

Touo leo miracleo de nre dame ſont ſi
beaulx et ſi precieux quil neſt hôme
qui leo peuſt touo raconter · Touteſſ
Ien vueil er raconter et reater vng qui moult
doit eſmouuoir geno ad ſeruir ſa doulce nefe
marie · Je trenue donequeo en eſtript quil fu
Iadio vng pbre riche dauoir ⁊ couuoiteur rc̃

In 1179 the third Lateran Council decided that usurers were not entitled to Christian burial.

Hell and damnation awaited them. This 1456 miniature, *The damnation of a usurer,* gives a graphic illustration of this doctrine.

In reality merchants already openly charged interest on their loans in the thirteenth century.

Paris, Bibliothèque nationale de France

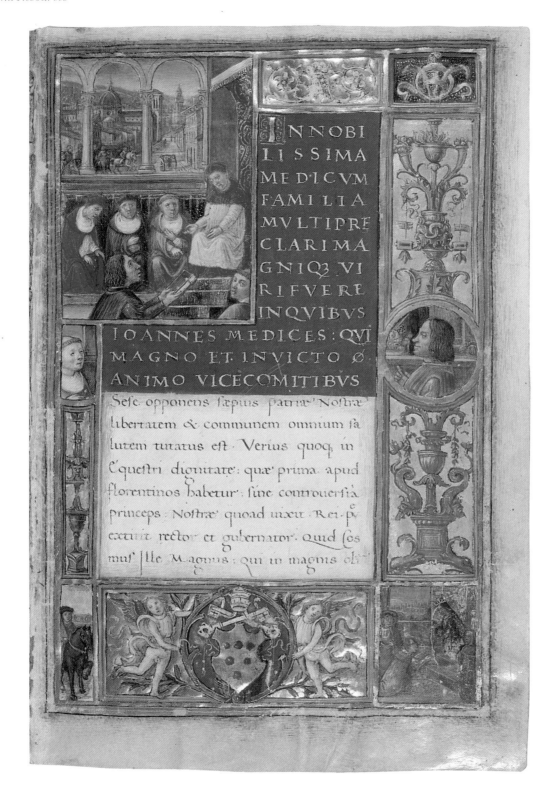

Lorenzo de' Medici, il Magnifico, offers a copy of his biography to Pope Leo x, his second son.
A sixteenth-century miniature which illustrates the complex relationship
between the interests of the merchants, bankers and rulers of Florence with those of the Vatican.
Florence, Biblioteca Laurenziana

among the prelates. Commercial profit was suspect and was therefore by preference left to non-Christian foreigners such as Jews and Arabs. The Church harped on the pernicious nature of the accumulation of capital, and stood by many a deathbed with threats of hell and damnation, from which pious bequests and the miraculous salvation of the generous merchant's soul resulted.

The antithesis was sharpest on the question of whether interest should be allowed on loan capital. The theologians held that time belonged to God alone, and that man might therefore put no price upon it. Moreover, from Christian love of one's neighbour it was fitting to give help to the needy without looking for any return. During the twelfth and thirteenth centuries successive councils fulminated against what was perceived as usury. In 1179 the third Lateran Council decided that usurers might not receive Holy Communion and could make no claim to a church burial. Papal decrees of the period defined usury as the receipt of a higher amount than the capital lent; for transgressions excommunication was proposed for laymen and removal from their office for ecclesiastics. Franciscan preachers inveighed in speech and writing against the trade in money and excessive profits. During the fifteenth century the Church in fact accepted that compensation for costs incurred or lost income was legitimate, but was still unhappy about pure interest. Because of this emphasis and repetition of the ecclesiastical prohibitions, it is the more remarkable that the practice of the wholesale trade took so little account of it. Originally the problem was avoided by camouflaging the interest in the recorded amount of the debt to be repaid, or by using methods of concealment, such as a mortgage (in which a yield-bearing property served as security). In the leading commercial areas around the Tyrrhenian and Adriatic Seas they made no bones about it around 1250: the Marseilles magistracy decided then in a ruling that usury was indeed forbidden... and that a reasonable interest was 5 per cent. The way in which in 1275 the merchant-bankers of Siena ignored every obstruction imposed by canon law on much higher interest rates has already been mentioned. The world of wholesale trade and high finance happily carried out transactions for the popes, but paid little heed to their prescriptions. In time these came to be regarded as an antiquarian survival. Certainly when between 1513 and 1521 scions of the great merchant-banking family of the Medici wore the papal tiara as Leo x and Clement vii, there was no longer any mention of the

earlier principles of canon law. The autonomy of commercial capitalism was still greater *vis-à-vis* the Church than it was towards the princes. This was to make its continuous growth possible.

The yield of taxes

Princes were landowners, kings those who had collected together a very extensive demesne and could therefore mobilize more resources and followers than their opponents. The incomes of princes were originally no different from those of other feudal lords, just larger. The far-reaching decentralization of state power during the previous centuries presented the kings of France in the eleventh century with the formidable task of recovering the rights which had originally belonged to the royal prerogatives. Naturally in doing so they found the feudal lords their competitors, since certainly the most powerful among them – such as the dukes of Normandy and counts of Flanders – had with good effect usurped royal powers, such as the right to mint coinage, to levy tolls, to grant privileges and to exercise the highest judicial power, with all their associated incomes. About 1190 their material position was certainly no weaker than that of the king of France, they only lacked his aura. Indeed, a duke of Normandy had already become king of England, and in 1204 a count of Flanders was to be elevated to no less than emperor of Constantinople.

With their traditional demesne incomes the Holy Roman Emperors of the Ottonian dynasty (936–1002) still succeeded in establishing a strong position of power. Furthermore they were able to profit from royal rights which were not generally available to all kings, those of levying tribute from the conquered equestrian hordes and the yield of the silver mines in the Hartz mountains. Similarly the Hungarian King Béla iii (1172–1196) managed to collect twelve tons of fine silver from his monopolies on the mining of salt, silver and gold. His other sources of income from tolls, tribute and his demesnes (these last were almost all of uncultivated land, which makes the conversion somewhat speculative) are estimated to have accounted for a further nineteen tons of silver. King Stephen had after all appropriated two-thirds of all the land in Hungary, which then included Croatia and Bosnia. In comparison with the income of his brother-in-law King Philip Augustus of France in 1203, which is estimated at more than seventeen tons of fine silver, these were enormous sums. Their political effect

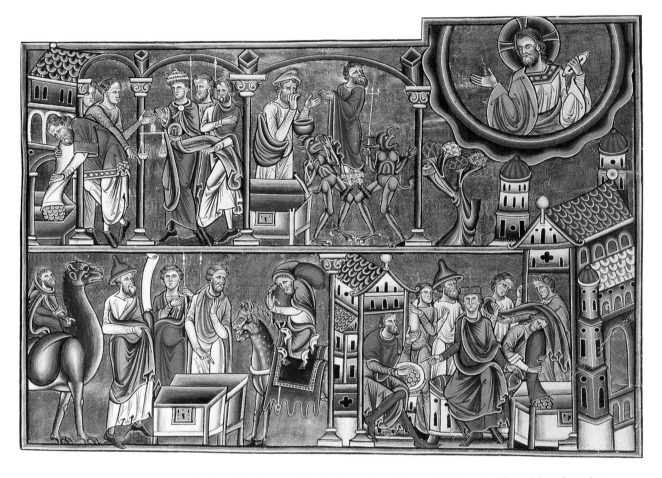

Kings drew their incomes not only from their demesnes but also from various levies and tributes raised from defeated peoples.

In this thirteenth-century miniature Jewish tax collectors are filling the royal treasure chest.

Not being members of the Catholic Church, Jews were employed early on as financial experts;

princes could easily dismiss them and put all the blame on them if anything went wrong.

Paris, Bibliothèque nationale de France

was, however, limited as a consequence of a complex of factors, including grants of land to the independent nobility and fluctuations in the yield of the mines. Later kings had to make do with much less, and, in addition, when in 1470 King Mathias I again reached a total income of thirty-one tons of silver, the share from the mines was only 3.5 tons, less than a third of their yield three centuries earlier. High demesne incomes were no guarantee of success: in the thirteenth and fourteenth centuries the Hungarians exported enormous quantities of precious metals for which they could find no productive use in their own country.

The long-drawn-out wars against the Muslims contributed to the levy of tribute at the expense of the losers, and in the long run this enabled the Christians to reward their warriors with large grants

of land. Yet after 1091 the Iberian crusades led to the introduction in Castile of a permanent tax, which applied also to Christians. Protection against the threat of invasion was a second reason for the introduction of general taxes. In order to cope with a new wave of Viking assaults, *Danegeld* from the time of the first invasions was reimposed in 991, this time on a permanent basis. It was retained, under the title of *heregeld*, after the defeat of the Danes, and also under the Norman rulers, up to the year 1160. It was a fixed assessment per area of land held, and was levied in coined silver, of which the issue was greatly increased in the same period. It can therefore be considered the earliest regular state tax in Europe, proportionate to land holdings. Other general state taxes were imposed in England much earlier than on the continent. In 1185, on the strong recommen-

King Bela III of Hungary (1172–1196), whose silver sceptre is shown here,
received a substantial income from his monopoly of mining silver, gold and salt in his country.
Budapest, Magyar Nemzeti Muzeum

dation of the pope, a tithe (10 per cent) was levied on movable property and incomes, in preparation for the third crusade. Fiscally it was a success, which is even more striking because a similar attempt in France not only came up against the immunity of the great territorial princes who were powerful enough to deny their collaboration, but also the objection of principle that the king was not legally entitled to tax movable property or income. In England shortly afterwards the principle of proportional taxation of movable goods was again applied, until the excesses under John Lackland which led in 1215 to the provisions against arbitrary taxation in Magna Carta. In the long term this seemed to be the chosen method by which the English crown was able to exercise its centralization of power.[5]

In 1275 the English parliament for the first time approved indirect taxes which fell mainly on the export of wool. They were to become a permanent source of income for the crown and a source of political conflict with purchasers on the continent, particularly the Italians, Flemings and north Germans. Parliament always determined how they should be raised, so that there was public discussion about important economic and political questions. The severity and frequency of taxes in the thirteenth century, when they were introduced in England as a permanent system – albeit based on age-old precedents – was determined by the rhythm of war. During periods of comparative peace with the Scots (1298–1306) and truce with France (1360–1369) no taxes were levied. On the other hand the intense warfare between 1294 and 1298, and the start of the Hundred Years War (1338–1342) led to explosive growth in the pressure of taxation. War enabled princes to demand extra money and support from their subjects on the pretext of the defence of the realm; that was, after all, the duty of every subject. The concepts of 'self-defence' and

'necessity' were dug up by learned councillors as reasons, when that of the crusade could no longer be used. But which country *had to be* defended so urgently, and against what aggressor? In 1297 the barons found that Edward's attack on Flanders could no longer really be called defence of the realm, but the campaigns in Gascony, Wales and Scotland evoked no such opposition.

From 1292 the *ayudas* or pleas for aid followed each other with increasing speed in the lands under the crown of Aragon as a result of the royal wars. The conquest of the Cerdaña in 1323 provided a legitimate reason; ten years later the war against the Muslims and the Genoese; in 1340 the dispatch of an armada of twenty galleys to the Straits of Gibraltar; in 1342 the recapture of Mallorca. The long war against Castile in the middle of the fourteenth century made the levy of taxes continuous and oppressive for all subjects of the crown. For instance, in 1363 in the *Cortes Generales* of Valencia, Aragon, Catalonia and Mallorca it was decided to impose a levy on textile production and on the export of trade goods.[6]

On the French side the war obviously also required new fiscal resources. From 1295 King Philip IV regularly summoned meetings of the provincial estates of Languedoc with urgent requests for money, using the legal argument of 'state rights'. The catastrophic course of the first phase of the Hundred Years War led, as in England, to immense demands for taxes from the crown, which for this had to make various promises and concessions to the States-General. Yet it was the monarchy which came off best by allocating itself permanent indirect taxation. It started in 1355 with the *gabelle*, a tax on salt and a levy of one-thirtieth on the value of trade goods; in 1435 this proportion was raised to one-twentieth. The great blow was struck in 1440 when a permanent annual *taille* was introduced,

The crusades against the Muslims led to the introduction in 1091 of a permanent tax in Castile on Christians as well.

It was mainly the increasing pressure of taxation which forced the prince to hold discussions with his *Cortes* in order to gain their agreement.

Meetings of the *Cortes* of Castile and León in 1188.

Cortes de Castilla y León

to be collected by royal officials. In contrast to the English Parliament, the French States-General and regional meetings had put themselves out of play as a political organ by giving up control over taxes. In the long term this had enormous consequences, resulting in the dominance of the crown in France as against that of parliament in England.

These systems continued to be applied as the basis of the royal tax policy until the French revolution. This does not mean to say that the system was a uniform one from which the entire yield flowed into the Paris treasury. Nothing is less true. In the eighteenth century the state had for long failed to have the taxes collected by its own officers, on the lines of the 1440 decree. To be able to gather in the taxes in good time and to a specified amount, there had in the course of time been a change by handing their

collection over to tax farmers. These paid the expected yield, determined by auction to the highest bidder, from their own capital. They then collected as much as they could, lining their own pockets first, and bleeding the subjects of the realm dry. The state also suffered double damage: its subjects, left to the avarice of the tax farmers, grumbled, while a large proportion of the taxes collected only went to enrich the tax farmers and never reached the state treasury. In addition the rates for the notorious *gabelle* were by no means equal in the kingdom of Louis XIV. The recently conquered provinces, such as Artois and Brittany, were completely exempt from the salt tax. Elsewhere the rates differed widely according to the effective power of the state. In the old core area around Paris people paid sixty livres for the salt for which only two livres were levied in the surrounding

In 1280 Guido, a Cistercian monk, was city treasurer of Siena.

On the binding of the Account Book for that year he is shown handling money.

Siena, Archivio di Stato

Session of the accountants of the Paris Exchequer in the year 1447.
The French States-General had put itself out of play as a political organ
by giving up control over taxes.
Paris, Archives nationales

The conversion of St Matthew was a favourite subject for sixteenth- and seventeenth-century iconography,
showing the environment of a tax collector's office. The amount of paperwork is striking.
A 1536 example from the southern Netherlands by Marinus van Reymerswaele.
Ghent, Museum voor Schone Kunsten

provinces. It is understandable that such differences gave rise to a flourishing smuggling trade. About 1760 this amounted close to three-quarters of the official sales. As the control of the black market was in the hands of private individuals who made a profitable business of it, everything went on as before, in spite of the high costs incurred by the state in trying to repress it.[7]

Wars drove up both taxes and the state debt. In Britain the national debt doubled three times in the eighteenth century; from 16.7 million pounds in 1697 to 36.2 in 1713 (the War of the Spanish Succession), again to 60 million after the War of the Austrian Succession (1739–1748), and 132.6 after the Seven Years War (1756–1763). In Holland the public debt also doubled between 1678 and 1713. Per head of population the weight of taxes in the three richest provinces of the Republic rose from 7.27 guilders in 1600 to 14.12 in 1650 and 20.18 in 1790. Strong economic growth in the first of these periods, and inflation during the second, accounted for the largest part of this nominal increase. In Spain the crown

achieved a doubling of its revenue between 1703 and 1713 primarily by a ruthless exploitation of exceptional income at the expense of the Church, by confiscating the property of insurgents and by repealing the tax privileges which had until then been enjoyed by Aragon, Valencia and Catalonia.

Under Louis xiv all records of the *ancien régime* were broken. By expanding the strength of the army to 400,000 men, military expenditure doubled from an average of 99 million livres per year between 1672 and 1678 (the Dutch War) to 218 million in 1708–1714 (the War of the Spanish Succession). To be able to maintain these military efforts new kinds of taxes had to be introduced in 1695 and 1710: first a poll tax; then for the duration of the war, a tithe (*dixième*).[8] In 1713 it was clear that all the great warring powers were exhausted, and they were forced into several decades of peaceful co-existence to lick their wounds, give some solace to their subjects, and pay off some of their debts. The systems of tax farming and of rising state debts had enriched the wealthy middle classes. They at least had money to

Signboard of the office of an Amsterdam collector of chimney taxes.
It dates from about 1580 and is by an anonymous painter.
Amsterdam, Rijksmuseum

invest, at the expense of the ordinary taxpayers. In what has been called absolutist France or Spain the state by no means had a monopoly of taxation, though they might claim one. Until shortly before the French revolution traditional immunities, the exemption from taxes of the aristocracy and of church property, continued to be respected. The state did not interfere, but left the landowners free to levy such taxes as were usual. In Castile 45 per cent of his subjects escaped the authority of the king in this way in the fifteenth century. In the course of time the burden of the *latifundia* grew steadily: from the fifteenth to the early twentieth century their average area increased fourfold.[9]

Money is the sinews of war, said Cicero; it is by implication also the touchstone of relationships between those who take decisions about war and ordinary mortals. The more a prince let himself be drawn into waging war, the more taxes he had to impose upon his subjects. As soon as these requirements rose above those a liege lord might expect from his vassals as feudal service, he had to ask for a voluntary contribution. However, princes made a habit of this as early as the thirteenth century, and in doing so used each other as justification for their calls for the defence of the realm or their legitimate claims. The frequency and rising volume of these princely appeals were among the reasons for the rise of systems of representation for their subjects, who negotiated the conditions of any provisions. This is an extremely important development which, however, in many countries – such as France, but also in Poland, Hungary, Sweden and Denmark – came to a halt some time between the fifteenth and the seventeenth centuries. The ability of the princes to introduce a system of taxation that could work independently of the agreement of popular representation played an essential role in this.

The possibility of this occurring was again dependent upon the type of economy in a country. In England and in Catalonia it was already apparently possible in the thirteenth and fourteenth centuries respectively to impose levies on exports. An export-oriented economy could therefore form the basis of a fiscal system which did not tax its own subjects but taxed the foreign buyers. This system reached its apogee in the Republic of the United Provinces, the commercial power *par excellence* of the seventeenth and eighteenth centuries, which could therefore match itself as a great power with more extensive and thickly populated countries. Where this possibility did not exist, then only the taxation of its own subjects remained, with the risk of revolt if the burden was felt to be unjustified. There was a sensitive link between increases in requests for taxation and the strengthening of opposition to them on the part of the representatives of the people. In France and most other states princes were able to reduce the representative institutions to a modest, almost ritual role in the course of the fifteenth century. In other regions they in fact offered effective resistance to the erosion of their rights, and therefore also to those of all subjects, particularly with regard to the allocation and distribution of taxation. The example of the lands of the Aragon crown has already been mentioned; they had a tradition – increasing in strength until the thirteenth century – of extensive liberties and rights, particularly for the richer trading towns. Only a full-blown war waged by the Madrid government was able to breach these regional liberties in the early years of the eighteenth century.

There was a comparable situation in the Low Countries, where most regions also enjoyed an ancient tradition of representation, primarily exercised by the large towns. By spirited negotiation on every appeal for help they were able to obtain a large degree of compliance with their wishes, and in this way to take part in determining the policy followed. When their prince requested money for a war of conquest which did not seem to them necessary or desirable, they did not pay. They effectively withstood increases in the rates of the prince's tolls because their vital trading interests would be harmed by them. No wonder, when one remembers that in 1445 the duke of Burgundy received 13,000 pounds from his tolls at Gravelines on the border between Flanders and Calais, where all the English wool for the Low Countries was imported, while his whole county of Namur scarcely provided 8,000 pounds income. For the same reason, and to prevent their own representation being trimmed, the large towns of Flanders in 1447 obstinately and effectively opposed a plan of their duke's to follow France's lead by introducing a permanent salt tax.

In the first half of the sixteenth century the Dutch towns five times successfully opposed the plans of the Habsburg regime to raise the levy on exports of grain. Here, too, it was a matter of vital interest to them, as the grain trade formed the basis of the Dutch international economy. This it was to remain – thanks to their opposition – till the eighteenth century. When the government, again following foreign examples, tried from 1542 to introduce various indirect taxes, such as the hundredth penny (1 per cent) on exports, and a tenth penny (10 per cent) on trading profits, opposition was so strong that the plans were abandoned again after 1545. Only the strict and repressive initiatives of the duke of Alva, when he was governor-general, were able to

reimpose such levies in 1569. Opposition was again so strong that the yield was very disappointing, and this plan, too, disappeared with the duke after a few years. Meanwhile it had contributed to the strength of rebellious feelings against the Spanish oppression. Later, however, in the United Provinces such taxes on consumption and trade would provide the major part of the revenue, but then primarily at the town and provincial level and under the control of their representatives. Just as in England, and particularly in the Swiss confederacy, supervision of fiscal affairs by representative bodies meant that there was a brake on their increase above what the subjects could bear.

During the fifteenth and sixteenth centuries the Low Countries produced a volume of taxation that increased substantially faster than the population, economic growth or inflation. Although the area may at that time have taken the core position in the world economy, this creaming off by the state in spite of an active popular representation definitely affected the roots of its prosperity. About 1445 and from 1531 to 1535 the state's income was on a peaceful level, but a comparison of the average figures at these two dates shows an increase of 65 per cent over ninety years. The share of the special levies *vis-à-vis* the traditional demesne income had risen from 38 per cent to 80 per cent. After 1535 the exigencies of war drove them up on average by a further 58 per cent. Such great flexibility in so short a time could only be envisaged in a very rich country. But at the same time it was also the best way to plunder it of its economic advantages.

If one sums up taxation policy as a means of exercising power, then the major factor is the direct and enduring relationship between wars and taxes. Wars always invited new and higher taxes, and even active representative institutions could not really withstand them. Princes did not let themselves be influenced by macro-economic considerations, which only began to play a role in the eighteenth century with mercantilist theories. In reality they did not properly understand the consequences of their actions, because they had no reliable statistical information available about their own finances and those of their subjects. Reviews of population numbers and of economic indicators were lacking at state level till 1688 (when Gregory King made an estimate for England); before then only fragmentary data were available. Not until the sixteenth century did they start thinking in terms of budgets. Time and again unplanned expenditure on military objectives threw the whole state finances into chaos.

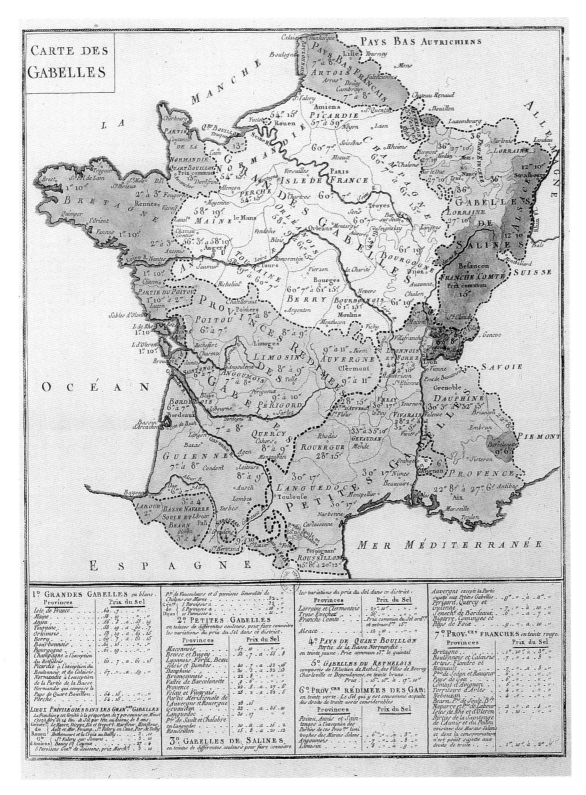

Map of France of c. 1707, divided into the various tax zones for the salt tax.

It shows plainly that the king was unable to impose a uniform system within the frontiers of France.

Smuggling could therefore be very lucrative.

Paris, Bibliothèque nationale de France, Estampes

La Taxe Par Teste

D'une taxe legere la douceur on impose.
A un peuple tout prest d'en accepter la loy.
Heureux s'y l'on pouvoit pour si modique chose.
Achepter une Paix aux voeux de notre Roy.

A Paris chez le Roux af [...]

The never-ending wars of Louis XIV ensured that his successors inherited an empty treasury.
The poll tax, illustrated in this 1709 print, must be seen in this context.
Paris, Bibliothèque nationale de France, Estampes

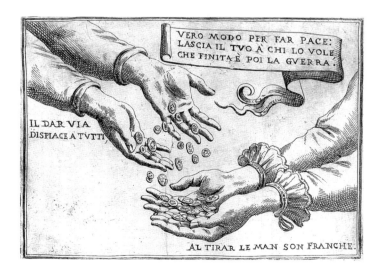

Vero modo per far pace. Not only war, but also negotiating and purchasing peace required large sums of money.
Italian satirical print of 1692 by Giuseppe Mitelli. Bologna, Cassa di Risparmio, Collezioni d'arte e di storia

The extent of expenditure – once a conflict had actually started – could not be controlled, because in war it was not economic efficiency but winning which counted. Therefore large sums of money always had to be spent which had been borrowed at high rates of interest; their repayment and interest would for decades press like a millstone on expenditure. However, only states that looked creditworthy could lay their hands on credit. In Poland interest was appreciably higher than in the United Provinces, because the availability of capital and the expectation of speedy repayment worked out to the advantage of the capital-intensive regions. There were few towns where the taxes on consumer goods or the sale of rents guaranteed by the total possessions of the town (as was said in Paris: 'on the town hall') offered a guarantee for the solvency of the state. Put in another way: a properly functioning system of taxation increased the chances of credit, which then in turn threatened the stability of the system.

In this way the economic system affected the chances of the state acquiring money from two aspects: in a commercialized economy appreciably more surpluses could be creamed off more quickly through indirect taxation – at whatever level it was levied – than in an agricultural economy; moreover, in the former credit was easier and cheaper, which made a rapid expansion of liquidity possible, while the latter remained in principle dependent upon the slow, limited and relatively inflexible yields of demesnes.

Most taxes under the *ancien régime* were very unevenly distributed, because exemptions were granted to the wealthy but influential nobility and ecclesiastics. Very seldom was the pressure of most taxes proportional to wealth, as it was in England during the eleventh and twelfth centuries. The better-off always opposed them, from pure and sometimes short-sighted self-interest. Indirect taxes, which made up the bulk of the levies in the towns and of the consumer taxes imposed by the state on food, bore unfairly heavily on the lowest income groups. The more taxes – and particularly the public debt – rose, the more this worked to the advantage of the rich at the expense of the poor. Hence state action drastically increased social inequality.

In states in which representative institutions with proper representation of commercial interests continued to function, more attention was paid to the economic effects of policy than in the so-called absolutist monarchies. Thus they could temper the negative social and economic effects of the monarchic policy of war. Obviously these were also the

regions with the highest urbanization where commercial capital had an appreciable role. So one can observe that the monarchic states' policy of war, fiscal pressure and repression formed a serious threat for flourishing centres of trade. Most of them reached their peak in times of mild or even non-existent state authority, such as in the case of the north Italian or Flemish towns, Barcelona and Valencia, the south German towns in the fifteenth and sixteenth century, the Dutch towns and London. The strangulation of metropolises by the increasing power of the state can be seen in Bruges in the late fifteenth century, Antwerp after 1566, and Florence and Lübeck in the sixteenth century. Autonomous metropolises, however, were only components of a European system of states in which they happened to be contained. Hence they did not escape the conditions imposed upon them by their environment, and they were also caught in the spiral of violence and ever more thorough milking of the economy for destructive ends.

Perhaps this matter has been set out too simplistically here. Traders – such as the Venetians and the Genoese – battled with each other as much as did knights, and fought it out to the point of exhaustion; some monarchs followed prudent economic policies. In the last resort the trading towns were concerned with the prospect of eliminating competitors themselves or achieving their long-term material ends in other ways. For princes this motivation, if not absent, was at least much less tangible. The key question therefore remains the same: on what was a prince's right to wage war based? Why did his subjects again and again accept generally and in the long term the horror of war and all its consequent fiscal and economic miseries, to say nothing of its human suffering? Is it not remarkable that in almost all countries and down the centuries people have assented to wars at least passively, and very often actively? Had they no choice? Did they really believe in the good cause of their prince? Were they indeed prepared to suffer appreciable material losses for it? With such questions we reach the province of political systems and their legitimation, which will be discussed in subsequent chapters.

1   De Vries 1984, 29–77, 163
2   Van der Wee 1994, 103–114
3   Van der Wee 1994, 160–180
4   Körner in Bonney 1995
5   Barta & Ormrod in Bonney 1995
6   Sanchez Martinez in Bonney 1995
7   Hocquet 1989, 151–167
8   Bonney 1995
9   Ladero Quesada 1983, Bernal 1988

CHAPTER III
From Private to Public Power

The feudal pyramid and local rule

About the year AD 100 the Roman historian Tacitus described in a famous passage, given below, the customs of the Germans, based on information from soldiers and traders who had visited Germany. The question obviously arises of how far this picture – assuming it was correct in the first century AD – could still apply five hundred or a thousand years later. Archaeological research of thousands of burials has, for example, shown that a cultural change occurred in the eighth century, involving among other things the disappearance of the typical pre-Christian grave gifts. On the other hand, the transition to Christian rituals in no way implies that all the values, norms and customs of the earlier culture were abandoned. What is fascinating in Tacitus' account is the finely drawn characterization of the warrior mentality that we recognize so well from high-medieval sources. For that reason there is a great temptation to see in the lifestyle and ethics of the Germanic warrior class – in which positions of honour and power were granted on the basis both of birth and of personal achievements – one of the roots of the later European aristocracy.

Particularly noble birth or the great merits of their forefathers confer the dignity of leader even on very young men; they are attached to other stronger adults who have already proved themselves, and it is no shame to be seen among the retinue of a leader. These retinues have their own hierarchies, determined by the judgement of the leader whom they follow. Among his followers there is great rivalry for the first place next to the leader, and among the leaders for the largest number and most valiant followers. If a leader is always surrounded by a large crowd of selected young men this confers upon him respect and power, in peace for honour, in war for his protection. If his retinue are conspicuous in their number and valour, this not only gives him fame and renown among his own people, but also among neighbouring nations. These leaders receive embassies and are honoured with gifts; they often win wars through their reputation.

When it comes to fighting it is shameful for a leader to be surpassed in valour, and for his followers not to equal their leader in courage. It is most ignominious and a lifelong disgrace for a follower to leave the field where his leader has been killed: to protect him, defend him, and to ascribe their own feats of valour to his fame is the most solemn obligation of a warrior; leaders fight for victory, their followers for their leader. If the tribe of their birth stagnates in a long period of peace and quiet, many well-born young men leave for other nations who are engaged in war, because among these people peace is undesirable and fame is easier to obtain in the midst of perils, and it is only possible to maintain a large host of followers by war and violence, because they expect from the generosity of their leader a

The defensive towers of private houses, and the tower of the Palazzo Publico in Siena, are symbols of the power of the great families and of the urban community.
Detail from *Bullfight in the Piazza del Campo in Siena*, painted in the sixteenth century by V. Rustici. Siena, Monte dei Paschi

Leaders fight for victory, followers fight for their leader from whom they then expect generosity.
This dependent mentality played a great role in feudal society.
Mutual loyalty and the performance of military obligations were essential in their code of honour.
Antonio Pollaiuolo (1432–1498), *Battle of the nude men*, Engraving. Manchester, Whitworth Art Gallery

warhorse and a blood-stained and victorious spear. As reward they accept feasts, and plain but gene- rous maintenance; war and plunder offer them the opportunity for generous gifts. They are not so easi- ly persuaded to work the land and to await the har- vest as to challenge an enemy and sustain injuries. For them it seems tame and cowardly to acquire with sweat what they can achieve with blood.[1]

Notes: see p. 159

During the Carolingian period – roughly the eighth and ninth centuries – an original and in theory co- herent system, the feudal system, was formed out of the various kinds of dependent relationships, some of which went back to the late Roman empire. The origin of it lies in the demands made by the Mayor of the Palace, Charles Martel, on the property of the Church to reward his heavily armoured knights in the fight against the Muslims, who had by then pen- etrated into southern France. For the Church it meant giving away land in fief for the benefit of the battle for the faith, which was finally to deliver vic- tory at Poitiers in 732. Against the not entirely incomprehensible inclination of the bold warriors to want to keep the land assigned to them, a ruling was made saying that a tenth of the yield from the land held in fief should be handed over to the Church. Formally the Church remained in full pos- session, and the fief could be claimed back in the case of disloyalty to the liege lord. After the death of the vassal it should also return to the liege lord.

Charlemagne extended this structure into a sys- tem designed to bind the officials and warriors in his far-flung empire to him. The logic is evident: in a society where land – including the men and beasts who worked it – was the most important form of wealth, and where very little money was in circula- tion and certainly no gold coinage, this was the way to distribute rewards to faithful followers and ser- vants. The king had large amounts of land at his dis- posal, thanks to his successful wars of conquest. From this he was able to distribute sections in fief, in the hope that by so doing he would still retain some control over his vassals. As a system of rule the feudal system consisted of a series of bilateral contracts between liege lord and vassal, both fully capable of acting in law, but unequal in status. The liege lord offered his protection and required ser- vices in exchange; in compensation he gave a source of income – usually a demesne, but it could be a toll or a whole territory, even a whole kingdom – in fief. In return for the protection and the benefice – the property in fief – the vassal offered his faithful service, counsel and homage. This con- tract was personal and not normally transferable. It could indeed be dissolved subject to specific condi-

sine man · ab iener in sine manschaft also ge
boten habe · Alse hem czu manne mit rechte
sulle emphan · Weigert in denne sine man
orteil czu vindene ane sine schult · vn mvge
si des mit rechte volkumen · d herre is ane
schult kegen den man · V nde d man ir wir
bit mit deme sinene nicht me wen als in
d herre dar nach schuldeget daz he sich
kegen im vorwaret habe · daz he im vnschult
da vor deste werlicher geruen mac · S wen d
hire deme mane girliet daz he mit rechte
an im bracht hat · daz is he phlichtic im czu
hant czu benennene daz hes weiz · des he
ab nicht en weiz · daz sal he im benennen
vb vierczen nacht · da sal he im d herre ver
dingen vor sime man · swaz he da nicht be
neuet · da en hat he nicht rechtes me an · vn
daz he im benennet al im des d herre nicht
en bekennet · daz behalde he mit gezuuge
al czu hant ab he mac · ab he nicht en mac ·
so habe he vrist vierczen nacht · sine gezuu
sal aber he czu hant benemen des herre
manne alse vil alse he wil · der sal d her
re sibene brengen · der d man geit · vnde
nicht did herre wil · S welcher dirre si
bene da czu kegenwert si · den en darf d
herre nicht brengen · ab hem vrager vm
me den gezuik · S welch ur deme czu de
me tage nicht en kumet dr ter herre
brengen sal · mit deme hat der man sine
gezuik vollbracht kegen sine herren.

A vassal paid homage by placing both hands in those of his liege lord.

Three other hands point symbolically to the vassal himself and to the fiefs which provide the vassal with an income.

Early fourteenth-century miniature.

Heidelberg, Universitätsbibliothek

Knights on horseback, ivory chessmen carved in southern Italy in the late eleventh century.
The knights with pointed helmets and long shields are Christians, the one with a round shield is a Muslim.
Chess is thought to have been introduced into western Europe by the Muslims.
Paris, Bibliothèque nationale de France

tions, which amounted to a breach of the mutual trust or non-compliance with the agreed obligations. A vassal could declare the contract cancelled if his lord took up arms against him, took his fief from him, or committed adultery with his wife. A liege lord could declare it cancelled if a vassal fell short in his obligations for faithful service and, for example, sided with another lord in war.

Feudalism was a valuable instrument for incorporating the local rulers in a wider national union. This still remained a union of separate individuals, though one that could be developed by handing down the feudal service in a series of steps into a whole pyramid of mutual links of protection and service. Charlemagne also made the great bishoprics and abbeys his feudal dependants, by which he gave substance to his protection of the Church and at the same time secured the service as sub-vassals of all the vassals who in their turn held fiefs from the bishops and abbots. It has been estimated that he could call on the services of 2,000 vassals and 30,000 sub-vassals.[2] Certainly linking official positions in his empire – such as count or margrave – to a fief that could in theory be called in, introduced the beginning of an administrative structure. The medieval Latin term *comes*, which survived into the Romance languages (*comte, conde, conte*) is strikingly that used by Tacitus for 'follower' or 'retinue'.

The feudal system functioned both centrifugally and centripetally. So long as wars of conquest were waged, as they were under Charlemagne, there was continually land to distribute and the king could bind plenty of vassals to him. His army constantly grew, so that his military superiority increased ever more. His empire was certainly extremely extensive, from the Pyrenees to Saxony, which made the mobilization of vassals only possible on a regional basis. This also meant that the punishment of a disloyal vassal by leading an army against him could take up a lot of time, and might well be impossible to achieve in the light of other priorities. In the West-Frankish empire feudalism was a strong influence for the fragmentation of power from the ninth to the eleventh centuries. Land is after all fixed property so that its control requires a local presence. Vassals displayed an inclination to stay in their most important feudal properties and to ally themselves with local families, so that their estates in the region grew larger. At the same time, however, their lack of interest in their original lord also grew. The divided inheritances and dynastic difficulties of the Carolingians reduced their ability to control their vassals. Wars seemed to go less successfully, to produce less booty, and therefore less motivation for the vassals. Already by 877 Charles the Bald had to promise his vassals that their sons might inherit offices and fiefs if they themselves lost their lives in the expedition to Italy for which he was summoning them.

Step by step the inheritance of fiefs became a fact, and the objective of linking possessions with

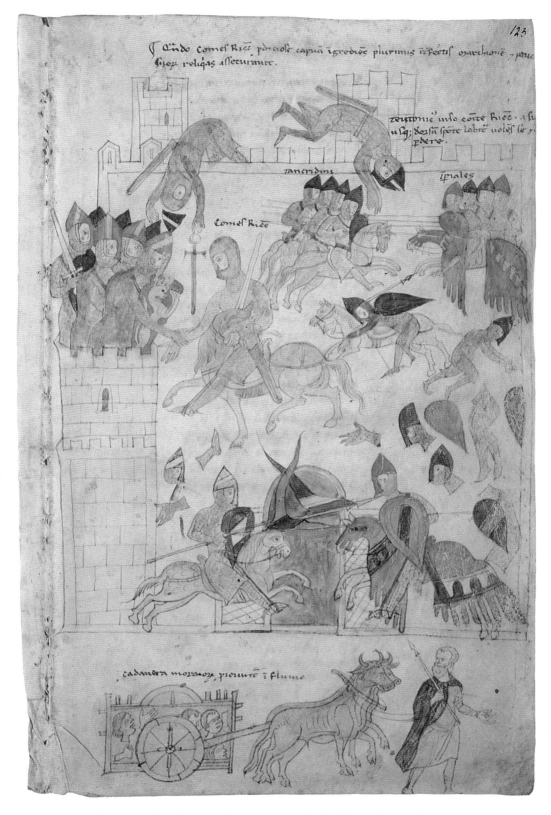

Knights in action at Capua during a campaign by the Holy Roman Emperor Henry VI.

Right at the bottom mortal remains are carried away from the battlefield in a cart. Coloured pen drawing, early thirteenth century.

Berne, Bürgerbibliothek

It was mainly local lords who on their own authority built castles for the defence and protection of their land
and its population as a result of the unpredictable raids and invasions by the Vikings.
By doing so they appreciably strengthened their position as against that of their liege lord and the king.
John Sell Cotman, *Norwich Castle,* watercolour *c.*1808. Norwich, Castle Museum

Ruins of the Cistercian Kirkstall Abbey in Yorkshire, dissolved by Henry VIII in 1539.
By actions such as this he enlarged the crown demesne with vast estates and income.
Watercolour *c.*1800 by T. Girtin. London, British Museum, Prints and Drawings

the proper performance of feudal obligations was lost. What had originally been intended as an instrument to bind regional and local rulers to the central authority was watered down into the *de facto* inalienable right of possession of the vassal. What remained of a royal army proved completely unable to withstand the Viking invasions which assailed the periphery of the Empire with new military techniques and at unpredictable times and places. Local lords took on the defence, and thereby strengthened their hold on their region. They took possession of the fortresses which had earlier been built with imperial resources, or had new ones built on their own authority. By doing this they offered protection to the surrounding population and built up an independent and very direct position of power for themselves.

From the tenth to the thirteenth century the most real power was local. Emperors, kings, popes and bishops were dependent upon the co-operation of local potentates. In the famous conflict between the German King Henry IV and Pope Gregory VII, the king's authority was immediately shaken when in 1076 the pope released his vassals from their feudal obligations. Large vassals and small ones rose in revolt and elected a new king. This example may demonstrate the effect of the papal bull, which will be discussed in more detail later, but also that the feudal link could very easily be turned round into a weapon against their liege lord by local and regional rulers. To understand this phenomenon it is worth setting out precisely the content of the rights available to a vassal when he received land in fief. At this stage other forms of feudal holding than demesnes are left out of consideration.

Demesnes formed the basis of the economy of western Europe from the fifth to the thirteenth century, and until the eighteenth and nineteenth in central and eastern Europe. This was the extensive exploitation of agriculture which usually, but certainly not exclusively, consisted of a concentrated core of property with an area equivalent to that of several modern villages. As a result of the circumstances under which it was acquired, or of its specific function, the demesne could be made up of several very widely distributed properties. Large areas of woodland could be added to the estate for hunting, vineyards because there was a favourable location for them, fenland for digging peat.

The lord of a demesne in practice exercised all forms of power there; he had the right to issue orders and to call up the population to follow him in his wars, he was judge, he appointed the priest,

he ran the estate like a business, and any surpluses were at his disposal. Local power was personal, direct and total. It was not arbitrary because right and custom, even if not laid down in writing, defined the rights and duties of every inhabitant, according to his or her status. Some enjoyed personal freedom, which meant that they could go wherever they liked, but were still bound to perform a well-prescribed amount of work and to supply produce, which was a burden on the farms their families worked. The unfree inhabitants were mostly descendants of former slaves or serfs, part of the booty conquered with the land. They were hereditarily bound to the land and had an appreciably heavier labour performance imposed upon them – up to half of a year's work. The work of peasant families on the demesne produced a surplus which was intended to enable the lord of the demesne to live according to his station. In abbeys and chapters the needs of the lord, the priestly community, were precisely prescribed: a rich lifestyle, but no more. Various specific sections of the demesne were responsible for the supply of food, clothing, wine, parchment, fuel and so on.

When the yield rose as a result of improved agricultural techniques, abbeys did not know what to do with it, because the rule did not allow for it.[3] For laymen the prescriptions were less strict, and we also know much less about the management of their estates than about that of the religious foundations, for which much more documentary evidence has survived. For the lords and their immediate retinues the basic needs were first of all the provision of good warhorses and expensive armour. Beyond this one can imagine that the laymen knew quite well what to do with any excess yields. Yet it is mainly the treasurers of the church demesnes who by frugal and rational management increased the productivity of the land, and so laid the foundations for the development which – at least in large parts of western Europe – made the demesne system come apart at the seams by the twelfth century: the sustained increase in the population. This made it no longer necessary, or even possible, for the peasants to be bound to the land, so that working conditions became more free and less hard; and those for whom there was no longer any room on the demesnes went away to develop new land, or to the fledgling towns.

As for all fundamental phenomena in Europe, it is again necessary here to point out the great regional differences which, for that matter, affected each other. The increase in population after the tenth century was concentrated in the most productive

An artist from Ferrara painted this farm worker with spade and hoe as the muse Polyhymnia in *c.* 1450.
The rows of vines symbolize the wealth produced by the harvest in the Po valley.
Berlin, Gemäldegalerie

Eighteenth-century entrance gate to the Cortijo Guzman in Seville.
There were large latifundia in this area even in classical times. Great estates or *haciendas,* administered from a central court or *cortijo*
by powerful landowners, still determine a high proportion of the Andalusian landscape.

agricultural areas near the coasts and the great rivers. Just because of this demographic growth and urbanization, commercialization also permeated agriculture, and exploitation of demesnes based on serf labour and force could no longer be maintained. As early as the thirteenth century, leases – which had their conditions regularly adapted to the circumstances of the market – began to replace serf labour in these regions; but in the more thinly populated parts of Europe – the interior of the Iberian peninsula, France, Germany, and almost all of central and eastern Europe – the system based on serf labour went on functioning until the great social and political revolutions of the late eighteenth and nineteenth centuries abolished it there, too. The

contrast between the Europe of the towns and that of the landowners seems to match differences in the structure of the population and of the economy. Where towns were close together, the strongest and most comprehensive dynamism developed; outside these areas the rivalry between the great landowners remained the fundamental determinant of the fate of the community. It was therefore only the revolutions of 1848 and later which brought serfdom to an end in central Europe.

By our present-day concepts the power of a landowner should be described as pertaining to private law: he received demesnes in fief to hold title to them personally, he could manage them and leave them as his personal patrimony. Demesnes

The Emperor Frederick II (1211–1250) handing over an enfeoffment
document for the duchy of Brunswick to Duke Otto, still a child.
In his turn Otto grants a charter to the representatives of Lüneburg.
In the margins are the coats of arms of the ruling families
at the time of this manuscript. Miniature by Hans Borneman
in a Lüneburg version of the *Sachsenspiegel* dated 1442.
Lüneburg, Ratsbibliothek

As a specialized warrior class medieval landowners
were primarily interested in the retention and expansion
of their inherited holdings. Skill in the use of arms
was therefore essential and a source of great prestige.
The chevalier Wolfram von Eschenbach with his squire,
Swiss miniature, early fourteenth century.
Heidelberg, Universitätsbibliothek

formed immunities, areas of law where higher authorities such as the king could not exercise direct authority. On the other hand, the landowner exercised rights which we now consider to be entirely the domain of public law: he could call up for military service, administer justice and levy taxes. This mixture of private and public rights characterized this sphere of seignorial rights and feudalism for the whole of the *ancien régime*. As the seigneurie formed the basis on which the whole structure of rule rested and from which it developed, it is essential to emphasize the 'totalitarian' character of the framework of contemporary thought. The lord of a demesne – a concept which could refer to an institution such as an abbey, which was, however, naturally represented by its local vassal or its treasurer – was lord and master over all aspects of the life of those living on his domain. In religious matters he did indeed have to recognize the autonomy of the priests, but his power of appointing them tempered this to some extent.

The mixture of private and public ideas applied at the level of the seigneurie as much as at that of the wider structure of rule. A king, who was also a feudal lord, linked the grant of a patrimony – originally a royal or ecclesiastical holding – to the exercise of a public function: the performance of military service, giving counsel, or carrying out the duties of an office. Tribute or the booty of war was, however, not public but private property, and this was to remain the case for centuries; even when – from the late Middle Ages – ransoms for captive princes and nobles were provided from tax money, those benefiting accepted them as personal enrichment. Princes, too, only gradually made a distinction between their private wealth and the property of the state. In the relations between feudal lords the personal element was always very important; there were direct relationships of loyalty or enmity between them. Inevitably these elements played a part in wars, just as the personal honour of those involved was at risk. When the lords fought a battle among themselves, then it was in their eyes primarily for such questions of status, as well as claims on property or rights, which again they counted as their personal, or better still, family wealth. As a

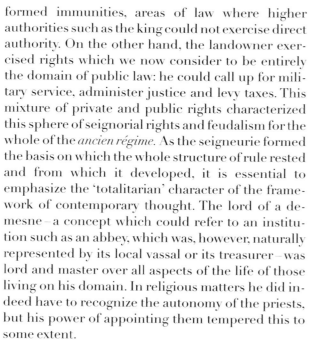

specialized warrior class – they were called knights – medieval landowners considered the fight to increase or hold on to their patrimony as an essential task, by which they upheld their status. In this situation war was also in essence a way to sort out private conflicts of interest.

The most successful of the contestants emerged from these continual conflicts of interest as new ruling dynasties. Their pattern of thinking did not differ in any way from that of other landowners: their finest achievements consisted of increasing their family patrimony. Princes continued to think of their role in this way up to the eighteenth century: on this they based their exclusive claims to the declaration of wars or leadership in them, and on the conduct of external relations. They related their personal ambitions and feelings of honour to the state over which they reigned. They were its complete incarnation and personification. In their vision of the exercise of power, renown and martial success were emphatically stressed. Up to the fourteenth century written history still consisted primarily of the description of the heroic deeds of the princes, while painting in a picture of the importance of their followers with lengthy lists of valiant knights.

The model of the Church

In the centuries following the break-up of the Roman empire the Church was the only coherently organized institution left surviving on a universal scale. In fact, together with the Byzantine empire, it was the most important heir of the Romans. It went on using Latin, which emphasized its universal aspirations the more as people expressed themselves in it less. Thus the language lifted the Church above any specific community, increasing its ritual distance from the common believer. For the organization the unity of language, however, offered the immense advantage that ecclesiastics could in fact be recruited from any part of Christendom without any problems of communication, and could be posted anywhere.

The Church took over the administrative subdivisions of the late Roman empire as its own, which involved the acceptance of a whole range of concepts, such as the territorial nature of authority, the hierarchy of official competences and functions and, more fundamental still, the concept of office itself. These were all abstract ideas which the Germanic and Slavic peoples had not yet reached by the tenth century. When – from the fourth century – the Church could legally set up its own organization, it naturally established its administrative bases in the provincial capitals, the *civitates*. From there bishops could exercise supervision – the literal translation of the Greek word *episkope* – over the cure of souls. The term is used as being an obvious one by Augustine, one of the Fathers of the Church, in his famous work *De Civitate Dei* (413–426), in which he compares the Kingdom of God with the sinful kingdoms of earth. The words derived from *civitas* in modern languages refer to the central position of a town or city.

In 292 the emperor Diocletian had divided the empire into prefectures, dioceses and provinces. These three levels can also be found in the ecclesiastical organization. The metropolitans or archbishops had supervision over a number of dioceses, and the patriarchs enjoyed comprehensive dominion over a wide ecclesiastical territory. The precedence claimed by the bishop of Rome rested purely ecclesiastically on his position as the only patriarch in the west vested with the authority of St Peter. In addition the prestige of the former imperial capital naturally played its part, particularly in rivalry with Constantinople, which had not inherited any apostolic function and had acquired its patriarchate later (in 381, as opposed to 325). The maintenance of hierarchically arranged and well-defined territorial offices was of such importance because in the period from the fifth to the eleventh century the mass migrations of peoples had blurred all ideas of frontiers. Among the Germans, and even more among the equestrian hordes who overran central Europe and the Balkans, power was linked to individuals and not to specific territories.

The Church also took over from the late empire the concept of exemptions, which the senatorial class of large landowners had deployed to protect their patrimonies from taxation by the state. Pleading its otherworldly mission, the Church claimed immunity for its property and sacrosanctity from worldly judges for its servants. By doing so it created for later ages its role as a special order, the First Estate. Apart from its separate legal status, this also rested on education and consecration. These two components added to the interpretation of the concept of office, which the Church took over from the Romans. As an abstract concept this consisted of a well-defined sum of qualifications which the holder needed to satisfy, and powers which he might or might not exercise. The role of an office-holder is strictly defined, and quite separate from the individual filling it. The criteria he has to satisfy, the

Princes of the Church were hardly distinguishable from secular princes during the Renaissance.
Portrait of Cardinal Lodovico Trevisano by Andrea Mantegna, second half of the fifteenth century.
Berlin, Gemäldegalerie

procedure for appointment and, where necessary, for dismissal from his office if he exceeds his powers or neglects his duties all exist quite separately from the individuals who have to fill the roles. This kind of abstract thought was wholly alien to the Germans and Slavs; their vision was a direct one of individuals who by virtue of the trust placed in them were given extensive but vaguely defined opportunities for exercising power. Dismissal was barely thinkable without a bloody conflict with those challenging them.

Officialdom implied literacy, another tradition which the Church alone upheld in Europe for centuries. It also involved a fixed reward; for the higher ranks this often took on the character of a *beneficium*, a benefice or demesne with

the incomes proceeding from it and the feudal rights attached to it. The Church also administered other forms of reward in the shape of prebends, actual gifts or rents, or even simply subsistence. The principles of poverty and celibacy prevented the formation of personal patrimonies, which continued to go to the institution.

The Church also upheld the great legal tradition of the Romans. By *c.* 500 the popes were already proclaiming church law, and in the eleventh to thirteenth centuries there was a new drive towards the collation and systematization of all the canons and decrees published up to then by councils and popes. While the worldly rulers tried to maintain a few legal relations based on a great variety of mainly unwritten customary laws,

Miniature of c. 1100, showing the Kingdom of God as represented by St Augustine, one of the Fathers of the Church. Just as in the Kingdom of God Christ sits enthroned over the angels and the apostles, so Ecclesia, personifying the Church, is enthroned over the kingdoms of this world. The Church, as a reflection of the heavenly kingdom on earth, is surrounded by saints, kings and emperors. Florence, Biblioteca Laurenziana

the Church had a codified system which could be understood and applied everywhere, centuries earlier than any western state. Canon law was indeed inspired at the abstract level by Roman law, but it differed from it emphatically both as regards the individuals concerned and cases. The Church retained to itself jurisdiction over its own servants and applied its own church law to them. In addition the Church claimed the authority to give judgement in all cases involving the sacraments it administered, of which that of marriage naturally produced the greatest social effect. Through its highly developed legal doctrine it was – after the eleventh century – gradually able to impose its norms on society, at first on the princes and the warrior class, with respect to the indissoluble monogamous marriage, and excluding connections within the fourth degree of relationship and renunciations on grounds of childlessness or a more attractive match elsewhere.[4]

As a large-scale organization the Church also increasingly gained in diversity. In addition to the secular hierarchy from pope through bishop down to parish priest, the monastic orders also developed. Each of these sub-systems had its own written rules, hierarchy and assemblies to achieve the implementation of the rule in the circumstances of the time. The church tradition of synods, councils and congregations of particular orders caused the emergence of a method of decision-making via delegated representatives. The rest of society learnt from this, too. The learning process was a very direct one, because priests moved in the retinues of lay princes in order to support them, often by drawing up administrative documents. Moreover, as heads of large demesnes, bishops and abbots carried out an appreciable part of public administration, the bishops in many cases also being charged with the secular authority within their diocese. More than the feudal lords, they were trained to think in abstract concepts such as institutions and norms, and could make their opinions felt in decision-making or at least in the written records of it. The Ottonian Imperial Church was the most extreme example of the subservience of a church to the secular government.

A contrary tendency, but also one opposed to simple malpractice and the alienation of ecclesiastical offices and property by feudal lords, was the reform movement which started in the tenth century. It began with the founding of the abbey of Cluny in Burgundy in 910, at which the founding donors expressly wished to escape from the strong inclination of neighbouring lords to interfere with abbey business; they were therefore given immunity from the authority of the bishop and placed directly under the pope. The intention was to follow the original Benedictine rule in all its glory and simplicity entirely for the worship of God. Donations flowed in, and the experiment was an impressive success. By 1049 Cluny headed its own congregation of sixty-five monasteries. There were similar movements in other regions. One of their effects was an internal cleansing of the Church which was able to elevate its status *vis-à-vis* secular rulers and put them back in their place. The conflict between the popes and the emperors about the right of appointment of bishops, the investiture contest, was a direct consequence. In it the Church marked out its autonomy and even its ambition for supremacy over the world of feudalism. From then on religious matters were to remain exclusively in its hands, priestly celibacy was imposed more strictly, and the hegemony of the feudal dynasties over the Church was to be broken. The Church also had the final judgement at strategic moments in a knight's life: the validity of his marriage, the legitimacy of his heirs, the force of an oath taken on sacred objects – in short the right or wrong of all he did.

An important expression of the new normative position of the Church was its opposition to feudal acts of violence. In their mutual rivalry it was quite normal for knights to deal with their opponents by plundering and sacking their demesnes, in which many a simple peasant lost his life. From the late tenth century diocesan synods in the south of France, and later in more northern regions, supported the peasants' yearnings for public order and safety. Because bishops enjoyed territorial authority, they could under the pretext of the Peace of God forbid certain forms of violence within the boundaries of their jurisdiction under pain of excommunication. The sanction was religious, but the aim political: the establishment of peaceful protected areas in a world full of violence. In this way acts of violence against defenceless peasants and travellers were resisted, and later truces were imposed for specific days and periods of the year for ritual reasons in the form of the 'Truces of God'. This action hit the world of chivalry at the foundations of its way of life, which had traditionally been characterized by the unrestrained use of force. The Church's peace movement was copied by princes who also saw in it a means of curbing the turbulent feudal lords who undermined their authority. So God's Peace became also the King's Peace or the Count's Peace, and in the Holy Roman Empire also often

Enthronement of Pope Boniface IX in Rome in 1389. In his time little of the authority of the bishop of Rome, who occupied the seat of St Peter, remained. An antipope reigned in Avignon.

Rome, Biblioteca Apostolica Vaticana

The Church continued some of the traditions of Roman law, and by doing so tried to acquire a hold on the social order.
For marriage they laid down prohibitions on marrying within the seventh degree of consanguinity.
Late thirteenth-century table of kindred and affinity.
Toulouse, Musée des Augustins

In the world of feudal violence the Church imposed the Peace of God. This was often converted into the count's peace, the king's peace,
or the country's peace. As a result violence against defenceless peasants was very gradually brought to an end.
This miniature illustrates an idealized atmosphere of peace. It adorns a prayerbook of about 1452 to 1460,
belonging to Etienne Chevalier, treasurer of France. Paris, Musée du Louvre, Arts graphiques

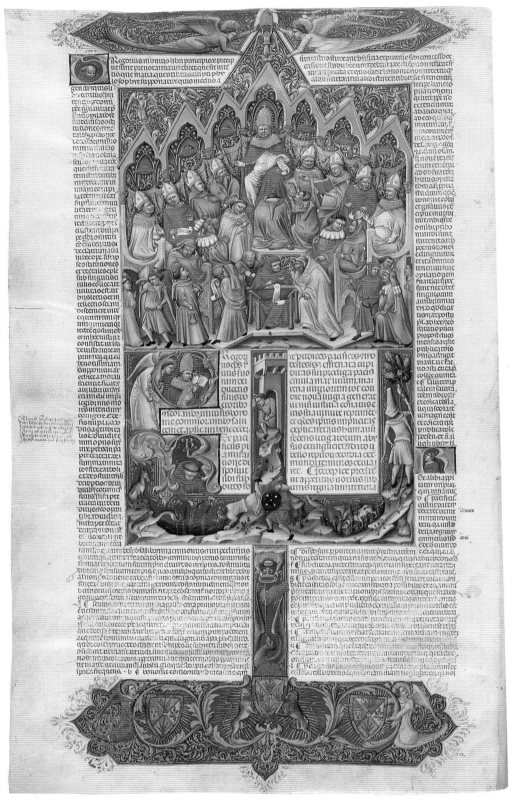

Decisions within the Church were taken in synods and councils. This laid the foundation for delegated representation.

The decisions were recorded in writing afterwards. General Council, c. 1350.

Rome, Biblioteca Apostolica Vaticana

View of the cathedral church of Bamberg, one of the Empire's administrative centres from the eleventh
to the thirteenth century. Detail from the 1483 apostles' altar, probably painted by Wolfgang Katzmeier the Elder. Bamberg, Historisches Museum

Official portrait of Richard II, king of England from 1377 to 1399. It includes every imaginable symbol of power:
throne, crown, sceptre, orb and necklace with the rose of the House of York, which is repeated on the robe
which also displays the crowned monogram RL. London, Westminster Abbey

the Territorial Peace. The Church's example had succeeded again.

After the thirteenth century the influence of the Church on the monarchies and towns diminished. Internal movements of reform no longer produced the social effects they had achieved in earlier centuries, simply because meanwhile other social structures more capable of administering themselves had arisen. From the fourteenth century the Church was for centuries in crisis from internal schisms and again – but from now on at the level of the states which had meanwhile developed – became dependent upon secular rulers. The role of the churches became a supportive one, their pioneering days were over.

The Office of King

The pioneering role of the Church shed brilliance on the highest secular offices, those of emperor and king. In 962, for the coronation of Otto the Great as emperor, a prayer of blessing was composed among his retinue at Mainz, which reads in part as follows:

Lord... enrich the King who stands here with his army through the abundance of Thy blessing, grant him strength and stability on his royal throne. Appear to him as Thou didst to Moses in the burning bush, to Joshua in battle, to Gideon in his camp, to Samuel in the temple; fill him with the constellation of Thy blessing, saturate him with the dew of Thy wisdom, received by the blessed David in his psalms and which his son Solomon could thanks to Thy mercy receive from heaven. Be his armour against his enemies, his helm against disaster, temper him in the days of his success, be his eternal protective shield; ensure that the people stay faithful to him, and that the mighty keep the peace; may they from love of their neighbour reject greed, proclaim righteousness and preserve truth. May all his people be filled with Thy eternal blessing, so that it will remain joyous for victory and in peace.[5]

God was therefore directly involved in the maintenance of Otto's supremacy, which in the eyes of his contemporaries must have given the emperor a very elevated power status. By the two-fold procedure of election as German king and the endorsement of the pope by his coronation as emperor, this function acquired a quasi-sacramental character. As soon as in the second half of the eleventh century energetic and scholarly popes led the Church, they tried to limit this position, particularly where it interfered with church matters.

In the eleventh century great conquering kings, such as Canute of Denmark and Stephen of Hungary, were canonized for the miracles they performed personally, as was also the case with Charles the Good, count of Flanders, who was murdered in church in 1127. From the twelfth century the priestly counsellors of the kings of France tried to invest this office with an inherent sacramental character which among other things included – on the analogy of Christ – the power to heal scrofula. A quasi-priestlike status, acquired through being anointed with oil during the coronation ritual, elevated kings above their contemporaries and, particularly, above their rivals. They claimed to have received authority by God's grace, so that no man could undo this without incurring the wrath of God. The Church lent its support to the sacring of princes in the hope of their support and protection. By doing so an attribute determined by the Church was added to a warlord. They were equally able to discredit a ruler by refusing this blessing.

Religious thought exercised a still more penetrating influence on the concept of kingship. Being anointed king was defined – partly due to religious inspiration – as the assumption of a role which became separated from the individual holding the office. In other words, while the Germanic tradition of kingship was still based on the outstanding military performance of a leader acknowledged by his band of warriors, the Church added to this other elements referring back to biblical models, as can be seen from Otto's blessing. Here it was a case of the king who maintains peace and thanks to his position as a mediator with God makes his people happy. The function remains, even when the individual who fills it dies. By seeing the function as separate from whoever happened to fill it, church thinking made the function an abstract one, with duties and resources attached to it. The office described in this way took precedence and the holder of it was chosen in this context. This approach saw kingship as another office, just as the Church had defined its own functions as offices. This system was completely at cross-purposes with the personal and less formalized idea of kingship or other forms of the exercise of wordly power which dominated feudal society.

The eminent historian Ernst Kantorowicz has commented that Christian doctrine offered an intrinsic model for distinguishing the living and mortal king and the enduring office which he fills. After all, the mystic body of Christ carries on eternally after the living person of Christ has left this earth. Other religions do not have this dichotomy,

The Church lent its support to sanctifying kingship.
By analogy with Christ, a king of France could cure sufferers from scrofula by touching them.
This scene from his Book of Hours shows Henry II after his coronation at Rheims in 1547. Paris, Bibliothèque nationale de France

A king was thought to occupy a position as mediator with God, which could benefit his subjects.

Fibula, also a reliquary, with a crowned eagle;

once the property of Charles VI, king of Bohemia and Holy Roman Emperor.

Paris, Musée de Cluny

so that they see power still as a personal attribute, and have not envisaged the same continuity in the exercise of power proceeding from the function.[6] In this way it became possible for the kings of France and England to assume rule immediately upon the death of their predecessor, even if the actual coronation followed later. Although during the fourteenth and fifteenth centuries the new reign in England only started a day after the death, in the sixteenth century this became the same day, so that even this brief interregnum was eliminated. This reduced the risk of intervention by rivals or subjects and enforced the succession, at least in theory.

Depersonalizing the kingship and making it into an office was, of course, not brought about solely by concepts propagated by ecclesiastics. Their ideas underpinned an evolution which was probably inevitable from a purely organizational point of view. Through expansion of territory the most successful participants in the competition for power were forced to form some administrative structure in the interests of stabilizing the territory they had acquired. Pacification was their first interest: the suppression of potential internal opposition by rivals or other subjects. By doing so, however, they were able to assign themselves the aura of someone who serves not a private interest but the common weal, in the knowledge that they would have the support of the Church. The priestly counsellors and court officials in their train would have encouraged them in this, just as did those who shared the renewed interest in Roman law after the twelfth century.

Castles were the bases of operations and safe refuges of feudal rulers, and were also impressive power symbols. Their appearance alone commanded respect and submission. August Holmberg, *The castle of Füssen in Allgau*. Berlin, Gemäldegalerie

For pacification loyal servants were needed, who in the earliest phase of territorial expansion were settled in castles in all strategic locations to offer security to the population and to keep the country under control against internal or external enemies. For the ruler it was of pre-eminent importance that he should be the strongest in his territory, and to achieve that goal on a long-term basis he was dependent on an apparatus of faithful servants: first and foremost the lords of his castles (burgraves or viscounts), in later stages also his tax collectors and judicial officers. In short, an official apparatus was the necessary route for the administration of a large territory. By creating that, the king placed himself at the head no longer of an informal warband, but of a hierarchical apparatus of offices, in which he himself simply filled the highest office.

The town as a hothouse

The growth of towns, which started in Italy in the tenth century and spread over the whole of Europe with great variations of timing and intensity, was in its origin a wholly alien phenomenon for the feudal world. For the demesnes to produce a greater yield and in the long run become overpopulated, due to increasing peace and intensive management, was not as such the desire of the warrior class. In fact to some extent it was against their interests, because the whole system of extensively self-supporting demesnes risked being disrupted by it. Now that with more favourable general conditions more people survived than in previous centuries, not all could stay bound to the soil, and some freedom of movement had to be allowed to the superfluous labour force. Once that right was acknowledged,

One of the liberties of a town was that a citizen could move without hindrance,
which in the feudal world was impossible for most of the population.
Andrea Mantegna, Predella di San Zeno, detail of the *Crucifixion,* painted in the second half of the fifteenth century.
Paris, Musée du Louvre

To acquire its liberties a town had to fight against the lord of the demesne where it was located.

The town hall was the primary symbol of the municipal autonomy it had gained. Gustavo Strafforello, *Palazzo dei Priori in Perugia*, 1889.

Ghent, private collection

appreciable differences arose in the status of peasants on land newly taken into cultivation, and on the older estates, which increased mobility still more. Henceforward not only did the labour force become more oriented towards the emerging market, but so, of course, did production for the market, so that commercialization also started in the agrarian sector. This all happened without the orders transacting the business – such as the warriors or the priests, who as large landowners were the leaders of society – being conscious of it. It was in fact the unintentional effect of the cessation of the invasions, the creation of more security, and meticulous management of the demesnes.

The towns grew because of the influx of people for whom within the established exploitation structures there was no longer room in the countryside.

Many had abandoned a position of serfdom, not without some difficulty as at first a great many lords tried to chase down the fugitives and to restore the old order by force. In this way communities were formed of a kind of outlaw, of individuals who had placed themselves outside the established order and whose first interest consisted in keeping themselves safe by acting in concert against the attempts of the feudal lords to bind them to their traditional obligations. These early townsfolk swore oaths, *coniurationes*, which literally means 'swearing together', in itself a respectable legal term were it not for the pejorative overtones given to it by princes and feudal lords. They bound themselves under oath to mutual support and assistance in a social order which for the time being had no place for them. That place they now

When a new city administration took office, the magistrates would take an oath of office on sacred objects.

Derick Baegert, *Taking the oath in the north German town of Wesel*, 1493–1494.

Wesel, Städtisches Museum

had to put up a fight for, against the lords whose authority was being thwarted.

The battle for the liberties of the towns took place in the eleventh and twelfth centuries – often violently, because that was after all the chivalric style. The Lombardy towns had developed early, and about 1100 had already under the leadership of self-appointed consuls fought for their freedom from episcopal territorial power; their conflict with the emperor Frederick Barbarossa is famous. In spite of his victory at Milan the emperor was unable to maintain his authority over the league of Lombard towns, and in 1183 he had to recognize their autonomy as a very theoretical fiefdom. In the twelfth century the German kings recognized the rights to

freedom of the individual residents of the old episcopal towns along the Rhine, but there was no question of recognizing autonomous towns there for a long time. The kings of France at that time granted liberties with municipal autonomy to many places in the north of their kingdom, partly with an eye to strengthening the monarchy against the great feudal lords who had up till then held these territories in their grasp.

Bishops who from the founding of their dioceses were lord and master of the town where they had their seat were least inclined to relinquish any of their rights to the urban community. In the first place the battle was for the personal freedom of all residents in a town: the recognition that they were

To maintain public order and create a favourable economic climate town administrations
took strong action against family clans who fought out their mutual feuds frequently and bloodily.
Armed clansmen, detail of *San Bernardino,* painted by Perugino in 1473.
Perugia, Galleria Nazionale dell'Umbria

Town governments tried gradually to limit acts of vengeance and to bring conflicts to an end
by imposing reconciliation on the rival clans which could only be broken on pain of a heavy fine.
Fifteenth-century altar of reconciliation erected for the salvation of the Ulrich Schwarz family.
Augsburg, Städtische Kunstsammlungen, Maximilianmuseum

no longer bound by the duties and constraints which they had borne as serfs. Agreement was reached that after living in a town for a year and a day residents of a town should acquire freedom under the law. This freedom included the right to move about without hindrance, for which urban society introduced the principle of solidarity, the second constituent of the town rights now being generated. A member of the sworn urban community could count on assistance if he fell into difficulties outside the town. As a legal persona the community could achieve more than individual citizens.

A third step in the movement towards the emancipation of towns consisted of their claims to autonomy, the right to formulate their own laws and regulations for their own community, and the right to exercise jurisdiction on these laws themselves. This meant that the lord of the district where the town developed had to relinquish all or part of his authority. Most lords knew how to set their price by arranging to be compensated in the form of eternal rents or excises, other material rights and a share of the income from administration of the law. The result of this battle varied greatly from place to place, depending on the nearness or distance from, and the strength of, the town's lord, and the weight that

the urban community itself could put in the scale by its size and its wealth. In the Holy Roman Empire a number of towns acquired the status of Free City of the Empire, which apart from formal subordination to the king or emperor meant in practice self-government, sometimes of the town itself, sometimes – as for instance at Ulm and Nuremberg – of an area around the town. Some bishops found life too hot in their own *civitas* and – like those of Cologne – elected to reside outside in Bonn and Bruhl. In other cases the urban community gradually bought more rights from their lord. In all cases members of the individual urban community, its citizens, ran the town. The richest merchants, entrepreneurs and proprietors always monopolized power in one way or another. Town administrations were mostly plutocracies who kept the power in the circle of a few families by co-option. They exercised political as well as judicial and legislative power in the name of their lord; this was a consequence of the delegation of power by princes who united all these aspects in their position. The linking of executive and judicial roles was maintained in European towns until the late eighteenth century. In the Middle Ages it made it more difficult to legitimize some politically laden judicial pronouncements, which made town administrations vulnerable to accusations of serving mainly their own private interests.

In the urban community, and the area of jurisdiction defined as a town, peace was the prescribed rule in the sense of excluding the typical feudal law of retaliation and taking the law into their own hands. The communities acquired from their lords well-defined rights which in the course of time were written down in the form of privileges, statutes and bye-laws. In these the exclusion of violence and feuding became prime concerns. In the privilege granted by the count of Flanders to the town of Ypres in 1116, he allowed the citizens, in place of trial by combat or trial by ordeal of hot iron or water, to adopt the more peaceful and rational manner of resolving conflicts by letting five honest men give witness under oath for a plaintiff. Of the twenty-eight articles making up the privilege granted by Count Philip of Alsace to Ghent and six other large towns of his county of Flanders between 1165 and 1177, half were devoted to the prevention of acts of violence; ten more were about procedure in the courts. One of the clauses laid down that no-one within the fortification walls might bear a sword unless they were a merchant in transit or one of the count's judicial officers; citizens of Ghent might only gird one on if they were about to leave the fortifications. Transgression of these rules incurred the maximum fine. The same concern is apparent in the imperial peace proclaimed by the emperor Frederick Barbarossa in Rhenish Franconia in 1179.

> *If anyone pursues a fleeing enemy to the vicinity of a town and he, by the action of his horse and not of his own volition, should stray into the town, then he must throw away his lance and his weapons at the town gate. In the town he will be required to declare under oath that he came into the town not of his own will, but by the strength of his horse, otherwise he will be held to be a peacebreaker.*[7]

The significance of the town walls and gate is clear from this quotation: they protected the town community with its own legal system and its own way of life from the violent surroundings where chivalry had the first – and last – say. In urban societies there was, of course, a constant threat of conflicts, some of them in fact forming the direct succession to the law of feuding which the knights had appropriated to themselves. Until the end of the Middle Ages – and in central Europe even longer – all towns wrestled with the tendency of prominent families to behave according to the code of chivalry and fight out their mutual disagreements as private wars.

Exacting vengeance, conducting feuds on a basis of purely personal law, was the archetypal method of restoring damaged status. There was then no government to mete out punishment, but parties – whole families with their supporters – who found themselves in a relationship of reciprocal violence. Damage suffered, even when it had only affected one's honour, had to be repaid according to an accepted code. This originally only applied to those with the right to bear arms, in other words, to free men. Feuding parties could often not be reconciled quickly because the enactment of revenge held the risk of overcompensation, hitting back harder than was justified, so leading to further imbalance in the other direction. As a consequence feuds dragged on even longer, until both parties were eventually exhausted. Once a mediated reconciliation had been brought about – with all the associated compensations, retributions, restoration of honour, pilgrimages for the good of the souls of the victims, and pious foundations – then the parties were supposed to behave towards each other as friends again, because they no longer had reasons for resentment.

The privileges of the principal Flemish towns of 1165–1177 dealt very carefully with the right of retaliation and did not challenge the right of carrying on feuds by *probi viri*, 'honest men' of the town, by which undoubtedly the elite was meant. However, the magistrates who ran the town did try to reconcile the parties – under pain of a fine – and to bind them to an agreement.

> *If anyone with regard to any dispute refuses to guarantee peace to two or more magistrates or peacemakers, then it will cost him sixty pounds [the maximum fine]. If among the honest men of the town any tension, discord, war or any other wrong arises, and the rumour of it comes to the ears of the magistrates, these will, subject to the rights of the count, settle it and bring about peace. Anyone, however, who rejects the aforesaid settlement or peace proposed by the magistrates shall be penalized sixty pounds.*[8]

Neither magistrates nor officers of the court were therefore as yet obliged to prosecute feuding, and they could not interfere in it as criminal judges either; they might only punish a refusal to accept conciliation. The parties maintained the right of mutual compensation for damage in accordance with private law, either by causing equal damage to the other party, or by obtaining financial and moral satisfaction from them. As long as the town magistracy could not forbid and punish private feuding, they were in a very weak position *vis-à-vis* the most important families within their walls, who in any case themselves usually provided the magistrates

In towns of north and central Italy the *podestà,* a professional judge from outside their own community, presided over the law courts.

Scenes from the fifteenth-century judicial process in Florence, *Santa Maria del Sacrilegio*:

the arrest, the imprisonment, the court proceedings, and the execution of the sentence.

and therefore had an interest in keeping the law in their own hands.

The large and powerful towns in north and central Italy had to cope with this structural weakness in relation to their own elites well into the fifteenth century. In the twelfth and thirteenth centuries they were run by consuls from their own community, presided over by a judicial officer, the *podestà,* a professional judge who came from outside the town and was therefore thought to be able to stand above parties and so maintain the peace and cohesion. The term of office of a *podestà* was usually six months. On taking office he swore an oath on the

town's statutes, the regulations and the administration of justice of the magistracy. On this occasion the new laws of the previous period were always added to the statute book. Thus a strong juridical tradition developed, supported by written texts. In Bologna in 1264 a committee of ten legal scholars needed no less than eighteen months to create order in the maze of regulations, laws and rules which in the course of time had been deposited in the eighty-five statute books of the town. Education at renowned faculties, such as that at Bologna, gave officials, lawyers and judges a basis which made it possible for them to introduce a supra-local legal culture. This high level of professional jurisprudence in the administration of justice was for a long time confined to the towns of north and central Italy.

Yet the great families continued to dominate and terrorize the towns. They were organized as clans, with the members of the family at their core, following a strict hierarchy of descent in the male line. Around them were more distant relations and supporters also belonging to the elite. A third class was formed by the squires, paid employees. All behaved in accordance with a code which reflected that of chivalry, though the use of violence had a less professional but rather more instrumental character. Members of the clan were mutually bound by reciprocal loyalty, which could be of vital importance in combat. To see the clans parade in the Italian and Flemish towns, decked in the heraldic colours of the family, exhibiting the reckless virility of the group as a means of affirming their honour and status – and when it came to the point, making sure they were the strongest – is a reminder of Tacitus' description of the Germanic *comites*. The grand stone houses of these families dominated the townscape. With their sturdy contruction, battlements and towers they were a symbol of power for everyone, equipped as they were to resist a siege. In the north Italian towns all the aristocratic houses were built with high towers, intended both for a military function and to show their importance.

The ultimate explanation for the continuing clan rivalry in the Italian towns must be sought in the spread of the instruments of violence. As long as the magistracy as a collective government had insufficient superiority of power to impose public order, the clans ruled the streets. So long as they provided the services of the town administration, nothing changed. An external, superior power could possibly impose peace: for instance, about 1170 the count of Flanders gave some degree of support to the town magistrates. In practice in the course of the thirteenth century the counts had even less superiority of strength over the powerful towns, and the town administrations remained in effect privatized.

It was the same in Italy: even the mighty Hohenstaufen emperors had to acknowledge their powerlessness against the Lombard towns. Factions in the towns tried to make use of the divisions between the emperor, the pope and later also the kings of Naples and Sicily to strengthen their position through coalitions. Put in another way – divisions at the territorial level worked to the advantage of the townsfolk. Factions were originally grafted onto the differences between the two rival German ruling families. The Hohenstaufens, whose castle of Waiblingen gave the name of Ghibellini to their supporters in Italy, were the figurehead of one party, while the opposition to the emperor in the Lombard towns called themselves Guelph after the Welf family, and in reaction supported the papacy. After the death of Frederick II in 1250 a new power contest broke out for the mastery of Sicily. The Ghibellines ruled Siena, the Guelphs held Florence; in 1261 they were driven out by the Ghibellines. After the victory in 1268 of Charles of Anjou, the papal candidate for the crown of Sicily, the Guelphs were also victorious in the towns of Tuscany. The Guelph coalition – Sicily, pope, Florence – held for more than a century. They were to reap the fruits of it in banking too.

Once embedded in the political culture, it was hard to get rid of these party conflicts: through long tradition they were firmly rooted in the ways in which problems were defined. During the fourteenth century the ruling Guelph party in Pistoia and Florence split into Whites and Blacks.[9] In this complicated situation the elites had a common interest in the maintenance of their oligarchic power, particularly when in the fourteenth century they were overtly threatened by the claims of the craftsmen. Against this challenge the town magistracies deployed their legitimacy by activating their role as mediators and presenting themselves as the defenders of the public weal. Various terms expressed this abstract concept, linking it to the principles of Roman law: *bonum commune, utilitas publica, quod interest civitati*. The interest of the town justified interference with special interests and sometimes with some legal rules. As magistracies were better able to call on such general principles in individual decisions, their intervention acquired more authority, while the cohesion of the elite and the town was also served by it. The support of the magistrates by professional jurists helped them to raise themselves as an institution above parties. Their judicial role was decisive in this because it demonstrated effectiveness and credibility in the establishment and maintenance of public order in an unambiguous way. The officers of the law began to bring criminal prosecutions by virtue of their office on the grounds of offences *against the authorities* – such as disturbing public order – which imposed higher requirements on the authorities' ability to hunt down offenders and build up valid evidence against them.

Any correspondence between the procedure for reconciliation under private law, in which the city

Injustice, represented with a grappling iron as sceptre, gives free rein to thieves, rapists and highwaymen.
Examples of these three classes are illustrated beneath his feet. Fresco in grisaille, painted by Giotto c. 1305.
Padua, Capella Scrovegni

The town walls were the dividing line between two kinds of society with different legal rules.
In the *Capture of Lierre by the Spaniards* in 1595 both the old and the new concentric circles of walls can be seen.
Brussels, Musées royaux des Beaux-Arts

authorities could purely appear as mediators and supervisors of agreements reached, and criminal prosecutions under public law by virtue of their office, was to disappear everywhere in western Europe in the course of the fourteenth to sixteenth centuries. This assumed, however, that peace, which in the eleventh and twelfth centuries was still a very clearly defined exceptional condition, would in the future be considered as the normal situation. These conditions could only be effectively maintained if an authority possessed sufficient superiority in power, based on the recognition of its use of force as legitimate. The criminal code proclaimed by Charles v in 1532 formally made an end of tolerance of the *lex talionis*, the law of retaliation. In regions where governmental authority was weak, such as the Tyrol, southern Italy, Sicily and Corsica, blood feuds continued to be standard practice for centuries.

The gradual process by which the practice of the leading families of taking the law into their own hands was subjected to the impartial authority of government, depended very much on the combination of political control and control of the courts, typical of the *ancien régime*, and of the involvement in the exercise of power of just those prominent families whose authority needed to be restricted for the common interest. When personal firearms were invented they were obviously forbidden first in the towns. In France royal legislation tried in the early seventeenth century under threat of high fines, exile and execution to forbid the carrying of small firearms, in order to deprive their subjects of dangerous instruments of violence. From 1589 the kings took measures against the nobility taking the law into their own hands in the form of duelling – yet the burghers of Ypres had banned it as early as 1116. As the aristocrats regarded the ban as an attack on a privilege of their order, sanctions such as execution, relegation from the ranks of the nobility and confiscation of goods could do little against a deep-rooted sense of their rights. Only towards the end of the seventeenth century did the sovereignty of the king begin to tip the balance, at least in France.[10]

In less sensitive areas the towns were able to establish public functions much more quickly. As a sworn association the original community became a legal person, demanding and giving solidarity, an abstract concept in comparison with the direct and personal links of loyalty by which individuals were bound, which were typical of feudalism. In the conflict with their former lords the territorial jurisdiction of towns became precisely demarcated, with churches and princes within the walls maintaining their immunities. However, the town walls provided for one and all a visible dividing line, which was easy to police, between two areas of jurisdiction and two forms of society, even if the town's jurisdiction, its liberties, already applied within a radius round the walls and although there were regular expansions of the town's area of jurisdiction – particularly in the period up to 1300 and again in the sixteenth and seventeenth centuries, when there was a strong growth of towns everywhere.

Building walls required an enormous effort of a town, as it involved a solid construction of several kilometres' length – in Ghent as much as twelve. A system of taxation had to be created for this purpose, mainly raised by levies on consumer goods. The burghers were therefore aware that they were making efforts on behalf of their community, just as they used to do for the collection of excise duty or ransom money for the former or even current lords. The management of the common resources was already in the late thirteenth century a point of conflict between the established oligarchy and the craft guilds, who were organizing themselves and demanding accountability for the way in which money collected in taxes was spent. After risings by the craft guilds the count of Flanders in 1279–1280 forced the authorities of his large towns to keep accounts of public income and expenditure, and so to be accountable for their policy. This was also the time when towns started raising their own militias, organized by districts and by crafts. Marshalled behind their banners and in their colourful tunics they gave very forceful expression to the self-esteem of the burghers.

In addition to the town walls, more public buildings were erected: a town hall, of course, but also often free-standing bell towers, called *belforts* in France and Flanders. They served various purposes: that of watch tower, pealing their bells to mark public events, or the times of starting and stopping work; they bore sundials or mechanical clocks; the

chest containing the town's privileges was kept there under lock and key; and in themselves such impressive towers also became a symbol of the town itself. Other building works with a public function were the trade halls, halls for the sale of foodstuffs, warehouses, harbours, canals, locks, bridges, roads, cranes, weigh-houses, water supplies and fountains. The town also created public open spaces, in the first place for the markets which fulfilled the primary purpose of the town, and streets and squares which were the stage for public demonstrations or for the everyday urban life. In function the churches served equally as public buildings, and were to a large extent financed by the resources from the urban community, though they were managed by the clergy. As an architectural whole the town formed a frame for a lifestyle which provided a very material and visible shape to the abstract concept of the community.

It is interesting to examine the extent of the public interests in the towns. Social care was originally in the hands of the Church, but foundations by the citizens brought it increasingly under the control of the representatives of the town authorities. These supervised the administration of their property, and also laid down some rules; their triangular relationship with private donors and religious charitable care continued to be honoured. This also applied to hospitals, whose management was left to the religious orders, and to alms for the poor which were mainly based on parishes. The care of old people, widows and orphans, in so far as it was not covered by the two previous categories, was the province of guilds and fraternities. In all these cases the town authorities exercised a supervisory function. The guardianship of the mentally ill was then seen as a problem of public order that was shouldered by the town, as was that of a prison. In the fifteenth century the towns also employed doctors and midwives to offer help in cases occurring in the public domain.

During the first decades of the sixteenth century town authorities all over Europe could be seen taking on a more emphatic organizational function in order to co-ordinate the widely distributed forms of social care and impose strict controls on it. The new increase in population made the need for rationalization keenly felt in the first economic depression. During the fourteenth century several towns had already founded one or more schools, clearly an invasion of a traditional ecclesiastic monopoly. The spread of the Reformation brought acceleration in this, because all denominations now rushed to capture the souls of the children.

In towns the need arose for buildings with various public functions.
As well as the town walls, town hall and market halls,
a prison was sometimes built. In Zürich this was a tower in the river, free-standing and difficult of access.
Hans Leu the Elder, *View of Zürich*, about 1492–1496. Zürich, Landesmuseum

This long list of areas in which towns were active until the sixteenth century makes it clear that they – or at least the larger ones – formed a socially very differentiated environment with a high intensity of human contacts. This perhaps heightened the discordance, but undoubtedly also the creativity, by which the towns achieved a lead in modernization over the feudal world surrounding them. In particular the idea of *res publica*, a republic, again acquired a real – and its original – meaning for the first time since Roman days. The medieval concept of a commune actually refers in more concrete terms to the community, which forms a collective identity and regulates its affairs in the public interest, than the phrase *res publica*, derived from the classical vocabulary by scholars. With this the towns went much further in the development of public power than the abstract ideas the Church had inherited

from the Roman constitution and legal system. It also put them centuries ahead of the monarchies who had only with difficulty begun to distinguish the public domain from their private heritage.

Networks of towns

Not all towns primarily filled commercial functions: several arose, or were founded, to provide services for a cathedral or some other administrative centre. The Iberian towns derived their great liberties from the *reconquista* led by the kings, and also functioned as bases for conquest and centres of occupation. During the Middle Ages towns with such a one-sided function were usually relatively small, like the archiepiscopal seats of Canterbury, Sens and Esztergom. Large capital cities, built to a plan, usually in the centre of a realm, date from more recent times, when states had more centralized resources available to make such a project successful: Madrid and Warsaw are examples in the sixteenth century, Berlin in the seventeenth, and St Petersburg in the eighteenth.

What is striking is that until the eighteenth century the largest commercial metropolises enjoyed a wide degree of autonomy compared with the states surrounding them. Often they were situated in small states in which they themselves exercised a strong influence on the government. They had been able to expand this position of relative autonomy in so far as their own development preceded the consolidation of royal power in the coastal areas. Moreover the concern of these metropolises was primarily with other interests, such as the safety of trade routes, the protection of travelling merchants, reaching agreements about commercial transactions with various partners, and the provision of an efficient disputes procedure. Neither the feudal lords nor their ecclesiastical counsellors knew much about such questions, so that it was the merchants directly involved who developed the relevant institutional rules and put them into effect themselves, sometimes with the formal seal of a nearby prince.

Between the tenth and the thirteenth centuries, in the growth phase of both kingdoms and towns, all these matters led to the large commercial towns themselves providing all kinds of institutional provisions to protect their vital interests against feudal lords who were often striving for directly opposed material interests, or against princes who had very little idea or interest in them. In the van were the Italian ports which had already expanded in the Mediterranean from the tenth century. Trading settlements were founded and later, from the twelfth century, whole towns along the Greek and Dalmatian coasts, in the Levant and on the Black Sea, came under their colonial authority. In particular Venice and Genoa built up immense networks of trading colonies, for which they fought each other to the death. After fierce competition Pisa and Marseilles had to accept that they could not make the grade. Barcelona developed its network during the thirteenth century, mainly in the western Mediterranean, with settlements in the Balearics, Sardinia and Sicily, but also consulates in Tunis, Bougie and Oran. These involved in the first place the organization of markets and the protection of their own citizens abroad. For this purpose concessions were agreed, including some in Muslim areas, though the support of Christian potentates – who in the twelfth century had founded their own kingdoms in the Levant and in parts of the Byzantine empire – was of some help. Where circumstances allowed, as along the coasts of Dalmatia and Greece, the Venetians went on to impose their rule on strings of towns, and during the fifteenth century even on countless islands, of which Crete, Euboea and Cyprus were the largest.

The Italian system of trade settlements was in the Middle Ages by far the largest in Europe. From the twelfth century a similar system – though on a much more modest scale – developed in the North Sea and the Baltic with trade settlements of North Germans in Scandinavia and the Baltic coastal regions. The most important centre was the island of Gotland off the east coast of Sweden. Danes and north Germans from the Lübeck region, and later also from Westphalia, made contact with local traders there and from there carried on trade with Novgorod (where the Germans already had a settlement by about 1190), England and Flanders. Traders from various regions organized themselves for their own protection on specific routes. Similar trading organizations were formed elsewhere in the twelfth and thirteenth centuries; for instance, for the Flemish trade with England, and for the trade from Flanders, Artois and Brabant to the annual fairs in Champagne. They were private law organizations for mutual assistance, who acquired privileges from the rulers in the target markets. Some of these organizations bore the name of guild, others of hansa. The most famous is the German Hansa, a league formed in the thirteenth century of older regional trade associations from the areas round Lübeck, Westphalia, Saxony and Prussia. In 1356 the German Hansa formed itself into a league of towns, with at its peak almost two hundred member towns, from Novgorod via the coast of Scandinavia to the Low Countries. Until 1669 this league operated on an interregional scale to promote the trading interests of the citizens of its member towns, and outside them acted as a collective body in public law.

In this way interregional networks were set up for the protection and advancement of trade relations, which found expression among other things in several forms of commercial and maritime law. The oldest of them developed in the eastern Mediterranean region, but from the eleventh century the region between Pisa and Marseilles developed its own legal tradition. A third was that of the consulate of Barcelona which, in this string of special commercial relationships, is the link with the

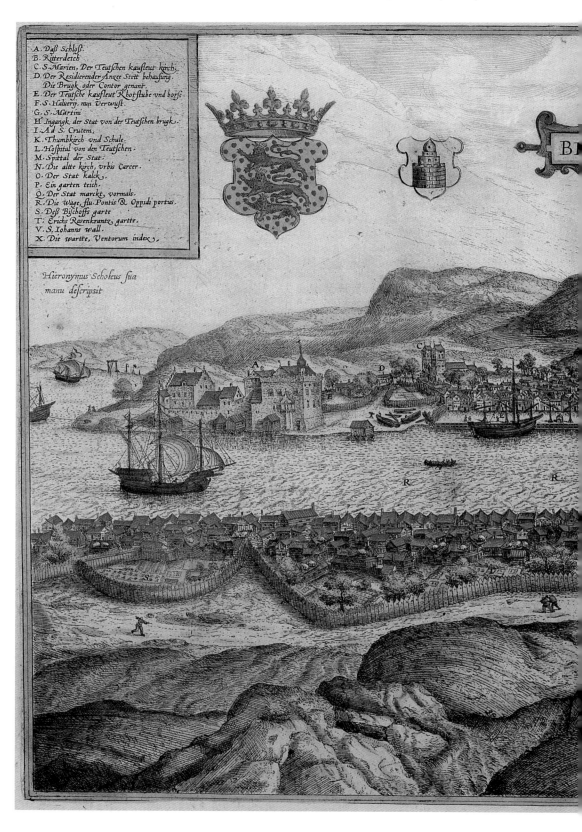

A. Daß Schloß.
B. Ritterdetch
C. S. Marien, Der Teutschen kaufleut kirch.
D. Der Residierender Anzee Stett behausung
   Die Brugk oder Contor genant.
E. Der Teutsche kaufleut Rhotstube vnd borse.
F. S. Halwey, nun Vertwust.
G. S. Martini
H. Ingangk der Stat von der Teutschen brugk.
I. Ad S. Crucem.
K. Thumbkirch vnd Schule.
L. Hospital von den Teutschen.
M. Spittal der Stat.
N. Die alte kirch, vrbis Carcer.
O. Der Stat kalck.
P. Ein garten teich.
Q. Der Stat marckt, vormals.
R. Die Wage, flu. Pontis & Oppidi portus.
S. Deß Bischoffs garte
T. Erichs Rosenkrantz gartte.
V. S. Iohanns wall.
X. Die wartte, Ventorum index.

Hieronymus Scholeus sua
manu descripsit

The Norwegian Hansa town of Bergen in 1581 by Frans Hogenberg and Hieronymus Scholeus:
at the head of the harbour stands the Gothic Hakonshall, where in the thirteenth century the king was crowned.

To its right the wharf with unloading cranes of the Tyskebryggen trading settlement of Hansa merchants is clearly visible.
Across the harbour sheep graze on the turf-covered roofs.

The trading metropolis of Venice depended on a good information network
to keep in touch with her colonies.
The senatorial foreign affairs committee supervised
the correspondence of the ambassadors sent out by the republic.
Vittorio Carpaccio, *Departure of an ambassador from Venice* (fifteenth century).
Venice, Galleria dell' Accademia

Atlantic legal traditions. Along the coasts of the Atlantic and the North Sea a thirteenth-century code operated – called after the island of Oléron – which applied in the whole area where the wine of Gascony was sold. A translation of this was made in Bruges in the early fourteenth century, and then became the model for a number of transcriptions in the area of the German Hansa. Around 1200 yet another tradition was encoded in the Schleswig town law. All these examples involved systems of customary law developing out of the way justice was administered in a specific trade circuit. No particular prince had prescribed it in legislation, it had arisen from the arguments of the lawyers involved who belonged to the trading environment and knew what they were talking about. Nowhere in Europe were commercial legal systems the business of princes and their lawyers. The initiative for them lay entirely in the organizations of inter-regional traders. They formulated the rules, negotiated agreements and administered justice.

In various ways groups of towns made arrangements for their own protection in a world which – because of the fragmentation of effective authority – was extremely unsafe for travellers. Because towns were dependent on close traffic links with their hinterland and other markets, the safety of the roads was their continual concern. There was always a great temptation for small feudal lords to take advantage of their control of a piece of country through which a strategic route passed by threatening travelling merchants with robbery and violence if they did not pay the tolls they imposed. In this way rulers who had a military superiority sold restraint in its use. Tolls were in fact pay-offs in what might be called a protection racket: if the toll was paid, the trader could count on a safe passage. The extent of the levy could, however, be a controversial matter: arbitrary decisions on the part of the ruler or his toll collector were difficult to avoid.

A vital traffic axis such as the Rhine was strewn with authorities who took their share from the crowded river traffic. Towns in this region, in Alsace and in Swabia, from the thirteenth to the fifteenth century regularly formed leagues for their common protection against assaults on their safety, on that of their citizens and of their commercial traffic. In some cases they were even able to include feudal lords in their leagues, or they were granted, in exchange for financial support, guarantees or rights by the German king or by the emperor. The first great league of the Rhine towns dates from 1254, when the Interregnum brought about problems of

public order. In the form of a *coniuratio* (swearing together) which placed them directly under the protection of Christ, the towns tried in the first place to maintain peace, settle conflicts by means of the legal system or by arbitration, to arrange the common prosecution of peace breakers, and to set limitations on tolls on rivers and roads. The points in this programme were clearly in conflict with the actions of the nobility, but the movement was still successful in persuading some archbishops and bishops, the count palatine and some counts and lords to join their league. In this way the league assumed a task which was in reality the king's, the maintenance of peace and justice in the common interest, and against the nobility's practices of feuding and taking the law into their own hands.

Such leagues of towns did not, however, last long, and their rare joint military actions achieved only limited successes. The Swabian league suffered a defeat by the feudal lords in 1388. The disparity of interests and the motley diversity of coalitions were obstacles to cohesion in extensive geographical areas. For example, in Swabia the great league consisted by the end of the fourteenth century of towns spread over 300 kilometres from north to south and 240 kilometres from east to west. The relatively low degree of urbanization made effective political and economic activity difficult here, but this organization still offered alternative forms for the exercise of public power against the initiatives of the princes. Thanks to their league the Swabian towns were also able to retain their status as Free Towns of the Empire, and to preserve their independence against the territorial princes of Württemburg.

Apart from the safety of the roads, protection against extortion and specially adapted regulations for settling commercial differences, the towns created still more power systems in the areas they controlled. What united the towns was their mutual trade. But towns also needed to maintain a proteced flow of men and goods to and from the surrounding countryside to provide for their livelihood. The food supply usually had to come from the immediate environs, which made market regulations necessary to guarantee against shortages. Many townspeople invested their capital in land outside the town, often to engage in cultivation for the market, and commonly stipulated that their income from this should be delivered in kind, so avoiding the fluctuations of the foodstuffs market. At the same time each town tried to protect its own products by banning similar activities in the vicinity. The investments and regulations of the townspeople bore

Barcelona developed a network of trading posts in the western Mediterranean.
Her pioneering position found expression in an independent system of maritime commercial law.
Miniature from the Customary of Barcelona, 1448. Barcelona, Museo de la Ciudad

From the twelfth century the Germans also developed a trading network, the Hansa,
in the regions round the North Sea and the Baltic;
this was a league of virtually autonomous towns.
Von Schikinge unde Vorderinge is a miniature illustrating Hamburg's commercial courts in 1497.
Hamburg, Staatsarchiv

The security of the roads was fundamental for merchants.
This votive painting by Stephan Praun was made in 1511
in gratitude for his survival after being attacked by brigands in Italy.
Nuremberg, Germanisches Nationalmuseum

In the past tolls were often levied along the great rivers, which not only cost traders much money, but also much time.
Once a toll had been paid the merchant could, however, count on a safe passage. Albrecht Dürer, *View of Trent.*
Bremen, Kunsthalle

Even in the Middle Ages an urbanized region was dependent on supplies of food from more distant areas.
The largest urban areas were therefore on the coast or along the great rivers.
Fra Angelico, Triptych from Perugia, predella: *Scene from the life of St Nicholas* (1437). Rome, Pinacoteca Vaticana

Sixteenth-century tapestry, *The month of October,* woven to a design by Bartolomeo Suardo, called Bramantino;

in the borders are the coats of arms of the seigneuries which supplied goods in kind to the duke of Milan.

Milan, Castello Sforzesco, Museo d'Arte Antica

heavily on the residents of the countryside. The vicinity of an urban market led to agriculture becoming commercialized, which benefited the productivity of the land. However, the town imposed its supremacy on the peasants and subjected them to all kinds of discrimination and expropriation.

Mutual relationships between towns were even less idyllic. They were strictly defined by their mutual interdependency in a hierarchy of markets. Larger towns usually exercised a suffocating hegemony over smaller ones, just as they did over the countryside. These relationships are most clearly

demonstrated in the most urbanized region, northern Italy. During the fifteenth and sixteenth centuries regional states were formed here, spurred on by the largest towns – Venice, Florence, Genoa and Milan – which then became their capital cities. The subordinate towns – a subordination which, as in the case of Pisa, was really the result of a conquest by Florence, finally giving it control of a seaport – came under an administration appointed by the capital city. The law courts of the capital enjoyed precedence in the whole *contado,* in legal matters citizens were given preferential treatment over

Towns were quick to see the need for an efficient official administrative system.
They often subsidized the academic studies of talented young men,
who were afterwards obliged to enter the town's service.
Portrait of Jacob de Vogelaer, town secretary of Amsterdam in 1655,
painted by an anonymous master.
Amsterdam, Amsterdams Historisch Museum

country folk, rural goods were more heavily taxed than those produced in the towns, town guilds enjoyed precedence over country crafts, and urban landownership penetrated deep into the countryside. In this way political hegemony rigidified market relationships, which still offered more scope to the larger than to the poorer centres. The north Italian regional states demonstrate yet another model of a socio-economic and political order which arose without – and sometimes in opposition to – monarchic interference.

Various political systems were therefore possible through the dynamism of the towns, of which the Italian model, with an overseas and a domestic component, was able to develop freely with the largest demographic and economic concentrations of the late Middle Ages, and relatively few monarchs in the vicinity. Even the invasions, first of the French armies in 1494, followed by those of the Empire which caused heavy damage to the country in the first half of the sixteenth century, could not essentially affect this system of regional states; at the most they could reduce it to a number of virtually autonomous vassal states. Elsewhere power relationships were less emphatically to the advantage of the towns, particularly the larger ones, and they formed other configurations.

The provisional conclusion from this brief examination is that districts of an urban or rural character in certain parts of Europe where the formation of feudal or monarchic power had not penetrated early or very deep, had developed their own political and social structures in order to look after their vital common interests. Under the watchword of peace they organized protection for their trade, independently, locally, and on the routes linking them. Where they enjoyed a superiority they formed hegemonistic market systems with a colonial dimension. As kingdoms and territorial principalities expanded their territory and power, they naturally came in contact with the power systems already built up by the urban networks in some areas. Conflicts of competence and open power struggles arose between the two sides. Meanwhile, however, co-operation in various forms also proved possible.

Farming communities

A fascinating example demonstrating the ability to form political systems on a much smaller scale out of towns and groups of villages is the Swiss one. Unlike in Italy not all the rural cantons here became subservient to the towns. Uri, Schwyz and Unterwalden even led the struggle for independence in 1291. It is true that in the urbanized cantons the main towns dominated the villages. Between dominance by feudal lords, and that by burghers, there lay yet a third road along which communities of farmers created forms of public power from the ground up. Special geographical circumstances, which made the traditional demesne exploitation impossible, and an economy based on cattle farming, supplied the particular conditions for freedom in such communities.

In districts where grazing was scarce because of the mountains and the dry climate, as around the Mediterranean, cattle farmers sought their livelihood by exchanging high pastures in the summer with winter pastures in the plains. The twice-yearly migration of herds made a special form of organization necessary. This was most clearly institutionalized in Iberia, because there in the course of the *reconquista* the Christian kings granted special rights in the conquered country to communities of herdsmen from the mountainous districts in the north. For instance, in 1273 King Alfonso X of Castile recognized the *Honrado Concejo de la Mesta*, an association of the owners of migrant cattle. He granted them the right to let their cattle graze freely along prescribed drove roads, which might be hundreds of kilometres long and dozens of metres wide, linking the summer pastures in the mountains and the winter pastures in the recently conquered and thinly populated south. Staging areas were provided at regular intervals, and halfway, near Segovia, there were stations for shearing. The pasturing rights could even prevent landowners on the route from cultivating crops on their own land. The privilege also protected the *Mesta* against increases in tolls. It levied its own taxes on its members, using them to pay officials and arbitrators who had to supervise the observance of the privileges. Naturally the crown took its share of these taxes, too. This system, which survived until 1836, at its height in 1780 controlled the movements of five million sheep. Similar organizations existed elsewhere, but on a smaller scale because of the more fragmented power structures than those in Castile. On the Foggia plateau in central Italy in the fifteenth

**In the south and west of the Holy Roman Empire
farmers organized their own communities for the protection of their rights.**
Village with wire-drawing mill on the Pegnitz, coloured drawing by Albrecht Dürer.
Berlin, Kupferstichkabinett

century this kind of transhumance was arranged for the movements of some three million sheep.[11]

Cattle farming is capital intensive and requires the maintenance of commercial contacts. Whenever because of geographical conditions this industry was carried on outside the great demesnes, the conditions for the development of institutions answering the specific needs of free farmers were inherent in it. In the Swiss context these did not develop into a large-scale organization as in Castile, but they gave rise to the formation of a league of autonomous communities of farmers – and later also of townspeople – in a confederation, the legal form in which collective rights were normally safeguarded. There were no differences in principle between the farming communities and those of the townspeople; in France, too, villages sometimes gained charters of freedom showing many similarities with those of the towns. Because of their small scale, assemblies of all the free men of the village continued to work

effectively as decision-making – and in some cases also judicial – bodies, a practice which soon became unworkable in the towns. However, this direct democracy hindered professionalization and modernization which, when added to their small scale, would prove to be a disadvantage for the survival of many farming communities.

Quite apart from a mountainous environment, problems of water management also gave communities and organizations of free farmers occasion to operate over long periods as public bodies on a larger than local scale. In Catalonia and Murcia irrigation systems were maintained by an autonomous administration with its own legal jurisdiction, which still meets in the north porch of the cathedral of Valencia. This was a matter of a specialized public provision, with limits which for natural reasons did not coincide with other jurisdictions. The need to construct an infrastructure for large areas in the interests of many landowners and land users,

In the safe shelter of their Alpine ranges the Swiss farming communities kept their independence.

From 1294 they were united in a sworn league for the protection of their collective rights.

Albert Anker, *Assembly of a local council* (nineteenth century).

Berne, Kunstmuseum

and to lay down regulations for the cheap and impartial distribution of benefits and burdens, led to collective interest groups of a public law nature.

Similarly free farmers in the low-lying areas along the North Sea created autonomous organizations whose object was collective defence against flooding. The substantial investments of labour required for digging drainage canals and raising dykes, and all the measures needed to carry out these works and maintain them, were achieved by organizations with specific objectives, the water boards. In the twelfth century they were first organized by villages, but by the thirteenth century the problem already needed to be approached on a wider scale. Territorial princes were also involved, though usually only to mediate or to confirm the groundwork already achieved by those more immediately concerned. As in Valencia, from the thirteenth century the water boards had various administrative rights in their specific field, such as levying taxes, administering justice and law enforcement. The organizational and administrative tasks became increasingly complicated in the course of

centuries, particularly in Holland, Utrecht and Friesland, because the land sank increasingly below sea level, so that ever more complex systems were necessary to stay dry-shod. The water boards therefore increasingly became professional organizations at the technical level, with extensive public powers. They were still based on the principles of proportional sharing of benefits and burdens by everyone and on the representation of those involved. This solidarity was the easier to impose because nature added its own sanctions in various disasters to the humanly imposed ones.

Outside the regions where transhumant cattle farming or water management set specific problems for which the farmers themselves had found solutions, farming communities were also sometimes able to make their voice heard. In extreme circumstances, when there was absolutely no organization to which they could have access for institutionalized consultation, they made their feelings felt by revolting. They then generally demanded justice, and no more. In Scandinavia it seldom reached this stage, because communities which

Polder areas in the northern Netherlands,
like this one near Enkhuizen (c. 1600)
had to be protected against the continuous threat of flooding.
This required collective efforts on a large scale.

From these emerged water boards
which since the thirteenth century have functioned
by participation and allocation of costs in proportion to holdings of land.
Enkhuizen, Stadhuismuseum

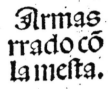

In Spain the six-monthly transhumance or migration of great herds of sheep
was already institutionalized by the thirteenth century through the *Honorado Concejo de la Mesta,*
a union of the owners of the trekking sheep.
Madrid, private collection

Six Orders of medieval society, from a miniature of *c.* 1375. Nicolas Oresme, councillor of Charles v of France,
in his translation of Aristotle's *Politics,* clearly sets out the relative authority of warriors,
councillors, clergy, peasants, artisans and merchants. Both clergy and knights were large landowners.
The world of industry and trade to which the townsfolk belonged was largely alien to them,
and they regarded it with great suspicion.
Brussels, Bibliothèque royale de Belgique

El Tribunal de las Aguas, The Water Tribunal, still sits every week in the north porch of Valencia cathedral.

This court, which goes back a thousand years, decides on all disputes involving control of water in the Huerta,

a fertile stretch of country which has for centuries been intensively irrigated.

Ferrandis recorded one of these sessions in 1865.

Valencia, Palau de la Generalitat

discussed matters in their *ting* could appeal to the crown with their complaints and find a hearing there, so that negotiation and mediation were possible. Similar traditions of complaints procedures for farming communities are widely met in southern Germany.[12] It is, however, still true that their small scale, thinly populated areas, limited accumulations of capital and restricted access to market systems gave fewer opportunities to farmers than to townspeople to develop large configurations of power.

Cui bono?

In this chapter princes have been examined primarily from the viewpoint of their feudal origins: large landowners aiming at the acquisition of yet more land by traditional methods, matrimony, inheritance, mortgaging, or as fiefs. In the case of

argument immediate resource to the use of force was the accepted method of salving one's offended honour. As the lords of castles rose to kingship, they could find inspiration in and make use of the administrative concepts and methods offered them by the Church. Ecclesiastics and knights were, however, all large landowners who had based their position on their dominion over large demesnes. The world of trade, crafts, seafaring and finance was equally alien to both.

This is why the new needs presented by the development of a commercial economy were initially provided for without any major problems by the communities of townspeople or farmers involved. At first it was a matter of marginal phenomena—not least from the point of view of geographical location—in the predominantly rural society. However, the reach of a prince's power and that of the towns grew towards each other. Some

In Scandinavia farming communities could address their complaints directly to the crown.

Alaert van Everdingen, *Scandinavian landscape with sawmill*, 1675.

Rouen, Musée des Beaux-Arts

In the late Middle Ages large trading towns had to give way to the princes, who were becoming increasingly more powerful.

urban networks, particularly overseas settlements, were able to survive for a considerable time just because they lay outside the zones of territorial expansion of the European princes. The German Hansa had to square up to this vigorously between the fourteenth and sixteenth centuries, but lost its case. Most Mediterranean colonies were absorbed by the expansion of the Ottoman empire in the fifteenth and sixteenth centuries. Within Europe all the large towns came into direct contact with the demands of the states which were also strengthening themselves internally.

Of the leagues of towns in the Holy Roman Empire, only one, the Swiss Confederation, had been able to remove itself entirely from feudal dominion by military victories. Individual centres of trade such as Genoa, Bruges, Lübeck, Antwerp, Barcelona, Milan or Florence gradually had to give way to the increasing power of princes with whom they had been able to do profitable business in better days. Yet these towns, particularly the larger ones in the most urbanized regions, had set off an appreciable process of modernization, by which they had achieved the exercise of power in a whole range of fields within the public sphere. An essential characteristic of a community was the fundamental equality under the law and solidarity of its members, which signified an innovation in the field

of world history. In spite of fine rhetoric Greek 'democracy' was after all based on the exploitation of slaves. There is no doubt at all that the Christian basis of western culture has moved this goalpost. Equally Christian in origin, but supported by self-interest, was the communities' quest for peace and the elimination of the violent application of the law in one's own interests, in favour of a rational system of jurisprudence. The legalization of social relationships implied that governments were parties in the legal argument and that they, rather than the victims, could be the prosecutors.

The Achilles' heel of the town's legal systems lay, however, in their restriction to the area of their own jurisdiction. Leagues of towns, including by far the largest and most enduring of all, the German Hansa, were not successful in transcending the private interests of individual member-towns and their actions often ran aground on internal conflicts. Nor were the towns any more able to expand their citizens' rights into the hinterlands which they dominated economically, and in some respects also administratively and judicially. When the princes had achieved sufficient superiority of power to pacify their territories, the leagues of towns lost their *raison d'être*. At sea their usefulness lasted longer, but here, too, the princes became the predominant power under arms from the sixteenth

Leagues of towns such as the German Hansa then became much less effective. *View of Lübeck, c. 1660.*
Lübeck, Museum für Kunst und Kulturgeschichte

century. By the fact that princes could claim that they, and not the towns, were serving the common interest – which they could substantiate by their consideration of interests on a wider than local level – the towns, in their competition with the princes, lost much of their advantage of modernity. This was the balance reached in the sixteenth century.[13]

1   Tacitus, *Germania*, c. 13–14
2   Prinz 1993, 254–258
3   Duby 1973, 237–251
4   Duby 1981, 35, 40–42
5   Folz 1967, 284–285
6   Kantorowicz 1966
7   Böhmer, *Acta Imperii Selecta*, 130
8   Van Caenegem & Milis 1978, 235
9   Heers 1977, 49–50, 57–60, 147
10 Muchembled 1992, 149–150
11 *La Lana* 1974
12 Blickle, Neveux-Oesterberg, Imsen-Vogler in Blickle 1997
13 Dilcher in Blickle 1997

CHAPTER IV
Cut-throat Competition

Knights and foot-soldiers

Demesnes were organized to give their lords the opportunity of carrying out their exalted tasks for the community – of praying for it or fighting for it. This, too, is how Bishop Aldalbero of Laon saw it, when about 1020 he divided society into three classes of which the third consisted of those who by the work of their hands maintained the first two. These were peasants who could be called out for battle by their lords, but otherwise did not have the right to bear arms. Knights enjoyed an important advantage in the distribution of instruments of violence: only they were able to provide themselves with expensive steel weapons and armour, ride powerful chargers, and regularly practise military skills. Every knight who went to war was accompanied by at least two squires, a shield-bearer and a man-at-arms – both horsed – as well as several foot-soldiers.

In accordance with his feudal duty a vassal followed his lord to battle. In regions where the laws of inheritance only recognized the oldest son as the heir, younger sons had to try and shine through valiant performance in battle, and thus to be accepted into the service and favour of a powerful and generous lord. Consequently armies were made up both of vassals and of other followers. Knights enjoyed an overwhelming superiority of power over ordinary peasants, who were often blatantly terrorized. It was usually assumed that one heavily armed horseman was the equivalent of ten foot-soldiers. Methods

of war consisted mainly of plundering expeditions in enemy country or in the region to be conquered, and of sieges. Pitched battles were the exception: in such cases both armies had to be prepared to expose themselves to risk. Much more profitable, however, were the smaller surprise raids which brought home plunder. After all, a ransom could be asked for a knight taken prisoner, which could mean a substantial source of income for the crafty warrior. The peasant population was virtually defenceless against such raids, and they often saw the fruits of their diligent labour go up in flames. Even the emperor Charles IV (1346–1378), lover of arts and letters, in his autobiography recorded in unvarnished words the motives and considerations influencing the highest ruling families, in which only their own strategies, honour and interests counted; he did not consider his subjects worthy of any mention, let alone that any thought should be given to the harm they suffered.

In that time [the 1330s] our father charged us to set out with a substantial army against Duke Bolko of Silesia, the lord of Munsterberg, because this duke was no prince and vassal of our father's and of the kingdom of Bohemia. Our father had, of course, acquired the town of Breslau from Duke Henry VII of Breslau who had no direct heirs ... After our father had taken possession of the town of Breslau, all the dukes of Silesia and also the lords of Opfeln submit-

Adriaan Pietersz. van de Velde,
The burning of the English warships by the Dutch navy, on 20 June 1667 off Chatham. The victory at Chatham, the main English naval base, was a psychological boost for the Dutch navy.
A century later Britain had the unmatched mastery of the seas.
Amsterdam, Rijksmuseum

Plundering arms and armour on the battlefield was a lucrative business,
as was taking knights prisoner.
It was possible to get a high ransom for important prisoners.
Albrecht Dürer, *The Bohemian trophy.*
Vienna, Graphische Sammlung Albertina

Notes: see p. 201

ted themselves to his dominion and to the crown of Bohemia, to be protected and defended. The duke of Silesia and the lord of Schweidnitz, and also Lord Bolko of Munsterberg, however, took no part in this. We therefore laid waste Bolko's lands, as was described in a chronicle. They were so severely ravaged that he felt forced to negotiate and just like the other lords to become vassal of our father and of the

kingdom of Bohemia … The king of Hungary now settled the conflict. On this occasion he, too, allied himself with our father and promised him help against the duke of Austria, who had seized the dukedom of Carinthia from our brother, and against Ludwig [of Bavaria, deposed by the pope in 1346], the self-styled emperor.[1]

Castles offered effective protection to lords and

The acquisition of a suit of armour was a very expensive affair.

However, armour had the disadvantage of being heavy and not very manoeuvrable, which often indirectly led to a defeat.

In the sixteenth century armourers refined its design to make it more comfortable for the wearer as well as giving better protection.

Albrecht Dürer, *Study of a helmet*. Drawing and watercolour, 1514.

Paris, Musée du Louvre, Arts graphiques

The main lethal weapon was the crossbow.

Knights considered it a dishonourable way of fighting.

Antonio and Piero del Pollaiuolo (ascribed), *The martyrdom of St Sebastian*.

London, National Gallery

The longbow was a very rapid and effective weapon in battle.
It was responsible for a good many of the English successes in the Hundred Years War.
Late fifteenth-century drawing, ascribed to the Master of the Parement of Narbonne.
Oxford, Christ Church Picture Gallery

their 'families', a term which also included their retinues and their servants. They formed an excellent operating base from which to control recently conquered or threatened territory. Sometimes they also had accommodation for the peasants of the demesne and possibly also their livestock, to provide protection against raids. They were built on natural or artificial high points offering good views of the surrounding country and putting attackers at a disadvantage. The latter were best advised to try to gain the upper hand by subterfuge and negotiation, since it was often difficult to maintain a complete blockade for long. The availability of a supply of water and stocks of food and munitions was a major consideration for the besieged. On the whole, however, the protection of thick walls was an advantage, and so castles were also pre-eminently the symbol of the power of the dominant warrior class.

The great demographic and economic changes between the tenth and the thirteenth centuries naturally had their effect on the arts of war. The thirteenth century saw the appearance on the battlefield of more archers, who fought on foot and were often mercenaries from the British Isles. Both the longbow and the crossbow were used; the first measured 1.6 to 1.8 metres and was rapid in use, capable of delivering ten to twelve arrows a minute over a range of not normally more than 200 metres. Crossbows were slower in action; they could only shoot two or three heavy bolts per minute, but their aim

Safe return in 1167 of the Milan militia, armed to the teeth.
Relief dating from 1171, originally from the Porta Romana, Milan.
Milan, Castello Sforzesco, Museo d'Arte Antica

was accurate and their range up to 300 metres. The larger types, mounted on a stand and with a thick cord, could cover up to 450 metres. As their bolts could even penetrate armour, knights regarded the crossbow as a dishonourable weapon which violated the code of chivalry. Knights after all observed a code of war, they did not kill each other, and above all it was dishonourable for an ordinary archer of peasant origin to be able to do so. It was even worse when towns and communities of free farmers put militias in the field.

In the course of the thirteenth century these were sometimes enrolled as auxiliary troops, but about 1300 they began to be encountered on their own behalf. The Swiss farmers who in 1291 and 1315 defeated the army of the Habsburg knights were writing history – as were, on a much larger scale, the members of the Flemish craft guilds, and peasants, who in 1302 crushed the army of French chivalry. The new concentrations of population gave them the advantage of numbers: the Flemings, helped by the marshy nature of the ground, fielded 11,000 men in 1302 against 7,500 French. One third of these were heavy armed cavalry, of whom the Flemish side only had about 500. The Scots who defeated the English at Bannockburn in 1314 were also mainly infantry. The infantry were armed with bows, pikes, clubs and stabbing weapons. They used them to great effect, and were no respecters of persons, as they were often clearly inspired by motives of emancipation: the rejection of what they felt was foreign rule.

Large-scale peasant revolts challenged feudal authority three times in the fourteenth century: in Flanders, France and England. The town militias used their military strength to establish the authority of the towns over the countryside, and that of large towns over small ones. In the urbanized regions like Lombardy the towns even dominated their environment by taking advantage of the remnants of the feudal system. Warlords took mercenary troops into their personal service for pay, and hired themselves out with their companies to the highest bidder. The phenomenon of the *condottiere*, actually a mercenary leader, is closely associated with the rivalry between the small, but wealthy, regional states of north and central Italy. In the armies of rulers, infantry – either called up or on paid service – gained a more important place. In 1346 Welsh archers made a great contribution to the English slaughter of 1,500 French knights at Crécy. The age of chivalry had passed, certainly with the advent of the cannon in the 1330s.

War, a sacred duty of the state

If war was a private affair for feudal lords, from the eleventh century the Church, with its appeal for a holy war against the Muslims, introduced a more general dimension into the exercise of violence. At the same time as it opposed the use of force among Christians – which was particularly practised by feudal lords and knights – the Church channelled aggression towards the peripheral areas of Christendom. The interests not only of private individuals, but also of kingdoms and peoples, were over-

Francesco Sforza, the successful Milanese condottiere, had himself painted by Giovanni Pietro Birago,
debating, with visible satisfaction, with illustrious predecessors from classical times such as Scipio, Pompey, Caesar and Hannibal.
Fifteenth-century fresco.
Florence, Gallerie degli Uffizi

shadowed by the higher importance of the battle for the propagation of Christianity and for the liberation of the Holy Places. Bishop Ivo of Chartres (*c.* 1040–1116) included in his collation of canon law, made shortly before 1100, the following quotation from a letter of about 860 from Pope Nicholas I to the Bulgars:

> *To anyone who dies in this war in faith, the kingdom of heaven shall not be denied. The Almighty knows indeed that he amongst you who dies does so for the truth of faith, for the salvation of his fatherland and the protection of Christians, for which thanks to the Lord his reward shall be forthcoming.*[2]

This prospect of salvation was in those days also held up before the departing crusaders. With some – if short-lived – success the popes persuaded the greatest secular princes of the twelfth century to forego their mutual rivalry and to march together for the faith. In 1190 not only Emperor Frederick Barbarossa but also King Philip Augustus of France and Richard Lionheart of England took the cross, though their contributions to the liberation of Jerusalem were disparate and unsuccessful.

However, the concept of the Holy War appeared to catch on, because it provided the leaders with the justification of a higher goal for their actions, and so made it easier to motivate their warriors. The Christian princes in Spain cashed in grandiosely on their 'holy' war against the Muslims, which scored some notable successes in the first half of the thirteenth century. Under the banner of conversion the Teutonic knights terrorized the Slav population of Prussia and occupied their lands. The kings of France launched crusades against the Cathars, damned as heretics, in Languedoc. In 1208 Pope Innocent III summoned warriors to this venture with the following encouragement:

> *Awake, knights of Christ! Awake, valiant members of the Christian community!... You must endeavour, as God has revealed to you, to root out the treason of heresy and its adherents by attacking the heretics with strong hand and outstretched arm, with even more conviction than if you were to attack the Saracens, because they are more dangerous than them.*[3]

The ruthless war of elimination against the Albigensians, which reached its sorry apogee in the sack of Montségur in 1244, gave the king the opportunity of subjecting the county of Toulouse to his direct authority. Because Charles of Anjou, the papal client, had lost the crown of Sicily to Peter III of Aragon during the Sicilian Vespers of 1282, the pope urged his nephew, Philip III of France, to start

Boabdil, the last Muslim king of Granada, surrenders to the Catholic kings.
The Muslims leave the Alhambra in chains and with hanging heads.
Altar relief by Felipe Vigarny made in 1520 for the Royal Burial Chapel in Granada.

what he called a crusade against Aragon. Unfortunately this time God does not appear to have been on the side of the crusaders, and in 1285 the king paid for the campaign with his life.

The link with piety was to be cherished by the kings to legitimize their wars. One way to achieve this was through the cult of their patron saints: in France St Denis – the first bishop of Paris, who gave his name to the war-cry 'Montjoie Saint Denis' – St Michael and St Louis (Louis IX). War heroes enjoyed the same privilege as their kings of burial in the mausoleum of St Denis where the *oriflamme*, the standard that was unfurled on the

The duke of Lancaster with St George, portrayed as Templars (shortly before 1322). The Templars were the oldest order of chivalry, founded in 1119 in Jerusalem with the object of protecting pilgrims and the Holy Places. They also operated as bankers during the crusades.
Oxford, Bodleian Library

royal campaigns, was kept. The long confrontation between France and England in the Hundred Years War (1337–1453), and particularly the mobilization of French resistance by Joan of Arc (1429–1431), undoubtedly contributed to the consolidation of a kind of national consciousness in both countries. As leaders of a war of liberation against a foreign invasion, the kings of France could claim to be serving a higher interest than the great territorial princes. The king's war could in this way be presented as the only one in the common interest of the kingdom, the only one that was legal and holy. The defence of the motherland, presented as

Blazons of knights, mainly from Flanders, the Rhineland and
the northern Netherlands, on crusade against
the Slav population of Prussia, c. 1382–1384. Illustration from
the *Armorial Bellenville,* made in the Netherlands c. 1364–1386.
Paris, Bibliothèque nationale de France

Joan of Arc on horseback with the *oriflamme,*
the royal banner of France,
which inspired the national spirit on campaign.
Miniature of 1505 from Antoine Dufour, *La vie des femmes célèbres.*
Nantes, Musée Dobrée

a mystic body, was worth a courageous death, as writers of propaganda increasingly proclaimed in the fifteenth century. Christine de Pisan, the poetess closely associated with the royal court, comforted the widows of the many knights who died at the battle of Agincourt (1415) with the thought that their beloved heroes:

> *…were chosen to be among God's martyrs in their just defence through battle, obedient unto death to maintain justice and the rights of the French crown and their sovereign lord; about them, and for them, the Gospel said: 'Blessed are they who suffer for righteousness'.*[4]

After regaining Normandy from the English in 1450 Charles VII published an order to hold a solemn Mass and public procession every 12 August, the anniversary of the capture of Cherbourg, in all cathedrals and collegiate churches. Kings left nothing undone to give their wars an exclusive justification, while those of the territorial princes were downgraded to private quarrels, if not actual rebellions against lawful authority. On some occasions the enemy could be attacked as heretics. The war against Bohemian independence from 1411 to 1436 was waged by the Holy Roman Emperor under the pretext of a crusade against the heretic Hussites.

Where a king did not succeed in keeping his nobles occupied on Christian ends, he ran a great risk that they would let their deployment depend on purely opportunistic considerations. This was clear in Hungary, threatened by the Turkish advance, where the archbishop's appeal was

St Louis of Toulouse, son of the king of Sicily, Charles of Anjou,
had refused the throne in 1296 in favour of his brother Robert.
He became a Franciscan and bishop of Toulouse,
in which dignity he was immortalized by Simone Martini in 1317.
Robert, shown in profile, commissioned this picture,
which unmistakably demonstrates dynastic and political propaganda
for the House of Anjou.
Naples, Museo Nazionale di Capodimonte

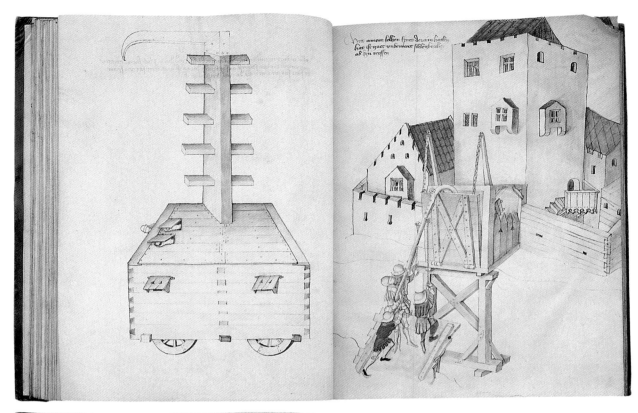

New assault techniques and the increasing use of heavy artillery gradually raised the effectiveness of siege warfare from about 1400.

Illustrations from Johannes Hartlieb, *Iconismi bellici* (c. 1400–1468). Rotthalmünster, Antiquariat Tenschert

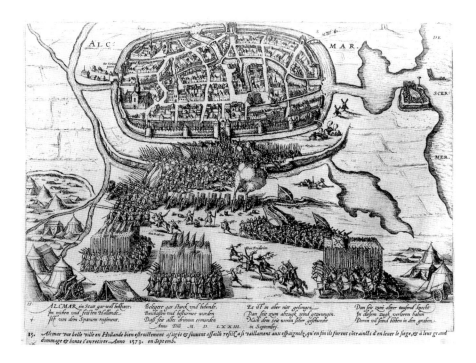

This print by Frans Hogenberg, *The unsuccessful siege of Alkmaar by Spanish troops* in 1573, clearly shows that the cavalry formations have been moved to the flanks.
Antwerp, Museum Plantin-Moretus, Prentenkabinet

answered by the peasantry, but not by the nobles. The army therefore lacked its natural leaders, with the result that the peasants cooled their ire on the castles of the nobility, whom they regarded as having betrayed them. In this precursor of the German peasant revolt ten years later, the nobility chose to wage war against the peasants, who were forced back into long-lasting oppression. In 1526 the Turks overran most of Hungary.

The arms race

The development of the legitimation of war as an exclusively royal activity was strengthened by the evolution of military technology. With the construction of their walls the towns had adopted, on a larger scale, the principle of the fortified castle. The attacker was vulnerable, the defender remained protected as long as his supplies held out. The long circumference of the towns made their effective blockade very difficult, because it required large numbers of troops over a long period, which often drained the financial resources of the besiegers. From the last decades of the fourteenth century, however, cannon turned the advantage in siege war-fare into a disadvantage for the towns. Their walls were calculated to resist battering rams, not the force of cannon balls. They were built high to give a view over a wide stretch of country, and to withstand projectiles from catapults and siege towers. About AD 1400 *ballistae* could throw stones of up to 600 kilogrammes for a distance of 400 to 500 metres, so that they could be set up outside the range of the defending archers. However, it was difficult to make breaches in the walls in this way; at the very most it was successful only in the gates and battlements. It was precisely their height which made the walls particularly vulnerable to cannon fire. Until the sixteenth century their enormous weight, slowness and poor accuracy limited the effectiveness of cannon on the battlefield. Against defensive walls, on the other hand, they could make wide breaches, so that castles and towns from about 1400 were no longer safe havens against an army equipped with artillery. Stone cannon balls weighing up to 700 kilogrammes could then be fired up to a range of 600 metres, which was not very different in range or weight from the largest catapults, but very different in force and accuracy. However, the whole operation could only be carried out once, or at most twice, a day. It was a military revolution, but a very slow one.[5]

From the fifteenth century Swiss mercenaries built up a formidable reputation for themselves
as invincible infantry. Urs Graf, *Swiss soldiers,* 1515. Basle, Öffentliche Kunstsammlung, Kupferstichkabinett

In the sixteenth century progressive princes introduced mobile phalanxes in their armies to counter the growing strength of the infantry.
Peter Bruegel the Elder, *The battle of Mount Gilboa and the suicide of Saul,* detail.
Vienna, Kunsthistorisches Museum

Tobias Stimmer,
*Portrait of the Zürich banneret
Jacob Schwytzer,* 1564.
In his left hand
he holds a Swiss dagger.

This steel weapon could
without difficulty penetrate
a mail shirt and easily
cut through leather
helmet straps.
Basle,
Öffentliche Kunstsammlung

The walls of medieval castles and towns were shot to pieces by cannon.
In the sixteenth century the new Italian style of fortification
filtered through to the rest of Europe, influencing the design
of fortifications and the strengthening of town walls.

During the fifteenth century there began to be a discrepancy in military resources which gave a substantial advantage to the besiegers, in so far as they could afford the very expensive cannon. It is clear that towns and feudal lords were at a disadvantage compared with princes; most of them lacked the financial resources to acquire many cannon with their specialized attendants and, more importantly, they could not use them as effectively as their be-siegers. The new technique was a card in the hands of the big players, who could afford the costly innovations together with their technically trained staff.

Bombardment of a badly defended north-Italian *palazzo,*

with in the distance a town within a protective girdle of fortifications.

Fresco by Giovanni Stradano.

Florence, Palazzo Vecchio, Sala di Giovanni delle Bande Nere

Princes soon saw the opportunity of dealing a definitive blow to their most formidable rivals, the local and regional concentrations of power. In France, the Low Countries and northern Germany the large towns lost their autonomy to the king, or to their territorial princes. The most spectacular example was the capture of Constantinople by the Turks in 1453: the legendary high walls which had withstood besiegers for centuries were reduced to rubble by artillery. In northern and central Italy there were no large territorial monarchs except the pope to exploit the situation, so that the advantage fell to

In the course of the sixteenth century war became a permanent
business and as a consequence large standing armies were raised.
Well-equipped professional Spanish soldiers, the *Tercios*.
Mural painting in the palace of Cruzat, Navarre, sixteenth century.
Pamplona, Junta de Navarra

Louis XIV, with his brother 'Monsieur',
visiting the trenches on the French front before Mons in 1691.
The art of war is represented here as an aesthetic affair.
Paris, Bibliothèque nationale de France, Estampes

The introduction of the pistol for cavalry dates from *c.* 1550. Battle with new and traditional weapons.
Jan Martens, *The assault,* 1639, detail. Amsterdam, private collection

In the sixteenth and seventeenth centuries France made regular attempts to capture the coastal town of Gravelines on its frontier with the Spanish Netherlands. Its ingenious defensive system, shown in this painting by Pieter Snaeyers, was designed by Vauban, who took part in the successful siege of 1658.

Madrid, Museo del Prado

the largest towns, which succeeded in substantially extending the area they controlled. The most successful was Venice which, confronted with the loss of its colonial empire to the Ottomans, assured its safety and prosperity by bringing the Po valley under its authority and conquering an area of more than 30,000 square kilometres, reaching to within 30 kilometres of Milan.

On the battlefield, too, the offensive gained the advantage in this period, as military organization adapted to the new challenges. In order to cope with massive infantry strength, the most progressive princes organized their infantry into mobile phalanxes, equipped with long pikes. These could bring enemy cavalry to a halt and force them back, and could lead the advance against the opposing infantry. The role of cavalry shifted more to the flanks, from which they could make sudden attacks at intervals. The initiative for this modern order of battle was given in France, where in 1439 the king for the first time allocated money to raise a standing army. In contrast to feudal practice, where the vassals were called out during the campaigning season for limited periods of perhaps as much as forty days, war became a permanent industry demanding the constant availability of trained troops. The French king now took 20,000 to 25,000 officers and soldiers into his permanent paid service as *gens d'armes*, combining various types of weapons. This initiative coincided with the final offensive of the Hundred Years War, and contributed to the definitive expulsion of the English. France's most important antagonist, Duke Charles of Burgundy, in his turn raised *compagnies d'ordonnance* in 1471. With this initiative both princes brought about a permanent increase in the level of their countries' taxes. In Castile, where there was no tradition of heavy cavalry, compulsory service was in force for men aged between 20 and 45, of whom one in twelve had to serve. Towards the end of the sixteenth century this system evolved into a professional volunteer army.

Standing as well as temporary armies were

Large numbers of soldiers and the use of firearms demanded iron discipline of the troops.
This 1665 medal by Thomas Bernard glorifies the drill of the French army as their means to victory.
Paris, Bibliothèque nationale de France, Médailles

made up on a very international basis until the late eighteenth century. Although some countries, such as Spain and France, were usually able to find sufficient recruits from among their own populations, their princes often made use of mercenaries too; these were trained and rapidly available, and could also be easily discharged once their services were no longer needed. The proportion made up by permanent troops paid directly by the exchequer remained in the long run extremely small. War became increasingly the business of a special kind of entrepreneur who offered his services to anyone who would pay for them, regardless of religion, nationality or past contracts with the other side. Italian *condottieri* prepared the way which during the sixteenth and seventeenth centuries was trodden with glory by small territorial princes who developed into major contractors in the business of death and destruction at someone else's expense, such as the Bohemian Count Albert von Wallenstein, Count Ernst von Mansfeld, Count Jean Tilly and Prince Bernard of Saxe-Weimar. As general of the imperial armies during the Thirty Years War (1618–1648) Wallenstein became immensely wealthy, because he ran armaments production and sup-

plies for the army as a gigantic private enterprise. Their troops were recruited in the poorer rural parts of Europe which could offer no employment for their surplus population: central Germany, the Scottish Highlands, the Alps. Since their military successes against the Habsburgs in the fourteenth century and the Burgundians in the fifteenth, the Swiss had built up a firm reputation as formidable infantrymen. Their method consisted of forming squares with long pikes; when they advanced they could put the best armed cavalry to flight. Their availability for the service of all warring parties brought peace and wealth to the Swiss cantons, and also contributed to the fact that no power has yet attempted to penetrate their territory, since no-one could get on without their *Suisses*. No less important were the *landsknechten* from various parts of Germany, originally provided by minor members of the nobility with their followers. In the early sixteenth century some of them were able to start developing new battle drills with diversified combinations of arms such as cavalry, artillery, pikemen and musketeers.

It was in Italy, which in the first half of the sixteenth century was the most important theatre of war in Europe, that the defensive answer to the cannon was thought up. In 1534 Alessandro de' Medici, duke of Florence, commissioned the construction of the *Fortezza da Basso*, the first application of the new invention which came to be called the *trace italienne*. Walls were packed with earth and became appreciably thicker, and were provided with triangular bastions from which fire could be directed on the besieger from all sides; earth ramparts and wide moats kept the attacking artillery at a distance. In the course of time this system was improved by building out advanced bastions and pentangular ravelins, crown and horn works, connected with the main fortification by a network of underground tunnels. In this way the attacking artillery was not only held at a distance, but might itself be subject to aggressive actions from within the fortification.

The breakthrough of firearms on the battlefield only occurred about 1530. In 1534 the Spanish *tercios* were organized in units of 3,000 men, made up of equal numbers of musketeers and pikemen, compared with the previous proportion of one musket to six pikes. The use of personal firearms made comprehensive training essential. Because of the time necessary for loading and taking aim, the different ranks fired in succession. To achieve this there had to be drill, so that the troops could carry out all their movements in an orderly and co-ordinated way: load, kneel, aim, fire, and step back. Neither cavalry nor pikemen could stand against these successive volleys; until about 1600 the only role of pikemen was to protect the musketeers from hostile cavalry charges. Consequently in the long run the pike was converted into the bayonet fixed on the firearm. This evolution in battlefield technique was perfected in the late sixteenth century by Maurice of Nassau, who so ensured the military survival of the Republic of the United Provinces. He invented a formation of long ranks of musketeers, up to ten files deep, flanked by pikemen and cavalry. His tactics demanded strictly disciplined troops; this was both necessary and possible because the Republic had plenty of money but was relatively short of manpower. As in the design of fortifications and trench systems, waging war became a strictly professional affair, in some respects extremely technical and even scientific in character. The higher the demands of competition, the less those engaged in it took risks.[6]

These ingenious techniques substantially increased the scale of wars, both for the attacker and for the defender, and also made them last longer and cost far more than ever before. The size of armies increased steadily: in 1552 the Emperor Charles v had about 150,000 troops in his service, while by the 1620s the king of Spain had 300,000 under arms. During the sixteenth century the size of armies grew twice as fast as the total population. About 1475 France, England and Castile-Aragon together had about 85,000 men under arms, but by 1760 this had increased by six and a half times to 550,000, while the population of the three countries had hardly grown by a half. The number of soldiers per inhabitant had therefore quadrupled: from three to twelve per thousand. On a European scale the proportions were not very different: between 1500 and 1800 the population doubled, but the number of soldiers increased tenfold. A computation of the intensity of war shows a value of 311 for the fifteenth century, 732 for the sixteenth and 5,193 for the seventeenth.[7]

From the sixteenth to the end of the eighteenth century wars consisted mainly of sieges of towns. Their fortifications required substantial capital expenditure, and large garrisons were necessary for their defence. On the other hand, attacking armies had to have tens of thousands of men. The Spanish conquest of Flanders and Brabant between 1582 and 1585 was only possible because the general, Alexander Farnese, had 86,000 well-trained, and mostly well-paid, troops. He forced town after town to submit after sieges sometimes lasting months. The largest city of north-western Europe was Antwerp, defended by 7.5 kilometres of the most modern fortifications. After fifteen months of blockade, with the Scheldt closed, it fell in 1585, without a shot being fired at its walls. The Spanish siege of Breda in 1624–1625 required the investment of a town with two rings of fortifications consisting of ninety-six redoubts, thirty-seven forts and forty-five batteries. The whole network was extended by entrenchments, and attempts by the Dutch to flood the fields were matched by the Spaniards, who constructed drainage canals. The town finally fell because after nine months of siege stocks of food were exhausted. The Dutch siege of 's-Hertogenbosch in 1629 required 25,000 men to complete the forty kilometres of encirclement.

In Louis xiv's days the French frontiers were strengthened by a girdle of fortifications with enormous outworks designed by Vauban, his military engineer. Troops were in this way all concentrated near the frontiers, where they could be used either in defence or offensively to carry out the king's expansionary policies. The Treaty of Utrecht in 1713 provided for the Republic of the United Provinces to maintain garrisons in the buffer area of the Austrian Netherlands as a *barrière* against France. In this way territories became firmly demarcated, at least by those states which possessed the resources needed to construct fortifications.

To keep these masses of men under arms, drastic modernization of army organization was essential. This was achieved by the introduction of a centralized bureaucracy for the control of resources, of a strict hierarchy based on merit, and consistent discipline for the troops. This last has already been mentioned in connection with the introduction of personal firearms. It involved the harsh necessity of enforcing strict obedience on individual units so that they could manoeuvre effectively on the immense battlefield, so placing higher demands on the officers than in the past. If previously it had been enough to be of gentle birth to command a company, effective personal qualities of leadership with tactical and strategic understanding now became essential. In the artillery and the navy technical and scientific knowledge became increasingly important; it was in these arms therefore that most young commoners obtained commissions. All this also meant a tighter hierarchy for those in a military career from the lowest commissioned rank, with clear requirements of ability for the higher ranks. Map-making developed as an important resource for large-scale operations. Officer training therefore became standardized, so that the same procedures and methods could be applied in all components of an army. The Ottoman army, whose organization was not modernized after the successes it had achieved in the fifteenth and sixteenth centuries as a result of the use of gunpowder, therefore lost its competitive edge over its Habsburg and Russian rivals. The Polish army, too, in which the autonomous aristocracy retained their role as cavalry, was destroyed in the course of the eighteenth century by the more modern and numerous armies of all its neighbouring states.

Meanwhile it had become clear that only large-scale concentrations of military resources would have any chance of affecting internal power relationships. There were then two basic possibilities. One applied when a state had a large population which could be mobilized for military service by means of an effective bureaucracy and the ability to impose strong pressure. Russia offers a striking example of such a state: Peter the Great (1689–1725) by compulsory service for the peasants and his feudal aristocracy could put 370,000 men in the field; Catherine (1762–1796) could deploy as many as a

million. On the other hand, less populated states could hold their end up in the competition if they had enough money to hire mercenaries from elsewhere. The English state systematically used Hessian troops, which became an essential source of livelihood for this small German landgravate and granted the English a peaceful existence. The age of independent towns and small seigneuries had indeed gone. Powerful rebel towns were brought under the control of princes by imposing fortresses upon them. Alexander Farnese, when he became Pope Paul III (1534–1549), built his *Rocca* in Perugia on the ruins of the sacked town. Charles V did the same in Utrecht and Ghent. Great garrisons were camped there, ready for use against the king's enemies at home or abroad.

The price of war

The strong correlation between war, public debt and taxation has been emphasized earlier. The link was reciprocal: wars such as that of the Spanish succession (1701–1713) had to end when the credits of all the warring parties were exhausted. The burden of debt had increased to the total of their normal incomes for five to seven years.[8] But there were other costs than financial ones: economic disadvantages in the sense of disadvantages for trade, destruction of property, disruption of economic life, and the withdrawal of capital and labour from productive investment. And, of course, the cost in human life. The heaviest sacrifices before the twentieth century were those of the Thirty Years War, which in all cost more than two million deaths on the field of battle. Altogether the Empire lost five million people, a third of its population. In Württemberg, the most seriously affected duchy, only 100,000 were left in 1634 against a population of 450,000 in 1618; this latter total was not reached again until 1750. More than half the population disappeared in the regions traversed by the Swedish army, from Pomerania via Mecklenburg, Brandenburg, Thuringia, western Saxony, the Palatinate and Wurzburg. South Germany, from Alsace to Bavaria, lost between a third and a half of its population.[9] In just those pitched battles costing more than 100,000 deaths in the great wars, 3,694,000 men died in the seventeenth century and 3,457,000 in the eighteenth. And yet the eighteenth century knew *only* seventy-eight years of war, as against ninety-five and ninety-four in the two preceding centuries. European wars may have become shorter, and perhaps less lethal, but they involved

From the seventeenth century professionalism also made itself felt in the high command.
It was no longer enough to be of aristocratic birth to become a general;
personal leadership qualities and a good strategic understanding were all-important.
Jan Bronchorst, *Portrait of General Ottavio Piccolomini* (1599–1656).
Bayonne, Musée Bonnat

The Thirty Years War (1618–1648) was particularly devastating.
Two million soldiers died in action and the Holy Roman Empire lost five million dead, a third of its population.
Italian school(?), *Dead soldier,* **seventeenth century. London, National Gallery**

more states.[10] War was the normal condition of European states, peace was the exception, and could be ascribed to exhaustion.

Since the fourteenth century warfare had increasingly become the exclusive affair of states and even the primary function of states: by far the highest proportion of their resources were devoted to it; it was for war that the apparatus of the state expanded with ever more functionaries and officials; war made it necessary to define the frontiers of territory. No single state could withdraw from this increasingly bitter rivalry without running the risk of being overrun by its aggressive neighbours. After Hungary, Poland offers the best example of this. It was a large, relatively wealthy and strong monarchy during the fifteenth and sixteenth centuries when it successfully incorporated Prussia and Lithuania. Its aristocratic republican system, which not only elected the king but could also block every decision by virtue of the free right of veto in parliament, weakened the monarchy. Unlike the western states, centralization of the state and building up a modern army were therefore ruled

out. In the course of the seventeenth century the country also became the target of Swedish expansion, until finally in 1697 a solution was sought in the election of Augustus the Strong, Elector of Saxony, as king. He, however, was removed from his throne by the Swedes as early as 1701. Successive partitions between its great-power neighbours, Brandenburg-Prussia, Austria and Russia, in 1772, 1793 and 1795 wiped Poland completely off the map. From a purely economic aspect these developments were perhaps not so disastrous for the Polish people as they are, from a national historical point of view, usually portrayed. The nobility, who were large landowners, chose to keep the rents from their land to themselves rather than to hand them over to strengthen the state. This meant that the Polish peasants were more gently treated than their fellows in Russia, Prussia, Denmark or Sweden, who were also not spared invasions by foreign troops.

State budgets were inflated under the increasing pressure of military expenditure, which was largely financed by loans. However, the effect of the loans was an associated rise in taxation as they came to

Frutti di Guerra, the fruits of war, a biting satirical print by the Italian Giuseppe Mitelli in 1692.

Bologna, Cassa di Risparmio, Collezioni d'arte e di storia

War disrupted economic life and took a heavy toll from the population.

Engraving after Willem Tybaut by Herman Muller, *The civilian and the soldier, c.* 1580.

Amsterdam, Rijksmuseum, Rijksprentenkabinet

term. In the mid-fourteenth and early fifteenth centuries the city state of Florence waged a series of wars against the pope, Milan and Pisa. At the start of this period the normal expenditure of the republic came to 40,000 florins, but the wars cost them 2.5, 7.5 and 4.5 million respectively.[11] At the height of its military achievements between 1560 and 1620 the Spanish crown saw its direct military expenditure rise from two to eight million ducats, respectively 40 per cent and 60 per cent of its total expenditure, of which, however, the burden of interest absorbed another 32 to 51 per cent.[12] During the period of military operations between 1689 and 1714 the great powers devoted 75 per cent of their expenditure to the conflict year after year. It is interesting to see that in that period France could afford to challenge England, the United Provinces, and the most important princes of the Empire at the same time, because her state income of 300 million livres came to as much as that of her great opponents combined.[13]

Not a single monarchy could be accused of having a sense of responsibility at that time. In England, under Charles II (1660–1688), military expenditure normally oscillated between 40 and 70 per cent of all state expenditure, with peaks to 77 per cent in 1665 and 1666. The great naval wars against the United Provinces, a formidable opponent, proved to be purely loss-making activities, in spite of the visionary profits forecast from the capture of Dutch ships. The Second Dutch War (1664–1666) cost £5.25 million sterling, against prize money to the value of £281,000. Moreover, the naval war reduced the normal income of the crown by 19 per cent (£159,000). The Third Dutch War, between 1672 and 1674, cost £2.43 million, but brought in £450,000 in French subsidies, £110,000 in prize money and £47,000 compensation from the Dutch – a net loss of more than £1.8 million. Parliament had approved a request for an extra £1.18 million. The same parliament in 1678 approved a supplementary request for £1,385 million for a war against France on condition that the troops, who had already been raised, should be demobilized; altogether there was expenditure of £2,165 million for a war which fortunately was never waged. Without parliamentary resistance the cost would certainly have been higher.[14]

Late entries in the competition between the states enjoyed the doubtful advantage that, in favourable circumstances, they could undertake the organization of state power more systematically. Thus the Swedish expansion from the late sixteenth century could profit at a stroke from the new weapons and strategies. In 1544, after a revolt by Catholic peasants against the Protestant king who had taken over church property, a standing army was raised that, contrary to the practice in the rest of Europe, was recruited entirely from the native population on the basis of conscription. Using the data in the population records – in itself a political innovation – one peasant in every five or six could be called up for service. In the course of time this system was refined so that groups of farms were made collectively responsible for the mobilization of a recruit. Each group of farms (*rotar*) had to provide the national serviceman with a building plot, a meadow and a standard military house, and during his absence in the field had to look after any family he might have. Soldiers, of course, received such low pay that they still remained dependent on the income from their farm. In this way the agricultural economy was called into the service of the military objectives of the state. The state built roads to link the garrison towns and districts efficiently with the embarkation ports.[15] The local peasant communities were even disciplined in their reproductive behaviour by the system of national service (the *indelta*, which remained in force until 1901): if a soldier died on active service, it was in the interest of the community to be able to supply a replacement, as the duty to provide a recruit remained in force.

Because of its relative isolation there was less need for investment in fortifications in Sweden than in France, where enemies were lurking in all directions. Local mines could provide all the requirements of the armaments industry, and there was no shortage of timber for shipbuilding. The Swedish monarchy established itself in the Baltic with the support of the very dynamic United Provinces which in this way strengthened their own interests in competition with Denmark and the Hansa. The weakened Hansa towns tried to play the surrounding princes off against one another, while Muscovy began to flex its muscles more effectively.

The great age of Swedish expansion started in 1617 with the conquest of Karelia and Ingemarland on the Gulf of Finland, regions bordering Finland, already under Swedish rule. More conquests in this region followed over the next few decades, such as, for instance, that of Livonia in 1629. Swedish participation in the Thirty Years War produced a campaign as spectacular as it was destructive right across the Empire, but resulted only in relatively small gains of territory in Hither Pomerania and the duchy of Bremen. In the 160 years after 1560 Sweden experienced only forty without war, and an

There were usually great delays in paying soldiers.
The troops often cooled their anger at this on the local population and robbed them of everything they could get hold of.
Karel Breydel (1678–1733), *Raid on a farm.*
Antwerp, Museum Mayer van den Bergh

average of 1.6 wars per annum during the others. As long as these were accompanied by gains of territory and plunder, roughly until the Treaty of Westphalia in 1648, the enormous expenses could be shouldered. After that time the monarchy, involved in the international competition, continually had to increase the exploitation of its own population in order to maintain its position as a great power. The fact that the wars were almost all fought on the territory of other states only lightened the financial burden on Sweden to some degree. Against this was the fact that its army consisted exclusively of Swedes and Finns, and therefore represented a heavy drain on its manpower and its economy. In 1709 the Swedish troops reached their maximum strength of 110,000 men, 7.1 per cent of a total population of 1.4 million, quite the highest proportion in Europe at the time. Louis XIV's army of 300,000 represented only 1.5 per cent of a population of 20 million, the United Provinces with 100,000 only 5.3 per cent, the Russians with 170,000 men 1.6 per cent, and the English with 75,000 barely 0.7 per cent.[16] Half a million Swedes and Finns died on active service between 1620 and 1719, 30 per cent of all adult males. Only 10 per cent of these were killed in action or died of wounds, and another 10 per cent in captivity. The remaining 80 per cent succumbed to the hardships of a soldier's life, mostly in the form of infectious diseases, among which syphilis was prominent. In the seventeenth century an active military career on average lasted no longer than three or four years, which made it necessary for the state to recruit from a quarter to a third of new blood every year. As a result boys of 15 in Sweden had a life expectancy of only 47, whereas girls could expect to survive to 59.[17]

Two other aggressive late entrants to the European system of states were Brandenburg-Prussia and Russia. The electorate of Brandenburg came out of the Thirty Years War strengthened. As compensation for the damage it had suffered it acquired the substantial addition to its territory of Further Pomerania on the Baltic, including Stettin, and also took in Magdeburg and Halberstadt to the south-west. The Great Elector modernized his state with a standing army and a centralized bureaucracy. This enabled him to act with increasing aggression, first against Sweden, which he drove out of Hither Pomerania by 1675. In 1701 he assumed the title of king of Prussia, by which – in the context of the Empire, severely weakened throughout – he laid a decidedly new accent on the future.

Like Sweden, and later also Russia, Brandenburg-Prussia gradually introduced general conscription from 1693. At first numbers of recruits were prescribed for each province; later all unmarried men were declared liable for service unless they could not be spared as large landowners or serfs. The system was based on the *Kanton*, describing an area which had to supply a regiment; for the infantry this consisted of 5,000 'hearths' or families, for the cavalry 1,800. At the age of ten boys were registered as *Obligat*, and when grown up they had to undergo a training period lasting from eighteen months to two years. For the whole of the rest of his life each had, as a *Kantonist*, to serve two to three months every year in the army. Here, too, the military apparatus was based on the agricultural economy, as an income from the land was needed to supplement the low pay, both for officers and for other ranks. The difference from Sweden was, however, that in that country there was an established class of free farmers, whereas the regions east of the Elbe had been systematically colonized with large estates based on plenty of serf labour, partly by the Teutonic knights. The circumstances of the international market had caused serfdom to expand there still further from the fifteenth century, when the growing demand for rye in the west stimulated the monocultural production of grain for export in these districts.

Prussian militarism was drafted onto this late-feudal structure in the course of the eighteenth century. King Frederick-William (1713–1740), nicknamed 'the Sergeant', succeeded by iron discipline

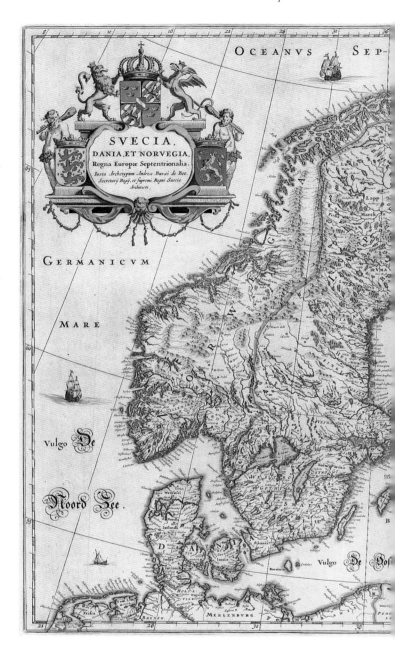

Map of Sweden, Denmark and Norway, published by Willem and Johan Blaeu, *c*. 1635. **This map had been drawn a few years earlier by Anders Bure de Boo**

in making his relatively backward and impoverished country into a great power. Towards the end of the century Prussia was tenth in order of area among the states of Europe, and thirteenth in size of population, but it had the third or fourth largest army. Although the feudal infrastructure made developments possible which would in Italy, for example, have been unthinkable, the strong-willed

(Buraeus), commissioned by King Gustavus Adolphus II (1611–1632).
Maps like this made it possible to maintain better administrative
and political control over subject populations.

abroad, declaring it to be treason. The nobility were even obliged to remain in the country, on pain of confiscation of their property.

A *Junker*, just like a *Kantonist*, was pressed into the army. In 1722 the Cadet School was founded in Berlin, where the young nobles were sent for their officer's training. Austerity was also essential for an officer. For this reason the state strengthened their position as landowners, made alienation of *Rittergut* (their estates) subject to the king's permission, and prohibited their sale to commoners. Nobles should not get involved in trade, or in leasing crown property, so that they remained dependent upon their income from their estates and their official offices. The combination of the economic, judicial and political power of the nobles as feudal lords and landowners, with the power they acquired over their peasants as officers, compensated them for the loss of their freedom *vis-à-vis* the king. Officers decided which recruits to take, they had to give their permission for a soldier to marry or to go on leave – for which they gradually began to demand money. Captains received a carefully calculated allowance for the upkeep of their companies, so that they started to behave like small businessmen, saving on expenses and drawing additional income from, for example, the purchase of rations. In garrison towns the army was after all not only the main market but also the main industry, and its captain moulded the world to his will. The king had tamed the nobility, but left them free to oppress the peasants. Low military pay, however, set a limit to the exploitation of this country which was still relatively poor: a *Kantonist* always had to have enough of his own income left to live on.

Prussia offers an extreme example of the militarization of a society. Military structures and patterns of thought permeated civilian life. Of the male nobility 60 to 68 per cent were in the officer corps. Ex-officers held administrative positions. In 1760 the Prussian army was 260,000 strong; one soldier to every fourteen inhabitants, a proportion that had only been equalled in Sweden in 1709. In spite of the very heavy restrictions on their freedom, as well as the financial and physical burdens imposed by the system on all ranks and classes, it was accepted because it delivered success in the form of victories. The general growth in agricultural productivity also gradually made this exploitation slightly more tolerable.

In Russia Peter the Great introduced a similar system of conscription, which provided a regiment

approach of successive Prussian princes produced a radical change of course in the whole of Prussian society. One remarkable act of interference was the introduction of military service on a national scale, even for the nobility. About 1700 the great Prussian landowners, the *Junkers*, like all the other nobles in Europe, served in whichever army paid them best. Prussia was the first state which prohibited service

Family tree of the House of Brandenburg (*c.* 1610).
Detail: Elizabeth, daughter of King Johan of Denmark, with her husband Joachim i Nestor, Elector of Brandenburg.
Part of a genealogical table of King Christian iv of Denmark.
Copenhagen, Slot Rosenborg, Coll. Danish kings

per district on the basis of demanding one recruit per 250 (in 1726) or 121 (in 1742) inhabitants. It was, however, less rigorously enforced than in Prussia, largely because of the impossibility of applying a centralized administration, as in Prussia, to so large a country. The expansion of both these powers founded on domestic oppression would determine their development up to the end of the twentieth century. First they pushed Sweden back, and next, in combination with Austria, they erased Poland from the map. Austria and Russia between them started the demolition of the Ottoman rule in the Balkans. As typical monarchic realms, their goal was the conquest of territory, and their means the oppression of their subjects.

The sharpened competition between states, started in the west, exerted an increased pressure on those societies which were less developed and less differentiated from the economic and social point of view. The old monarchies in Poland, Hungary and Bohemia succumbed to it, but others, peripheral areas until then, proved capable of a powerful expansion. By making domestic exploitation harsher, the subjection of yet more peoples could be achieved. In the agrarian economies east of the Elbe no other resources existed for the concentration of power than their own populations and their meagre harvests. These authoritarian regimes therefore fossilized productive relationships in their traditional forms of feudal serfdom and so deepened the gap in development between east and west, which had existed for so many centuries.

Control of the seas

Only occasionally did medieval princes worry about control of the sea. Scandinavian kingdoms were founded on military service in ships, and the counts of Holland, too, could call upon their subjects for specific numbers of ships and oarsmen. Up to the sixteenth century it was the communities of merchants and fishermen who had the greatest interest in ensuring the safety of specific shipping

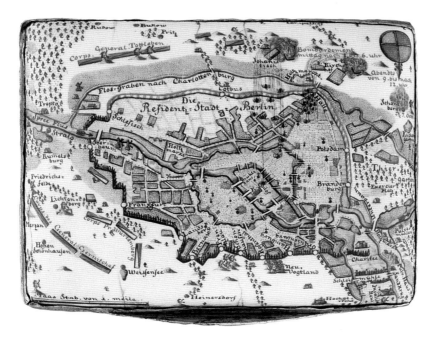

Porcelain snuffbox (*c. 1760*) with town plan of Berlin and the dispositions of the Prussian and Russian troops on the lid.
Doorn, Museumstichting Huis Doorn

The new eighteenth-century drill hall for the Prussian elite units. Coloured print by Peter Haas.
Berlin, Kunstbibliothek

On 1 September 1697 the Amsterdam Admiralty arranged a spectacular demonstration battle on the River IJ for Tsar Peter the Great,
who had a modern fleet built in St Petersburg with Dutch help. Engraving by Carel Allard.
Amsterdam, Rijksmuseum, Prentenkabinet

routes, fishing grounds, channels and ports, and took the first steps towards achieving this. Private arrangements or controls by communities, individually or jointly, usually came down to sailing in convoy, and arming a few accompanying ships manned by soldiers.

In the Mediterranean it was mainly the large Italian city states who were in mutual competition and had repeated naval engagements. Pisa lost its fleet in 1284 against Genoa, and never recovered from this blow. The competition between Genoa and Venice was fiercely waged with four naval wars between 1257 and 1400. In 1298 nearly 200 galleys were involved, but neither of these two great imperial powers was ever able to force the other completely out of any sector of the sea-going trade. They in fact exhausted each other in a conflict which grew beyond rational proportions. By 1475 the Ottoman conquests on land had cost the Genoese virtually all their fortified stations in the eastern Mediterranean and the Black Sea. In 1470 the Venetians lost the island of Euboea with the fortress of Negroponte, the base from which they had con-

trolled the Aegean. They were also defeated at sea by the Ottomans in 1499, which within a few years cost them all their forts along the Albanian and Greek coasts. The Venetian and Genoese fleets were after this never able to operate independently on a large scale. In 1571, in the famous naval battle of Lepanto, where the Ottomans were defeated, both still provided important squadrons, but most of the ships and the commander – Don Juan – were Spanish. This enabled the Habsburg monarchy to establish its hegemony over the Mediterranean – for some time at least.

In the Baltic the straits between Denmark and Sweden formed a strategic bottleneck over which the Danish kings systematically tried to exercise control to their financial advantage. The merchants both along the shores of the North Sea and of the Hansa naturally objected. When in 1360 King Waldemar IV, after the conquest of Skania and Gotland, raised his levies on the passage trade and imposed restrictions on Dutch seafarers, all the Hansa towns from Narva to the Zuiderzee, together with the towns in Holland, formed a league that in 1370

In the sixteenth century heavy galleons were no longer able to moor in the naval arsenal at Genoa,
where the war galleys were traditionally accommodated. This made substantial work necessary on the infrastructure of the port.
Cristoforo Grassi, *Dredging of Genoa harbour* in 1597. Genoa, Musea Navale di Pegli

forced him to allow free passage and took the fort-resses of Helsingborg, Skanör, Falsterbo and Malmö as pledges of good faith. The mobilization of a large fleet none the less depended on a specific challenge, and required special arrangements and taxes. As soon as peace was declared the alliance became much looser. About 1400 anarchic bands of Frisian *likedelers* (who shared out plunder equally among one another) harassed the trade both of the Dutch and the Hanseatics. Naval action against them was not enough, and the count of Holland also under-took land campaigns. In the years 1438 to 1441 the Hollanders enforced their free passage and harbour rights in the eastern Baltic in a naval war between associations of towns. The Wendish towns under the leadership of Lübeck unsuccessfully tried to put all kinds of obstacles in the way of these competitors.

Leagues of seafarers found occasion for forceful intervention, both offensive and defensive; for the eviction of competitors from trade routes and har-bours, or protection against such actions by others; for resisting levies, hijacking or piracy by princes and other warlords. Certainly until the sixteenth century there was on the seas of Europe a great diversity of actors organizing protection – or the use of force – either privately or jointly. Only occasion-ally did princes play an active maritime role in this context. Even the kings of England, who had to have a large fleet available during the Hundred Years War, did not use it for naval battles. In 1340 the Eng-lish broke the French blockade of the harbour of Sluis in a hand-to-hand battle and by setting fire to the ships. In 1372 Castilian barges assaulted an Eng-lish convoy with reinforcements for La Rochelle. In 1386 the French did not venture out of Sluis with the fleet they had assembled there; in order to get together several dozen ships, they had had to build, requisition and charter from private owners from Castile to Zeeland.

This was to remain the pattern until the six-teenth century, and even into the nineteenth it was often the case that a fleet was assembled partly from chartered merchant shipping. The industrialization of war, and particularly the advent of highly techni-cal steamships, would finally bring to an end inter-changeability of merchant and naval shipping.

Ectypoma classis bis mille octingentarum navium Ductore Illustrissimo Principe MAVRITIO Nassovio in Flandriam appulsa XXII. Juny. M.VI

The high cost of maintaining a navy frightened off rulers. For a long time navies consisted of armed merchantmen.
In 1600, for instance, 2,800 private vessels in the Western Scheldt were in league with Maurice to raise the Spanish siege of Nieuwpoort.
Contemporary engraving by Henricus Vroom. Rotterdam, Atlas van Stolk

This also applied to their crews, which in the age of sail could in peacetime easily switch to the civilian sector. Not only did states strive to control the seas much later than they did the land, the enormous expense involved in the maintenance of a fleet meant that most states were reluctant to form a permanent navy. During the seventeenth century this process got into its stride in several states, but temporary solutions still operated simultaneously in the form of chartering ships and their crews, hiring mercenary troops, and compulsory or agreed supply by towns and villages.

The reluctant involvement of monarchies in seapower can be explained by their origin – discussed earlier – as rulers over land, while the sea was for a long time left to the initiative of the towns. When from the fifteenth century states gained more control of their coastal regions, the incorporation of existing practices for the protection of sea traffic was the obvious answer. The invention of cannon, however, brought change here too. If earlier it had been enough to fill some merchant ships with soldiers to create a navy, the introduction of gunpowder posed some specific requirements. The great weight of cannon, and their recoil, made it necessary to make a careful study of the distribution of weight over the whole ship, and the walls of the ship also needed to be stronger to withstand hostile fire. The formation of a

With the victory over the Ottoman fleet
at the naval battle of Lepanto (7 October 1571)
the Habsburg monarchy gained the hegemony
over the Mediterranean for some time.
Giorgio Vasari painted these events on a wall
of the Sala Regia of the Vatican Palace in Rome.
Rome, Museo Vaticano

permanent fleet of warships was a logical consequence, which because of its high cost was only reluctantly undertaken by a small number of sea powers. Apart from the ships themselves, with their upkeep and replacement, considerable investment was also necessary in naval bases and dockyards.

During the second half of the seventeenth century there was a phenomenal growth of navies in Europe: from a total tonnage of 200,000 in 1650 to 450,000 in 1680 and 769,000 in 1705. After that the volume declined to 614,000 in 1720. Ships became substantially larger: from an average of 630 tons in 1650 to 900 in 1680. The growth was primarily to be blamed on the armaments race between England and the United Provinces from 1650 to 1674 and during the 1690s between both of them and France. The rulers of the Commonwealth under Cromwell, inspired with militarist spirit, thought that a monopoly of sea power was an essential condition for the enforcement of their mercantilist Navigation Act in 1651. As their first object was to threaten Dutch maritime supremacy, a reaction from that direction was inevitable. On a more limited scale there was a similar race in the Baltic between Sweden and Denmark, brought to a head in Denmark in 1660 by Sweden's threat to their national sovereignty. In the Levant and the Black Sea, Venice and the Ottoman empire maintained large navies up to

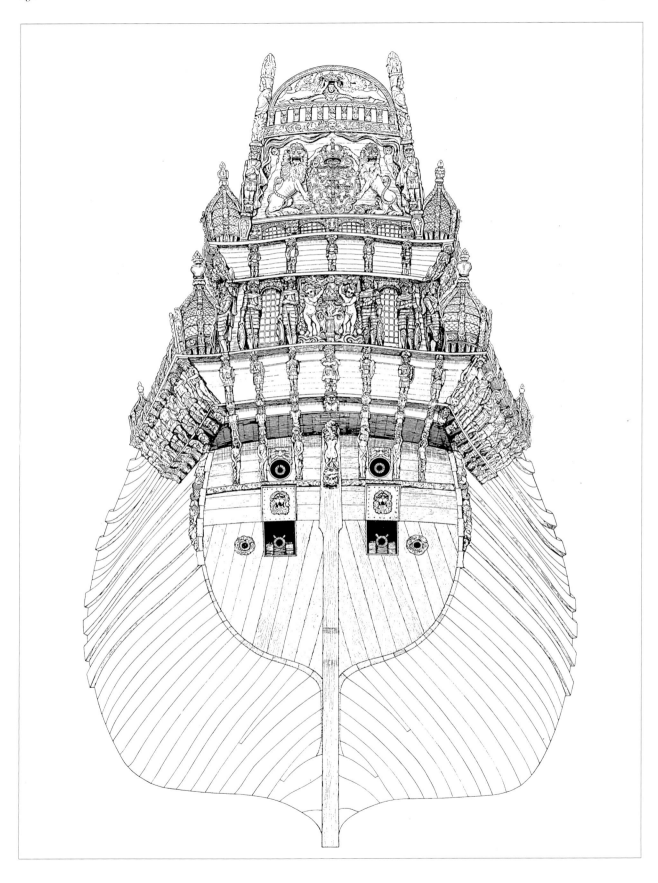

View of the Sound with the Danish castle of Frederiksborg, also called Kronborg,
located at Helsingør at the junction of the North Sea and the Baltic.
A print by Frans Hogenberg of 1657.

about 1730 for mutual deterrence; later Russia made an aggressive entry into the competition. During the second half of the eighteenth century England, France and Spain were involved in a fresh armaments race in their rivalry for colonies and long-distance trade routes. Actually only a few powers also built large navies in peacetime: England, Denmark, Sweden and Venice. In France the fluctuating balance of power was responsible for a capricious policy for the navy, which was reduced in the first half of both the seventeenth century and the eighteenth to very modest proportions. In spite of the strength of the Spanish world empire, they did not succeed in defeating the revolt of the Netherlands with an adequate navy after the

English had magnificently chased their Armada to the bottom of the sea in 1588. The arms race drove the states to substantially higher expenditure than could be justified purely on the basis of ensuring the safety of the seas. The United Provinces could lean strongly on the conversion of their enormous and partly armed merchant fleet, in addition to which they had enough shipbuilding capacity to launch some ten new warships a year.[18]

Since the late sixteenth century the Danish and Swedish navies, and a century later the Russian, had ensured the safety of the Baltic to protect their vital trade interests. The Prussian merchant fleet could for that reason also sail there without the protection of a navy of its

Reconstruction drawing by Björn Landström
of the salvaged Swedish royal battleship Wasa.
She sank on her maiden voyage in 1628 in Stockholm harbour
as a consequence of a gross error in ballasting.
The motifs and figures on her stern
were overlaid with gold leaf
and constituted a whole iconographic programme
for the glorification of the royal power.
Stockholm, National Maritime Museum

own. The Russian navy was developed mainly for political ends. The three Anglo-Dutch wars had by 1674 established a similar monopoly of power in the North Sea for England, the United Provinces and France. It is very probable that the fall in transport costs resulting from the elimination of uncontrolled violence in these seas may have had a favourable influence on the conditions for economic growth, but that was certainly not the reason for expanding the national navies. These three sea powers also invested a great deal of energy in the protection of the western Mediterranean against pirate strongholds in north Africa, against which the separate Italian, Maltese and Spanish fleets had not been able to operate effectively. The three short but sharp and very costly sea wars between England and the United Provinces between 1652 and 1674, and that of both of them against France in 1692, left England as the strongest surviving sea power. From 1665 the navy was the largest item of British government expenditure. After this the positions had become established; the zones were marked out, the strategic zones of the European waters were protected, and the struggle for new advantages, largely conducted by private companies, moved to the colonies. It is no wonder that the warships themselves were decorated with a superfluity of heroic ornamentation, and that marine paintings are among the most valuable and prestigious works of Dutch painters.

The new guard house,
arsenal and royal palace of the king of Prussia in Berlin,
painted in 1853 by Eduard Gärtner.

The outcome: powerful states

In this chapter the competition between men – indeed, women are hardly ever mentioned in it – for land, commercial profits and authority over people was our point of departure. Feudal lords were essentially concerned with land and people: if a knight unexpectedly came across a pile of money, he knew no better use for it than to share it out and squander it.[19] Competition was a permanent driving force in which up to the eighteenth century the use of force was in many regions regarded as a legitimate means to supplement traditional strategies. It always profoundly characterized the mentality of the noble and princely elites. Until the nineteenth century ownership of land remained the main objective of every elite. This led to the expansion of their spheres of power until they balanced each other in some regions for considerable periods. The ability of elites to take advantage of new materials and organizational techniques developed by their

opponents determined their chances of survival. The composition of some elites changed as a result of altered circumstances: the participation of the citizens of towns in the urbanized areas from the thirteenth century and their exclusion from the fifteenth century in larger more unified states. Where elites did not adapt – as in Poland, Hungary and the Ottoman empire, and until 1917 in Russia – this led to the elimination of the state itself.

Competition led to the formation of greater areas of power, absorbing, eliminating or taking over smaller ones; independent towns and baronies ended up in territorial principalities, which in turn were incorporated in kingdoms or empires. Between 1300 and 1800 the frontiers in western and northern Europe were rearranged less dramatically than in central, eastern and south-eastern Europe. Even then there were obviously appreciable differences in developments and rhythms, explained earlier by means of population densities, levels of urbanization and economic structures. If the frontier changes agreed between states after years of warfare are examined, then time and again there

In the centre of the square
stands the equestrian statue of Frederick the Great.
Berlin, Gemäldegalerie

seems to be a surprising discrepancy between the determined application of immensely violent means and their result. Take, for instance, the Hundred Years War: this cost the English and the foreign purchasers of English wool tons of gold for 116 years and imposed on the French a permanent burden of heavy taxes; for decades it laid waste large areas of north-west France. The results for England, the aggressor: the loss of the duchy of Gascony and the possession until 1559, as the only remnant of all their conquests, of the town of Calais. And what of the murderous Thirty Years War? France gained Alsace, Sweden Hither Pomerania, Brandenburg Further Pomerania; the Swiss Confederation and the United Provinces – in fact already in existence for a long time – were recognized as sovereign states; the Empire lost power compared with its constituent principalities; religious divisions were confirmed. Could this outweigh five million dead? Admittedly, contemporaries could not take the same overview that we can now, particularly not at the outset of the adventure. Louis XIV exhausted his country over half a century for a marginal gain in territory.

The list could be lengthened, and perhaps it should be said that wars were trials of strength which sometimes led to stabilization and sometimes to shifts in earlier relationships. Even then it is still true that violent methods to achieve the redistribution of power relationships were extremely expensive.

Why did subject populations tolerate such heavy burdens for the sake of shadowy objectives? It must be granted that they did not always do so without some grumbling: representative institutions created delays, set limits and imposed conditions. Where these were ignored by monarchs as in most states from the sixteenth century onwards, rebellions sometimes indicated the aversion of the populace to the immediate consequences of wars, which usually resulted in their being exploited more. Three things must be taken into consideration here. It is possible that the subjects were convinced, in whole or in part or for the time being, of the justice of the cause for which they were fighting, and therefore supported it, even when it cost such a high price. Another possibility is that they thought of their own situation as one that could not be altered by themselves, and the trials they suffered as being unavoidable. These two interpretations will be examined in chapter VI.

A third explanation is concealed in the fact that war did not just mean death and destruction: there were always those who had a direct interest in it, nobles with an eye to a lucrative career as an officer, soldiers eager for a more interesting existence with a chance of loot – regardless, of course, of the fact that they were often disappointed in their expectations. There were contractors who made fat profits from military efforts and all those who gained personal benefits from military action. Much, of course, depended on the theatre of operations: Sweden and England were great heroes in other people's countries, as long as everything was quiet at home. This was quite the contrary in rich agricultural regions such as the Po valley, Poland, western Germany and the Low Countries, where massive armies always 'lived off the land' – in other words, maintained themselves by plunder, a strategy openly advocated by Wallenstein, that great entrepreneur. Even less cynical generals such as Louvois and Marlborough did not succeed around 1700 in carrying more than 10 per cent of the supplies they needed with them from their home base. This meant that after at most nine days an army descended on the peasants, looting and extorting their needs from towns and villages. Subject populations exposed to such invasions were easily convinced that the

When the war quietened down in the winter months and the armies were disbanded,
parties of soldiers descended on the country and oppressed the defenceless villagers.
Gillis Mostaert painted this scene in the late sixteenth century.
Vienna, Kunsthistorisches Museum

defence of the realm cost money, and that if necessary an enemy should be pursued further. Lengthy conflicts such as the wars of religion in the sixteenth and seventeenth centuries created an emotively loaded image of the enemy which made subject populations prepared to make great sacrifices.

A variant on this last interpretation is that the formation of larger and stronger states, as well as producing losers in the feudal castles and within the walls of the towns, also produced winners – at least in some parts of western Europe – such as the class of free yeomen who could expect more justice from a distant state than from a neighbouring exploiter. More generally the consolidation of territory and its protection with belts of fortresses meant that violence by the state was in principle kept outside the frontiers. Within its frontiers the state protected its citizens, and demanded a price for this in the shape of military service and taxes. States, if they functioned effectively, produced peace at home and exported violence. Only, what is 'home' to one state is 'abroad' for another, which made this interactive model as a whole so pointless. Long and exhausting trials of strength, with only minor shifts of frontiers in western Europe, were the result. It must, however, not be forgotten that

this same western Europe also exported its violence to the colonies, an activity of which the less developed parts of the continent were deprived, except for Russia which found room for immeasurable expansion in Asia.

So the competition led to a continuous expansion of the surviving units. Not only did their territory expand, both within Europe and outside, but in the competition it also gained a permanent shape, that of states. For centuries these were still very diverse in size, composition and character. Until about 1800 autonomous country districts continued to exist in Switzerland, and autonomous towns – with or without territory – in Switzerland, Italy and the Holy Roman Empire; in the United Provinces towns and provinces still enjoyed their own sovereign rights besides those of the Republic as a whole; there were still dozens of ecclesiastical and secular principalities which were in reality autonomous, while others were included in a very loosely unified monarchic state. However, the states were ever more plainly fulfilling the essentially public functions which were earlier to be seen only in the towns. Above all, the larger states, which not only had access to a numerous population but also to substantial sources of capital, appeared best able

As armies grew larger, they could only be supplied with provisions by living off rich agricultural areas.
David Vinckboons (1578–1629), *Enraged peasants chasing soldiers out of their house.*
Amsterdam, Rijksmuseum

to concentrate the most modern means of violence of their time. Both on land and at sea they therefore had more opportunities of enforcing their objectives with physical force than their challengers, competitors or opponents at home and abroad. The state grew in size and in the means of exercising power as a consequence – unnoticed by most participants and often also unwanted – of the competition from which it itself had been born. It derived its territory and its identity from its opponents; the expansion of its own state institutions was a necessary accompanying phenomenon, which would contribute further to the strengthening of its self-image.

1   Hillenbrand 1979, 125–126
2   Contamine 1986, 13
3   Riley-Smith 1981, 84–85
4   Contamine 1986, 21–22
5   Waale 1990, 153–160
6   Howard 1976, 25–55
7   Parker 1972, 6; Parker 1988, 24; Aho 1981, 195
8   *The New Cambridge Modern History* vi, 1970, ch. ix
9   Press 1991, 248, 270
10 Tilly 1990, 72–73, 165–166
11 Molho 1971, 9–21
12 Thompson 1976, 69–71, 288
13 *The New Cambridge Modern History* vi, 1970, ch. ix
14 Chandaman 1975, 196–241, 332–333, 348–363; Brulez 1979
15 Corvisier 1976, 62–70
16 Corvisier 1976, 126; Tilly 1990, 79
17 Lindegren in Contamine 1997
18 Glete 1993, 158–160, 199, 241
19 Duby 1984

CHAPTER V

The State Apparatus

Righteous judges

Law and order: if the concentration of the means of violence described in the last chapter was to achieve some kind of order, at least within specific territories and waters, the question inevitably arose of how this power could be justified. Predominance in the means of violence was certainly a necessary condition for any lasting exercise of power, if not enough in itself. If large sections of the population did not accept the government imposed upon them as legitimate, this invited opposition which drove up the rulers' expenditure on control, affected their pretensions to offer protection to all subjects in their dominions, and made their government vulnerable to coalitions between internal and foreign enemies. If we accept that every human society, as well as a considerable dose of aggression, also displays a fundamental need for peace and stability, one would expect to see mutual efforts by rulers and by their subjects to achieve some lasting arrangement. Inevitably these would involve the fundamental factors of existence: distribution of goods in short supply, establishment and maintenance of some kind of social order, and provision of a purpose in life.

Control of internal discord is always, and in every society, a primary function; for order to be enforced permanently and with a minimum of tension and expense, it must not just be imposed, but must be recognized. To elevate power into authority it is necessary that certain common values

should be respected in a society, and particularly one made up of a ruling elite and large groups of subjects. Norms can then be socialized and absorbed from childhood by every individual, so that his behaviour complies with the norms and is predictable to his fellows. Departures from the norm are identified and punished.

Long before states existed, societies applied systems of law. From the sixth century lawyers made the first written versions – in Latin – of the rules that were accepted among the various German tribes, to make some kind of orderly relationships possible in the extremely varied situation after the great migrations. In fact the situation after that only became more complicated, because more and more regulatory bodies appeared on the scene. The Church tried to impose its norms and sanctions, a large proportion of which dealt with matters of private and criminal law such as marriage, theft and acts of violence. Lords of demesnes administered justice over their serfs in accordance with specific conventions. In the context of feudalism the law of fiefs developed and when dealing with cases distinguished between the nature of the person and the act. In the towns and free villages special laws applied, defined in their privileges and customs. There was a specific system of law with its associated judges and procedures for every individual, depending on his personal status.

Francisco Rizi, *Auto-da-fe* ceremony presided over by the king of Spain in 1680 on the Plaza Mayor in Madrid. During this spectacle heretics were burned at the stoke by the secular law authorities after being condemned by the ecclesiastical Inquisition.

An *auto-da-fe* was therefore a demonstration of both religious fanaticism and the power of the state. Madrid, Museo del Prado

To prevent situations of internal conflict governments also tried to impose moral values by artistic means.
In the eighteenth century Jan Ovens painted this allegory of Prudence, Justice and Peace.
Eighteenth-century allegorical design for the Amsterdam town hall, now the royal palace. Amsterdam, Stichting Koninklijk Paleis

Kings and territorial princes tried to establish their higher authority above all these forms of judicial procedure, but until the late eighteenth century they still had to take account of a great variety of legal systems within their territories. As these were expanded, this variety increased, not only regionally, but also by the inclusion of institutions with separate codes. Kings could fall back on the sacramental nature of their power, which had after all since the seventh century been derived from their anointing. References to priest-kings in the Old Testament underpinned this justification of the elevation of kings above ordinary mortals. From the examples of Samuel and David, and naturally also of Christ, they presented themselves as supreme judges and the source of justice. Their spiritual advisors added the patronage of the Church and everything that went with it.

The efforts of princes were directed towards giving their laws precedence for all the subjects within their territories, and to giving their administration of justice if not a monopoly, then certainly the supreme legal power. In view of the conflicts of interest involved this was a far from simple process. Force could be an effective aid in establishing the ruler's supremacy in the field of law by, for instance, curtailing the autonomous rights of the losers after suppressing a revolt by a town or region. In the course of the fifteenth and sixteenth centuries monarchs restricted the judicial powers of large towns and local lords in this way. The Low Countries provide a clear example of this because of the long tradition of autonomy of their large towns in the face of a diversity of relatively small territorial principalities. When these became united under the common authority of the dukes of Burgundy, the dukes had a substantial superiority in the means of violence which they repeatedly used in arguments about the extent of powers, arguments which they deliberately allowed to escalate into long wars. With each triumphant subjection of one of these large towns to ducal authority – Bruges in 1438, 1485 and 1490; Ghent in 1453, 1467, 1485, 1492 and 1540; Malines in 1467; Brussels in 1488 and 1532; Utrecht in 1483 and 1525 – the prince took action to cripple their judicial autonomy.

Elsewhere princes tried to get the supremacy of their courts accepted, using more gradual methods. England was the most advanced in this, as in so many matters affecting the establishment of the state. Already in the thirteenth century the king's central courts enjoyed precedence over all others and enjoyed the exclusive right of sitting in judgement on serious crimes. The kings of France had much more difficulty in reserving to themselves specific 'royal cases', such as counterfeiting coinage, lese-majesty, and appeals. The Paris Parliament, which from about 1250 they set up as the highest court of the kingdom, had an increasing number of cases to deal with as confidence in the independence of the judges grew.

In the most progressive parts of the kingdom of France – the duchy of Normandy, the county of Flanders and the crown demesnes – royal legal offi-

A 'Germanic' murderer is condemned to have his hand cut off. He is a Saxon, recognizable by the weapon *(sax)* in his hand. Sketches from a version of the *Sachsenspiegel* of *c.* 1330, one of the most widely disseminated codes of customary law. Heidelberg, Universitätsbibliothek

Force was an effective aid in establishing princely supremacy. After the revolt of 1539–1540 Charles v restricted the judicial power of the town of Ghent and its magistracy. *Citizens of Ghent kneeling before the Emperor Charles v in the Prinsenhof* by F.J. Pinchart from a sixteenth-century original. Ghent, Stadsarchief, Atlas Goetghebuer

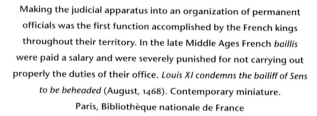

Making the judicial apparatus into an organization of permanent
officials was the first function accomplished by the French kings
throughout their territory. In the late Middle Ages French *baillis*
were paid a salary and were severely punished for not carrying out
properly the duties of their office. *Louis XI condemns the bailiff of Sens
to be beheaded* (August, 1468). Contemporary miniature.
Paris, Bibliothèque nationale de France

The many regional codes of customary law
obstructed a systematic homogenizing of the laws
on the authority of the central government.
Illustration from the *Grand coutumier de Normandie* (c. 1330–1340)
in which King Louis x of France hands the text of the Charter
of Normandy to the archbishop of Rouen and his train.
Paris, Musée du Petit Palais

cers, bailiffs and seneschals in well-defined areas of
jurisdiction (*baillages* and *sénéchaussées*) were from
the second half of the twelfth century responsible
for the prosecution and correct trial of criminals.
Their income no longer came from a fief, but from
an official stipend, a salary, or a proportion of the
court costs and fines. Turning the judicial apparatus
into an official organization was the first function
which would spread a prince's jurisdiction over the
whole kingdom. Until then there had only been
officials in the immediate surroundings of the
prince, in the hierarchy of his household and in his
chancellery. Traditionally such offices had been

filled by vassals or, if they demanded intellectual
knowledge, clerics. Expanding the prince's administration of justice to cover the whole country
therefore meant an important step towards the
modern bureaucratic state.

The supremacy of the princes' administration of
justice over the many competitive legal circles
depended on several factors; in the first place, of
course, on pure power relationships. Powerful local
lords and rich towns were able to offer effective
resistance until well into the eighteenth century.
Venice allowed every town submitting to her in the
terraferma she conquered in the fifteenth century

The modern civil process derives in essence from medieval canonical procedure,
which itself originated in the late-Roman form of legal process in which written evidence predominated.
During the case, the justices' clerks recorded what was said.
In this miniature, St Peter is supervising both canon and civil law courts. Fifteenth-century miniature.
Geneva, Bibliothèque publique et universitaire

to keep their own privileges and institutions, but still made them subject to her political authority and fiscal discrimination. For the peasants the Venetian hegemony meant liberation from the class-based courts of the citizens in the smaller towns. Elsewhere the possibility of appealing to the princely courts of law also offered new opportunities for parties in a weaker political or economic position than those of the main towns. The princes' administration of justice tried to place itself above the local and regional customary laws and in this gradually applied more general procedures and principles, often derived from jurisprudence. In the Spanish kingdoms, from the fifteenth century onwards, peasants increasingly appealed to the

crown as arbitrator on complaints against exploitation by aristocratic landowners. Royal judges, the *alcaldes* and in some cases the *Audiencia* had a growing number of cases laid before them by peasant communities against their lords about the excessive feudal rents. In the long run the crown courts strengthened the peasants' position, and with it also that of the king as the ultimate guarantor of justice.[1]

Both canon and Roman law–which from the twelfth century had spread from Bologna and was being intensively studied again at many of the emerging universities–contained many elements which the princes could usefully employ in their attempts to justify their actions. The Roman law

Notes: see p. 265

The 'Bed of Justice' was originally the bench on which the king of France took his seat in formal sittings of the Parliament.
Later it became the title of the court of justice held by the king in person. Jean Fouquet recorded for posterity the *lit de justice*
presided over by Charles VII in Vendôme in 1458.
Munich, Bayerische Staatsbibliothek

which had come down to them was the early sixth-century codification, and had a strong centralizing and absolutist bias, with principles such as 'the prince is not bound by the law' and 'what pleases the prince has the force of law'. Emperor Frederick Barbarossa quoted this axiom after his defeat of Milan in 1162. Lawyers at the court of the kings of France used similar formulae in the thirteenth century to justify decrees in which they claimed to promote the 'common interest'. Reliance on Roman law, however, also inspired opposition – for instance, at the English court which did not wish to consider itself subordinate to the emperor. Henry Bracton, priest and judge of the King's Bench in the mid-thirteenth century, wrote a treatise about the laws and customs of England, basing it on a compilation of some two thousand judgements. He defended the superiority of the English public trial by jury and natural law, since, he claimed, Roman law favoured the interest of the king, reduced a freedman to slavery again for reasons of ingratitude, forbade a woman to appear on behalf of anyone or to make a will, or for a child to acquire property without the permission of the father of the family. English law, on the other hand, protects the interest of the people, forbids the return

of a freedman to servile status, and allows a woman to give evidence and a son to acquire property freely. There is no doubt that Roman law was a basic subject in the education of lawyers internationally, though the kings of France were able to ban it at the University of Paris from the thirteenth century until 1679. Concepts such as that of the *res publica* filtered through to their thinking and the language of the administration and, although there was no precise contemporary equivalent, still sharpened the ideas of statesmen and the distinction between public, civil and criminal law.

Attempts at codification at the level of kingdoms were still exceptional during the Middle Ages: once in the second half of the thirteenth century in Castile, soon after substantial expansion of the kingdom's territory at the expense of the Muslims, and again in similar circumstances in Poland in 1347. The breakthrough of systematic codes of law would not, however, occur until the sixteenth century, in a gradual and generally laborious assessment of the many local and national customary laws. In France there was an extremely slow response to the royal decree of the mid-fifteenth century to adopt an official authorized code of the

This altarpiece, painted c.1450 by an anonymous Flemish master, hung in the Parliament of Paris, then the court of appeal for disputes for the entire northern part of the kingdom. On the left St Louis and John the Baptist can be identified with the Louvre in the background, and on the right Charlemagne and St Denis, carrying his head in his hands. Paris, Musée du Louvre

many regional customary laws. A century later most of the code had been published in north and central France, but not in the south, with its much stronger Roman tradition. Full codification, a systematic ordering and homogenizing on the authority of the central government, was never achieved. The Sun King succeeded at the most in unifying the civil and criminal procedures throughout the country by his decrees of 1667 and 1670, but the so-called absolutist monarchy proved to be unable to give expression to the power of the state by a uniform system of legislation. Local judges retained great freedom in practising the administration of justice.[2]

Rather than Roman law, the influence of canon law permeated the administrative and juridical practices of the young states. Rational research by the judge into the facts before anyone was charged, as against the Germanic custom of the accusatory indictment and single combat, found its model in the Church: the *inquisitio*. The fourth Lateran Council in 1215 condemned trial by ordeal as a method of proof, officially because it was irrational and the result was often doubtful. The Carolingian kings had at one time introduced it in order to decide cases in which the evidence or witnesses did not provide sufficient certainty, a situation which must often have occurred in the multicultural society over which they ruled. In the thirteenth century religious and secular authority had developed so much further that they eschewed the unpredictability of a trial by a publicly proclaimed ordeal and preferred more rational inquisitorial methods, carried out by professional judges specially trained in them.[3] The emphasis on investigation was already included in urban legal systems such as those of the large Flemish towns of about 1170.

It is of fundamental significance for western thinking that at the young universities law (meaning Roman and canon law) was recognized as a separate discipline, distinct from theology. Although the universities still came under the authority of the Church, they still offered – unlike, for example, the Islamic schools – the opportunity to develop an approach to law that was without dogma, and free from religious prescriptions. From this the rational approach to western legal thinking evolved. The technique of interpreting the text of the law made continual renovation and adjustment to changes in the real world possible. In this way the principles of Roman law were also reworked in fresh applications.[4]

Originally members of the local patrician families presided over the town law courts. In the course of the fourteenth century representatives of the craft guilds joined them. They gave judgement according to the customary law of the town, and had no specific legal qualifications. Miniature from the *Lawbook of the town of Hertford* of c. 1375. Hertford, Town Archives

The professional class of university lawyers trained along common lines acquired key positions in all public administrations, within the state and outside it. In Italy and the south of France their role in the public life of the towns was from the thirteenth century very great, both in the town magistracies and in those of the regional and ecclesiastical authorities, and as practising lawyers. The courts and legislative bodies were increasingly staffed by academically trained lawyers, *consules iustitiae.* Their activity contributed to the legitimizing of public life, in which the principles of scholarly jurisprudence were also evoked for the defence of the interests of individuals against authorities, particularly with respect to the protection of private property, its disposal by will, the freedom of contracting parties, and the protection of widows and orphans. The concept of the collective person at law, *universitas,* was applied in towns and districts, in their mutual unions and in their collective organs such as guilds. Like so many other matters, the spread of modern rational legal thinking was closely linked with the urban environment, alongside and in opposition to that of the great princely courts. From the social point of view university studies opened up the chances of rising socially for commoners who thanks to their technical knowl-

edge could acquire influential positions in the towns and above all at court, so that the knights' monopoly of power was broken. In those parts of Germany and of central and northern Europe characterized by long-lasting aristocratic and feudal relationships, the new rational forms of law only penetrated slowly and partially, but during the sixteenth century university-trained lawyers of commoner origin were appointed to key posts all over the Empire.[5]

The administration of justice and its practice encroached far more deeply on the real world of society than did the princes' legislation. In this last field local rules were much closer to reality, and were often simpler to enforce through a combination of social control and common interest. In this context the situation in England was at variance with that on the continent, on the one hand through the long tradition of trial by a jury of laymen, and on the other through the early expansion, from the twelfth century, of a system of professional crown courts with far-reaching powers. In England the common law, the law based on custom, remained intact – with only minor influences from the academic lawyers, and a great weight of juridical precedents – so that it was really the courts that laid down the law. Nor should we assume that the legislation of the kings of France

Under the *ancien régime* serious criminals were displayed in a central place in the town after sentencing.
This *Ecce Homo* illustrates the course of events in fifteenth-century Brunswick. Brunswick, Herzog-Anton-Ulrich Museum

With the increasing importance of written documents in disputes, university educated advocates and notaries
were much in demand in the course of the sixteenth century. Pieter Bruegel the Younger, *The advocate with difficult cases,* 1621.
Ghent, Museum voor Schone Kunsten

Reputed portrait of the lawyer Francesco Righetti, c. 1626–1628, painted by Giovanni Guercino.
In the scholar's bookcase a number of authoritative books of law are displayed,
such as Pope Gregory's *Decretals* and Justinian's *Digests*.
Fort Worth, Texas, The Kimbell Art Museum

Shame and remorse, caryatids on the Amsterdam High Court, carved by Artus Quellinus in 1648.
Amsterdam, Stichting Koninklijk Paleis

was just a simple act of will, the sovereign's *bon plaisir*: the great majority of royal decrees were issued in response to requests, through petitions by a pressure group. These were comprehensively examined, and after a writ had been issued the final formulation of the government's act still required the approval of various officials and of the supreme court, the Parliament of Paris. As early as the fourteenth century bureaucratic controls were a brake on arbitrary decisions.

The interests of parties to litigation were an important stimulus to the expansion of the prince's administration of justice, particularly because of their independence and the associated potential professionalism that they offered. For example, the Great Council of the Netherlands pronounced forty judgements a year about 1500, and 135 by 1550. The central courts were created by specialization and splitting the original judicial council of a prince into separate chambers and councils. The more cases came before the crown, the more the need arose for expansion and specialization of the highest judicial bodies. Their object was to function as a court of appeal for all the lower courts in the country, in doing so sometimes by-passing ancient privileges which had granted all levels of jurisdiction to

towns and seigneuries. In composite territories such as the Low Countries and the Empire this meant that three levels of courts were piled on top of each other in a hierarchy: local, territorial and central. In France in 1552 the king added some fifty *présidiaux*, appeal courts between the *baillages* and the Parliament. By the eighteenth century there were a hundred of them. Finally the prince himself continued to exercise his sovereign judicial power – in France during the sixteenth century surrounded by the special ceremony of the *lit de justice* – and retained his right to grant pardons and so to annul any legal decision. Because of the number of regional parliaments, the royal councils – ultimately the *Grand Conseil* – took over the supreme jurisdiction in cases of infringement of legality. In England, in addition to the new supreme court of the Star Chamber for criminal cases we see the unique creation of the Court of Requests for people who were too poor to bring their cases before the normal courts.

Princes had an interest in monopolizing the highest judicial power within their territories. That implied the protection of their subjects against interventions by external judges such as episcopal officials, university law faculties, or the courts of higher princes. The interests of the princes and those of their subjects, or at least of that part of them who had a voice, coincided here. Through their representative organs the subjects indeed persistently stressed the demand to let everyone in the first instance be judged by their 'natural' judges (by which were meant the traditional local powers) and to bar foreign courts. Their arguments for this were the higher cost of proceedings in a place located at a distance, often in a foreign language, and following a largely unfamiliar procedure. Of course, disputes about their competence compared with the local courts also had a role to play. The competence of the Parliament of Paris in the counties of Artois and Flanders, which were part of the kingdom, but were under Burgundian – and from 1477 Habsburg – authority, was a point of issue between the rival monarchies. In 1529 Charles v was able to free his territory from the sovereign judicial power of his rival, even though modern research has shown that the Parliament of Paris was not influenced by political motives in its judgements. Similarly Charles later attempted to make the boundaries of dioceses coincide with those of his secular authority, to avoid interference from outside. In Protestant countries the Reformation substantially reduced the importance of the ecclesiastical courts, but they lost ground to secular judges even in Catholic areas.

In the Holy Roman Empire the emperor made use of his *Reichsacht* to make it possible to take reprisals against the community – town or country – to which a criminal belonged, a procedure which was quite normal anyway in commercial law. After 1495 the establishment of the imperial supreme court, the *Reichskammergericht*, offered wide opportunities of appeal over a large area. It was, however, typical of the weakness of the Empire that the emperor had to allow powerful territorial princes exemption for their subjects, because they had set up their own central courts in their territories. In France, too, regional variation could be seen with the setting up of parliaments in districts with a strong tradition of autonomy: in 1600 there were already nine, and under Louis xiv thirteen. In Languedoc, for instance, the king allowed the regional oligarchy of *clientèles* to retain the financial administration in return for their recognition of the political and cultural hegemony of the state. The monarchy was able to adapt itself to the regional diversity and enforced its own pattern to the extent that circumstances allowed.[6]

Expansion of the judicial apparatus made the presence of the authority of the state, with its norms,

more visible to more of its subjects. The judges represented the sacramental authority of the anointed prince in its most emphatic form, that of maintaining public order and punishing transgressors. In monarchic states this was from the sixteenth century increasingly done with theatrical display, in which public executions particularly became grandly staged mass spectacles. There was a strict ritual for the physical humiliation and destruction of the wrongdoer, often applied in successive stages according to the seriousness of the offence. The responsible government bodies supervised the execution of their sentences and displayed themselves to the people in their full panoply as the solemn guarantee on behalf of the king of the divine right. In Amsterdam, then the largest town in north-west Europe with a population of 200,000, sixty-eight executions were carried out between 1650 and 1750. In Artois, under Charles v and Philip ii's judges, there were 649 in eighty-two years of the sixteenth century, an indication of their proportionally much harsher repression.[7] However gruesome these public ritual executions may seem to the twentieth-century western observer, they fulfilled their purpose in the drive for civilization of the monarchic states. By isolating and publicly humiliating transgressors of the law, the government emphasized the power of the law to the assembled masses. The public felt itself to be distanced from the accused, and so had the norm imprinted in a deeply emotional way. From the point of view of creating a disciplined and internally peaceful society, public judicial rituals fulfilled their function of internalizing the norm. A rough way of 'civilizing', perhaps, for which there was obviously considerably less need in the more urbane world of the United Provinces than in that of the absolute monarchies. Perhaps there were already sufficient internal pacification mechanisms at work in urban communities, whereas in the villages order still had to be imposed from above.

The state as employer

As early as the twelfth century the emerging monarchs experienced the need to surround themselves with increasing numbers of experts in administration. The growth into the *Beamtenstaat* can best be illustrated as a concentric expansion, starting from the royal household of a territorial prince or king. The most elementary functions developed into a diversity of court offices, whose structure survived fairly generally until the seventeenth century. Every

Jean Fouquet, *Portrait of Guillaume Jouvenel des Ursins*, Chancellor of France, c. 1460.

Paris, Musée du Louvre

Charles Le Brun, *The French Chancellor Séguier,* **c.1655.**
Paris, Musée du Louvre

court was divided up into a few basic functions onto which these offices were grafted: responsibility for the stables, the kitchen, the wine, the bread, the meat, the personal apartments of the prince, his lady and his children, the chapel.

The more important the central figure, the more he surrounded himself with a greater diversity of court offices. To draw up and publish written documents the earliest princes simply called on the priests in their train, who were after all the only ones who could read and write, and in Latin too. In 1308 the king of Norway agreed with the pope that his chancellery should form one organization with the chapel royal. It was a general phenomenon for princes to hand over their paperwork to priests. Every monastery had a centuries-old tradition of literacy in Latin, sometimes associated with running a school. The cathedrals, too, ran their own schools and from the tenth century achieved even greater intellectual excellence. In the course of the centuries the use of writing for recording the actions of the government and contracts increased rapidly. The original oral, personal and direct judicial and administrative procedures gradually evolved into methods of recording, communicating and producing evidence in writing. The spread of the use of

writing made more detached, objective, comprehensive and better arranged forms of justice and administration possible than those based on being present in person and on memory, spoken testimony and oaths. Through the calls on the priests by illiterate warlords, who were feudal lords, to record their administrative acts, judicial pronouncements and agreements, Church Latin also became the administrative language of the early states throughout Europe.

About the mid-thirteenth century vernacular languages began to appear in official documents in the west. In Hungary Latin, partly because of the completely different roots of the Hungarian language, retained a function in the administration until the nineteenth century. The adoption of the local vernacular went together with the increasing role commoners began to play in administration, as it helped to some extent to bridge the gulf between the world of chivalry and that of urban society. A fundamental consequence of this opening up of government circles to the native tongue and to officials from commoner origins was that, unlike in the Catholic Church or the Chinese empire, the government of the country in all its aspects became accessible for its subjects. It was no longer con-

Hans Holbein, *Robert Cheseman,* falconer to Henry VIII of England, 1533.
The Hague, Mauritshuis

cealed behind a strange, esoteric language and culture which distanced it from the people. Princes, officials and representatives of the people could speak to each other directly – whence the term 'parliament'. It must not, of course, be forgotten that in every language area there were a multiplicity of regional tongues and that High German was regarded as a foreign language by the Low Germans, just as the *langue d'oil* differed from the *langue d'oc,* and many other local tongues were in use, such as Breton and Frisian. In Iberia the families of languages were divided into three strips running north to south which roughly agreed with the institutionalized maritime or continental orientation of the different kingdoms. In the Norman tradition the English court retained Norman French as the primary language for various functions until the sixteenth century, which was not unassociated with its claims on the French crown. As administration and justice used more and more written procedures, use of the official language won social importance. So various representatives of the Estates protested successfully in the fourteenth and fifteenth centuries against the use by their rulers of a foreign language – German in Bohemia and French in the Low Countries. Administrative centres

reduced the gulf between them and the people by using the native language, so that this vernacular won a wider circulation than any other – even if only in official documents. In Protestant areas the unifying effect of the obligatory reading of a standard translation of the Bible contributed to this.

Nevertheless the ecclesiastical origin of western literacy for long left its traces in the clerical status of the heads of princely secretariats, their chancellors. From 1070 the counts of Flanders regularly recruited as their chancellors the provosts of the chapter of St Donatian in Bruges. Chancellors of the German kings were usually bishops or became bishops soon after their appointment. Not until 1424 did the first layman hold office as German chancellor. From 1280 until 1331 all the French chancellors were bishops of the wealthy cathedral of Laon. In the fourteenth century the Avignon popes promoted various French chancellors to cardinal; one of them actually achieved the papacy himself. In 1390 the king of Navarre's chancellor also received a cardinal's hat. Cardinal Wolsey, as Lord Chancellor and papal legate, combined the highest ecclesiastical and secular offices in England. After these became incompatible as a result of Henry VIII's quarrel with Rome, and Wolsey in 1530 suffered his

tragic end in royal custody, only two more ecclesiastics were briefly to fill the office of chancellor. In Catholic Poland on the other hand one of the two royal chancellors was an ecclesiastic until 1795. In France secularization had set in much earlier: from the mid-fourteenth century there were lay chancellors and by 1500 only 8 per cent of the royal secretaries were ecclesiastics.[8]

Apart from their original monopoly of expertise, the service of ecclesiastics offered still further advantages to princes. It was important that their ecclesiastical dignity already provided them with an adequate income, making them cheap for princes to employ. The Church freely granted dispensations to its servants for these kinds of service, undoubtedly out of love for their fellow-men and a care for the good government of the faithful. Their service also meant, however, that the Church had an excellent opportunity of promoting its own interests, and in a manner as direct as it was discreet. No wonder that the overwhelming majority of all the pre-1300 deeds that have survived are concerned with church property. It was also important for the princes to be able to count on the support of the Church, which in any case was almost everywhere the largest landowner and could bring influence to bear on the souls of the faithful. Their celibacy also meant that ecclesiastics were less inclined than secular lords to put their personal and dynastic interests first. In theory they had no sons to push as their successors in office, and as they grew elderly, or if there was any argument, could be dismissed back to their spiritual duties without problems. The famous first ministers – in its original sense of first servants – of the French kings in the seventeenth and eighteenth centuries, Richelieu, Mazarin, Dubois and Fleury, continued this tradition. In the sixteenth and seventeenth centuries 15 to 17 per cent of the seats in the Spanish royal councils were still filled by ecclesiastics.

The advance of the ecclesiastics in the first stages of the formation of states was pure necessity. There was, however, implicit in it a strong influence on policy which was particularly felt from the mid-eleventh to the thirteenth century when the prestige of the Church was at its highest. Powerful popes had set in motion internal reforms and purges and formulated high requirements of the secular rulers. The struggle with the Holy Roman Emperors was the most bitter, particularly in the time of Henry IV and Gregory VII (1073–1085),

El Greco, *Portrait of a cardinal*, probably Don Fernando Nino de Guevara, Grand Inquisitor in Toledo from 1599 to 1601. New York, Metropolitan Museum of Art

who deposed and humiliated each other. Against the kings of England and France the popes also asserted their claims with respect to the ultimate highest authority, particularly when it came to the appointment and investiture of bishops. Just because the administrative structure of the Empire was so firmly grafted onto that of the Church, and the emperors had invested the bishops with considerable secular power, they wanted to have a say in their appointment. This went right against the new vision – entirely correct from the ecclesiastical point of view – of the reforming popes who wished to regard the choice and investiture of bishops as a purely church affair. In the end both parties were weakened by this conflict: relationships between popes and emperors often continued to be extremely tense up to the time of Frederick II; the imperial office lost much of its power in Germany, but the popes, too, had to allow princes in most western countries to be involved in appointments to high ecclesiastical offices. Meanwhile the popes with their influence on the early states had, of course, launched the crusades, in which they had managed to make their priorities prevail above those of the monarchs. In this context it was also possible to launch a reign of terror against other enemies of the Church such as Jews and heretics. Precisely at the moment that the ecclesiastics had a firm grip on the young state administrations and the Church had reached the peak of its ambitions, both together launched campaigns against the Jews. Because of their higher intellectual and commercial development, the Jews had until the twelfth century frequently performed financial, medical and administrative services for western princes. In the early thirteenth century, however, the crusade against the heretic Christians in the south of France, the Albigensians, was justified in part by the argument that Count Raymond VI of Toulouse was too dependent on Jewish officials. The simultaneous witch-hunt against Jews and heretics was a side effect of the new and temporarily monopolistic hold the ecclesiastics had on the young states; making heretics out of their enemies and competitors proved to be an effective means for the princes of rooting them out with the blessing of Rome.[9]

From the fifteenth century kings and, for instance, also the powerful dukes of Burgundy acquired, first in practice and in 1515 and 1521 by virtue of a papal bull, extensive influence on the appointment of bishops, abbots and provosts

Queen Elizabeth of England receiving ambassadors from the Low Countries.
Kassel, Staatliche Kunstsammlungen

within their territories. In addition they had plenty of canons' prebends to give away to loyal clients or members of their families. Not only did this mean the Renaissance popes giving away the great prize of the 'Freedom of the Church' for which they had fought so hard in the eleventh and twelfth centuries; in effect they also lost the universalist ideal of their predecessors. After the late Middle Ages the Church became increasingly bound to the vigorously growing power of the state. In the 1290s both the English and French kings had taxed church property in their territories very heavily. Papal protests produced the reaction on the part of Philip the Fair of preventing remittances by the French churches to Rome. The argument escalated further about the competence of the pope or of the king to judge a bishop accused of heresy. Territorial sovereignty was again at odds with the universality of the Church. This time, however, the pope had to yield, at which the day dawned of the 'Babylonian exile' of the popes to Avignon, the Western Schism and the conciliar movement, which brought about a fatal weakening of the Church. Various princes eagerly made use of this vulnerable position of the popes to strengthen their hold on the Church's material and manpower resources.

The Catholic kings, Ferdinand and Isabella of Castile (1474–1516), during their final offensive against the Muslim kingdom of Granada, integrated the Inquisition into a real organ of the state, with which to attack the problem of their active Jewish and Muslim minorities. During the advancing Reformation, the interaction between state and Inquisition increased, in which the state proclaimed decrees against heretics, handed over the prosecution of them to the diocesan or central Inquisition, and then carried out the execution of the sentences.

As well as the chancellery and various council functions, diplomacy was a field of activity favoured by ecclesiastics. Their internationally standardized education and knowledge of Latin were obvious reasons for this, as well as the sacrosanction of their legal position, and the trust engendered by their priestly status. Most diplomatic delegations therefore included ecclesiastics, and their rank and numbers were determined by the weight a government wished to attach to a mission. Not until the fifteenth century in the complex of Italian political relationships did the institution develop of reciprocal resident embassies. About 1500 the western monarchies gradually began to adopt this regular form of mutual communication. In that period the

Hans Holbein, *Portrait of Charles de Solier,* Sieur de Morette, French ambassador to England, 1534–1535.

Dresden, Staatliche Gemäldegalerie

Thomas Howard, third duke of Norfolk. In one hand he holds the white rod of his office of Lord Treasurer,
and in the other the gold baton of the Earl Marshal of England. Portrait painted in 1539 by an unknown artist.
Windsor Castle, Royal Collection

Lee trésoriers.

At first north Italians held the high post of Treasurer in the service of almost all European princes. About 1400 they were replaced by local experts. Officers of the French Treasury, miniature of about 1505. Paris, Bibliothéque nationale de France

Habsburg dynasty saw its sphere of interest suddenly expand enormously by the prospect of inheriting the kingdom of Spain, so that the need for permanent lines of communication between the various princely courts made itself acutely felt.

Experts such as the ecclesiastics who were competent to operate in the fields of administration, the secretariat and diplomacy were less evident in the financial field. The clergy often left the management of their own demesnes to lay stewards, though these were still of course accountable to them in writing. During the second half of the thirteenth century Italian financial specialists came to the fore in the princely courts of north-west Europe, an obvious extension of their activities as bankers and moneylenders. Until about the mid-fourteenth century they filled high offices in the service of princes as tax collectors, treasurers or mint masters. In these posts they rationalized the management of the fast-increasing princely finances, and in so doing doubtless kept an eye on the safeguarding of their own interests. Towards the end of the fourteenth century the reaction against foreign officials, coupled with an increase in native skills, pushed the Italian financiers from their official level to that of councillors or advisors.

Just as much as other aspects of the state apparatus, that of finance developed out of the management of the prince's family demesnes. Like any great lord, princes received rents in kind and in money from the demesnes they held, together with the income from the exercise of their seigneurial rights such as administering justice and levying tolls and dues for their serfs. The English Domesday Book of 1086 is the earliest – and a unique – review of all the royal incomes from the vast crown demesne of the Norman conquest throughout England. Exactly a century later – in 1187 – in Flanders, a summary of all the count's incomes was drawn up, subdivided systematically by receipts from each locality. Unlike the Domesday Book, which owed its existence to the exceptional circumstances of a foreign conquest, the Flemish *Grote Brief* appears to reflect a normal administrative procedure. An inventory was made of the income of the French Dauphin between 1250 and 1267, with difficulty and relatively late, but it was done. Nowhere was there a standard procedure for making these kinds of reviews.

Masters of the Mint processed metal into a quantity of coin, prescribed for them by law.
They received a fixed remuneration per coin supplied to cover their production costs. *Portrait of a German mintmaster,* 1501.
Munich, Bayerische Staatsgemäldesammlungen, Alte Pinakothek

Apart from being the holder of his own demesne, a prince by virtue of his sovereignty exercised certain rights throughout his territory. The incomes he enjoyed as ruler over land which he did not exploit economically himself – such as his profits from granting privileges, minting coinage, a proportion from the administration of justice, tolls and various other levies – were only with great difficulty distinguishable from his private income as lord of a demesne. As a prince's council only gradually formed from among the train of loyal vassals who surrounded their liege lord, and functions at court gradually acquired the character of public offices, eventually there was a differentiation between the finances of the prince as lord of a demesne, and those he received as holder of the office of ruler.

Dukes, counts and bishops were recruited from the powerful, and potentially dangerous, regional high nobility to represent the authority of the crown in that region, and therefore became the natural mediators between central and regional or local interests. In France and the Low Countries there was a

El Greco, *Portrait of Rodrigo Vasquez de Arce.*
Rodrigo came of a prominent family of lawyers.
Under Philip II he was from 1584 to 1592
president of the Financial Council,
and also a member of the Royal Council.
Madrid, Museo del Prado

change in the sixteenth century when the old territorial princedoms were redesignated as provinces, under the charge of a governor or stadtholder (literally *lieutenant*) from the high nobility. Inspired by the example of the Roman empire, this suggested a higher degree of administrative integration.

England was far ahead of the rest of Europe in administrative and judicial organization, as a consequence of the strong organization of the Anglo-Saxons, and the Normans' need to keep a tight grip on the conquered country. Certainly as early as the twelfth century two specialized courts were split off from the royal council in the two basic areas requiring specific expertise: the Court of Common Pleas, the central royal court for free men, and the Exchequer, the court where the king's financial officials had to answer for their accounts. This model can be labelled a common European one, which developed in various periods and to a varying degree depending upon the social development of a region: progressive specialization and bureaucratization by hiving off parts of the original unitary council of great

In the fifteenth century secretaries of state began to head separate departments of the papal Curia.
In western courts this specialisation only occurred in the course of the seventeenth century.
Fresco painted c. 1500 by Pinturicchio, *Aeneas Silvio Piccolomini submits to the papal authority and the Curia.*
Siena, Duomo, Libreria Piccolomini

vassals of the crown. Advisory functions were expanded and established in separate institutions run by officials. In the papal Curia secretaries of state appeared in the fifteenth century at the head of separate departments, an evolution which spread through most western courts from the seventeenth century. During the eighteenth century public examinations were held for the first time for appointment to offices of state, in the technical financial sectors and in the army. Bavaria and Prussia were in the forefront of this development.[10]

Although it is plain that in the course of this process increasing numbers of officials started working in the king's service, thus creating a state apparatus, not many overall statistics can as yet be found about it in academic literature. An example of its evolution can be found for the central administration in France; in the early fourteenth century it had eight accountancy officials, in 1484 nineteen; in 1286 ten notaries were working in the chancellery, in 1361 fifty-nine, in 1418 seventy-nine, and by the early sixteenth century 120. The king of England had fifteen messengers in his service about 1200 and about sixty about 1350, allowing the sheriffs in the counties to receive mail from the capital once a week.[11] After that there was an enormous acceleration in bureaucratization: around 1515 the French state in its entirety already had more than 4,000 *officiers*, officials; a century later there were perhaps 25,000 and about 1665 at least 46,000.[12] In England there were undoubtedly fewer state officials per head of population, partly because many functions, such as that of justice of the peace, remained unsalaried.

The collection of taxes required a widely ramified net of collectors, beyond the capability of the kings and territorial princes to construct, partly because all the areas with fiscal immunities – such as the seigneuries, the ecclesiastical demesnes and the towns – insisted on maintaining their autonomy. They preferred contributing a total sum for the whole of the district they covered, mainly so that they could keep in their own hands the actual collection and so the control over what the population could bear. The system of levying customs in the ports made it possible for the English kings to instal their own collectors there; this was a matter of new crown rights mainly affecting foreign purchasers. The introduction of general and permanent royal taxation, under the pressure of the Hundred Years War, gave the king of France by the middle of the fifteenth century the opportunity to keep the collection of taxes largely in his own hands. In Castile, too, because of the expansion of its power by conquest at the expense of the Muslims, the crown had acquired the right of direct appointment of officials in the towns, the *regidores*. None the less in the rest of Europe the monarchies experienced great difficulties in centralizing the collection of taxes by their own officials in the whole country.

The privatization of public offices

In 1427 the papal Curia introduced the practice of putting up for sale the offices of the writers of the papal correspondence. The steadily recurring need of the states for quickly available liquid finance was the most important reason why the tendency towards the creation of skilled and reliable bureaucratic apparatus went astray nearly everywhere in Europe. Under pressure of cut-throat competition every state unrelentingly opted for quick money for the sake of its wars at the expense of the proper functioning of its own apparatus. The states therefore began bit by bit to put up for sale what they had laboriously built up in previous centuries: offices which answered to an existing need. The functions which had to be carried out for the state and for society became subordinated to what greedy interested parties were willing to pay in hard cash. Three things interested them in exchange for their capital: the power which an office granted, and which the holder, having bought it, could use reasonably freely without too much fear of control by his superiors in the hierarchy; the possibility of getting a return on his invested capital from the incomes associated with the office; and the status that went with a high office. From the fifteenth century, in France particularly, the tendency developed to grant titles of nobility to high officials. The commoner origin of many of the academically educated among them was thus blurred by drawing them into the hierarchy of status as equals with the traditional upper classes. What in the fourteenth century was done by promoting an ecclesiastic to bishop or cardinal, now applied to the secular world. A good example is the Burgundian advocate Nicholas Rolin who in 1422 became the duke's chancellor and was immediately ennobled by him so that he would be on the same footing as the other members of the Council. This *noblesse de robe* gave the offices a particular cachet and therefore made their price more valuable, to the benefit of the prince as much as for the applicants.

From the sixteenth century local elites in Castile bought offices from the king. This meant that they acquired the status of *hidalgo* and were integrated into the state apparatus. Charter to bear arms with *hidalgo* status, granted in 1569 to Don Diego Aranguiz by the *Audiencia* of Valladolid. Pamplona, la Diputacion de Navarra

States went over to the sale of offices on a massive scale when they were in acute need of money, in other words, in wartime. Thus in Spain from 1560 to 1640 there was a wholesale disposal of the royal demesnes, of offices and of judicial functions. In Castile it was mostly offices under the crown in towns which were sold, so that along this way the local elites were integrated into the states and acquired the rank of *hidalgo.* In France the sixteenth century saw the first great wave of sales. After the Treaty of Westphalia (1648) there was everywhere some slowing down in the tendency to privatize, because in peacetime the states' need for money was reduced. The burden on the treasury was relieved by keeping only part of the domestic bureaucracy in salaried service and transferring the remainder to the expenses which the user of public services had to pay to the office holder. For drawing up a public document, for the initiation of a case at law, for the purchase of salt, the good citizen had to pay a supplement to the collector on behalf of the state, not to the state but to the office holder in person. He received it as if it were interest on the purchase price of his office. As the state did not look too closely at precisely what sums were received, there was a grey area from which an office holder could enrich himself substantially at the expense of the citizen by virtue of the monopoly of office, granted him by the state, of which he could call himself the owner. As there was no requirement to exercise an office in person, anyone could become the owner of more offices, which he could rent out in order to enjoy their income and status, without any effort on his own part.

There are naturally only estimates of how much any office brought in. However, these show that during the sixteenth century and the first decades of the seventeenth there was a strongly increasing

In 1661 Juan Pareja depicted the office of a Madrid tax farmer under the title *The calling of Matthew.*

Tax farmers were hated by the people because of their unbridled profiteering.

Madrid, Museo del Prado

demand for offices, mainly from the bourgeois elites, while the states created an even greater supply of them. Ownership of land usually produced a return of 5 per cent per year, but the minimum return expected from offices was 8 per cent. In Rome in the 1480s the sale of offices was regulated by law. A clerical office in the Apostolic Chancery produced 10 per cent in 1495; about 1560 offices would on average yield 12 per cent. There seems to have been a steep climb in the kingdom of Naples in the second half of the sixteenth century, with prices increasing three, four or even sixfold in nominal terms, depending upon the kind of office. Even after discounting steep inflation this meant strong growth, after which the yields stagnated. Under Henry IV, from 1594 to 1610, the gross national product and the demand for offices grew strongly in France; there was at that time no inflation, but the price of office increased threefold.

The ways in which offices were sold varied from country to country and from time to time. In Venice offices were sold as fiefs, with the highest reserved to be co-opted from among families of the patriciate. In the papal Curia and in France legal prescriptions lent an official character to a practice to which a blind eye was usually turned elsewhere in spite of various prohibitions. On the feudal model the owners of offices even acquired the right to pass them on by inheritance. Court functions and officer ranks in the army were reserved for the nobility, who already thought themselves passed over by the *nouveaux riches*. One answer consisted in the requirement of a kind of entry fee, an amount which the candidate had to pay into the treasury to validate his candidacy; he or his heirs then had to try and recover this from his successor. After the initial benefit to the state, it lost its control of the office and the income resulting from it; the holder could not be dismissed from office without the state repaying the initial entry fee. Another answer was for the government to farm out its offices for a limited period to the highest bidder. This method was

The collection of sacks of grain on a royal demesne carried out under the supervision of a official. Sixteenth-century French miniature.
Paris, Bibliothèque nationale de France

used mostly for collecting taxes, enabling the state to bank the estimated yield for the period in a lump sum – although it naturally meant that the collectors did all they could to pull in considerably more.

Against the limited benefits of an assured yield and immediate liquidity was the risk that the tax collectors would squeeze the subjects to the point where they rose against the state. The tax farmers soon started forming cartels which also put pressure on the state income. Associations were also created by office holders forming pressure groups to promote their interests. Profitable offices were often allocated to favourites or clients in those countries where their sales were not officially regulated – everywhere in fact except in the Papal State and in France – enabling powerful lords such as courtiers and private secretaries to reap a rich harvest. In the reign of Charles I (1625–1649) the English treasury paid on average £350,000 per year in salaries out of

a total budget of £900,000 to £1 million. The 'spice' paid to officials by subjects seeking office came, however, on average to some £300,000 per annum. In Portugal in the mid-seventeenth century emoluments from offices always contributed more than their salaries, so that officials were only dependent for their material needs to a limited degree on the state which they were supposed to be serving.[13]

The privatization of the public sector can be interpreted as a failure of the states to achieve the objectives which they had set themselves for the public administration. The reason for this was clearly an internal weakening as a consequence of the priorities dictated by the competition between states. The benefits to the state were short term and limited; their subjects suffered considerable aggravation from the pressure from those who like a swarm of locusts sucked the country dry in the name of the state, but to their own advantage. Reactions

Peter van der Meulen immortalized the Colbert family, *c.* 1680. In the centre is Jean Baptiste Colbert, the famous chief minister of France.

The prelate on the balcony is Jacques Nicolas, appointed archbishop of Rouen in 1680. To the right of Colbert is probably Charles,

from 1668 to 1674 ambassador to England and from 1679 minister for foreign affairs. The figure on the far right may be Colbert's son,

Jean-Baptiste Antoine, who assisted his father in his administrative work. London, The Wellington Museum

were not lacking: in France, during the 125 years from 1662 to 1787, there were on average thirty-eight popular uprisings every year, half of which were directed against the taxation and repression by the state.[14]

On the other hand, the bureaucracy started to form a new elite mainly of bourgeois origin, which represented an alternative form of administration to the ancient supremacy of the large landowners. As relatively independent officials they led the state in a way that did not *per se* exploit the subjects any more than any other regime might at that time have done. With their qualifications, and relying on the fact that they could not be dismissed and even held hereditary title to their office, they also provided a check to the royal power, since, in spite of all high-flown talk of absolutism, Louis XIV in fact had direct control

over very few officials. In order to recover its control in spite of the privatization, the French crown introduced the office of *intendant*, an inspector surrounded by his deputy and assistants, with authority in a province from which he himself did not come.

On the whole the new rich – since their offices all too evidently enriched them – were better educated and more interested in the cultural products of the French Golden Age (the seventeenth century). Moreover, beyond any doubt the central governments in most European states – France, Spain, Portugal, Great Britain, most of the German and Habsburg lands, Milan, Savoy-Piedmont and even Russia – had in the eighteenth century developed more effective methods of implementing their policy at the local level, and by doing so maintaining internal order better. This order was based on the

Portrait by Diego Velasquez of Don Diego de Corral y Arellano, Chief Councillor of Castile and secretary of Philip III of Spain, 1624.
In exchange for the indispensable loyalty of the grandees or high nobility,
the king allowed them in practice to exercise complete power over their estates and their serfs.
Madrid, Museo del Prado

Title page of Richard Brathwaite, *The English gentleman,* engraving by Robert Vaughan, c. 1630.
Note all the good qualities required of a gentleman surrounding the central figure.
London, British Museum, Prints and Drawings

social order and pacification which the earlier smaller circles of power, which had gradually been incorporated into the states, had achieved over the centuries. The whole difference between the still very diverse forms and dimensions of public powers lurked in the relationships between the local, regional and central concentrations of power. In the eighteenth century not a single monarchy could gain respect down to the villages without the active assistance of the intermediary powers. It was precisely the lack of any tradition of urban or district structures which made it impossible in Russia to introduce the Prussian *Polizeiordnung* as the empress Catherine the Great (1762–1796), with her German origins and as a fervent admirer of King Frederick the Great, had wanted to do. The social order was in any case still that of the great landowners, whether or not they had feudal rights. Even the most enlightened absolute monarchs did not interfere in the direct and quasi-total power of the landlords over their serfs. In exchange for the essential loyalty of the nobility, and here and there also of the high bourgeoisie, allowances had to be made. In this way kings also responded to a constant pressure from these elites. In comparison with the high ambitions to which the kings had given vent during the fourteenth century – and still more during the sixteenth – based on the doctrines prompted by their scholarly lawyers, the monarchies of the seventeenth and eighteenth centuries were much less centralized, homogeneous and absolutist than they themselves pretended, and than most historians have rather naively accepted from their propaganda.

The submission of Granada, with Boabdil kneeling before Isabella of Castile in 1492.
Theatrical tableau erected beside the route followed by Joanna of Castile into Brussels at her Joyful Entry there in 1496.
Berlin, Staatliche Museen Preussischer Kulturbesitz, Kupferstichkabinet

The expulsion in 1609 of more than 275,000 *moriscos* from Spain meant a substantial drain on the economy of Valencia, Aragon and Murcia.

Design sketch for a painting by Vicente Carducho in 1627 as his entry in a competition

arranged by Philip IV of Spain for the redecoration of the royal palace.

Madrid, Museo del Prado

The services of the Church

Until the seventeenth century politics and religion continued to be very closely linked. During the Middle Ages some monarchies in Europe were Catholic and others Greek Orthodox. The Catholic Church's system of norms and values formed the self-evident ideological frame of the western monarchies. Spain was a notable exception in the sense that, despite phases of bitter conflict between Catholics and Muslims, there was for a long period very intensive interaction between Muslims, Jews and Christians. This was expressed in the society – albeit segmented – of the towns and villages, in the maintenance of active economic and cultural relationships and in mutual assistance. The continued use of the Moorish style was entirely natural in the palaces built for the Christian kings in the Alcazar of Seville after the *reconquista* (1248). This tolerance should certainly be ascribed in the first place to the Muslims, who in all the areas they conquered, including the Balkans when the Ottoman empire advanced there from the fourteenth century, permitted the practice of the 'two other religions of the book', Judaism and Christianity.

Catholicism was, however, in general fanatically universalist and also fought against heretical Christian tendencies with fire and sword. The crusades and the repression of the Cathars and their sympathizers in northern Italy, southern France and Aragon were extremely bloody in the thirteenth and fourteenth centuries. John Hus' reforming movement in Bohemia in the first half of the fifteenth century was suppressed under the sign of the cross by the armies of the emperor, who naturally strengthened his own political authority in the process. There, just as during some other revolts, such as that of the Flemish peasants between 1323 and 1328 and the English peasants' revolt in 1381, the subjects perceived links between an oppressive social order and its justification by the extremely prosperous Church whose top hierarchy leaned heavily upon the holders of secular power. The repudiation of social order therefore also included a denial of the Church's view of the world, which led to unmistakably anticlerical utterances.

The Reformation put the interrelationship of Church and state, of which the personal and institutional aspects had already been questioned, under extreme pressure. On the one hand this can be understood because the fragile position of the papacy since the start of the fourteenth century, the deterioration of monastic discipline and of the lifestyle of priests, the crude sale of indulgences, the instrumentalizing and formalizing of piety, gave as many reasons to broad sections of the population to desire a thoroughgoing reformation of the Church. Because of the secular orientation of the hierarchy, and particularly of the Renaissance popes, the Church did not offer a satisfactory doctrinal answer to the desires for authenticity on the part of the faithful. Hence the reforming movement, unlike in former centuries, was not limited to certain regions, but soon found itself spreading all over Europe.

On the other hand this crisis of belief came to a peak in the framework of the states, because they were so closely interwoven with the Church, both in personnel and in rituals and ideas. During the sixteenth century all states were enthusiastically moving towards expanding their institutional cadres and sharpening up the intellectual, or rather ideological, legitimation of the strengthened monarchy. Precisely in this situation royal tolerance of religious – and by implication also political – dissidence was nil. The efforts of the kings to establish themselves in their territories were directed in fact towards the exclusion in their area of all competitive powers, such as the extra-territorial jurisdiction of princes or bishops. In the Low Countries the emperor Charles v and his son Philip ii were successful in three stages. First Charles v made a treaty with the king of France by which France in 1529 gave up all its sovereign rights in Artois and Flanders. Next in 1548 Charles v isolated his territories from the Burgundian heritage in a separate legal circumscription within the Empire, but without effective obligations. Finally in 1559 it was possible

to restructure the dioceses in the Low Countries so that their boundaries henceforth coincided with those of the secular authorities, by which the exclusion of the area from formal foreign interventions became a fact. This completed the control of the state over the hierarchy of the Church, as the involvement of the king in high ecclesiastical appointments had been achieved some time earlier: in 1515 the pope had granted this right to the recently installed prince and later emperor Charles v, and a year later to the French king Francis i. In exchange a year's income had to be handed over to Rome for each office to which an appointment was made. The popes of the time of the Gregorian reforms in the eleventh to thirteenth centuries denounced such practices, but in the sixteenth century their ambitions were on a considerably lower level.

In Spain the link between Catholicism and the formation of the state grew closer in the last decades of the fifteenth century as a consequence of the final phase of the *reconquista*. The union of the kingdoms of Aragon and Castile was achieved in 1469 by the marriage of the Catholic kings, Ferdinand and Isabella. They conquered Granada, the last of the Muslim dominions, in January 1492. Scarcely three months later they published the decree that all practising Jews who did not convert to Christianity within four months must be driven out of Spain, abandoning most of their possessions. In Castile there must have been 200,000, in Aragon 60,000, respectively 3 to 5 per cent and 6 to 7 per cent of the population. They filled strategic functions in the economic, cultural and administrative life of the country, and had even contributed generously to financing the conquest of Granada. The Catholic kings thus relieved themselves of having to repay that debt, but the symbolic significance of the decision was unmistakable: there was only room for a single religious faith within the new unified Spain. Towards the Muslim population, which to a large extent consisted of peasants and manual workers and was therefore less the object of Christian jealousy than the Jews, the Catholic kings remained tolerant for some time. In 1499 the Muslims in Castile were given the choice of converting or moving out, but that did not apply in Aragon, Valencia and Granada. In 1508 Muslim practices and dress were forbidden. Further discriminatory measures led in 1568 to a revolt in Granada, which ended in 1570 with a pardon linked with deportation for the *moriscos*, many of whom fled to Valencia, where by around 1600 they made up a third of the population. 'Reasons of state', however, led to their mass expulsion

An illustration of the death at the stake in 1415 of John Hus, the Bohemian reformer.
His 'heretical' writings were also burned at the same time.
Illustration from the Berne Chronicles by Diebold Schilling, 1483. Berne, Burgerbibliothek

Condemned heretics burned at the communal stake in Schwarzenburg.
Illustration from the Spiez Chronicles by Diebold Schilling, 1485. Berne, Bürgerbibliothek

Sixteenth-century satirical Protestant print on the vulgar sale of indulgences by the 'Romish fisherman', the Pope of Rome.
Rotterdam, Atlas van Stolk

The Elector of Saxony supported the Reformation of Martin Luther.
On this 1554 tapestry by Peter Heymans the theologian preaches before princes of the Houses of Saxony and Pomerania.
Greifswald, Ernst-Moritz-Arndt-Universität

too, when King Philip III in 1609 had to sign his humiliating truce with the Protestant rebels in the Netherlands. On the strength of an invented complaint often also used against the Jews, that they were plotting an uprising, an estimated 275,000 Muslims were in 1611 forced to cross to North Africa on ships of the navy, as a kind of imaginary compensation for the king's political defeat.

The Spanish state which had developed from the *reconquista* defined itself during the sixteenth century pre-eminently as *the* Catholic monarchy. It is easy to see why Charles V and Philip II as kings of Spain had problems with the strong Protestant movement in their northern dominions, the Low Countries, and Charles V also in the Empire. Since political unity was assumed to mean unity of belief, those who no longer saw salvation in the Catholic Church clashed fatally with the power of the state. However, where monarchs became convinced by the doctrine of reform, they imposed the new faith on their subjects from above. In this way Lutheranism spread quickly in some territories of the Empire and in the Scandinavian and Baltic countries. It was the *de facto* independence of the free cities and principalities of the Empire that made the imposition and preaching of the reformed ideology possible in many places, in spite of the imperial edict published in 1521 at the Diet of Worms, in which Luther was exiled and the propagation of his ideas labelled as heretical and forbidden. John the Constant, Elector of Saxony (where Luther lived), and Philip the Magnanimous, the Landgrave of Hesse, supported the Reformation by 1525, while the Grand Master of the Teutonic Knights, Albert of Hohenzollern, turned his demesnes into a secular state and from now on had himself called duke of Prussia.

In 1529 six princes and fourteen free cities of the Empire 'protested' against the revocation by King Ferdinand, of the Romans, of his earlier guarantee of safety to the Lutherans. During the next few years the duke of Württemberg (1534) and the kings of Sweden (1536) and Denmark (1537) went over to the new doctrines, and established national Lutheran churches. This involved the confiscation of church property in their dominions, which gave an enormous stimulus to the treasuries of the young Protestant states. In Hesse and Württemberg it came to 30 per cent of their total income, enabling among other things the University of Marburg to be founded. Moreover, this again meant a highly symbolic act which not only underpinned the glory of the dynasty and the new identity of the state, but also emphasized the intellectual and rational outlook on

the world of Protestantism. In most states, the church property benefited mainly the prince's treasury, reducing his financial dependence on the representatives of the Estates.

The political battle about Protestantism followed the traditional characteristic course in the Holy Roman Empire: alliances and non-aggression treaties. The peasant revolt in southern and central Germany in 1524–1525 was partly inspired by the Anabaptist ideas of Thomas Münzer and rejected by Luther for doctrinal reasons. The rulers smothered the movement in blood and so strengthened their position in the long run. Towns and princes formed a political alliance of Luther's sympathizers, the League of Schmalkalde, which was defeated in 1546–1547 by Charles V. Yet in 1555 the Diet had to declare a religious truce on the basis of freedom of religion for the Lutherans (following the Augsburg Confession set up by Melanchthon in 1529) by which in effect territories and towns acquired the right to establish their own independent religions and churches. With this the territorialization of religion in the Empire became a fact and the imperial ambition of universality was erased.

It was not only the Empire which was too extensive and administratively too little unified to withstand the Reformation as a politico-religious union. The Spanish imperium, too, was unable to suppress for long the strong support for the various reforming movements in the Low Countries. The repression of the Inquisition – though of increasing harshness and extent – could not prevent important segments in the large towns, up to a third of the population, opting for Calvinism, Lutheranism, or some other persuasion. Particularly in the most urbanized and economically influential south, sympathy for Calvinism grew strongly after 1560. After the failure of attempts by the nobility for reconciliation between the government and the Protestants, violence escalated. A cyclical economic crisis in the rural textile industry produced the massive iconoclasm which, starting in August 1566 in south-west Flanders, swept over the Low Countries. King Philip II opted for the repression of the rising of large sections of the population. Sixty to eighty thousand soldiers under Spanish command only succeeded in forcing the southern Netherlands back under royal authority by 1585, eighteen years later, after which the Protestants were still given two years in which to leave the country. The estimated 200,000 – 10 per cent of the population – who took that opportunity belonged largely to the economic and cultural upper classes. Most went to the

The Emperor Charles v presiding over the Diet in Augsburg in 1530. On his right hand are representatives of the Catholic Church, opposite them those of the Protestant congregations. The Augsburg Confession was read aloud during this ceremony.
Coburg, Kunstsammlungen der Veste

northern provinces, which – in spite of a war which continued until 1648 – managed to maintain their position as a bastion of Protestantism.

The shift to Protestantism here was not through imposition by the government as it had been in the principalities of the Empire, since the revolt had in fact been directed against 'oppression of conscience' by the state. Until far into the seventeenth century the Calvinists were an influential minority who kept religious toleration alive – in spite of restrictions imposed on Catholics, and quarrels between orthodox and moderate parties. The Republic of the United Provinces followed rather the example of the Swiss and German urban republics, led by Geneva and Zurich, which were based on the towns' autonomy. At the local level that implied in principle religious pluralism based on the various congregations.

The marital adventures of King Henry viii lay at the origin of the break – in the first instance political – with the Roman Church in England in 1534,

when Parliament approved the bill making the king the head of the Anglican Church. He demanded an oath of loyalty to this Act, which cost his chancellor Thomas More his head. Henry viii appropriated and sold church property, out of which the exchequer and the landed gentry did well. Radical religious reformation only started through the Calvinist inspiration of the Puritans. In 1563 the Anglican Church adopted Calvinist doctrines and there was an outbreak of persecution of Catholics. This was accompanied by the imposition of Protestantism on Ireland. The risings against this in 1579 and 1598 were bloodily suppressed, and in Ireland the land began to be distributed to English Protestant colonists. This politico-religious imperialism was to create a problem which was to be a thorn in the flesh of the British state into and throughout the twentieth century. England and Scotland in any case experienced their own wars of religion as a form of protest against the attempts of Charles i

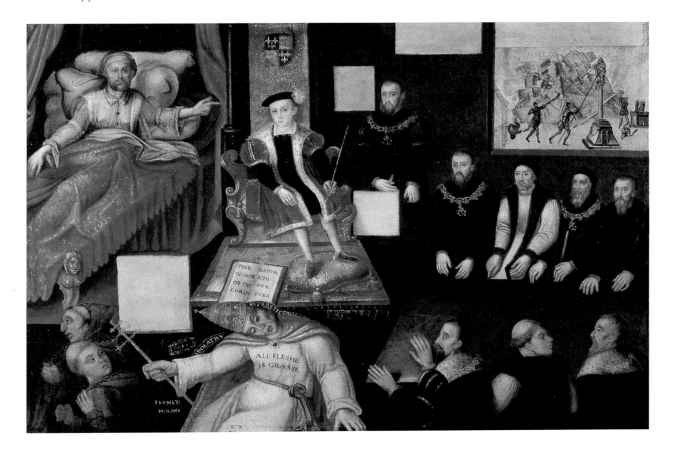

Allegorical painting of about 1548
showing the dying Henry VIII of England,
succeeded by the young Edward VI in a strongly anti-papal atmosphere.
London, National Portrait Gallery

(1625–1645) to impose absolute rule. Puritan Calvinists and Scottish Presbyterians accused the Anglican Church of papacy. The subsequent Civil War settled both Anglicanism and absolutism. During the 1660s Puritans and Presbyterians were persecuted (the Killing Time). Only with the coronation of the Dutch Stadtholder as William III (1689–1702) was a Toleration Act passed which granted freedom of religion to all Protestant denominations as long as they accepted the Trinity and held public services. The Scots re-established their own Church.

In France the Calvinist sympathies of a section of the nobility in some regions led to fierce wars of religion (1562–1598) in which the degree of toleration in the kingdom was the stake. The attempt of the court to smother the Huguenot trend by murdering its leaders escalated into a fearful bloodbath in the famous Massacre of St Bartholomew on 24 August 1572. The population of Paris and of other towns revenged past ills by murdering and plun-

dering 22,000 Protestants in the course of a few days. Both the monarchy and the Huguenot movement came out of this conflict weakened. Two kings in succession, Henry III and Henry IV, were to be murdered by Catholic fanatics. Henry IV had tried to find a reconciliation between the religious differences in a way unique for the monarchic Europe of that time. He had himself enjoyed a sound Protestant upbringing, and assumed the leadership of the Huguenots, but *pour les besoins de la cause* he had twice been received back into the bosom of the Catholic Church, in 1593 actually in the royal mausoleum of St Denis. By his military successes he was able to bring to an end the religious wars which had afflicted France for nearly forty years. His siege of Paris, then in the hands of the Catholic League which refused to acknowledge him as the legitimate king, still cost 45 000 deaths out of a population of 220, 000 in 1590. Exhaustion was then, as so often, the reason for the war coming to an end.

Setting out from the church of Saint-Jean en Grève
(destroyed in the revolution) in the heart of Paris,

a large number of armed supporters of the Catholic League demonstrate in 1590.

Paris, Musée Carnavalet

In 1618 Protestant Bohemian rebels threw two Habsburg deputy governors
and a secretary from a window of the Hradschin Palace in Prague, as a protest against the emperor's Catholic faith.
View of the royal palace in Prague, a watercoloured drawing of 1836 by Eduard Gurk.
Vienna, Graphische Sammlung Albertina

The famous Edict of Nantes in 1598, in which Henry IV laid down the compromise between the faiths, granted the Huguenots freedom of worship in some places, while forbidding it elsewhere. Corporate privileges, special jurisdictions, military fortresses (La Rochelle, Montauban *et al.*) and civil rights guaranteed the Huguenots a safe existence, which a class society founded on privileged groups was able to provide. This recognition was made easier by the large concentrations of Huguenots in Languedoc, where they are estimated to have been a million strong, particularly in the towns and among the male, literate, and to some degree wealthy sections of the population. In the total population before the beginning of the wars of religion there are estimated to have been a maximum of 1.75 million Huguenot sympathizers, 8.75 per cent of the French population, with around 1,400 congregations, of which 800 were concentrated in the south.[15] Can it be a coincidence that the concentrations of Huguenots coincide roughly with those of the Cathars in the twelfth and thirteenth centuries, in a region where urbanization had since Roman times been much denser than in the rest of France? Thus in one sense Henry IV applied the territorial right to self-determination in religious affairs as it had been

Despite the spread of printing, the pulpit remained
a powerful weapon for influencing the faithful.
Sermon by the papal nuncio C. Musso
given before the Emperor Ferdinand I
and his court in the Augustinerkirche
in Vienna around 1560.
Painting by Jacob Seisenegger.
Vienna, Graf Harrach Kunstgallerie

Satirical print of the *Roman idolatry*, the Catholic liturgy.
Coloured woodcut of 1573 by Tobias Stimmer, reprinted in 1576 by Bernhard Jobin. Zürich, Zentralbibliothek

recognized since 1555 in the Empire. However, by 1627 Cardinal Richelieu had reconquered the refuge of La Rochelle, and broken the military power of the Huguenots. As the monarchy acquired more absolutist traits under Louis XIV, religious toleration again became unacceptable in France, and the persecutions resumed. They led in 1685 to the revocation of the Edict of Nantes, with a prohibition on public demonstrations of Protestantism except in recently conquered Alsace, where the imperial legislation protected Lutheranism.

Louis' repression led to an exodus of an estimated 200,000 to 270,000 Huguenots, 1 per cent of the total French population, and 20 per cent of the Calvinists. They left for Protestant areas, mainly to the free imperial city of Frankfurt, from where many

went on to Brandenburg, where the Electors hoped that this bourgeois immigration would help their traditional economies to advance. Large numbers also settled in the United Provinces and in England.

The most terrible war of religion broke out in a reaction by the Catholic Habsburg Emperor Ferdinand II against the rising of the Protestant Estates of Bohemia. In 1618 in their opposition to the strict imposition of the Catholic faith by Vienna, they had thrown the two Habsburg regents and a secretary out of a window of the Hradcin palace in Prague, repeating with this symbolic act one committed two hundred years earlier during the Hussite revolt of 1419. Perhaps the Prague Protestants also wanted to avenge the Protestant leader Gaspard de Coligny, who had been flung out of a window of the Louvre

Supported by the state, the Church was able to give expression to its philosophy by a strong campaign for civilization in the form of art, education and social care. *San Diego de Alcala and the poor,* painted in 1682 by Murillo. Madrid, Real Academia de San Fernando

during the Massacre of St Bartholomew in Paris. Whatever the reason, the Habsburgs were not prepared to put up with losing an important part of their *Hausmacht,* quite close to Vienna, which was the prospect when the leader of the Protestant Union, Frederick, the Elector Palatine, was chosen as king of Bohemia. The flagrant lese-majesty of the Prague rebels brought into operation a system by which a broad Catholic coalition provoked an equally broad alliance of Protestant princes. In 1620 the imperial and Bavarian army defeated the Bohemian Protestants on the White Mountain.

There was yet another rising of Bohemian nobles and peasants in 1626–1627 against the imposition of an absolutist Catholic rule, but again the Bavarian army was the stronger. The result was the confiscation of the nobles' estates, and the emigration of 250,000 dissidents. Meanwhile a colossal trial of strength had started between Protestant and Catholic princes, which was to last till 1648. Of the 28 million Protestants in 1600, only 15 million were left in 1648. Catholicism had consolidated its position at the cost of enormous human suffering.

The forced emigration of hundreds of thousands

In the course of the sixteenth century governments in Catholic countries took harsh action against alleged witches.
Impoverished and single countrywomen were the target of the witch hunt.
Illustrated pamphlet distributed on the occasion of a sensational witch trial in the German town of Derneburg in 1555.
Nuremburg, Germanisches Nationalmuseum

of Jews, Muslims and Protestants between 1492 and 1700 strengthened the religious homogeneity of the European states, so that they each took on their diverse territorial identities more plainly. England, the United Provinces and Sweden were the Protestant great powers; Spain, Austria, and eventually also France, the Catholic ones. Churches were from now on state churches. In Poland the Orthodox Church even came under papal authority but retained its doctrines and rites. In the overwhelmingly Orthodox areas there were distinctions between the Greek, Bulgarian, Serbian and Russian Orthodox churches. The Russian one had since 1589 been under its own Moscow patriarch, who had close links with the tsar's political interests.

Every state with its homogeneous religion established a system for influencing its own subjects, directed at the formation of an exclusive confessional identity in which the authority of the government implied that of both the state and the Church. The exclusion of heterodox influences was a condition for this, and that required censorship and political control. The importance of this had increased appreciably because the dissemination of

new ideas in the sixteenth century could proceed much more rapidly than in previous centuries as printed propaganda texts, pamphlets and all kinds of symbolic illustrations could now be used. Translations of the Bible and theological writings were soon distributed, in print, by the reformers. In addition Humanism had considerably heightened the interest and belief in the effects of education, so that in the first place the Protestants, and later also the Catholics, tried to imprint their ideology through a proper school system from an early age. Control over these new powerful influential media therefore demanded all the attention of the 'caring' authorities. Through its Index of Prohibited Books, first published in 1559, the Catholic Church tried to protect its faithful adherents from unorthodox influences, and it organized public burnings of books thought to be heretical. In the unitary confessional system the loss of religious independence was coupled with the destruction of political rights.

Political and cultural elites combined to impose a new system of norms on subject populations, with all the instruments available to them, including where necessary deterrence and force. Clergy, university professors, teachers in the new Latin schools, judges, censors and publishers prepared the way for a new social and political consensus which was unleashed on the population like a real civilizing offensive. On the Catholic side parish priests, in accordance with the prescriptions of the Council of Trent (1545–1563) were better trained and more tightly controlled by their bishops; the Jesuits, established as an order in 1534, were in the van of the highly disciplined scholarly ecclesiastics who took over education, and the papal power was reinforced. Similarly Catholics and Protestants used the care of the poor, the sick and the needy to bring these dependants safely into the fold and keep them there. Disciplining the faithful as loyal subjects and as members of a congregation was the manifest objective of all denominations, although the reformers did this even more strictly in the smaller territories where they shared power with the Catholics.

The interweaving of Church and state within the state frontiers made a much firmer influence possible than had ever been the case before, and this benefited both parties. The Church knew that it was supported by the strong arm of the state in the expulsion of unorthodox individuals, writings and pictures, and was given full scope to impose its philosophy on its congregations and parishes, in education and in social care. The increase in numbers of these institutions of social control, which were managed by the churches and were paid for by the faithful themselves, or by the yield of the church patrimony whether it had been secularized or not, cost the state nothing.

The peak of this confessional civilization campaign was reached between 1570 and 1650. For the state it helped to implement the hierarchy of society on the model of paternalist authority, emanating from God to the king, through his cultural agents (judges, preachers, priests, teachers and so on) to the father of the family. Each of these levels fitted functionally into a pattern of obedience: wife and children obeyed the father, all of them obeyed their spiritual leaders, they in their turn obeyed the king, who claimed to be granted his authority directly from God's grace. The Church, with its close ties to the state, saw a unique opportunity to drum into the population a suitable awe of God and fear of evil; the state gained an ideal host of unpaid employees for the social disciplining of its subjects. The state, with its legislative and judicial role, marched on a broad front into the territory of the Church, by publishing decrees about heresy, witchcraft, blasphemy, moral-

ity and even against ugly and dishonourable expressions, as Charles v did in 1554.

The Catholic Church and the states sympathetic to it acted forcefully against what they called heretics (Protestants) and, particularly from 1570 to 1630, against alleged witches. Thousands of stakes were kindled for these two categories, because only fire was thought capable of eradicating their sins entirely. Designating scapegoats appeared to be an effective means of enforcing discipline, sometimes instigated by local authorities, but always encouraged by Church and state, even in Protestant countries. Those branded as criminals were mostly single country women who at this time of economic crisis had lost their incomes and were marginalized. In the general climate of religious bigotry they were easily suspected of carrying out heathen practices, which were interpreted as consorting with the Devil. Midwives, too, ran a risk of being stigmatized in this way. Since the appearance in 1487 of *Malleus Maleficarum* (Witch Hammer) by two German inquisitors, based on a papal bull of 1484, trials of witches were thought to be legitimized by canon law. Society was able, under the pressure of politico-religious oppression, to project its anxieties onto vulnerable women who fitted the template created by the Inquisition, so contributing to the tightening of discipline which governments were so anxious to impose. These saw their opportunity clear to make the imposition of their standards felt into the farthest corners of the country by persecuting witches. It is interesting to note that it was not only in states typically characterized as those of the Catholic Counter Reformation, such as Bavaria, the southern Netherlands and Lorraine, that there was an intensive persecution of witches. In Lorraine there were 3,000 witch trials between 1580 and 1630, 90 per cent of which ended in a judgement of guilty. In some Protestant areas, too, such as Scotland and Sweden, the persecution of witches facilitated the penetrative power of the Church. Their limited distribution in Spain, where the Moorish scapegoats had already been persecuted; and in the United Provinces, where religious toleration, the lack of an absolute and centralist authority, and economic prosperity provided little encouragement to adopt this terror, is striking.

This whole disciplinary activity naturally did not banish all heresy or unbelief, but did produce more obedient, docile, respectful and malleable subjects than the rather uncontrollable masses of previous centuries. This civilizing campaign made it possible for the cost of internal security to be

On taking up their office the magistrates of Lüneburg swore their oath of good faith on this costly 'civil oath crystal':
a silver gilt reliquary of 1443. Berlin, Staatliche Museen Preussischer Kulturbesitz, Kunstgewerbemuseum

substantially reduced, which was a remarkable and perhaps indeed essential achievement in the context of the steadily increasing size of states. Unfortunately the states continued to spend the energy saved in this way mainly on expanding their external dominions. During the eighteenth century the barbarity of state terror grew milder. The past campaigns had achieved their disciplinary effect, but they were subject to increasingly sharper criticism by enlightened philosophers who condemned the irrationality of the persecutions, so that finally the one-sided religious legitimacy of the state came under pressure.[16]

The voice of the people

The initiative for the continued competition for greater concentrations of the means of power, reflected in the formation of increasingly stronger armed states, obviously came from the individuals and institutions who already possessed a superiority of power: feudal lords, large landowners, princes, princes of the Church, and oligarchies in the towns. The result of this age-long conflict was not, however, decided only by these elites. The people on whom greater ranges of power had been imposed were not just passive observers; communities

Tapestry illustrating the oath of good faith sworn by Philip the Handsome on his Joyful Entry to Brabant in 1494. Brussels workshop.
Amsterdam, Rijksmuseum

formed their own political organizations which were for a long time an important factor in the general rivalry. Feudal lords who were no match for their more powerful rivals sometimes made alliances against their overlords, and in doing so sought the support of their natural opponents in the towns or in ecclesiastical institutions. In short, the formation of stronger concentrations of power provoked reactions in which the losers formed coalitions which could turn the tide at the first sign of weakness on the part of the oppressor. In this process of give and take forms of representation and opposition arose by which western Europe was to make a unique contribution to the history of the world: parliamentarianism.

The feudal contract was one of the foundations of this process by its condition that a vassal might refuse service to his lord if this lord did not fulfil his obligations to him. Both parties had sworn loyalty to each other, by an oath taken on sacred objects, so that even the weaker party could invoke this and, if necessary, offer resistance to the wrongful acts of the stronger one. These kinds of oaths implied that private agreements became sanctified, so that breach of contract also invited a spiritual sanction. They served as a model for agreements to which

Complaints boxes built into the wall of Verona town hall
for denouncing, anonymously or not, usurers and smugglers.

In the early seventeenth century the Parisian 'Merchant Provost' and the magistrates traditionally
had themselves painted kneeling and praying round a crucifix.
At the end of the century Nicolas de Largillière painted the same group of officials in this completely secularized context.
Amiens, Musée de Picardie

our modern thinking would ascribe a public law nature. The recognition of a town's privileges in the eleventh and twelfth centuries was also done under oath, in which the written record held less weight in law than the public ceremonial. The recognition of a prince, too, was solemnized in the form of a reciprocal oath of homage, in which first the incoming prince swore to protect and safeguard the rights of his subjects and of the Church, and then his vassals and other representatives of his subjects swore an oath of allegiance to him. This public law enlargement of the feudal oath of homage conceals the fundamental right of the real and pseudo-vassals – such as the privileged town communities – to decide freely on the acceptance of a lord or ruler, and to hold him to the obligations he had undertaken, on sanction of breach of contract.

As a result of the high mortality among the stalwart warriors, the designation of a legitimate successor provided a frequently recurring problem, about which there were often disputes because of the diversity of legal rules for succession, and the wide spread of branches of families. Rules of succession such as that of primogeniture, and the acceptance (England) or exclusion (France, the Holy Roman Empire) of women, in theory directed the choice, but gave no guarantee either against ambiguity or for a satisfactory solution. One succession in every two raised problems, either because there were too many equally qualified claimants, or because the lawful successor was a minor, incompetent, or a woman – which even in those countries where women enjoyed the right of succession, such as England, Castile and the Low Countries, always raised questions about their marriage partner and his claims. In these circumstances those subjects who were summoned to acknowledge a new prince had scope to express a preference and to lay down conditions for their agreement. This applied even more strongly in those areas where the crown was by definition assigned by election, such as in the Holy Roman Empire and in its original vassal kingdoms of Bohemia, Hungary and Poland. When after 1440 the Habsburgs in effect made the crown of Germany

When the English Parliament demanded supervision of King Richard II's financial policy, he replaced that Parliament
by a new one more favourably disposed towards him. The terror he then unleashed in 1398 led to a rising and his arrest at Flint castle
by Henry Bolingbroke in August 1399. He was killed in Pontefract castle soon afterwards. Fifteenth-century French miniature.
London, British Library

In 1591 Wolfgang Breny portrayed a trial at Niederbussnang. At the head of the table are the judge and the guardian.

Behind them the beadle and in front of them are twelve justices, whose coats of arms are shown in the border. Frauenfeld, Thurgau Museum

hereditary, the battle for election always provoked intense rivalry between the great princely families, so that the kingship as such remained weak.

After the twelfth century there is evidence all over Europe of the involvement of representatives of various orders, including the townspeople, in the recognition of princes and the formulation of ground rules for their administrations. Not, however, in France: until 1328 the succession stayed without major problems in the Capetian dynasty, and when this died out the barons, by themselves, decided that Philip of Valois enjoyed their preference over Edward III of England, because he was a 'natural prince', and in any case belonged to a family that had been born and bred in the country since living memory. Only on the disinheritance of the Dauphin in 1420 were meetings of the Estates and the University of Paris asked for their agreement, but this was soon overtaken by events.[17] The regency of Catherine de' Medici and the switch to the Bourbon dynasty in 1589, too, were effected without any representation of the people.

In 1135 Alfonso VII had himself proclaimed emperor of Spain before a solemn assembly in which as well as high ecclesiastical dignitaries and great barons, 'judges' also took part, by which may be meant the elected representatives of the towns. This was in any event the case in 1187 when the administrators of fifty towns took part in the session of the royal *Curia* of Castile when the right of succession of Berengaria was established, together with her marriage contract with Conrad of Hohenstaufen. A year later King Alfonso IX of León swore – after a disputed succession to the throne – before the 'archbishops, bishops, religious orders, counts and other nobles of the kingdom, together with selected citizens of the towns' to respect the good customs and to take decisions about war and peace only in consultation with 'the bishops, nobles and honest men'. In its turn the assemblage swore allegiance, and promised to maintain the law and peace in the kingdom.[18] In the neighbouring kingdom of Aragon general *cortes* of more than a hundred members, including some from the towns, had been operative since the mid-twelfth century. They discussed political questions such as the maintenance of order, the administration of justice, taxation and coinage. A general *cortes* consisting of 'barons, knights, citizens and fiefholders of the castles and villages' swore allegiance in 1214 to King James, then still a minor, in exchange for financial and juridical benefits. During dynastic crises, such as between 1275 and 1325 in Castile-León, the *cortes*

was able to formulate their complaints about all kinds of matters in the administration of the country, to exercise effective influence on the government and determine the choice of one of the rival pretenders to the throne.[19] The extensive rights which the Spanish nobility and the towns had acquired in the framework of the *reconquista* lent them a stronger bargaining position against the crown than that of their peers elsewhere in Europe.

In Flanders the representatives of the nobles and the large towns took the next step as early as 1127. From a count who had been imposed on them as their liege lord by the king of France, and who in no time at all violated all the privileges which he had granted on his inauguration and sworn to, they demanded the public repair of the wrong he had done. They proposed to commission a special court to give judgement on their dispute, assembled from wise men belonging to each of the three Estates. If this court should reach the decision that the count had violated the rights of his subjects and he still refused to repair the breaches, they should depose the count as an oath breaker and look for a more suitable candidate. The proposed assembly never took place, because the count, in accordance with the ancient tradition of chivalry, took arms and happened to be killed. However, the principle that the inaugural oath bound a prince to the agreed legal conditions, and that he, in accordance with feudal law, on violating it lost the loyalty of his vassals and his subjects – and therefore his office – was here clearly formulated for the first time with respect to an important principality. It would be applied again in the Low Countries in 1420 and in 1580, after which it was adopted – via the English revolution of the seventeenth century – into the American constitution as the impeachment procedure. Similarly the famous English Magna Carta of 1215 was really a summary of the complaints addressed to the king by his vassals about infringements of the feudal law. The deposition and trial of King Edward II in 1327 and of Richard II in 1399 were similarly supported by parliamentary procedures, although these were often prejudiced by rivalries between the great families.

In urbanized regions the citizens did not wait for the dynastic problems of their princes to establish on their own initiative structures for consultation on a regional and interregional scale. In this way they took care of their commercial interests with all their implications for coinage, judicial policy and security. If these interests were damaged by interference from their own or foreign princes,

In the Republic of the United Provinces representation of the Estates – without the priesthood – continued to play a decisive role in state affairs. Meeting of the States General held in 1651 in the Ridderzaal (Knights' Hall) of the Binnenhof in The Hague. The Hague, Mauritshuis

then they ranged themselves against them collectively with complaints and petitions which they persuaded them to grant, possibly by means of financial concessions and if necessary by boycotts or reprisals. Since trade routes, whether by land or sea, crossed several geographical jurisdictions, the administrators of the trading towns worked in alliances which operated far beyond their own territories. As long as the princes showed little interest in economic policy – which applied to most of them in the fifteenth century – the traders enjoyed considerable freedom in doing this. The princes' competition for territories, and the expansion of the state apparatus, brought them into conflict with the urban world. With their leagues, privileges and own legal systems the towns had established firm structures

Under the *ancien régime* the Swedish Diet was held in the *Riddarhus* or House of Nobles.
Of the four Estates the nobility had the best numerical representation. Engraving of 1783 by Johan Snack.
Stockholm, National Library

which functioned largely separately from the monarchies, and which could not simply be pushed to one side by the new state apparatus: they had the specialized knowledge and contacts and were not inclined to submit just like that. Governments therefore had to negotiate with the representative organizations of the towns, who were backed by a tradition of autonomy in protecting their own interests. The moment of their administrative incorporation into tighter state structures was an eminent occasion for this, from which developed their emphatic role also in such purely political events as, for instance, the succession crises in Aragon, Flanders and Brabant.

Together with the representatives of the Church and the nobility, the towns also developed a negotiating position for domestic politics. They were, after all, continually confronted with the problems and demands of territorial princes. Two types of regularly recurring situations lent themselves in particular to the submission of complaints and needs on behalf of the subjects: the procedure, already referred

to, of acknowledging a new prince, and his requests for financial and military assistance. We have already established that princes everywhere needed more money and more troops to defeat their rivals. The degree to which the representatives of their subjects could offer resistance to this depended in the first place on the intensity of the external threat. In France, most of which was flooded with English troops in the fourteenth and early fifteenth centuries, the king could rightly proclaim a state of emergency to get himself allocated special and permanent resources. In this situation the representatives of the Estates, however, gave away their most important negotiating cards and the kings were in the future able to save themselves the trouble of summoning them to meet. Under the very real threats of the Swedish invasion in the Holy Roman Empire between 1630 and 1634, or in Denmark in 1659, the princes of the Empire and the Danish king could give their governments a radically absolute character. However, in regions where there was an active and sound political organization of large towns, such *force majeure* did not work. Where it was tried, as in the Low Countries and in Catalonia, it provoked revolts. The final outcome was eventually decided by the complex of military, political and financial factors which always decide the course of wars.

The survival of effectively functioning representative bodies therefore depended on external pressure as well as on the social, economic and political structures in the relevant region. The English Parliament owes its exceptional continuity (despite interruptions – sometimes lasting for years – about 1500) to the fact that its representation was firmly rooted in the counties and boroughs, where the tradition of the participation of the subjects went back to the time of the Anglo-Saxon kings. In the Republic of the United Provinces, which was created out of a rising led by the States General and the Provincial States, the two levels of decision-making remained strictly dependent upon and closely linked to the autonomous power of decision of the individual towns. The Republic had founded its legitimacy on this threefold sovereignty. All threats, even those of the conquests of Louis xiv in 1672, could be dealt with by this pattern, so that there was little support there for any tendency towards a monarchy. Towards the end of the *ancien régime* even the most centralized states, such as France and Spain, could never entirely abolish strong traditional systems of regional representation such as, for instance, those in Languedoc, Burgundy, Catalonia and the southern Netherlands. In the dominions strung together piece by piece by the kings of France all newly incorporated territories retained their traditional rights, from the charter of the Normans in 1315 to Lorraine in 1766. After the revolt in Catalonia between 1640 and 1652, in which the *diputacio*, a standing deputation of the *cortes*, had taken the lead, the Spanish king had no option but to grant a pardon and reaffirm all the traditional rights and privileges of the region. The economically strong periphery, with its liberties and strong representative tradition, could not be treated like the more rural Castilian hinterland.

Where the balance of power between the prince and the various Estates induced regular negotiations, the representatives of the subjects appear to have developed a practical sense of territory. It was they who wrung promises from the prince not to relinquish any parts of the territory or to pledge them as securities, to take no foreign counsellors or officials into his service, and to use the language of the country in the courts of law. Such rulings are encountered in the national charters of Bohemia in 1310, Brandenburg and Prussia in 1345, Brabant in 1356, Utrecht in 1375, Normandy in 1381, Hungary in 1387 and so on. The representatives also always appear to have been ready for sacrifices to protect the country (but only their own country) against real or imagined threats. Their organization and awareness of a common cause without any doubt contributed importantly to the transformation of the regions conquered by their rulers into peoples with a sense of territorial identity. As inhabitants of a region maintaining a tight network of mutual relationships – it was naturally tighter where the density of population was higher – they showed more attachment to the land within their borders than did the princes. These avidly grasped any opportunity of expansion by means of marriage, inheritance, purchase, as security or by conquest, even at a thousand kilometres distance from their heartland.

Representative bodies reflected in their origins the real power relationships of a region. Like all human institutions, however, they displayed a tendency to become rigid and oligarchic. Established factions looked primarily to their own interests, if necessary even against other categories of subjects. For instance, after the fifteenth century representatives of the towns could certainly no longer generally be considered members of a dynamic merchant bourgeoisie; often they were by then so grafted into the structure of consultation that they had degenerated into local clients of the monarchy. In the lands of the crowns of Aragon and Castile this was certainly already the case when the revolts broke out there in 1519 and 1523, of the *Germanías* and the *Comunidades* respectively, which began as the political opposition of the urban knightly class, but quickly became more radical by the participation of the craft unions and peasants, and were subsequently harshly suppressed by the royal troops. Much therefore depended on how representative the representatives in fact were. If the towns were represented purely by *rentiers* who hankered after a title of nobility, then petitions of their subjects directly to the king – and in extreme circumstances revolts – put them at risk of getting their fingers burnt, so that their role as mediators in the state between the centre and the periphery took a sharp knock.

From the fifteenth century two kinds of factors heightened the pressure on such 'representatives': the expansion of monarchic power restricted their scope for trade, and the escalation of warfare heightened the fiscal and military demands of the crown. Both trends were simultaneous, although the extreme need for financial resources for the war was likely to restrain the state in the area of the domestic distribution of power.

During the sixteenth century the Low Countries offered a striking example of this dilemma. Charles v's pronounced efforts for absolutism were tempered in their implementation, even when it came to the persecution of heresy, during the periods of acute conflict with France in the 1520s, 1540s and 1550s. Because the pressure of taxation then went sky-high, the government thought it best to tread carefully to avoid more serious resistance. The representative organs saw real opportunities for negotiation in this, and contributed to the general good relations between government and subjects, in spite of the overall substantial rise in taxes and more centralizing government measures.

When, however, in the 1560s and 1570s the much more rigid Philip ii increased the oppression simultaneously in all areas, and did not even offer the opportunity of consultation to the top nobility, they formed a broad coalition of opponents who saw armed revolt as the only – and also the legitimate – way out. Referring to Philip's oath on the country's privileges at his inauguration, they accused him of countless breaches which he refused to annul. As well as violating various rights, allowing his troops to terrorize the people and denying his subjects fair recourse to law, the most serious accusation was that by means of the Inquisition he tried to rule the consciences of his subjects whom he considered as having no rights, as if they were natives of the colonies. As a result of the stubborn refusal of the king to discuss freedom of religion, the role of the representatives of the Estates evolved into that of leading the revolt and demanding satisfaction from the king. On the grounds of systematic and sustained violations of the rights of the subjects, in conflict with his inaugural oath, the States General in 1581 finally declared him deprived of his sovereign rights in the Netherlands, and chose the brother of the French king in his place. In the States General the representatives of the towns, particularly those of Flanders, Brabant and Holland, had a decisive vote, but even so they were acting with the open support of a large section of the nobility. The obstruction by the king of the consultation structures which could boast a long and solid tradition made them the natural leaders of a revolt which had long been waged within legitimate frameworks and lines of reasoning. Both in the southern provinces, where the Spanish armies car-

ried the day, and in the north, where the Spaniards eventually lost their case, the representatives of the Estates played a great role until the end of the eighteenth century; in the Republic of the United Provinces without the clergy (the First Estate) and as a sovereign body, and in the south as local and mediating oligarchies.

High demands for taxes, religious intolerance and absolutist tendencies were to bring the English king Charles i (1625–1649) similarly first into conflict with Parliament and, when he had sent them all home, next into encountering armed revolt. Like the burghers in the Low Countries, the London merchants stubbornly resisted the new royal levies on trade, which would have produced a permanent source of state income without parliamentary approval. Arbitrary arrests and abuse of judicial procedures aggravated the arguments over taxes. When the king wanted to impose an English prayerbook on the Scots which the Presbyterians regarded as papist, the Scots invaded England. Without the active co-operation of Parliament the government could raise no troops, so in 1640 it had to be recalled after a break of eleven years. This led to polarization, and actually to a civil war in which the king had to confront a parliamentary party based on the trading towns and the most highly commercialized and urbanized region of south-east England. In 1646 Scottish victory in the field decided the issue: Charles i had to surrender and fell into the hands of the army which, after fruitless negotiations with Parliament, had him put on trial before an extraordinary court, and executed. After the eleven years of the Commonwealth, the restoration of Charles ii, and the renewed problem of the crown and matters of religion under James ii (1685–1688), there followed the replacement – decided on by Parliament – of the king by the Protestant Stadtholder William iii of Orange with his wife Mary.

The role of the nobility and gentry proved to have been decisive in the lengthy trial of strength which weakened the crown permanently in comparison with Parliament. Expansion overseas and the growth of the domestic economy during the eighteenth century further strengthened the position of the gentry, and specially that of the commercial interests. The resulting balance of power and the new economic prospects increased the need for an efficient bureaucratic state apparatus. This situation enabled all the elites to improve their positions in their mutual relationships. This practice of a policy of compromise – certainly influenced in part by the trauma of the Civil War in the seventeenth century –

In 1537 the lesser Polish nobility rebelled against the king's plans for military modernization.
Their success in enforcing the free right of veto of every nobleman prevented the formation of a centralized state
and led to the country being overrun by its militarist neighbours in the second half of the eighteenth century.
Rembrandt van Rijn, *The Polish rider, c.* 1655.
New York, The Frick Collection

On the opposite bank of the Seine to the Louvre an aristocratic *Frondeur* in 1648
tries to incite the Parisians against the policy of Cardinal Mazarin, the Chief Minister. Seventeenth-century print.
Paris, Bibliothèque nationale de France, Estampes

made it possible for the political system gradually to adjust to the rapid and fundamental changes in the economy and in society. Parliament disregarded the open communication between the government and local magnates, which made possible the gradual opening up of the political system to the modern segments of society earlier and less dramatically in England than in most continental countries, where xenophobic elites held doggedly to their privileges until they were forced to lose them all through violent revolution.

Another country where parliament survived rebellions at the expense of the royal power was Poland. In 1537 the lesser nobles, who made up 10 per cent of the population, revolted against an attempt by the king to carry through a modernization programme for the army, with an eye on the competition from an expanding Muscovy. They proclaimed the principle of the right of veto of every man of coat armour against any innovation whatsoever, so that the Polish Diet degenerated into its proverbial anarchy, and the monarchy and the state were permanently weakened, which in the second half of the eighteenth century was to lead to the country being overrun by its militarist neighbours. During the seventeenth century countless smaller losses of territory in the Ukraine, Pomerania and Prussia had already revealed the decay of the power of the Polish state. It is fascinating to see that not every feudal

exploitation of a peasant society necessarily led to a centralized, absolutist and militarist state, as it did in Sweden, Denmark, Prussia, Bavaria, Austria and Russia. The difference lay in the interpretation of its functions by the Polish parliament, in which the bourgeois element after 1500 was no longer of any importance. Since the Polish economy was almost entirely based on the exploitation of peasant serfs on the estates of the nobility, while export trade was all in the hands of foreign merchants, no large concentrations of capital were formed. There was therefore no possibility of building up power outside the ranks of the large landowners.

In 1648, early in the minority of Louis XIV, the centralist efforts of Cardinals Richelieu and Mazarin to bring taxation and the provinces under control by the introduction of royal *intendants* came up against sharp criticism from the high courts of law, which in France were called *parlements*. When later the nobility unleashed the rebellion known as the *Fronde*, and there was a threat from Spain, an extremely risky situation developed. The court had fled, the Parliament of Paris had proclaimed Mazarin the 'disturber of public peace and enemy of the king and of his state'. The cardinal – learning from the experiences of Charles I in England – won the day by marching through the country with 6,000 mercenary soldiers from Brandenburg. He restored his authority and that of the king, still a minor,

Premiere Sceance Royalle du Roy Louis quatorzie, en son Parlement, ou assisté des Princes, Seigneurs, et autres Officiers de sa Couronne, il declare la Reine, Anne d'Austriche, sa Mere, Regente du Royaume, le 18 iour de May l'An 1643.

Robed in mourning, Anne of Austria, widow of Louis XIII and mother of the child Louis XIV, who sits enthroned in the king's place in the corner,
is installed on 18 May 1643 as Regent by the French Parliament. Washed drawing.
Paris, Bibliothèque nationale de France, Estampes

and advanced further along the road to absolutism. The nobility were tamed by forcing them to take part in life at court.[20]

Wars and revolts were closely linked: the same armies were employed against domestic as against foreign enemies, so that a state which was strong in the competition between states also had a firm grip on its own subjects. The goodwill of the subjects was an essential for any large military effort, but these helped to encourage the compliance of some of the subjects with a heavy hand. Steeply rising military expenditure imposed a heavy fiscal burden on the population, making them more inclined to revolt; this was the case, for example, in the Catalan resistance to the levying of troops by Castile in 1640 and the Portuguese rising in the same year which led to the restoration of their independence. Of the 5,125 revolts and riots which broke out in France between 1661 and 1789, 25 per cent were directed against the burden of state taxation, and 21.6 per cent against its repressive apparatus. Among the dozen or so other motives for revolt the only prominent one was the high price of food, which particularly during the last thirty years of the monarchy inflamed emotions and was responsible for 31 per cent of the riots. Rebelliousness seems to have been highest in the peripheral provinces with a long tradition of autonomy, such as Brittany, Languedoc and Provence.[21] This again meant that foreign powers could make use of the destabilization of their competitor, creating a further link between domestic and foreign conflicts. The long-lasting insurrection of the Cossacks from 1590 to 1734 thus fuelled rivalry between Russia and Poland, and in the long run weakened the Polish state.[22]

Peasant revolts supported by the lesser nobility were endemic in Russia with its constant expansion. By defeating these movements one after the

The Countess of Helfenstein with her little son appealing for mercy from the peasants who are setting fire to her husband's castle.
A 1619 engraving of an incident during the Peasant Revolt of 1525.
Berlin, Archiv für Kunst und Geschichte

other the central government strengthened its grip on the population. This was exploited indirectly because the government put estates at the disposal of nobility in their service which by the seventeenth century were already regarded as their private property, a situation finally recognized by the tsar in 1740. This created a patrimonial bureaucracy like that of western European feudalism seven or eight centuries earlier, but with modern techniques of appreciably larger scope and more permanency.

In this way the state apparatus was shaped by the reactions between the princes and their environment; they had undoubtedly been the most important driving forces and also the first to have an interest in the expansion of state power. The structures of society also determined the opportunities for development of the state-builders, as well as the form their efforts would take. The tradition of consultation was not normally highly valued by the princes. Most tried to eliminate parliamentary traditions completely; this led to revolts and the secession of peripheral regions. In those countries where the representatives still had substantial financial resources and sufficient clearsightedness not to surrender this financial power, they looked after the maintenance of regional privileges and of local clientèles. This combination of factors was, however, rarely found in Europe: only in the Low Countries, Catalonia, Portugal, England, and the outlying regions of France. Elsewhere – with the splendid exceptions of Venice, a few exceptional free cities of the Empire and in Poland – autonomous towns and parliaments disappeared from the scene. Monarchic states left the negotiating arena: they would in future be strong enough to impose their will, with the active support of the nobility and the clergy.

Sack of a castle.
Contemporary woodcut in: Thomas Murner, *Von dem grossen Lutherischen Narren*, 1522.
Berlin, Archiv für Kunst und Geschichte

The state had incorporated both, subordinated them to its own ends, and so survived as the dominant form of the concentration of power. In all this the voice of the people was only heard in those brief moments when they mobilized themselves in their bottled-up rage and cried out for justice, by which they usually meant a return to an idealized past.

1 VALDEON BARUQUE in BLICKLE 1997
2 BARRET-KRIEGEL 1990, 94–106; MUCHEMBLED 1992, 195
3 MOORE 1987, 124–130
4 PADOA-SCHIOPPA 1997
5 PRESS 1986
6 MUCHEMBLED 1992, 191–192
7 MUCHEMBLED 1992, 105–109, 155, 230–231
8 MILLET & MORAW in REINHARD 1996
9 MOORE 1987, 146–153
10 REINHARD 1996
11 GUENÉE 1971, 197, 201
12 LE ROY LADURIE 1987, 443
13 DESCIMON in REINHARD 1996
14 NICOLAS 1990, 185–198
15 LE ROY LADURIE 1987, 266
16 MUCHEMBLED 1992, 164–195
17 KRYNEN 1993, 328–336
18 ESTEPA DIEZ 1990, 21–39
19 BISSON 1986, 59; O'CALLAGHAN 1989, 79–93
20 BONNEY 1991, 232–238
21 NICOLAS 1990, 187–198
22 TILLY 1993, 232–237

Chapter VI
Persuasion and Sympathy

The exercise of physical force, levying tribute or taxes, and imposing law and order, all gained in efficiency as still further dimensions were added to them. After all, human societies do not function only on the basis of rational considerations, in the sense of a cool weighing up of material gains and losses. They also fulfil emotional functions such as the creation of feelings of security, involvement and dignity. In addition, the ways in which rulers communicate with their subordinates are not limited to instrumental, professional contacts; there have always been many more forms of human intercourse. In all societies symbolic and artistic media fulfil a fundamental role of clarifying positions and expressing values without having to do so in words. Particularly in societies such as those in Europe between 1000 and 1800, in which the vast majority of people were excluded from intellectual education or from direct or indirect participation in power, metaphorical forms of communication and emotional associations played an essential role.

The cult of princes

The origins of royalty in Europe were closely bound up with religion: it was his conversion to Christianity about AD 500 which assured Clovis of the support of the only large, well-established and highly developed institution of his time, the Church. It was the popes who in 751 elevated the Frankish mayors of the palace to be kings, and in 800 made them emperors for the first time. The Holy Roman Empire,

the most important secular power until the twelfth century, relied heavily on its close links with the bishops. The office of king of Germany was acquired by election from among the great princely families, but the emperorship was a sacrament that the pope could grant or withhold. In France the support of the bishops was essential to the young Capetian dynasty, who neglected nothing that might emphasize the sacramental nature of their office. After his consecration, Robert the Pious (✝1031) was one of the first to take part in a service of laying on of hands for sufferers from the king's evil, scrofula, a practice believed to be curative, which his successors were to cultivate in imitation of Christ. The ritual of anointing by the archbishop of Rheims placed the king above laymen in a quasi-priestlike status.

Looking at the chronology of their development of power, it is not surprising that the Holy Roman Emperors of the eleventh and twelfth centuries left imposing monumental traces. These were not so much secular buildings–the imperial palace, the *palts* at Goslar, has a certain style, but none the less bears witness to the modesty of their ambitions in this sphere. All their attention was then directed to the episcopal churches along the Rhine, the core area *par excellence* of the contemporary Empire. The emperor Conrad II (1024–1039) had the cathedral of Speier expanded into a mausoleum for the Salian dynasty. Just at the time of his conflict with the pope about the investiture of bishops, Henry IV in 1080 had a new design worked out which was to be a model for a whole series of imperial cathedrals. This was to be achieved in the most balanced way in the

Between 1482 and 1492 Andrea Mantegna worked for the Marquis Frederico Gonzaga of Mantua on the *Triumphs of Caesar*, a series of nine monumental canvases. In 1629 Charles I of England bought the paintings, and they left Mantua for Hampton Court near London. Detail of Picture IV. London, Royal Collection

In the eleventh and twelfth centuries *Kaiserdome* (imperial cathedrals) arose in the episcopal towns along the Rhine,
demonstrating the dimensions, worldly and spiritual, of the imperial Church.
Ivory reliquary in the shape of a twelfth-century Rhineland church,
with symmetrical emphasis of the east and west ends.
Brussels, Musées royaux d'Art et d'Histoire

archiepiscopal cathedral of Mainz, which was to function as an imperial mausoleum after Speier. This archdiocese was the largest in the west, with thirteen suffragan bishops, from Chur, through Prague, to Brandenburg. Links with the Empire were reinforced by the appointment of the archbishop as archchancellor, the highest secular office in the Empire. The dual structure of authority in the imperial Church was symbolized in these grandiose buildings by the symmetry between the east and west ends. Both were built high with an austere facade with two flanking and one central octagonal tower. The eight sides symbolized perfection, the three towers the divine unity of the Trinity. The east end, with the choir and the crypt containing the tombs of the emperors and the archbishops, was the spiritual domain, the west end the symbolic domain of the emperor, with a throne room. The great Benedictine abbeys which were supported by the emperors, such as Maria Laach in the Eifel, followed the same design concept. By their size and in their

design they silently radiated a clear conception of power. So did the succession of famous abbey churches at Cluny, the centre of the reform of the Church from about 1000, but in their case following their own design with no monumental westwork.

The French crown began to demonstrate its glory in an original way from the twelfth century. It started with the abbey church of St Denis, north of Paris, which acted as a base for monarchist propaganda, where the kings were buried and some relics of the Passion were kept. With their active support, and in their crown demesnes, there was an explosion of building employing a revolutionary concept: Gothic. It became all the rage: in 1144 the new chancel was consecrated at St Denis, and work had already started in 1133 on rebuilding the archiepiscopal cathedral at Sens. Within a few decades enormous building sites appeared in a whole range of towns for immense cathedrals with walls ever more open and airy, greater areas of window, loftier roofs, more pointed arches, sculpture in deeper relief,

Wand finial which is part of the treasure of the Sainte Chapelle in Paris.
The cameo in the form of the bust of a Roman emperor
dates from the sixth century and was mounted about 1368
by Hennequin du Vivier.
Paris, Bibliothèque nationale de France

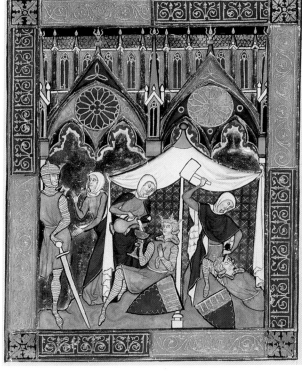

Miniature with scenes from the Bible,
illustrated in the architectural frame of the Sainte Chapelle, 1253–1270.
This palace chapel of St Louis was conceived as a monumental shrine
and intended as a French counterpart of the Palace Chapel in Aachen.
Paris, Bibliothèque nationale de France

more daring vaulting, and taller towers. They strove to let as much light as possible shine into the building, and to reach up as far as possible towards God. In the cathedral of Paris, begun in 1163, the nave was 32.8 metres high, in Chartres in 1194 they reached 36.55 metres, in 1212 Rheims climbed to 37.95 metres, and Amiens in 1221 to 42.3. Beauvais reached the record height of 48 metres, but the roof collapsed in 1284. The competition now shifted to the height of towers: Strasburg with its 142 metres in 1420 was to remain unmatched until the nineteenth century. This radical new building concept spread throughout almost the whole of Europe, and was not restricted to churches. It emanated from a monarchy which was consolidating its position in close association with its efforts to identify itself as the 'most Christian kings'. Their primary choice for cathedrals was therefore an element in a planned policy by which the kings, with the support of the popes, distinguished themselves from the waning efforts of the Holy Roman Emperors for hegemony. At the same

time this building mania was only achievable as a consequence of the growing surpluses from agriculture and the growth of the towns, whose population in mutual competition devoutly shared in paying for these prestigious projects.

The absolute pearl of Gothic architecture arose between 1239 and 1248 at the instigation of King Louis IX: his palace chapel in the Ile de la Cité in Paris, known as the Sainte Chapelle. It was built for the most precious of all the relics of the Passion, Christ's crown of thorns, which had been brought from Palestine in 1063 to the chapel of the palace in Constantinople. After the siege by the Bulgars and the Greeks the rulers of the contemporary Latin empire were in financial straits and had to sell this precious relic in 1238. The building was the model for further chapels in French episcopal palaces and in the royal castle at St Germain-en-Laye, conceived as a dual church on two levels, the lower dedicated to the Holy Virgin, the upper to the crown of thorns. As well as the shrine of the relic,

All the elements of the French coronation ceremony have been precisely described since the twelfth century.
For instance, the king of France first had to take off his old robes before being anointed. He was then dressed ritually;
in succession he received shoes with the French *fleur-de-lis,* golden spurs, the royal cloak, sword and sceptre, and finally the royal crown.
Golden spurs (twelfth-thirteenth century) and the sword, known as the sword of Charlemagne, which were used during the ceremony at Rheims.
Paris, Musée du Louvre

the treasure of the royal records was also deposited there. This consisted, among other things, of some eight hundred papal bulls demonstrating the special recognition of the Capetians as 'most Christian kings'. The legitimizing function of the relic and the concept of the chapel as a grandiose reliquary were only too clear, just at the time that the Byzantine empire was shaky and the Emperor Frederick II had been excommunicated for the second time. Who else than the king of France was worthy to assume the leadership of Christendom?

The building is a miracle of technical daring: the walls look as if they were made entirely of glass, there is light, sparkle and colour everywhere. This effect was produced by mirrorwork and precious stones, while iron clamps hold the narrow supporting walls firm. As in cathedral apses, the chancel is enclosed by seven windows (the holy number). The reliquary was positioned so high up that an observer could only see it against the background of the

leaded glass windows. The stained glass in the two lancet windows immediately behind the shrine portrayed the Passion. The others showed the delivery of the relics of the Passion, presented by the king himself. Niches were left open in the walls on each side for the oratories of the king and the queen. Christ the Saviour is shown on the wall of the royal stall. Had not Pope Innocent IV written to him: 'We believe it is deservedly that the Lord crowned you with His crown of thorns, the care of which He, in His ineffable power, has granted to your excellency'? The link with the 'most Christian kingship' reached its full expression in the departure of Louis IX on crusade in August 1249, scarcely two months after the consecration of the Sainte Chapelle.

This building completely fulfilled its propagandist function as a royal riposte to Charlemagne's palace chapel in Aachen, Frederick II's Palatina in Palermo, and the palace chapel in Constantinople—from which the crown of thorns had come. Count-

Scenes illustrating the French coronation ritual as laid down in the *Ordo* of 1250: the crowning by the king's peers and the 'kiss of peace'.
Paris, Bibliothèque nationale de France

less royal marriages were solemnized there, many crowned heads desired to kneel before the True Crown. The Joyful Entry in 1594 of King Henry IV, who had twice forsworn his Protestant faith, was accompanied by a solemn procession from the Sainte Chapelle to Notre Dame, with all the most holy relics. On Twelfth Night of 1378 the emperor Charles IV with his son Wenceslas, the king of the Romans, and King Charles V attended Mass there. Canon Sauveur-Jérôme Morand, who in 1790 wrote a history of his chapel for the National Assembly to save it from desecration and from being robbed of its relics, gives a lively description of the scene.

For Vespers on the eve of Tiffany, of Theophania, the feast that is popularly called Twelfth Night, two prie-dieus had been set out in the Sainte Chapelle for the monarchs, on the right for the king, on the left for the emperor. He, however, did not take his place there, but put himself right in front of the shrine. The next day they attended Mass, celebrated by the archbishop of Rheims. The three kings came to the offertory with gold, myrrh and frankincense. The emperor requested the king to show him the relics. Since he suffered from gout, he had to be carried, with great difficulty since the stairs leading to the treasury are very narrow. The emperor kissed the relics with deep respect and showed them to the princes and lords in his retinue. [1]

Charles IV was so impressed with the Sainte Chapelle that he had it copied at the palatine chapel in Aachen, and at Karlstein near Prague, his capital, where he had a fresco painted of the Passion relics of the Empire: the holy spear and the nails and pieces of the True Cross. In contrast to France, where the Capetian dynasty ruled from 987 till 1328 from Paris and neighbouring St Denis, the continual change of imperial families never brought the whole symbolic power of the Empire together in one specific capital. Aachen, Speier, Mainz, Nuremberg, Prague, Augsburg and many other temporary residences would never develop the cohesive power of Paris, a problem with which Germany in the late twentieth century is still wrestling.

Rheims – the scene of the consecration of Clovis, the first Christian king of the Franks, by St Remy, its bishop – was for that reason chosen to be the

Notes: see

location of the ritual of coronation by the archbishop from 1179 to 1824. The relics of St Remy, and the sacred *ampulla* in which according to tradition the oil he used to anoint Clovis had been kept, were in the care of the abbot of St Remy's Abbey. The abbot and his monks brought this most holy object of the ceremony in procession to the cathedral, where it was placed in the chancel under a baldaquin. The abbot and monks of St Denis, the church of the first bishop of Lutetia – later Paris – where the royal insignia were kept and the mortal remains of the kings rested, also had their role in the ceremony, placing the insignia on the altar where they were consecrated.

The French coronation ritual, which has come down to us in a description from 1250, corresponds closely to the imperial and to the Anglo-Saxon ones. Common elements were the presentation of the king to the assembled

people by the priests and his promise in the form of an oath to maintain peace, justice and mercy. The king next swore before God to defend the Catholic faith, to the Church to protect it and its servants, to the people to rule the kingdom which God had granted him and to protect it according to the tradition of justice of his forefathers. The acclamation *Fiat, fiat* by clergy and people sealed the three oaths. Then the king put off his old robes, to receive the shoes with the *fleur-de-lis*, the golden spurs and the sword. The anointing by the archbishop was done – as for the high priest and the king in ancient Israel, and for bishops – on the head, the chest, between and on the shoulders, and on the elbows and the hands. The archbishop asked God to behold this glorious king with his mercy. He then received the insignia: the hyacinth-blue cloak, the ring, the sceptre and the rod. The crown was placed on his head

Miniatures from the *Livre du sacre de Charles v* of 1365:
awaiting the arrival of Charles v
at the doors of Rheims cathedral;
the oath on the Holy Scriptures to keep faith
with Church and people; the crowning by
the archbishop of Rheims; and the elevation
of Charles v to the throne of France.
London, British Library

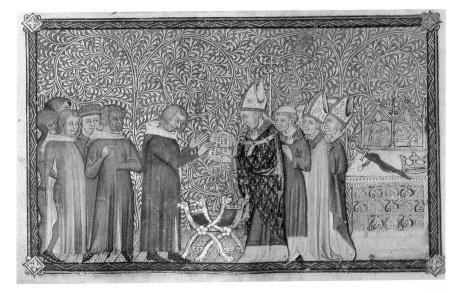

by his peers, literally his equals as territorial princes in the kingdom. The number of six priests and six laymen is a clear reference to the number of the apostles. By their participation they demonstrated the assent and submission of the great feudal lords to the new king. After the coronation they literally supported the crown by leading the king to his throne, where they gave him the kiss of peace. The archbishop, too, took off his mitre before the king, enthroned in his full power, and kissed him. The naked sword, borne by the seneschal, led the procession as they left the cathedral.[2]

During the Great Interregnum in the Empire, from 1250 to 1272, the image of the French 'most Christian' kings was dominant. Under Philip the Fair (1285–1314) the propagandists busied themselves tracing the Capetian dynasty back not only in the direct and legitimate line to Clovis, but even to the Homeric hero Priam. The switch to the Valois dynasty and the severe defeats in the Hundred Years War gave fresh stimulus to the endeavour for divine justification. References to the anointing granted the kings by God with the sacred *ampulla*, their power of curing the king's evil, the insignia of the *fleur-de-lis*, the *oriflamme* and, from Charles VII (1422–1461) onwards, the reaffirmation of the Salic law and the acknowledgement that the king of France had no superior in this world, had to support the self-confidence and self-reliance of the beleaguered people. The popes went so far as to grant indulgences to those who prayed for the king. On the other hand, from the thirteenth century speaking ill of the king was regarded as equivalent to attacks on what was sacred, and therefore blasphemy, against which various laws already fulminated, anticipating the later common and very elastic concept of lese-majesty. The concept of 'most Christian king' was therefore exploited to the utmost to underpin a monarchy which vied with the emperors but which later had to fight to maintain its position.[3]

During the Middle Ages princes mainly justified their often dubious and contested position and claims by appealing to divine authority, so much so that they themselves, and in the long run even their people, identified themselves with it. The weakening of papal authority from about 1300 also gave scope for this, which was mostly taken advantage of by the French kings. Others, however, did the same, each within their own territories, since for a long time there had been no more question of the universality of Christendom.

Entries Joyful and not so Joyful

In Rheims the common people were assigned a humble, assenting role. Nothing else was possible, because it was not the coronation ritual which made a man king but – at least according to the doctrine – first God's grace and second the legitimacy of his birth. He was king directly upon the death of his predecessor, according to the doctrine of mystic kingship; the coronation only confirmed and consummated that reality. Above all it was, of course, the political assent of powerful men – in France the peers – who decided whether a candidate should go to Rheims. After he had been disinherited in 1420, Charles VII derived his new legitimacy from the coronation in Rheims insisted upon in 1429 by Joan of Arc, who at the nadir of the monarchy provided a very significant symbolism.

From Rheims a French king went to Paris to make his Joyful Entry there, a custom he repeated on his first visit to every town in his kingdom. In the course of the fourteenth century this public and mainly secular ritual was developed further. On the one hand it displayed a popular, colourful and boisterous character; on the other the king was presented with increasing emphasis as a cult object, placed under a canopy like the Holy Sacrament that was carried round in procession.[4] Outside the Porte St Denis he was received by the highest dignitaries of the city: the counsellors of the royal Parliament, the bishop and canons of the cathedral, the university, the city magistracy. Along the Rue St Denis at a dozen or so fixed points *tableaux vivants* and theatrical performances were presented before him. The crafts, guilds, fraternities and rhetoric clubs were responsible for designing historical, religious and mythological presentations on raised platforms. By their themes they could deliver a specific message to the king; in any case the various sections of the urban community took part in a dialogue with the royal retinue, which passed slowly along the road to the cathedral and the palace.[5]

In the Low Countries similar ceremonies also carried constitutional significance, since the new prince after his enthronement was expected to progress through his territory to receive homage in each capital as duke, count or lord of that specific dominion. Apart from oaths, similar to those in France, before God and the Church, here it was a matter of swearing on the privileges, rights and customs of each country and each town separately. Representatives of his subjects concentrated on acquiring new commitments from the young prince

Amidst massive public excitement the procession with Charles V approaches the Porte St Denis of Paris in 1365.

About a century later Jean Fouquet re-created this scene

from the Joyful Entry in *Les grandes chroniques de France.*

Paris, Bibliothèque nationale de France

Turma Caterua phalanx properant Jruisere Martem.
Qui regit audaces ad fera bella manus.

From the top of a wooden stand Henry II of France reviews the march past of the inhabitants of Rouen.
At the head are the priests, followed by the town authorities, the members of the Parliament of Rouen, the town militia and the craft guilds.
Rouen, Bibliothèque municipale

on these occasions. In some regions with a turbulent dynastic tradition these commitments developed into yards of parchment documents which were revised at each succession as a function of the power relationships at the time. An account by a Saxon courtier from the retinue of the emperor Maximilian, who in 1494 accompanied his son, Duke Philip the Handsome, on his Joyful Entries in Brabant, shows the surprise at this custom of someone coming from a region where there was appreciably less political participation. He gave a full description of the splendid procession and the sumptuousness of the theatrical performances on the occasion of the feast of the birth of Our Lady, on 7 and 8 September, and was deeply impressed by a giant in full armour on horseback 'as tall as the Weimar town hall'. About the Joyful Entry of Philip the Handsome the next day he only commented that the emperor and his son first left the town and went into the country, then returned, were entertained and had to take their places on a dais in the market place, where the young duke 'had to make a great number of promises before all the princes [in the imperial retinue] and [the States of] the county of Brabant', before being acknowledged and sworn in as their 'lawful and natural prince'.[6]

Otherwise the Saxon eyewitness, full of amaze-ment, described with how much splendour, particularly with how many costly fireworks and rich colourful processions and performances, the princes were received in these towns. His description of the reception of Maximilian and his new bride Bianca Sforza in Malines a month earlier is witness to the genuine feeling of good cheer.

As is usual in these countries, the population of the town of Malines, for the honour of the queen [for whom it was after all her first visit] organized in the streets along which the company was to pass a great many plays and wonderful histories of antiquity, from the Holy Scriptures, and also contemporary ones. They expended much decoration and expensive equipment on this. The streets along which the procession would come were richly decorated on both sides with green branches and arched with costly banners of gold and silk. Hundreds of great bonfires and barrels of pitch had been lit and several thousands of candles, so that in all the streets, in the market place, on the facades of the houses and the towers, there was so much light that one could see as clearly as if it were broad daylight. As the bells pealed, all the priests, monks and all the people capable of walking, young and old, left the town in procession to welcome the queen and to escort her within the walls with many torches and candles,

Detail from the *Parade in Brussels on 31 May 1615,* painting by Denijs van Aelsloot.
In the foreground a triumphal car on which the archduchess Isabella is seated with the ladies of her court.
London, Victoria and Albert Museum

because it was already dark. It is impossible to describe how much joy there was, and this lasted from eight to ten in the evening.

When the princely company returned on 12 September, this time for Philip's Joyful Entry, there was, still according to the same authority, again an expensive (this was what struck the Saxon observers most) and splendid entry procession. For an hour and a half Maximilian presided over a tournament in the market place, until darkness fell. A week later the court was still in Malines—where the government of the Low Countries held residence—and there celebrated the wedding of an Austrian captain of Maximilian's court with a local beauty, about whom the writer heard it said 'that she brought him much money'. Again a great tournament was held for the emperor, the queen and the princess, their daughter Margaret. That evening there was to be a ball in the town hall, but that very soon appeared to be too small for the great mass of merrymakers, so that the whole company started dancing in the market place 'each after his own fashion, German, Dutch and French all mixed … The emperor and many of his train had provided themselves with masks and disguised themselves especially, and so joined the dance'.

This delightful account by a Saxon who apparently never got bored with the wealth and the customs of the towns in the Low Countries shows plainly just how free conventions in the late fifteenth century could still be between the royal court and the whole assembled population, then perhaps some 20,000 souls. Official entries and also ordinary visits offered the opportunity for a show, in the most literal sense of the word: the court circle showed itself in all its splendour and in its tournaments; some went hunting in the surrounding woods; ceremonies, church services and processions were all opportunities for the higher nobility to show themselves to the common people. In the Burgundian and Habsburg dynasties, as in many others, conclaves of the orders of chivalry were held in various towns, in this case the Order of the Golden Fleece. The high nobility and their princely fellows who were members of the order then stayed for several days in the town where they held their ceremonial gatherings, which would include a Mass for the Dead and a session of the Chapter. To celebrate the occasion the coats of arms of those members attending were hung up in the chancel of the church where these meetings took place, and they then stayed there in memory of an event which would certainly have been marvelled at by the townspeople. During formal meetings of the States

In some large towns of the Empire an imposing funerary ceremony was held in memory of Charles v who died at Yuste in Spain.
In 1559 Plantin in Antwerp printed an illustrated account of the ceremonial held in Brussels on 29 December 1558.
Detail of the funerary procession.
Antwerp, Museum Plantin-Moretus

In 1506, with shaven heads and robed in black,
prominent Genoese carried the baldaquin for their conqueror, Louis xii of France.
Kneeling girls humbly sang *misericordia* to him. Miniature from Jean Manot, *Le voyage de Gènes,* c. 1508.
Paris, Bibliothèque nationale de France

political negotiations were also carried out. On their side the urban community showed themselves in the way they loved most, and expended special care on their performance. The subject matter of theatrical presentations, inspired by biblical, historical or literary themes, was often adapted to the situation, and could be used to create, repair or maintain good relationships between the town and its princes. Towns usually presented a gift, often jewellers' work, and naturally a *vin d'honneur*. The use of much symbolism, fantasy and emotion helped to establish direct communication between a prince and his subjects. For the masses this was the most direct way to get to know their prince and to be acquainted with his policies. This mainly metaphorical exchange created emotional bonds and allowed the mass of the subjects to identify personally with the monarchic state which was otherwise so distant and abstract.

Communication between prince and subjects during a Joyful Entry could also, of course, assume a less cheerful character. When in 1301 King Philip the Fair of France and his wife Joanna of Navarre visited the towns of his newly conquered county of Flanders, the well-to-do citizens expressed their choice for or against the king by the colour of their clothes. The common people grumbled because they feared a return of the repressive rule of the merchants and entrepreneurs which they had earlier thrown off. They complained that the town administration had bought too expensive presents and spent too much money, at their expense, on the reception for the king, and that the increase in indirect taxes to pay for all this should be repealed. The king proved to be generous, and ordered the repeal of the new levy – much to the displeasure of the town administration who had to manage without it somehow. But the festivities and the tournaments could go ahead. Learning from this experience, the magistracy of Bruges, who were organizing an Entry a few days later, forbade the people, on pain of death, to submit any petitions to the king. The reaction was a stony silence in the streets as the royal parade passed. The row over the cost of the festivities broke out a few days after his departure.

Demands for the abolition of excises imposed by the town, and other grounds for complaint, also caused dissension during the Joyful Entries of Charles the Bold into Ghent and Malines in 1467. In Ghent the members of the crafts were particularly incensed because the Joyful Entry was held on the exact day of their own traditional procession with the relics of their local saint. The confrontation in the public market place was intimidating for the new prince because the furious craftsmen considered themselves protected by the relics behind which they were shielding themselves. He managed to extricate himself from the embarrassing confrontation, but afterwards punished the rebellious town both politically, by bringing its administration more tightly under his control, and symbolically, by stripping the craft guilds of their banners and publicly humiliating the delegates of the town. His father, Philip the Good, had found himself and his retinue in mortal danger in Bruges in 1436, and no less than Maximilian himself, when King of the Romans, was held prisoner there for three and a half months in 1488. Again these ill-fated entries were followed by formal punishments.

Most of the large towns in the Low Countries, all of which rebelled at least once and some more often, experienced such ritual humiliations. They restored the order which had been disturbed by a revolt by making the defeated rebels acquit themselves of a debt of honour (in addition, of course, to the punishment of their leaders and the payment of fines). They had literally to submit to the prince, kneeling before him and asking his forgiveness, bareheaded, barefoot, and in their shifts. In 1540 Charles v added an extra refinement to this by making the citizens of Ghent, who had revolted (again), appear before him with a noose round their necks, as a symbolic punishment. The public ceremony weighed heavily, it was fixed in the memory and was understood by others, who were not involved, as a warning. Demonstrative punishments served to discourage others from rebellion. The Christian prince did not just reward, he also chastised.

This ambivalent nature of Joyful Entries was particularly evident in the confused period of the wars in Italy between 1494 and 1529, in which the kings of France and Aragon, the emperor and the pope were all fighting for dominion over the wealthy, but competitively weakened, regional states. At this time when the Renaissance and the art of printing were spreading, the new forms and media of expression were everywhere pressed into service for political propaganda. At the time of the Entry of King Charles VIII into Naples in 1495 the printed accounts of it even anticipated the event. While – without much ostentation – the king had on 22 February entered the town with his troops along the ramparts right up to the castle, in the hope that the pope would lend his approval to this assumption of power, a pamphlet appeared in Paris with a completely invented account of a coronation, which

Maximilian of Austria had the Hofkirche at Innsbruck arranged as his funerary chapel.
Round the monumental tomb are twenty-eight more-than-life-size bronze statues of members of his family and illustrious ancestors,
such as Clovis and Theodoric. When the emperor died in 1519 eleven of the statues were ready.
Rudolph von Alt made a pen drawing of this in 1886. Vienna, Graphische Sammlung Albertina

would actually not occur until 12 May. Two children dressed as angels were supposed to have brought the crown of Naples down from heaven in the procession on the way to the cathedral. There the barons allegedly led the king to his throne and he was 'elevated in royal majesty, the sceptre placed in his hand, the crown set on his head, consecrated by the cardinal-legate and installed as the natural and lawful king of Naples'. After that the barons were supposed to have completed paying homage to the new king, kissing his hands and feet.[7] Propaganda purposes in France must surely have been served by the glorious gain of the kingdom of Naples. The French public would have recognized the ceremonial, because the author of the pamphlet had confined himself to copying the Rheims ceremony.

Charles VIII's successor Louis XII had a series of entries into north-Italian towns which, dependent upon the circumstances, were in turn constitutional (Milan 1499), peaceful (Genoa 1502), chastising tempered with mercy (Milan 1500, Genoa 1507), or triumphal (Pavia and Milan 1507). In these ceremonies purely French traditions (the king under a baldaquin, the reception outside the town gates, the change of robes, the laying on of hands) were mixed with elements typical of the Italian Renaissance. For instance, in Milan in 1499 Louis' baldaquin was borne in turn by thirty scholars and thirty knights, symbolizing the two Estates which supported the crown, gave counsel and carried out its decisions. Moreover, the king was elaborately addressed as the liberator of the fatherland, who had driven out the tyranny of the Sforzas.

After a few months a revolt broke out and Lodovico il Moro was brought back again as ruler. However, the French soon defeated him. These events were widely reported in poems and pamphlets in French, Italian and Latin, and, of course, the town had to suffer various kinds of humiliation. There were three ways of doing this: imposing a fine, beheading or exiling the leaders with confiscation of their property, and imposing a penance. This was performed on a day which was pre-eminently a day of mourning, Good Friday 1500. Four thousand children in hair shirts and bearing crucifixes had to file past Cardinal Georges d'Amboise crying 'Francia' and 'Misericordia'. On each side scholarly addresses explained the guilt of the rebels. The Milan lawyer, Michele Torso, referred to the founding of Milan by the Gauls, and to the Roman name for the region, Gallia Cisalpina. He acknowledged that the revolt meant nothing less than lese-majesty. The French orator referred to the subjection of rebellious Milan by the Emperor Frederick Barbarossa in 1176, and spoke disapprovingly of the delight of the common people at the return of Lodovico il Moro 'which could not have been greater if God himself had come down to earth from heaven'.

Pope Julius II arranged for his Triumphal Entry into Rome to be on Palm Sunday. This miniature of c. 1508 from the panegyric of Nagonius shows the papal triumphal car. Next to the pope stands the prefect of Rome; behind him are a cardinal and his relative Francesco Maria della Rovere. Rome, Biblioteca Apostolica Vaticana

The Virgin Queen, Elizabeth I (1559–1603) is carried in a litter under a baldaquin borne by courtiers.
In front are Knights of the Garter.
In 1576 she wrote to Parliament that she considered her personal happiness less important than the welfare of her kingdom.
This painting was done about 1600 by Robert Peake, but shows the queen as she was in the first years of her reign.
London, Simon Wingfield Digby Collection

Francis I steers the Ship of State with the *oriflamme* flying high from its mast. The ship is drawn by a white hart.
Illustration from the Joyful Entry into Lyons in 1515.
Wolfenbüttel, Herzogliche Bibliothek

In Genoa Louis celebrated an entry in 1502 as a voluntarily invited Protector. There his baldaquin was borne by twelve prominent citizens and escorted by twelve mounted trumpeters; the people cried 'Francia', the bells pealed, and the ships in the harbour fired salvos until the town shook with their roar. The streets were decorated with green branches and tropical fruits, and his host's palace was adorned with a triumphal arch of cloth. In 1506 the people of Genoa rose against the French garrison and chose a doge of their own. Louis led an army across the Alps and was able to subdue the town. French and Italian poets praised the heroic figure of the king in mediocre verse, comparing him with the military heroes of antiquity. His entry had to illustrate both the penance of his subjects and the generosity of their ruler. The representatives of the town were dressed in mourning, the baldaquin bearers had their heads shorn, maidens and young girls had to arouse the king's 'misericordia' by lining the windows along the processional route, others knelt and waved olive branches, begging the king for compassion. Louis did indeed demonstrate his generosity, for which his propagandists used the image of the king bee (the queen bee was then thought to be male) who refrained from using his sting against his subjects. The new rule was unambiguously marked on the *genovino*, the internationally famous gold coin, which had been in circulation for centuries; it now had the crown and three royal *fleurs-de-lis* stamped on the obverse. During an entry into Milan, shortly after that into Genoa, the town magistracy awaited Louis outside the walls with a four-wheeled triumphal car in typical Renaissance style drawn by four horses and bearing a personification of Victory surrounded by the four cardinal virtues. Round the car danced savages (a play on the coat of arms of the royal deputy Charles d'Amboise) and young men dressed in blue decorated with *fleurs-de-lis*, The figure of Victory greeted the king as conqueror and the father of his country and invited him to take her place in the car, saying he would then put every triumph of antiquity in the shade.

The emperor Maximilian, whose position in Brittany, the Low Countries and Italy was seriously threatened by the French advance, paid a great deal of attention to publicizing the symbols of his imperial status, as a riposte to his rivals' possible ambitions in this field. In his funerary chapel at Innsbruck Maximilian had busts of the Roman emperors placed round the walls, while his tomb, decorated with scenes of his heroic deeds and surmounted by his own image, was surrounded by more than life-size bronze figures of his princely forebears. His dynasty's links with the imperial aura were a message which could hardly be misunderstood by visitors, particularly by princes of the Empire and indirectly by other European monarchs. Maximilian used heraldic symbolism when in 1499 he had the Saggenpfort of the Hofburg in Innsbruck painted with fifty-four coats of arms of seigneuries in the possession of the Habsburgs, or to which he laid claim. In a humbler but for that reason more widely distributed medium this theme was also still more brilliantly developed by Dürer in a series of 192 woodcuts which, when assembled in the form of an enormous triumphal arch, made the glory of the emperor known throughout the world in words and pictures. The ageing emperor, who also had his autobiography written, relied more on publicity through the media than on personal contacts to spread his renown.

In the battle for Italy the martial pope Julius II was not to be outdone. At the head of his army he again subdued those parts of the papal states which had freed themselves under his more indolent predecessors. He eschewed no worldly means, not even his majestic entry into Bologna, conquered by him in 1506, which drew the disapproving comment from the peace-loving Dutchman Erasmus who witnessed it that 'Pope Julius wages war, conquers, has triumphs, in short, plays at being Julius Caesar'. In the triumphal procession the theme was the liberation from their former rulers who were branded tyrants, a theme that was repeated on specially issued papal coinage and on commemorative tokens, which were scattered among the crowd after the example of the Roman emperors. Julius organized his triumphal return to Rome for Palm Sunday, so that he was received like Christ with waving palm branches. In the town triumphal arches were decorated in classical style; the arch of Domitian was restored and repainted for the occasion, and on St Peter's Square the arch of Constantine was re-created with illustrations of all the glorious deeds of the pope. Everywhere there was an abundance of comparisons with the great emperors of antiquity in addresses, inscriptions and paeans.[8]

Joyful Entries thus acquired a character clearly adapted to the circumstances, in which a symbolic dialogue was carried on between prince and subjects in images, colours, gestures, sounds and words, written and spoken. All communication media of the time were applied in the form of 'public art' and as mass spectacles they could leave no-one

Caparison of wool and silk with the arms of Gustavus Adolphus II of Sweden.
It was manufactured in 1621 in the Zeeland workshop of Frans Spiering for the king's Joyful Entry into Stockholm.
Stockholm, Livrustkammaren

unmoved. Everything was directed towards the expression of a single dominant emotion; overwhelming joy or profound sorrow and fear. The masses cheered the exalted prince, peacemaker and victor, or they abased themselves in sackcloth and ashes, humbly imploring his mercy. If the people took a heartfelt dislike to their rulers, they expressed this spontaneously, and would refuse to be roped in to play their part – which was certainly not a passive one – in the rituals of the parades. Several princes experienced this in Ghent and Bruges, and Charles VIII was careful to avoid it in Naples.

During the sixteenth century public spectacles became more and more magnificent. Their exuberant presentation gradually gained the upper hand over their function of political mediation, their message was transformed into a paean of praise for the dynasty. Their organization gradually became the business of specialists in government service, eventually even of famous artists such as Peter Paul Rubens in Antwerp in 1635, and in Counter-Reformation countries was often controlled by the Jesuits. This meant that the guilds and fraternities, who originally had given all sections of society some voice, lost their input, and the dialogue between prince and subjects degenerated into a one-sided

orchestrated scenario for a passive public. During the critical period of transition from the fourteenth to the sixteenth century public ceremonial none the less facilitated the assimilation of growing numbers of subjects in the increasingly larger states with more and more distant monarchs. Emotional links could be forged between a king over millions of people through the subjects congregated in his towns. The urban stage offered the state the only place where princes could be in direct contact with the mass of their subjects. Through the agency of the town administrations who were gradually made more dependent on the central government, local traditions were transformed and directed wholly towards the prince, by which they lost their spontaneous reciprocity.

Although Francis I and Charles IX still found it necessary to make long progresses through France – Charles made one lasting from January 1564 to May 1566 – to carry out these reciprocal, pseudo-feudal rituals with their subjects. Louis XIV was able to establish himself permanently at his court. He left it only for his campaigns, the true field of honour, and only held a royal progress as the victor over conquered towns. His state was strong enough to force obligations and oaths on his subjects unilat-

Three great processions were held in Venice every year: on Good Friday, on 25 April – the feast day of St Mark, the patron saint of the city –
and on Corpus Christi. In his *Miracle on the San Lio Bridge* Giovanni Mansueti gives a fifteenth-century view of such a procession.
Venice, Accademia delle belle Arti

erally without direct signs of resistance to the 'absolute' king. His effigy and emblems were meanwhile visible everywhere in the kingdom in the form of statues, prints, paintings and decorations, and the gazettes were filled with accounts of his glorious campaigns.

The image of the town

Life in pre-industrial Europe ran by the rhythm of the church calendar with its highdays and holidays. In countries which had remained Catholic these included various festivals in honour of saints who had a special significance for a town or its corporation as its patron saint. The feast of St Mark in Venice, St John the Baptist in Florence or St Lawrence in Perugia gave an opportunity for splendid processions when the whole town came out to watch and to show itself off. The organization of the processions with all their accompaniments of tableaux, decorated floats, puppets, festive costumes and everything else, was looked after by fraternities, guilds and parish organizations, usually encouraged by a town administration, which sometimes also organized competitions. In some towns associ-

ations of this kind ran contests in which the young men of the various parishes tried to outdo each other, as in the famous *palio* in Siena, or the water battles of Pisa. General religious festivals such as Carnival and Corpus Christi also provided a canvas for displays which regularly gave fresh expression to the collective identity of the urban community as a whole and in all its sectors.

Although they had not by definition expressed a political statement with their local identification, mass demonstrations could naturally never be ignored by the rulers. From fear that the *arti*, the craft guilds in Florence, might find a medium for expressing an independent policy by their participation in the grandiose festivities during the fourteenth and fifteenth centuries, the rich merchants who ran the city only allowed the people to take part in the framework of other organizations, such as the town militia which was organized on a parochial basis. Equally, from fear of disturbance of the peace, if not of insurrection, the fathers of the republic excluded the young men as a group from taking part in the festival of St John the Baptist, when the constitutional annual change of magistrates took place. Separate equestrian tournaments were arranged for the turbulent young men, and

they were also charged with providing escorts for diplomats, so keeping them away from the politically sensitive scene. During the great social and political upheavals of the late fifteenth century until 1530, there was also pressure for participation in civic rituals by groups which had formerly been excluded, such as children, women, young men and the repressed workers. The Medici were able to regain their power supported by these new public adherents. Once established as granddukes, they started to impose strict controls on the parochial organizations. Secular relationships became controlled in the unaltered framework of a religious view of the world. The appearance of the *arti* on the stage of Florentine public festivals coincided with the loss of their political voice in a more bureaucratic, centralized and monarchic state system. Could their symbolic function be called a politically harmless and controlled safety valve? That would be an indication of the successful integration of the population through a symbolic participation in public life.[9]

In Protestant countries most of the church festivals disappeared, but some gained compensation in secular festivities. For instance, the annual installation of the new magistracy in London on 29 Octo-

ber grew into a splendid public ritual. The choice of a Lord Mayor was accompanied by a triumphal parade, starting by boat on the Thames from Guildhall to the Palace of Westminster, where the oath was administered. Returning to the city, he was then handed its keys and was met at St Paul's Cathedral by a *tableau vivant* with actors declaiming addresses and verses. As well as the usual allegorical praises of the cardinal virtues or qualities of the city company to which the Lord Mayor belonged, there were also commentaries on historical events and topical political occasions. Certainly during the periods of religious and political tension in the seventeenth century at least one 'papal plot' was exposed. The tableaux followed the Lord Mayor's coach and the procession of gentry, members of the city companies and other organizations through the town, which was decorated with triumphal arches. The whole spectacle was arranged for the

The scene is painted on a Florentine bridal chest of *c.* 1417.
It shows plainly how the riders, defending the colours of their parish,
ride each other off in the race, frequently a cause of accidents.
Cleveland, Cleveland Museum of Art, Holden Collection

public by the city company of the new Lord Mayor, and was carried out by professionals. There was no longer any question of a spontaneous interaction as there had been in the much smaller medieval towns. Illustrated accounts of the proceedings were immediately published, because in a town of half a million inhabitants it was no longer possible for everyone to see it all in person.

Apart from ceremonials, it was particularly in buildings that a visible and comprehensible political message was expressed to the masses. The size of buildings, their location, free-standing or surrounded by other buildings, elevated above the masses and accessible – or strictly not – and the height of any towers, are all elementary factors which carry a clear message to the observer. Moreover, buildings can be charged with additional significance, communicating a political message to the educated and the cultured when they take a closer look at them.

The earliest and most elaborate demonstrations of a purely civic symbolic universe are naturally found in the Italian towns. The central market was arranged as a public open space which would reflect the town's identity. In Perugia it lay between the cathedral, where the body of St Lawrence is kept as a precious relic, and the 'Palace of the People' – later rechristened 'Palace of the Priors' – on a somewhat lower site, but still imposing with its mass of masonry, battlements and monumental entrance. It housed administrative functions in the commercial field, such as the Exchange, the Chamber of Trade, and the Hall of the Notaries. Early in the fourteenth century the bronze emblems of the town, the lion and the gryphon, were placed on the facade of the cathedral above the main entrance.

In 1278 the great fountain in the middle of the square, on which the sculptor Nicola Pisano had worked, was completed. A spring is always a meeting place and in Christian symbolism it is a symbol of spiritual life and salvation. The fountain consists of three basins, placed one above the other, and smaller in size as they ascend; the two lower ones are decorated with an iconographic programme easily visible to passers-by, and also explained by

Canaletto painted the *Lord Mayor's Show on the Thames* about 1747. Every year the richly decorated barge
of the newly elected Lord Mayor of London was rowed up the Thames from Guildhall to Westminster, where he took the oath.
He then went in procession in the Golden Coach to St Paul's Cathedral and through the streets of the City.
Artillery salutes, rolls of drums and fanfares of trumpets completed the spectacle. London, Victoria and Albert Museum

inscriptions. The middle basin is twelve-sided, without question a comparison of Perugia with Jerusalem. The groups of figures symbolize the dual origins of the town: on the one hand as part of the Catholic Church, of which it is part without being subordinated to it; on the other hand as an urban community with its own heroes. The two central figures were respectively St John the Baptist as the harbinger of Rome, the centre of the world, and Euliste *(nobilis Heulixstes Perusine conditor urbis)* the mythological founder of Perugia, portrayed as lawgiver, priest-king and warrior. St John the Baptist is between two pairs of symbols and saints of the Church: the Catholic Church, the apostle St Peter, the sublime Godhead, and St Paul, the people's scholar. Opposite him Euliste is flanked by Melchizedek, the priest-king of Jerusalem, and the people's captain Ermanno da Sassoferrato; on the other side by the archangel Michael and the *podestà* Matteo da Correggio. The circle is completed by the two local saints St Lawrence and St Ercolano.

A few years later, in 1293, inspired by a local lawyer, the Eulistea, a historical epic, was written in Latin verse – a history of the town from its origins in which the development of the people and their constitutional role is emphasized. The confrontations with the supporters of Frederick II and with Rome, the creation of their own territory, are described in it in a reflection on the internal and external political position of the town. Its public law nature and the harmonious setting up of the urban community and that of its territory form the basic theme of the poem, which reflects for a more select public the background of the political message which could already be seen and read on the fountain. During the fourteenth century a vernacular history of Perugia appeared, in which the protagonist Ulisste appears as the hero of a chivalric romance, without the complex political constructs of the earlier scholarly epic, but purely based on associations with a glorious mythological past.[10]

A similar link between a town's political propaganda in text and in pictures can be established for the frescoes painted by Ambrogio Lorenzetti be-

At the end of the eighteenth century a painting by Francesco Guardi showed how the doge of Venice was presented
with his ceremonial headdress on accepting the highest office of the republic. At that time, however, the doge had hardly any power
and was bound by the decisions of the Council who had elected him.
Externally he was, however, surrounded by extravagant Byzantine-inspired ceremonial. Paris, Musée du Louvre

tween 1337 and 1340 in the *Sala dei Nove* of Siena town hall. While even for the superficial observer it is plain what the aediles intended by depicting good government on one side and bad on the other, the painter followed this inspiration up into the smallest details from specialized treatises on town administration in the second half of the thirteenth century. The pre-Humanist authors drew on the one hand on classical literature, particularly Cicero's *De Officiis*, about offices, and on Seneca, and on the other hand on their own experience of administration and justice. In particular *Li Livres dou tresor*, the encyclopedia assembled by Brunetto Latini in the early 1260s, based on earlier works, corresponds very closely with Lorenzetti's composition. There are also striking similarities with the constitution of Siena signed in 1309.

All these texts call the preservation of peace, concord and quiet the most precious value in public life, and the manifest goal of every good government. The *Novi Signori*, chosen from the merchant oligarchy ruling the town from 1287 to 1355, who used to meet in this very room, saw as a statement of their most important obligation 'to keep the town in enduring peace and pure righteousness'. Lorenzetti inscribed the word PAX right in the middle of his composition, in the central one of the three walls he painted. A belaurelled female figure with a palm branch, representing peace, sits in the middle of the central section of the cycle. On the left (sinister) side of the fresco he painted the enemies of peace: war, division (dressed in black and white, Siena's heraldic colours) and rage, represented by a three-headed monster. According to Cicero concord was one of the two fundamentals of public life. The female figure with this emblem is offering a double cord of red and grey to twenty-four (twice twelve) citizens, who stand at the feet of the figure of the ruler on his right (good) side. She is given this cord by the angels of righteousness above her. The citizens willingly hold it as a means towards unity; the other end is tied to the right wrist of the figure of the ruler, the hand in which he holds his sceptre. In this way he is linked in his rule

to the unity of the citizens, which proceeds from righteousness. Below him stand groups of warriors, the strong arm of the ruler. At his left foot two members of the nobility in full armour dedicate their castle to the town. Further on shackled criminals are being chastised – a right to left, good to bad composition which the whole of Christianity recognized from pictures of the Last Judgement. The ruler, inspired by the Christian virtues of faith, love of one's fellow men, and hope, is seated on a bench surrounded by six female figures, among whom Peace reclines slightly to one side, and the other five represent Seneca's five civic virtues: Prudence, Magnanimity, Fortitude, Temperance and Justice.

Between 1337 and 1340 Ambrogio Lorenzetti painted a fresco in the Hall of the Council of Nine of Siena town hall,

Thus the ruler is surrounded by a total of nine virtues, exactly the number of *Signori* in Siena.[11]

Particularly striking is the female figure enthroned under the quotation from the Book of Wisdom: 'Dispense justice, Ye who judge on earth.' Above her floats Wisdom, holding the scales before her; she gazes into the unknown. Two angels carry out her tasks: distributive justice beheads and crowns; commutative or restitutive justice brings about fair settlements and compensation between

on the subject of good government. The central figure is Peace.
Siena, Palazzo Publico, Sala dei Nove

parties. The strings coming from these two functions lead to Concord, who binds the citizens together. Wisdom is here therefore visibly separated from the other virtues; she sits apart from the administrators and distinguishes various forms of justice, separate from the traditional virtues. Here is a form of division of powers long before Montesquieu, in accordance with the distinction which applied in towns between the criminal courts and the civil arbitration.

Even this limited analysis of part of Lorenzetti's frescoes shows that the administrators of Siena about 1340 were capable of showing – for their own benefit and that of all visitors to the town hall – a completely clear, comprehensive and coherent vision of the establishment of a republican form of government on a mainly secular foundation. What was then illustrated pictorially had been developed in the texts of laws and the writings of legal scholars since the mid-thirteenth century. Other parts of Europe were not in a position to offer anything like as much in this field as the Italian towns and city states. The Gothic town halls of the Low Countries were certainly provided with iconographic

Pieter de Hooch painted the *Parlour of the Burgomasters* soon after the new town hall of Amsterdam was taken into use.
It shows what the room looked like originally. Above the mantel hung Ferdinand Bol's *Consul Fabricius and King Pyrrhus* (1656) which,
together with Govaert Flinck's *The Virtue of Marcus Curius Dentatus* – which the elegant gentleman is contemplating
from the opposite side of the room – invites the burgomasters to govern well.
Madrid, Thyssen-Bornemisza Collection

programmes, but these consisted primarily of fa-
çades covered with statues of princes and local
heroes. Plenty of scenes of justice being administered were hung in court rooms, paintings which
treated the subject of righteous judges through
biblical themes. Richly decorated chimney-pieces,
like those in Bruges and Courtrai, reflected the formal power structure through images and symbols,
but did not touch upon public values. In that environment political theory was applied pragmatically,
relying on local and regional juridical tradition
rather than on learned treatises.

The high point of the monumental expression
of a civic political theory in later centuries must be
the Amsterdam town hall, built between 1650
and 1655. The imposing building was erected soon

after the Republic of the United Provinces gained international recognition in the Peace of Westphalia, which brought to an end the Eighty Years War with Spain. After an explosive period of development the young state had almost reached its peak. The decoration of the exterior is on the whole sober and is confined to bronze figures of the cardinal virtues, of Atlas and similar representations. The decoration of the rooms inside was undoubtedly very luxurious, making use of various decorative techniques and of lines from the works of Vondel, the great Dutch poet. As for political content, however, we find little here that would have been new in Siena. In general the theme was strictly based on classical and biblical examples, more topically referring to situations which could occur in each specific office. Coats of arms of the earliest administrators decorated the rooms where they had exercised their duties. More than in Siena, in Amsterdam there was a heavy moral emphasis, concentrating on the incorruptibility of the officials, the honour of the office, and its moral obligations.

The office of the burgomaster was adorned with a mantel painting showing how the Consul Quintus Fabius Maximus ordered his father, himself a former consul, to dismount from his horse. Even the ceiling paintings referred in their emblems to the honour of the office. In the adjoining burgomaster's parlour the paintings illustrated the fearlessness and incorruptibility of Roman consuls. The mantel painting in the treasurer's room showed Joseph selling grain collected in the years of plenty to the starving people. In the magistrates' room a fresco showed Justice, Fortitude and Prudence. For the mantel Frans Bol painted *Moses with the Ten Commandments*, and Artus Quellien carved the relief of the *Worship of the Golden Calf.* The appropriate decorative theme for the commissioners of insolvent estates – thus responsible for orphans – is also striking. As well as an *Odysseus and Nausicaa* by Thomas de Keyser, and a ceiling painting extolling the charities of guardianship, the mantel painting showed Lycurgus who, by immediately recognizing his newly-born nephew as the legitimate successor to his throne, showed that he did not want to abuse his guardianship. It is not so much a restatement of political theory that strikes a note in the iconographic programme of the Amsterdam town hall as its consistent moralizing tone. This still compares favourably with the town hall of the free imperial city of Augsburg, completed in 1620. The building demonstrated an impressive monumentalism, partly by its location at the highest point of a spacious square. The sober facade is actually only distinguished by the imposing painted imperial eagle, and by the pineapple in the top of the gable – the emblem this town had taken over from its founder, the Roman emperor Augustus. The paintings in the vast Golden Hall show eight Roman emperors, with on the wall opposite their Christian counterparts. Allusions to the benevolent town administrators are witness to an identification with and subordination to the imperial idea, however theoretical this might be, rather than manifesting a political model of autonomous citizenship, as in Italy or Amsterdam.

In the urbanized regions of Europe detailed secular theories of public power therefore existed within both urban and territorial frameworks. They were based both on classical inspiration and on their own incremental experience of justice and administration. The rare urban republics – Venice, the United Provinces and, on a much more modest scale, the Swiss Federation and some free cities of the Empire – developed this tradition further. Within the towns of Italy, Catalonia, the Rhineland, northern Germany and the southern Netherlands, which were stagnating from the fifteenth century, the development of oligarchies gradually began to increase and political participation to diminish. In the earlier Italian city republics new monarchs determinedly took over the helm and acted like territorial princes, allowing the country nobility to develop again. The administrative elites, whose power was curtailed, were easily bought off by the seductions of princely patronage. From now on they were to see their role more as that of mediators between local and central interests than as that of promoting an autonomous city republic. From a symbolic aspect they allowed the spectacle of public ceremony in the town to be controlled by the princes who ruled the city and the country. When in the seventeenth century the supremacy of the monarchies over the towns had become a fact in virtually the whole of Europe, the winners no longer needed a direct dialogue with their subjects. The court withdrew from the towns which had been brought under administrative control.

Courtly society

Royal courts were always characterized by their artistic activities and their festive celebrations. They held literary recitals, music was performed, there was dancing, artistic gifts were exchanged and buildings were decorated. As the monarchies were able to establish their supremacy above all other powers in society more plainly, from the fourteenth and fifteenth centuries, they exhibited a stronger tendency to express this power symbolically. Naked power is after all not honourable; artistic metaphors served to elevate it above the ordinary. This sublimation made the roots of power less transparent and so helped to establish it more firmly.

From now on, however, the feast was no longer to be for the eyes of the people, but would be celebrated in the exclusivity of the court. In 1479 Lodovico Sforza, 'Il Moro', seized power by force in Milan; in his turn he would be chased out by Louis XII's army in 1499, and after his unsuccessful coup escorted back to France. He first introduced changes to the Milanese festival culture by distancing himself from the popular festivities on the square in front of the cathedral on the occasion of the fund-raising for completing its construction. Within the heavy walls of his *Castello* he organized cultured performances for the aristocrats about the Garden of Eden, which boiled down to a glorification of his princely person. To honour the new cult of the prince no less an artist than Leonardo da Vinci produced complicated theatrical effects, with movable scenery, far removed from the mass of the people whose masters they were, after all.[12]

The Humanist spirit of enquiry was fed by the craving for artistic brilliance. For young states and new dynasties founding a university was a means of gaining prestige. Frederick II founded his university in Naples, as Charles IV did his in Prague and other princes theirs in Coimbra, Vienna, Uppsala, St Andrews, Buda and Cracow. In the still fragile Republic of the United Provinces the States of Holland and the Stadtholder William of Orange founded the University of Leiden, still formally in the name of King Philip II of Spain. Significantly theology was one of the first areas of study. Breaking the Church's earlier monopoly of knowledge was manifestly one of the aims of these foundations. In the seventeenth and eighteenth centuries Academies and Learned Societies began to fulfil a similar function of lending brilliance to the state. Renaissance princes assembled art collections and exercised patronage both from their personal interest and in the conviction that such were the proper activities of a modern prince. Charles V of France assembled a library of richly illuminated manuscripts, an example his descendants in the Burgundian line were to surpass. Frederico da Montefeltro, duke of Urbino, not only liked to have himself portrayed as a classical hero, but also constructed a *studiolo*, a private room where he studied personally. Pope Julius II had Raphael paint rooms in the Vatican with glorifications of classical learning, in which he had himself painted as the equal of the great lawgivers of the world and the Church: the emperor Justinian, who commissioned the Pandects, and Pope Gregory IX, who published the Decretals. Cosimo I of the archduchy of Florence had Vasari paint the vast Hall of the Five Hundred, where the representatives of the former republic used to meet, in order to extol his princely glory. Italian influences brought a new elegance to the courts of Matthias Corvinus in Buda and of the Jagellonians in Cracow.

Since they had marched through Italy with their armies from 1494 onwards, the French kings came under the spell of the Renaissance palaces, and had a whole string of them built along the Loire. Francis I had a gallery built at Fontainebleau on the Seine for his collection of classical art, which he personally – in the character of 'Master of the Mysteries' – opened to his intimate invited guests. His earlier castles in the capital, the Ile de la Cité and the Louvre had for long not been used as residences. Kings moved out of town, to Hampton Court or the Escorial.

But first, of course, to Versailles.

The unprecedented programmes of building and decoration in the long reign of Louis XIV (1661–1715) created the model for courtly society that was to bewitch all European aristocracies in the eighteenth century. Intended as a model for society, it had to be presented not only in imagery but as a permanent series of spectacles, meant as an intensive civilizing campaign to attach the turbulent nobility to the court and hence to the state. The continual festivities, balls, horse shows, royal progresses, theatrical performances, concerts and fireworks were aimed in the first place at imprinting in the minds of the nobles a strict etiquette with a hierarchy tightly oriented on the king. The trauma of aristocratic rebellion during the *Fronde* between 1648 and 1652 produced its reaction in the form of a global scenario of seduction which would teach the turbulent nobility throughout the land to behave humbly and in a civilized way in their station in the service of an absolute monarchy. It was a compre-

The enchanted room in Maria of Hungary's castle at Binche during the reception of Prince Philip (later Philip II) of Spain in 1549.
For each course a table descended from the heavens all set for the distinguished visitors, and wine flowed from the painted rock face
to one's heart's desire. Small lamps with perfumed oils spread a pleasant fragrance to the painted ceiling.
Coloured pen drawing of the same year. Brussels, Bibliothèque royale de Belgique, Cabinet d'Estampes

hensive programme which provided employment for 36,000 in 1685 and to the indignation of many contemporaries soaked up millions of livres. For the whole period of the reign it cost 82 million livres, an average 1.8 per cent of the state budget, a trifle in comparison with the 52 per cent devoted to war. At least the whole of Versailles cost the state less than the *Fronde*.

The arrangement which was laid out in stages in the gardens, the palace and the town of Versailles was along a west-to-east axis centred on the king's bedchamber, the core of this symbolic universe. On the east side of the palace were the ministerial departments and the three axes, like three prongs of a fork, pointing towards the town. The west side consisted of the gardens, which symbolized the seasons, the monarchy and France. Nature with its four elements, time with its four seasons, man with his four humours, and the stars moved in perfect harmony, expressed by the symmetrical and clearly ordered design. Thus the function of the king consisted of safeguarding the harmony and permanence of the realm. The only rotation could be that of the stars, not that of men. The groups of statuary in the west end of the central axis, of Apollo, the god of the sun, and of Leto, who with the help of Zeus protected her children Apollo and Diana against the rebellious peasants of Lycia who were punished by being turned into toads (according to Ovid), are manifestly allegories for the king and for the *Fronde* during the years of his minority. The interior decoration of the State Apartments, which were built in the first decades of the reign, was based on classical mythology and history. The message here was still an indirect and general one about the qualities of a ruler: Trajan pronounces judgement, Ptolemy Philadelphus grants freedom to the Jews, Solon explains his laws to the Athenians, Alexander Severus has corn distributed to the people. Similar themes and allegories were in the same period painted in Amsterdam town hall, where Calvinist republican merchants ruled, albeit that they avoided worshipping monarchs.

After the Treaty of Nijmegen (1678) Louis gave a much more nationalist and personal turn to his iconographic programme. This is when the bronze figures were set up in the gardens in basins representing the rivers of France. French emblems were added to the capitals: the sun, fleurs-de-lis and the Gallic cock against a background of palms. Above all the painted ceilings in the Hall of Mirrors and the adjoining rooms portrayed the great deeds of the king. Eighteen smaller scenes showed the special activities of government, and six great compositions were devoted to the Dutch War and the conquest of Franch-Comté. In the two central panels the king himself was portrayed as a classical god holding thunderbolts: as Apollo crossing the Rhine in his chariot, and as Jupiter seated upon a cloud at the capture of Ghent. The other scenes show Louis before the battle, weighing up the risks, choosing courses of action, taking decisions, making preparations. In contrast to earlier iconographic traditions Versailles displayed no genealogical justifications, no descent from a mythical origin or from the founder of the country. It exhibited, gradually more directly and more recognizably, a completely contemporary period.

Already by 1684 explanations were being printed by royal command of the paintings in the Hall of Mirrors, so that no visitor should remain unaware of the meanings of the apparently complicated composition. It was after all not meant to be read in a straight line, but starting from the centre (the king) travelling in concentric circles to the periphery – where the enemy powers were located. Thus the order of the representations reflected the abso-

lutist order of the state. The political message was actually briefly summed up in the words of Bossuet, the court chaplain:

> *I do not know what divinity attaches to princes and awakes such fear in the people ... Ye are gods, ye have authority in you, ye bear a divine mark on your forehead ... O kings, exercise your power boldly ...*[13]

The universe portrayed was meant to attune the conceptual universe of the French aristocracy to the objectives of the monarchy. Architecture here underpinned a social and political structure heavily laden with significance. The indoctrinatory efforts to strengthen the royal authority over the aristocracy spoke so eloquently to other princes throughout Europe that Versailles literally became the pattern for princely courts from Lisbon to St Petersburg. French court culture became the general European culture of the elite in the areas of etiquette, language, literature, music and design. At the same time an intellectual reaction to the overwhelming indoctrination grew from this cultural trend. In aristocratic salons the intellectual level of debates rose as in the course of the eighteenth century these were increasingly fed by the social criticism of philosophers. It was along this road that the progressive section of the nobility and the bourgeoisie were to reject the ideology of absolutism.

Without any doubt court art, however serviceable it may have been, started an unprecedented creative élan in which the performing arts probably experienced the most innovative effects. The Italian princely courts, which in the fifteenth century already competed with each other, not only on the battlefield but also in cultural expression, remained the leading influence in this field until the nineteenth century. In their drive to astonish the arrogant court circles with continual new products, media and inventions, the internationally circulating artists created a strong cultural movement. Since every prince of any significance tried to maintain a court orchestra, the demand for musicians grew, as also for new scores and librettos. By its manifold applications music became, after architecture, perhaps the most functional branch of the arts. Because of their excessive costs, both were also the most exclusive. Court composers were engaged from far and near to compose pieces for every occasion. The most famous of them was probably George Frederick Handel (1685–1759) who worked for the prince of Tuscany and after him for the Hanoverians, in London after 1714. In the style of his time he wrote operas to Italian neo-classical librettos,

Garden party at the court of Catherine de' Medici on the occasion of the reception of the Polish ambassadors.

In splendid surroundings courtiers performed the *Ballet of the French provinces* for the queen and her guests.

Detail of one of the eight 'Valois tapestries' of 1573.

Florence, Gallerie degli Uffizi

as well as music for court festivities – *Coronation Anthems, Music for the Royal Fireworks, Water Music* – a *Te Deum* and chamber music. Only after he had become world famous was he able to devote himself entirely to his own preference – oratorios. However, the fact that almost all seventeenth- and eighteenth-century composers in the first place had to live on the commissions of their royal patrons, and that the form of their products had therefore to be adapted to their prince's resources and preferences, did not prevent immortal works of art being created which have for generations enchanted other publics far removed from their original court audiences.

Let us now examine one of the peripheral princely courts of the time in some detail: in this instance the Swedish court which during the seventeenth century was also at the peak of its power. The court painter, David Klöcker Ehrenstrahl, was the central figure here, who for a quarter of a century portrayed all the symbolism of the state. In the House of the

A royal visit, birth or marriage was accompanied by festivities which also involved the subjects.

The high point was a grand fireworks display.

Fireworks in June 1709 on the Elbe at Dresden on the occasion of the visit of the king of Denmark.

Dresden, Kupferstichkabinett

The Farnese theatre, entirely built of wood, was erected in 1618 in a single year on the upper floor of the ducal palace at Parma.

It had a painted ceiling and many niches holding statues. Three hundred lights gave the theatre a muted appearance

and the floor could be flooded for water spectacles by using an ingenious system of pumps.

Parma, Palazzo Bourbon, Galleria Nazionale

Versailles and the society of the French court were the model in the eighteenth century for countless other princely courts.
The Swedish royal summer palace at Drottningholm is seen here from the garden, with its fountain of Hercules (c. 1740).
The statues in the park, spoils of war from Prague and the Danish castle of Frederiksborg, were by Adriaen de Vries (sixteenth century).
Nyköping, County Administration

In the first 'quadrille' of the carrousel, a horse show in which the royal cavalry displayed their skills to music in the open air,
Charles XI of Sweden paraded in the uniform of a Roman general, followed by a troop of soldiers bearing fasces.
This carrousel was held at Stockholm after his coronation in 1672. Print by Georg C. Eimmart the Younger after David Klöcker von Ehrenstrahl.
Stockholm, Statens Konstmuseer

These frescos by Raphael in the Hall of the Signature of the Vatican Palace show the great reforming pope, Gregory IX,
with the features of Pope Julius II de la Rovere (1503–1513), handing over the *Decretals* to Raymond de Penafort.
The second fresco shows Justinian, the Byzantine emperor and lawgiver, giving his *Pandects* to Tribonian to be implemented.
Rome, Museo Vaticano, Sala della Segnatura

Nobles, where the Diet met, he provided the great hall in 1674 with a painted ceiling of the Apotheosis of Sweden. Personified as Svecia, she presides over a gathering of the virtues and is acclaimed by Fame. The royal palace at Drottningholm outside Stockholm was the scene of festivities, balls and theatrical performances. By now the subject matter should be familiar to us: Queen Christina was hailed as Minerva, the patron goddess of the arts and lover of peace. Justice, Prudence and Peace appeared with Wisdom on the stage during the coronation ceremony of 1650 – Lorenzetti had already included them in his complicated allegory in 1340 – and a triumphal car bore Fortune. Gustavus Adolphus was acclaimed as the new Augustus. About 1670 Charles XI was portrayed as Apollo, the astral symbol who as in France was to pervade royal panegyrics. Ehrenstrahl painted the sun god with the features of Charles XI, depicting him after his defeat of the dragon Python. On the occasion of the enlargement of royal power and the acceptance of female succession in 1683 Ehrenstrahl made a portrait of the royal family as an Apotheosis. The princes were clothed in classical robes, the little princess crowning her little brother in the traditional blue toga with a laurel wreath. In an allegory of the succession in 1693 the court painter expressed the humble loyalty of the Four Estates to the anointed kingship. In a central gallery of the palace realistic wall paintings offered an accurate picture of Charles X Gustavus' battles, both as a lesson in the art of war and a glorification of Swedish royal militarism. It was a more or less contemporaneous equivalent of the Hall of Mirrors in Versailles, but incomparably simpler in its dimensions, inspiration and design. Performances in the palace theatre at Drottningholm were equally outspoken in their praise for the dynasty. For the birthday of the young Charles XI in 1669 Count Erik Lindschold, one of the councillors, wrote the text for a

François Puget is thought to have been commissioned by King Louis XIV of France to record for posterity the court musicians of Versailles and Lully, his favourite composer, in this painting in 1687. The score on the table is an ode to the everlasting fame of the king, of whom it is known that he was cured of an illness in that particular year.

Paris, Musée du Louvre

ballet about princely genius, a subject also treated in contemporary paintings. Genius led the prince along the path of virtue; he was represented fully grown as Hercules faced with the choice between virtue and dishonour, after which Fame announces the future glory of the king.[14]

This work of art has not, however, achieved the glory ascribed to the works of Molière and Racine, which were being produced at the same time at Versailles. It was not so much a matter of absolute aesthetic quality, as of the effect achieved by this symbolism on the select audience for which it was created. Seen in this light artistic media contributed strongly to the consolidation and imprinting of the new, more authoritative and larger-scale power relationships. From the late eighteenth century the 'courtly' pattern of culture percolated by imitation down into the bourgeois middle classes. In the final analysis it also contributed in the modern mass society to the acceptance of an imposed order.

1 MORAND 1790, x; SAUERLÄNDER 1977.
2 LE GOFF in BAK 1990.
3 BEAUNE 1985, 226–229.
4 GUENÉE & LEHOUX 1968, 18, 26–29.
5 BRYANT 1986 & 1990.
6 BLOCKMANS 1994.
7 SCHELLER 1982, 47–48.
8 SCHELLER 1985.
9 TREXLER 1980.
10 GALLETTI 1988.
11 SKINNER 1989.
12 RACINE 1994.
13 SABATIER in *Culture et Idéologie* 1985.
14 ELLENIUS 1988.

CHAPTER VII
The Formation of
the European System of States

Eight hundred years of the development of European power systems have so far been unravelled into six components which seem to be equally essential. Dynamism led to the formation of substantially larger but no less penetrative areas of power. The accomplishment is indeed the more remarkable because the enormous expansion of the territories, within which power was exercised from a co-ordinated centre, was accompanied by the creation of appropriate control apparatus. These could on a steadily increasing scale exercise the various forms of power necessary to make a controlled social reproduction possible.

Fragmentation and segmentation of areas of power is characteristic of the whole *ancien régime.* This was also the case within the larger states of the seventeenth and eighteenth centuries which are often mistakenly labelled national and absolutist. All states before 1800, and many still after that date, consisted of countless privileged territorial and social entities – princedoms, provinces, towns, seigneuries, ecclesiastical immunities, the aristocracy, local communities and even the corporate bodies set up by the state itself, such as the royal courts of law – whose centuries-old rights and customs could not be interfered with without provoking resistance or rebellion. The central government had to negotiate with these bodies if it wanted to obtain more from them than the performance of those duties to which they were committed by virtue of a mutual contract. This segmentation of the European power systems was about 1780 still expressed in the manifold variety of sovereign and quasi-sovereign entities which made the map look so fragmented within states as well as between them. There were still at that time in Europe autonomous peasant communities, city republics, republican confederations, regional states dominated by a city republic, ecclesiastical and secular princedoms of many grades and sizes, kingdoms, and no fewer than three empires. Several of these powers also exercised colonial authority outside Europe in various ways.

This diversity of power systems was the logical reflection of the lengthy and irregular process of growth they had gone through over eight centuries. In this complex weave of competition, coalition, absorption and destruction, every unit had been formed by a large number of forces interacting at various times and with varying intensity. For this reason the same influences produced divergent outcomes on different units or at other times. The number of interactive factors in this process of social differentiation is so great that the number of outcomes is extremely varied, so that generalized

The armoury tower of the Hofburg in Innsbruck
was recorded for posterity by Matthias Perathoner
in 1777, just before its demolition.
Round the central portrait
by the painter Georg Kölder (1499)
are fifty-four coats of arms
of regions ruled by the Habsburgs.
On the left of the entrance stood a knight in armour
with the banner of Habsburg,
on the right another with the banner of Tyrol.
The arms of Hungary can be seen
above the second-floor window.
On the upper part of the tower, in the middle row
on the left the figures of Maximilian I
and his two successive wives,
Mary of Burgundy and Bianca Sforza,
can be identified,
and on the right those of Ferdinand I
and Anne of Hungary.
Innsbruck, Tiroler Landesmuseum Ferdinandeum

The apotheosis of Charles v is illustrated on this round Italian shield of the first half of the sixteenth century.

A Roman galley carries the belaurelled emperor over the oceans.

The Pillars of Hercules symbolize the cliffs at the western end of the Mediterranean which formed

the frontier of the known world in classical times.

The winged Victory on the ship's bow holds a shield with the motto of Charles, *Plus ultra,* in mirror writing.

This implied that his Empire reached 'much further', in fact to the two Americas.

Madrid, Real Armeria

statements can only be relevant to relationships between the factors themselves, and not to each outcome separately. Simple interpretations are therefore nothing but reductions and simplifications. What conclusions can still be drawn about the factors operating in the process?

Note: see p. 313 The mutual competitive conflict of feudal lords in early medieval society, which rested on an almost exclusively agricultural basis, has been identified as an initial driving force in the process of the enlargement of power.[1] Each of them strove consciously to expand their territory. Their joint efforts led to the elimination of their weaker rivals and a larger dimension for the surviving units. With adjustments, the feudal model influenced the ruling systems of Europe fundamentally. First of all because in central and eastern Europe until the nineteenth

century, and in many regions of the west until the end of the eighteenth, it continued to function as the primary, lowest level of the exercise of power; secondly, because it became a model for various public law relationships; and finally because the feudal ethic, oriented towards honour through valiant behaviour in battle and – partly as a result – enlarging one's holdings of land, fundamentally continued to determine aristocratic thought, and to a large degree also that of rulers.

Between the tenth and twelfth centuries this continuous competitive strife between feudal lords acquired an additional impulse from the rise in agricultural productivity. Pressure on the means of subsistence increased as a result of the consequent growth in population, helped by the ending of non-Christian invasions. This pressure led to expansion

In the second half of the fifteenth century Urbino, under Duke Frederico da Montefeltro,
was one of the most flourishing centres of art in northern Italy.
In c. 1475 Justus van Gent made a portrait of Frederico as a warrior-prince, reading.
Urbino, Galleria Nazionale delle Marche

On the *Campo* at Siena, the scallop-shaped area in front of the town hall, the Franciscan Bernardinus (1380–1444)
preached public sermons which had a great following among the rich as well as among the poor.
Sano di Pietro (1406–1481) was a faithful witness and shows that the listening crowd was arranged by sexes as if they were in church.
Siena, Capitolo del Duomo

In 1500 the patricians of the town of Augsburg held a ball on the upper floor of the town hall. Among the invited guests were also
non-patricians of both sexes who because of their prominent position formed part of the local association of 'High Society'.
Dancing gave both social classes an opportunity to meet, which often led to marriages and a rise from the lower to the upper class.
Painted record of the Augsburg *Geschlechtertanz* by Abraham Schelhas. Augsburg, Städtische Kunstsammlungen, Maximilianmuseum

as well as to implosion. Conquest and bringing new land under cultivation was, particularly in the thinly populated parts of central and northern Europe, the most obvious reaction. Increased competition, and particularly the rise of social mobility, characterized the more thickly populated and most progressive regions, so that the demesne system, on which the feudal power structure rested, was disrupted. The early monarchies, particularly in England and the Iberian peninsula, emerged from this dynamism. They can be regarded as power structures essentially formed from the socio-economic growth of Europe at this period, as opposed to the much older foundations upon which the Church was established.

In its organization, abstract ideas and universalism the Church still reflected the high stage of development achieved by the Roman empire. The adaption of its concepts – in many respects Roman – to the agricultural and even still nomadic types of society of the Germanic and Slav peoples could only lead to tensions. The frequently recurring ambition to restore the Roman (Christian) empire – actually from within the areas of the Germanic peoples who had only marginally been affected by

Roman colonization – never lasted longer than the fortuitous strength of a few successive generations of a dynasty. The institutionalization of the Empire through the superior organization of the Church led inevitably to a conflict of competences from which both the Empire and, some time later, the papacy emerged weakened.

Feudal monarchies after the twelfth century could only hold their own in their mutual competition if they (1) maintained a good working relationship with the Church, from which their authority could draw extra legitimacy and support; (2) possessed a sufficient *Hausmacht*, a dynastic power base to keep on top of their domestic feudal competitors; (3) could lay their hands on sufficient commercial capital in their territories as a new resource besides feudal service and their own demesne incomes. Support by the Church was in the initial stages essential for territorial princes for logistical reasons, because of the expert services of its highly educated staff. Moreover, after about AD 1000 the Church had launched a peace offensive, aimed at curbing the unbridled violence of the feudal lords. This benefited the princes, who eagerly took over this strategy of domestic pacification in order to

In this detail of his fresco *The angel appearing to Zacharias in the Temple,* Domenico Ghirlandaio (1440–1494)
immortalized four prominent citizens of Florence. They are Marsilio Ficino, Cristoforo Landino, Agnolo Poliziano and Gentile de' Becchi.
Florence, Santa Maria Novella

disarm their most important competitors. Naturally legitimization by the Church was also extremely valuable for princes, because it granted them sacramental elevation above ordinary knights. It meant that only they could employ religious arguments and means such as crusades and the protection of patron saints for their political ends.

The towns had grown as a result of the general increase in population. In their initial stages they enjoyed the support of the princes, for pay, particularly because they formed a counterweight or support for the princes against their real rivals, the great feudal lords. From the thirteenth century, in some commercialized regions of western Europe, trade capital represented a substantially larger volume of money than that which the princes had at their disposal through their traditional incomes from rents, excises, coining rights and fines. Loans from Italian or native merchants gave extra financial elbow-room to princes who could put pressure on merchants because they operated in their territory. This meant that they could mobilize more troops than their vassals, committed to feudal service, or their subjects. These were generally more reliable because they were now professional mercenaries who would stay in the field as long as they were paid, unlike the vassals who usually slipped away after forty days and also tended to put their own interests first. Princes who had no access to commercial capital of any size, as, for example, the

counts of Holland in the fourteenth century, were for that reason weaker than their competitors who could call on it, such as the dukes of Burgundy. Princes who could make effective use of the support of the Church and the financial resources and expertise of the merchants enjoyed an appreciable competitive advantage over their rivals, who had remained purely feudal. This could result in gains of territory such as those of the kings of England in the thirteenth and fourteenth centuries, the kings of France in the thirteenth and fifteenth, the kings of Aragon from the thirteenth to the fifteenth, the kings of Denmark and the dukes of Burgundy.

Towns were not just passive tools in the hands of princely strategists. Merchants administered the towns and insisted, if necessary by force of arms, on as much autonomy as possible. A striking example is offered by the Lombard towns, who by joining together in a mutual league were able to shake off the hegemony of the emperor Frederick Barbarossa. Most pronouncedly in Italy – and to a lesser degree in Catalonia, the Low Countries, the Rhineland and the Baltic coast – trading towns formed their own networks and associations for the protection of their mutual trade. In this environment commercial capitalism developed from northern Italy until from the thirteenth century it discarded more and more openly the restrictions which the Church ethic tried to impose on the accumulation of capital and levying interest on loans. The actions of the merchant capitalists were characterized by autonomy with respect to princely authority; in the early fourteenth and sixteenth centuries prominent examples demonstrated the disadvantages of putting too much trust in princes.

About 1300 a turning point in this development can be seen. Until then the various systems of power, each of which had its own resources, had developed relatively independently of each other. All had their points of contact, but Church, feudal lords, townspeople and princes in reality allowed each other the necessary elbow-room. From a demographic and economic point of view 1300 also meant an interruption to a trend: until then the population and production had gradually increased, but after that date a slow process of regression started. The shifts in power that accompanied this change in the long run strengthened the modernizing monarchies compared with their three great opposing powers: the feudal aristocracy, the Church and the towns.

The first to give way was the feudal aristocracy. The growth of a money economy had undermined their material basis, the expansion of the power of the princes had reduced their freedom of action, and finally the increasing importance of mercenary troops and local militias, all infantry, put an end to their military supremacy as cavalry.

During the eleventh century the Church was an autonomous power, able to launch a rebellion against the emperor Henry IV and leave him literally out in the cold, and by threats of excommunication forcing several French kings to revise their marriage policies, the umbilical cord of their dynasty, to fit the Church's prescriptions. However, the weapons of papal anathema, interdict and excommunication were deployed too often for obviously political reasons and lost their credibility. They no longer had any effect on the emperor Frederick II. King Philip the Fair took so little notice of them in 1302 – though he had first obtained the support of the States General – that he had the pope himself imprisoned. The issue was in fact a political one, the freedom of the king to tax church property. In spite of the establishment of the mendicant orders, who concentrated especially on preaching in the fast-growing towns, where a new class of poor had now emerged, the Church lost its hold on the urban communities. The mendicant orders proved to be rabid persecutors of heretics, which meant that the need, particularly in bourgeois circles, for a less formal kind of faith, but one more satisfying, authentic and liberal, was frustrated. The removal

of the Curia to Avignon, the Western Schism, and the secularization of the Church fundamentally affected its credibility. It survived as a result of small devout moves for innovation at its foundations and integration into the apparatus of the state at the top of its hierarchy. This meant the loss of the autonomy which the Church had previously enjoyed as an institution above the state, wielding the highest authority on norms, values and philosophy. The monarchies eagerly made use of the material, organizational, intellectual and ritual resources of the Church, not least to add to their own divine aura and that of the embryo state. The state churches, enclosed within their frontiers, were absorbed by the monarchies and set to work on political ends, ultimately on creating a social discipline. The wars of religion made this process more radical and more absolute: the churches which had to ascribe their survival to secular political power were reduced to supporting that power as their most prominent function.

The third factor opposing the monarchies were the towns, at least in those regions where towns represented a substantial proportion of the population and of wealth. In Scandinavia, central and eastern Europe, as in the central regions of France and Spain, the level of urbanization was so low that it had no political importance. This was not the case in northern and central Italy, Catalonia and the other urbanized regions. There the large towns had built up both regional systems of power and interregional networks, sometimes even colonies. They did not let themselves be drawn passively into the expanding monarchic states. The economic recession in the fourteenth century meant a temporary end to the development of the towns in general, with in some cases a dramatic fall in population. There were shifts in the international economy in which some regions fell sharply back, and others developed. These processes were not controlled by the princes, though they were partly determined by whether their policy with regard to trade was favourable or less so. The economic stagnation of some regions created opportunities for princes to make the weakened towns more dependent upon them. These opportunities occurred mainly where princes had so established and built up their judicial, financial and military organization that it became an administrative apparatus that operated to some extent separately from the individual ruler. This meant that dominion was no longer exercised on the basis of a purely feudal commitment between individuals, but by a depersonalized body of

Florentine senators paying homage and swearing allegiance to the young grand duke of Tuscany, Ferdinand II de' Medici (1610–1670).
Justus Sustermans recorded the event. Oxford, Ashmolean Museum

officials, professionally trained and following their own rules.

In this stage of development, between 1300 and 1600 depending on the region, states can be distinguished as separate institutions from the earlier court establishments of feudal lords, which had come apart at the seams. As impersonal institutions these states had neither been planned nor in fact desired by any of the participants in the earlier struggle for power. However, depending on the degree of success achieved by the feudal lords in their deliberate efforts to expand their territory, they had to adjust their resources of power in order to keep their ever larger holdings under control. They therefore had to create a state apparatus, with officials. These in their turn started to regard the interests of the state – often identified with those of the prince, but not *per se* under all circumstances – as the objectives of their own actions, and therefore by striving to enlarge the power of the state, they also served their own personal interests. Once it was possible to think of the state in abstract, the promotion of general prosperity could be ascribed to it, which within its own territory implied in the first place that public law and order must be guaranteed. The state could then claim to be weighing the mutual clash of interests of ranks and classes fairly against each other, implying a new, rational legitimization of power.

The states formed in this way offered safety under the law to more people because of their superiority in the instruments of violence and their

guarantee of fair treatment at law. Rule by city-states had never – even in the Venetian *terraferma* – meant that there was equal status under the law for the urban and the rural population, or even for citizens of the capital and those of smaller towns. Not a single ruling city granted the general right of citizen status, which had made the Roman state so strong. On the contrary, towns, like the clergy and the aristocracy, remained until the end of the *ancien régime* entrenched behind their walls of privilege, insisting on judicial, economic and fiscal advantages. This characteristic particularism made it difficult for the towns to maintain leagues with each other for long, because the necessary solidarity for this was always lacking. The princes' armies were therefore able to defeat them all one by one. The military superiority of the state was assisted from the fifteenth century by the development of firearms. The greater security and safety under the law which the state – after acceptance of its hegemony – could offer made many of the functions for which leagues of towns had earlier been set up redundant and also exercised an attraction on the areas dominated by large towns. Internal pacification and the establishment of a state system of law offered obvious advantages in the shape of lowering the cost of protection for distant trading by land and, after the seventeenth century, also for sea-going trade.

The subjection of towns and their spheres of influence to the hegemony of the state was not a purely political or administrative problem. As centres of interregional trade they were also the nerve centres of the market system. After 'discovering' loans as a means of increasing their financial resources, princes had in the fourteenth century gradually introduced systems of taxation which provided them with regular incomes creamed off from industry and commerce. The lack of economic understanding, if not the downright disapproval of everything associated with trade by the nobles and princes, meant that their military needs determined the level of taxation and the expansion of public debt. Waging war imposed its own dynamic and logic – it was the final result that mattered, not the price – which eventually came down to the personal ambition and honour of the prince. This meant that to slow down the creaming off of a prosperous economy by a warmongering prince, or by a prince forced to defend himself against aggressive competitors, there were no brakes except political representation of the commercial interests in an assembly of the Estates or a parliament with some power of taking decisions – or else an economic fiasco.

Since heavy tax levies and warfare generally affected opportunities for commercial profit, and government interference tended to prevent the smooth course of transactions, commercial capital generally tended to take flight from countries with a strongly centralized and militarist administration. The cities where commercial activity had developed most strongly – Venice, Genoa, Florence, Barcelona, Bruges, Lübeck, Antwerp, Augsburg, Danzig, Amsterdam and London – enjoyed, if not complete autonomy under an administration of merchants and their families, then at least a distant monarchy which refrained from interference. The power aspirations of princes – and in the long run the executives in the state apparatus could become involved in these – showed a tendency to impose no restraints on themselves, so that a point always came when a strong state strangled the opposing powers it had embraced. For the aristocracy this point can be located in the imposition of a court culture, for the Church in the secularization for state ends of religious rituals and values, and for the town bourgeoisie in the conversion of the town oligarchies into clients.

In the sixteenth and seventeenth centuries it therefore appeared that the dynastic states had absorbed their opposing powers one by one and had survived as the only dominating concentrations of power. Established churches spread the state ideology down to the smallest community or parish; opposition became soothed by propaganda, and if necessary suppressed by military supremacy.

Local churches, in their schools and in the institutions for social care which they controlled, had to imprint socially acceptable behaviour and the true faith. Deviant opinions and behaviour were persecuted in an increasing number of ways and excluded from society: first by the persecution of heretics and witches; then by making executions into public displays of power with the object of providing a deterrent; and next by confining vagrants, gypsies, beggars, the mentally deficient and other dissidents in institutions. In this respect there were no striking differences between Catholic and Protestant countries. What seems to have been more relevant was the degree of centralization of the Church and the organization of the church hierarchy; in this respect the Lutherans and Anglicans leaned towards the Catholic model, whereas Calvinism kept the movement for reform essentially at a community level. It therefore proved to be particularly successful in the United Provinces, Switzerland and southern Germany. The level of public violence was appreciably lower there than in the dynastic states, while there was even an attempt to give some economic and moralizing functions to penitentiary and disciplinary institutions.

The form and dimensions acquired by states in the course of their lengthy process of development depended on many factors: the strength and continuity of dynasties, the concentration and accumulation of capital, the pressure of surrounding political powers, the attraction of distant markets, and the level to which their subjects were organized. The tighter the structures absorbed by the expanding states, the more opposition they were able to offer from within; they gave shape to the state power by forcing it to respect intermediate spheres of power to a greater or lesser degree. Hence, and also because of the paucity of communications media, the cultural homogenization of their subjects was at first confined to the elites. Public ceremonial, which originally had a purely religious character but gradually underwent a process of secularization, showed that rulers were thoroughly aware of the need to confer an additional sacramental value on their position in the eyes of their subjects. In this way they created for themselves an elevated position of authority which their rivals could not challenge without equivalent resources of legitimization. This symbolic position of authority offered their subjects the opportunity to feel emotionally involved in a system of power that otherwise, because of its wide extent, would have been remote and impossible to identify with. In the

Port activities in the British East India Company Dock in London, *c.* 1800.
All discharges were recorded in detail before being warehoused. Anonymous painting.
London, Victoria and Albert Museum

course of the seventeenth and particularly the eighteenth century courts began to assume that the presentation of the state could be detached from the
public display of the prince and his entourage. His
officials and his emblems were after all by then
widely distributed throughout his realm. However,
their aura faded compared with that evoked by the
mass events that always produced a personally
experienced emotion, which was lacking in the
remote courtly state.

Dynastic states did not provide the only route to
the modern Europe. During the *ancien régime*
republics and constitutional monarchies with real
participation of commercial interests on a representative basis remained the political configurations in which the core of the European economy
could thrive. In their peripheral provinces in the
Balkans the Ottoman empire imposed a command
economy in which the state apparatus imposed on
districts the delivery of a specific production of
grain. In the long run this system resulted in cor-
ruption among the district officials and the provincial governors while it kept the productive forces
dependent and discouraged them. Western states
had already during the late Middle Ages carried on
an economic policy directed towards the retention
– and in so far as possible the attraction – of precious metals, a concern which would obsess monarchs into the eighteenth century. Grain and its
provision was the second product over which
towns and states from the fourteenth century
onwards watched by alternately opening and clos-
ing their frontiers temporarily.

The control of the Spanish and Portuguese
monarchs over their colonial trade remained very
limited and was in reality only directed towards
their own supply of precious metals. Colonial trade
was in general entrusted by the European states to
private companies who were equipped for military,
administrative and judicial tasks. Mercantilist opinions, which had spread and become more dogmatic
in the seventeenth and eighteenth centuries, in
reality only expanded the interest in precious metals and grain to cover a few other goods and services. In particular carriage in one's own ships had
great economic importance, as prescribed by the
English Navigation Act of 1651, followed by similar
French (1664) and Swedish (1724) laws which were
primarily directed towards the protection of their
own merchant shipping against the Dutch hegemony. Systematic encouragement of domestic pro-
cessing of their own raw materials appeared in
practice impossible because the laws of economics

could not be constrained by the states, which were
still quite inefficient. At the end of the eighteenth
century the inadequate supply of food shook the
ancien régime in France to its foundations.

Although by the eighteenth century dynastic
states of varying shapes and sizes had absorbed the
great competitive powers and little by little brought
them under their control, they did not have a real
hold on the economy, particularly not on the mass
of commercial capital. By definition movable, it
continually shifted to places which at any given
moment offered expectations of the most profitable
returns, and it could not therefore be confined
within the fixed frontiers of the states. The city
states and republics, administered by merchants,
offered the safest havens. Certainly capitalists regularly co-operated with princes and made their
profit from the relationship until some became victims of their meddling with power, and their more
fortunate colleagues took to their heels. On the eve
of the great revolutions the picture was therefore
far from being decided by absolutist power blocs, as
is widely assumed. Rivalry between states remained
a major characteristic, the segmentation and indi-
rectness of the domestic exercise of power a second, and the relative autonomy of commercial capital a third. In the next centuries completely new
configurations of power would emerge from these
three ingredients.

1   Elias 1969; Dhondt 1948.

CHAPTER VIII
Europe on the Move

Profound changes in various sectors of European society resulted in fundamental alterations to power relationships in the late eighteenth century. Those protagonists whom we identified as decisive in the pre-industrial period lost much of their influence. After being dominated by the great landowners and merchants, the continent, and soon the whole world, came under the mastery of industrial entrepreneurs and bankers; bureaucrats and elected politicians replaced hereditary rulers, the churches saw their authority and their adherents dwindle, while nationalism and other cultural identities created new emotional ties among the masses who had become more assured about their own identity.

During the eighteenth century a process of continuous and self-sustaining growth started in the economy of western Europe, initially in agriculture; this development was to revolutionize ever larger parts of the world at increasing speed. It resulted in a strong increase in population at an unprecedented rate, leading to substantial growth in the total population of Europe, coupled with heavy emigration to other continents. Extensive shifts in the distribution of population, greatly increased mobility throughout the world, and the growth of megacities produced a totally new type of society. The core of wealth shifted from the countryside to the urban areas, capitalism was from now on to find its most important accumulations in industrial establishments and expert services, and technological development increasingly broke through the barriers of tradition. All organizations and community relations became much larger and so more impersonal. Against this background the established power relationships of the *ancien régime* lost their legiti-

Edvard Munch, *Workers returning home*, 1913. An anonymous crowd of Norwegian workers go homewards after their daily work.
Oslo, Munch Museet

macy; as so often in Europe, first in the west and later in the east. The uneven degree and irregular timing of the changes heightened tensions in all countries by their cross-frontier effects.

The population explosion

Never before had the population of Europe grown so fast as between about 1730 and 1913: including Russia the continent had a population of about 115 million in 1700, 187 in 1800, 266 in 1850, 401 in 1900, and 468 in 1913 (of whom 122 million were in Russia). In 1950 the total European population came to 414 million without the Soviet Union, which then accounted for a further 195 million. Two world wars, continuous emigration and a decrease in fertility reduced the rate of population growth during the last century. After the Second World War, on the other hand, immigration from other continents became a very important factor; concentrated in large towns it created a new kind of multiculturalism there, but not without tensions. Meanwhile European influence had brought about a further population explosion in other continents, which is still continuing.

The pattern which had developed since the high Middle Ages of a varying density of urbanization remained much the same, but the opportunities for towns to grow became less dependent upon port activities. Capital cities, industrial and mining towns could – thanks to the development of railways – also attract large populations in the interior. Thus substantial variations in population density continued into the twentieth century. On the eve of the First World War these proportions were to

The population explosion in the nineteenth century led to waves of emigration and more impersonal community relations in the large towns.
The nuclear family, here idealized around 1867 by Albert Anker in *The new baby*,
was often put under heavy pressure by the factory work of women and children.
Lausanne, Musée Cantonal des Beaux-Arts

some extent different from those in 1600 because the process of industrialization had caused violent shifts in some regions, although the fundamental contrast between the densely populated and urbanized north-west on the one hand, and the much more thinly populated east and north on the other, remained striking. In the early industrializing countries of Belgium and England with Wales, there were 259 and 239 inhabitants per square kilometre respectively. The regions which had previously been ahead had now fallen rather behind: the Netherlands now scored 171, and Italy 121. Germany,

where some regions became industrialized fast, but large areas remained purely agricultural, averaged about 120. It is obvious that by this method of calculation small countries like Belgium were more likely to reach a high average than large ones; none the less there are some extremely striking variances. A middle category was made up by the Austrian empire (95) and Switzerland (91). France (74) was, apart from the industrialized regions in its north-western and north-eastern periphery, still largely rural. Low densities were shown by Hungary (64), Romania (55), Bulgaria (45), Spain (39) and Rus-

Vater und Mutter verlaßen mich.

Aber der Herr nimt mich auf. Pf. 27. 2.10.

Saltzburg

Königsberg

Muß ich gleich Haus und Hof, Freund, Eltern, Kinder laßen,
So wül mich doch der Herr in seine Arme faßen;
Er hält mich väterlich bey seiner rechten Hand,
Und führt mich wohl vergnügt in Friedrich Willhelms Land.

A Protestant Salzburg family emigrating to Prussia in their search for better living conditions.
There were often very great differences in incomes, even within the same country. Coloured engraving, c. 1800.
Berlin, Archiv für Kunst und Geschichte

sia (26). The Scandinavian countries were still at the bottom of the scale for population density: twelve in Sweden, eight in Finland and seven in Norway.

In 1910 Great Britain had forty-six towns with more than 100,000 inhabitants, Germany forty-five and Russia fourteen, while by 1851 in England and Wales more people lived in towns than in the country; this did not occur in Germany until 1891, in France till 1931, and in the Soviet Union until 1960. These figures give an indication of the social structure of the population as well as the speed with which it was changing. An urban population has a completely different way of life and thinking from a rural one. Its proportion of the total population forms the basis for the modernization of the economy and of social relationships. In the highly urbanized parts of western Europe the servile state of the great majority of the peasants had already disappeared under the pressure of the market economy in the course of the thirteenth century. In France serfdom was only generally abolished by the Revolution in 1789, in Austria in 1848, and in Russia in 1861. To put it bluntly: in the urbanized areas freedom under the law could be acknowledged quite early, because productivity could be exacted by economic pressure. In the thinly populated rural

REVEIL DU TIERS ETAT.

Ma feinte, il étoit tems que je me réveillasse, car l'oppression de mes fers me donnoit le cochemar un peu trop fort.

The Third Estate, which was excluded from all political decision-taking, found themselves in unprecedented straits through the prohibitive cost of food. On 14 July 1789 the mob who could no longer be restrained marched to the arsenal of Paris, seized arms and stormed the Bastille. *The awakening of the Third Estate* is a coloured satirical print of the time. Paris, Musée Carnavalet

areas on the other hand personal serfdom and physical force were still applied. This system of exploitation resulted from the scarcity of resources and the great distances between communities and markets. It contributed in its turn to the preservation of traditional societies. Among the traditions not affected immediately by external influences were the regionally nuanced religious beliefs, customs, vernaculars and other cultural characteristics.

The increase in population varied greatly from region to region, partly because it was to a large degree caused by migration. The most urbanized and industrialized regions showed the greatest growth: in the mining areas of Pas de Calais, Hainault and Liège, the growth between the middle of the nineteenth century and 1910 was from 127 per cent to 140 per cent, and in the Ruhr it even reached 284 per cent. In Germany at this

Notes: see p. 361

William Hogarth satirized the notorious
Oxfordshire elections of 1754 in four paintings.
The elected Tory is borne round in a triumphal procession.
Grotesquely, Hogarth shows above his head
not the eagle of victory but a silly goose,
while the inscription on the sundial:
'We are dust and ashes', with the bespectacled skull,
is meant to put the victory in perspective.
London, Sir John Soane's Museum

period the strongest growth was in Westphalia (132 per cent), Brandenburg, the Rhineland and Saxony, while the agricultural areas saw their young men leave and hardly grew at all: East Prussia only by 13 per cent, and Mecklenburg-Schwerin by 15 per cent. Migratory movements were driven by great differences in incomes. These were highest per head in Berlin, the Rhineland and Saxony, and lowest in the agricultural areas east of the Elbe, Bavaria, Baden and Württemburg. In 1864 incomes in Paris averaged 75 per cent more than in the country. In the Habsburg monarchy in the province of Lower Austria, which contained Vienna, the annual income per head averaged 850 krone, in Bohemia 761, in Galicia 316, and in Dalmatia 264.[1]

Over the centuries innovatory impulses have driven through Europe in waves, first from south to north, and later from west to east. Innovations in all

fields appeared earlier and spread more rapidly in the thickly populated areas than in the continental hinterlands. Concentration itself creates problems of a material and organizational nature which cry out for solutions and thus enforce inventiveness. Moreover, a high degree of human interaction also stimulates greater creativity. In central, south-east and eastern Europe the empires could maintain themselves for a long time because they were based on archaic societies. Their populations, very thinly scattered over extensive territories, had few external contacts and therefore went on believing absolutely in the unalterable values of their ancestral traditions. It was just the fragmentation, diversity and lack of mutual contact between their peoples which made their domination by an imperial power, supported by large landowners, possible. Apart from that, the empires lacked both the strength and the ambition to bring western culture to their subjects. In return for their support the centre of power granted the large landowners extensive licence to keep the peasants in their demesnes under the knout. The exceptionally large empires were therefore characterized by the extremely limited ability of their state apparatus to penetrate down to their own subjects. Because of this they were also incapable of bringing about much change in the local and regional cultures. In effect administration of the interior was left to the large landowners who carried it out as they saw fit, and mainly to their own advantage. Peasant revolts offered only occasional resistance and on a relatively small scale against exploitation, without being able to alter the system as such. In 1991, with the break-up of the Soviet Union, the last remnants of the imperial form of state seemed to have disappeared from Europe. In view of the oppressive nature of every empire such an evolution could be interpreted as a belated modernization. It is, however, still not quite clear whether the new rulers of Russia have yet entirely abandoned their imperial philosophy.

In the areas which had for a long time been thickly populated, political, economic and cultural structures were more strongly developed, and through their intense mutual frictions they had sharpened the subject peoples' sense of justice. It is difficult to indicate a closer connection between density of population and political processes since very many factors were involved simultaneously: socio-eco-

nomic ones such as the availability or not of what were thought to be appropriate living standards, and political ones such as the access to or exclusion from the centres of power to satisfy the desires of various categories of the population.

The contrast between Great Britain and France is an interesting one. Britain was ahead in terms of demographic growth and socio-economic innovation, but by a succession of limited adjustments the old elites were able to keep their political system in reasonable shape without revolutionary shocks. The monarchy, the House of Lords – composed of the old orders, the bishops and the peers – the old laws and privileges, administrative arrangements and traditions, all remained intact. Although in France industrialization and urbanization got underway much more gradually, and the pressure of population was also less severe, the political system there suffered for nearly a century under pressure from both revolutionary and counter-revolutionary movements. The exclusivity of the political and social system of the *ancien régime*, untempered by parliamentary representation and fenced around by the strict distinctions between the orders, invited the polarization of antagonisms. The lack of any readiness to adapt, for example, in respect of the fiscal privileges of the clergy and the nobility which were generally considered as fundamentally unjust, drove reform-minded aristocrats into the arms of the bourgeois opposition, who also profited from the popular rebellions caused by hunger. Radical seizures of power in their turn provoked reactions, so that for decades there was conflict directed at the constitutional distribution of power.

As a comparison there is Russia, where the population of Russia in Europe doubled in the fifty years between 1863 and 1913, and serfdom was abolished, starting a massive trek to the towns. The urban population tripled in this half century, with concentrations in the two largest towns, St Petersburg (one million in 1890, 2.2 in 1914) and Moscow (one million in 1897, 1.7 in 1914). As a consequence of their impoverished standard of living this accumulation of people created a real danger for the extremely traditionalist autocratic regime. The 84 per cent of the rural population also demonstrated very rebellious behaviour, but this was driven by other motives than that of the townspeople. The chasm between the political revolution in the towns and the

Clearly elevated above his work force,
the top-hatted entrepreneur, his hand raised in greeting,
attracts the attention of the observer.
A scene from Biermeister and Wain's
nineteenth-century steel mill in Copenhagen.
Contemporary painting by P.S. Krøyer.
Copenhagen, Statens Museum for Kunst

evolution of the countryside was to reach a dramatic nadir in the late 1920s. In both 1917 and 1930 the rule of the political system in respect of social problems was a repressive one. Unlike the tsar and the former capitalist government in 1917, the bolshevist rulers in the 1930s were able to suppress the peasants because they knew that they were sure of the support of the population in the towns.

The industrial boom

No single analysis of power relationships can ignore the impressive economic growth experienced in Europe since the start of the process of industrialization. Between the 1860s and the 1950s growth in the national product contributed an annual average of 3.6 per cent in Sweden, 3.1 in Russia/USSR, 2.7 in Germany, 2.2 in Britain, 1.8 in Italy, and 1.5 in France. With respect to the first three, one must take account of the fact that industrialization in these countries only got going after 1850, so that the proportionally strong growth was from very small beginnings, while the process in Britain had already been in train for a century. Per head of population the percentages of growth differed much less, at between 1.3 and 1.5 per cent per year, except for Italy with 1 per cent and Sweden with 2.8 per cent.[2] To an increasing degree the states drew the resources for the growing package of tasks they assumed for themselves from this general increase of the national product. It also led to accumulations of capital without precedent in the hands of private partnerships and companies.

There is a deep-rooted tradition of analysing socio-economic realities within the frontiers of individual states. There is an obvious reason for it: it was, and still is, overwhelmingly the states who have collected the data for their national statistics. It is much harder to comprehend the reality of regional developments because data at that level are scarce and heterogeneous. Even so, Europe, compared with, for example, North America, central Asia and Australia, is very varied geographically. Natural resources are extremely randomly distributed there, and environmental conditions soon vary over relatively small distances. Nothing would therefore be more natural than to start the presentation of European development from the basis of the ever-present regional diversity, which has only in this century been supplanted by larger homogeneous regions. However, our vision is so influenced by the effects of the nineteenth-century formation of states that it is difficult for us to detect the truth hiding behind them.

This certainly applies to the earliest phase when environmental conditions still played a decisive role. The first industries were established, as was agricultural cultivation, where the environment made this possible. Between 1750 and 1755 35 per cent of British coal was mined in the two north-eastern counties of England: Durham and Northumberland (Newcastle); in 1788 more than half the water-driven spinning mills were in the areas of Lancashire, Cheshire, Derbyshire and Flintshire; in 1823 south Wales produced 41 per cent of Britain's pig iron, and in 1840 still 36 per cent. Coal and iron ore seams were located across the state frontiers of France, Belgium, Luxemburg and Germany, so that these states could not do too much to hamper their exploitation on both sides, if they did not want to influence competition negatively. Hence early industrialization should not be interpreted so much within national frameworks, but in that of the regions which developed around specific geographical sources of raw materials, energy and transport facilities.[3]

Various social and political factors also played a role in starting up the industrialization process and in its success, sometimes as a brake and sometimes stimulating it. Thus states, with their taxation, foreign policy, legislation and possibly with their policy for investment on traffic routes, exercised varying degrees of influence on industrial development. The British state systematically saw to it that small tax payers transferred money to wealthy investors. The most important instrument for this was the national debt: creditors after all received interest which was financed from taxation. From 1715 to 1850 two-thirds of this came from levies on consumer goods, which fell disproportionately heavily on small consumers. In this way there was a massive transfer of capital from the less wealthy to the owners of capital, who could use it for private investments. The sharp increase in the national debt during the Napoleonic wars thus led to almost a doubling of the share of private capital in the gross national product (from 10 per cent in 1780 to 19 per cent in 1830). Interest on the national debt rose to unprecedented heights: to 8.5 percent of GNP per year during the wars, and in the long term to 4.7 per cent per year.[4]

The very fact that traditional monarchies were still deaf to the needs of entrepreneurs stirred these to political activism. In the *ancien régime* societies of France and Germany, political rulers from aristocratic circles displayed complete disdain for com-

Ironbridge in Coalbrookdale had the first cast-iron bridge. This arched bridge of 1777–1780 has a 30-metre span and weighs 278 tons.

The design, however, was still derived from wooden constructions: mortises, wedges and dove-tails were simply cast in iron.

There are numerous contemporary pictures of this technical marvel, like this one of 1788.

Telford, Ironbridge Gorge Museum

Between 1670 and 1830 the total length of canals, then newly dug in England and Wales, reached some 3,000 miles.

When the first cargoes of coal were delivered by canal the price fell by half.

Because of this commercial success England experienced a real 'canal mania' about 1790. John Constable (1776–1837), *Dedham Lock.*

London, Victoria and Albert Museum

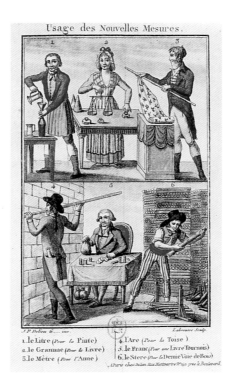

Weighing and measuring under the *ancien régime* was done with far from accurate weights and measures.
Measures in particular varied from place to place.
Coloured print of *c.* 1800 showing the metric measures as the revolutionary government
had introduced them throughout France, compared with their old counterparts.
Paris, Bibliothèque nationale de France, Estampes

The Peterloo massacre.
At a demonstration against the Corn Laws in Manchester on 16 August 1819
the use of troops by the government, which was drawn from the propertied classes,
resulted in a bloodbath; eleven dead and more than four hundred seriously wounded.

mercial and industrial enterprise, so that their policy did not concern itself in the least with the interests of these classes. The economic policy of the French government was at that time primarily determined by *raisons d'état*, which usually came down to dynastic and prestigious considerations, sometimes for the protection of the interests of the large French landowners. The feudal order which in pre-1789 France, as well as in Germany, still kept real territorial frontiers in being, hindered commercial traffic by enforcing a great variety of regulations, tolls, weights and measures. In this way the remnants of feudal segmentation obstructed the passage of goods, which in late eighteenth-century France made it impossible to resolve food shortages and so exacerbated social tensions.

The English state on the other hand had had a unified internal market since the Middle Ages, because it was the crown which, after approval by Parliament, levied tolls in ports and established the conditions of economic life. In this respect the laws approved in the course of centuries for enclosing land are typical; they allowed arable land to be converted into meadows, making them more cost-efficient for the owner. The numerous aristocrats in Parliament watched over their incomes, but commercial interests were also well protected by the representatives of the trading towns. The fact that ecclesiastical institutions, and particularly the lesser country nobility, the gentry, had been involved as landlords in sheepfarming for export or for the domestic textile industry since the thirteenth century, meant that since that time commercial interests were automatically a subject of discussion and legislation in Parliament. The English landed aristocracy had therefore none of the continental disdain for commercial activities. This situation, which itself arose from the particular situation of the English rural economy, meant that the English political system, in which, after the Glorious Revolution of 1688, Parliament enjoyed supremacy in the government, was open to reforms which encouraged industrial development.

In general the British government was able to preach free trade, by reason of the superior position of its economy and its overseas trade network. After 1815 the last remnants of mercantilism were folded up: the Navigation Act of the mid-seventeenth century, which had made carriage on English ships and the use of English ports compulsory for products from the home country and from the colonies, was relaxed and in 1849 repealed. Even the prohibition, never strictly adhered to, on the export of British

machinery and technicians was removed. An important exception to all this was the Corn Laws. In 1815, under pressure from landowners, levies were imposed on grain to keep domestic prices high. After violent working-class demonstrations, and after a reform of the political franchise in 1832 to include the new industrial towns, Parliament made the import of grain free again in 1846. Social laws, restricting the working hours and employment of women and children, but also imposing restrictions on associations of workers, reflected the favourable attitude of the state to economic life. Also essential for the development of industrial capitalism was the new company legislation by which the entrepreneur's risk could be spread and separated from the private wealth of those involved. In 1826 a new law allowed the establishment of joint stock banks aiming particularly at deposits and short-term credit. Since this could normally be extended without difficulty, they functioned in practice as providers of long-term finance for business. For the rest, the British government was conspicuous for its restraint, and as long as possible kept its apparatus small and cheap. Unlike on the continent it did not interfere to protect or support industry or even railway companies with fiscal or other regulations, nor did it plan or operate railway networks itself. At the most it was tempted to guide the ever more complex relationships between segments of society along the right lines by administrative regulations.

In Germany the effort to remove feudal obstacles became a divisive element between the industrializing Rhineland and the more traditional regions. The logical objective of the manufacturers, who were able to produce more by the new production techniques, was to make their market as extensive as possible. This required the removal of internal octroi barriers, and standardization of weights, measures and regulations. The French revolution had made short shrift of the old diversity by the introduction of the metric system and the abolition of princedoms going back to the Middle Ages. Centralization of the administration made the creation of a single market within the frontiers of the state easier. The German Confederation took these steps later and gradually, because bourgeois attempts at revolution had not been successful there. The Treaty of Vienna of 1815 restored the number of German principalities to thirty-five, and the number of Free Cities of the Empire to four. Each of these territories could still have its own policy for tolls and customs duties, which hampered the

Attempts at revolution in the confederal German empire had no success.
Until c. 1870 the country was battling against serious industrial backwardness in industrialization.
However, complaints from the military were to accelerate the process considerably in the last quarter of the century.
Warthmüller, *The king is everywhere*, 1886. Berlin, Archiv für Kunst und Geschichte

transport of goods within Germany even more than before. In 1833 a customs union between the German principalities was achieved, probably mainly inspired by the Prussian efforts for political hegemony and the exclusion of Austria. Frontier areas in the north, west and south still remained outside the union for decades, and the important ports of Bremen and Hamburg, more oriented towards Britain than towards the interior, only joined in 1885 and 1888. In 1839, in the kingdom of Prussia – which included the industrial regions of the Rhineland and Silesia which had developed early – legal restrictions were announced on child labour. Until about 1870 German industry was struggling to make up its backlog compared with Britain. For instance, between 1836 and 1840 70 per cent of the German cotton industry depended on imported yarn, and the rails, wagons and engines for the first German railways had to be imported from Britain. By 1869 only 22 per cent of yarn was imported, and in 1873 the reduction of the import duty on iron showed that the Germans were confident of being able to compete with Britain in the future. Until then protectionist measures against the import of industrial

products or components had done Germany more harm than good.

Wars and reparations between states also continued to be a fundamental influence on the balance of payments and the whole of economic life in the nineteenth and twentieth centuries. Taking up state loans and putting them into public circulation represented a substantial part of the activities of private bankers until about 1865. The French revolution and the wars that followed it led to a flight of capital to England. This made credit cheaper for the British government, who used it to finance the conduct of the war and subsidies to its allies. After her final defeat in 1815, £700 million sterling was imposed on France as reparations (the British state had spent £911 million on the war). It was the London bankers Baring and Hope who in 1816 agreed the first loans to the French state under the restored monarchy at an interest of 5 per cent on a price of Frs 52.50 for Frs 100 nominal. When the creditworthiness of the French state had been restored in 1821, the interest fell to 3 per cent with a price of Frs 85 for Frs 100 worth of stock. The Rothschild Bank guaranteed the repayment in London, at a

Old factory of the firm of Siemens in Berlin, which from its establishment in 1847
by Werner von Siemens and Johan Halske specialized in electrical products.
In 1848 Siemens produced the first telegraphic links in Germany.
Munich, Siemens Museum

In the euphoria of the financial speculation, which between 1870 and 1872 followed the Franco-Prussian War,
107 banks were founded in Germany. The private banks played an influential role in the establishment of the Deutsche Bank in Berlin in 1870.
Document recording the twenty-fifth anniversary of the Deutsche Bank.
Frankfurt, Deutsche Bank

In the nineteenth century iron was smelted in ovens fuelled by quantities of coke.
Even then the heavy emissions of smoke and gas seriously polluted the environment. Lovis Corinth, *View of the harbour basin*, 1911.
Hamburg, Kunsthalle, Marie Oppenheim Legacy

fixed rate of exchange and at regular intervals, of the loans to members of the Holy Alliance. In this way the massive concentrations of capital in London acquired influence on the political stability of the counter-revolutionary regimes. After 1830 this did not, however, prevent the bankers from seeing that liberal governments might perhaps succeed even better in advancing economic development and capital accumulation.

The 5,000 million francs reparations imposed on France by Germany in 1871 again offered international bankers such as Rothschilds an excellent opportunity to make a good profit on the commissions for subscribing to French state loans and to take advantage of their growth in value. In 1872 the Banque de Paris et des Pays-Bas was even specially set up for these operations by a consortium of German, Viennese, Belgian, Swiss and Dutch groups. These massive operations strengthened the international banking system and led to unprecedentedly high transfers of capital by French taxpayers to holders of capital in their own country and abroad. This conclusion puts the settlement of the Franco-Prussian War in a different perspective from that generally taken from a purely political and nationalist point of view. *Pecunia non olet;* money has no smell.

In the most highly industrialized states, banks started to control increasingly larger proportions of the total money in circulation. The central state banks gradually acquired the exclusive responsibility for the issue of banknotes as paper money. In addition they began to function as the bankers'

The high-quality steel produced by the Bessemer process was easy to cast and made larger-sized products possible.
This steel was ideal for use in building bridges, ships and the railways. With *On the Europe bridge, c. 1876–1880,*
Gustave Caillebotte expressed his admiration for this achievement with the new material in Paris. Fort Worth, Texas, Kimbell Art Museum

bank, to guarantee loans in the last resort. Bank deposits made up 55 per cent of total money in circulation in Britain by 1844, while in France they only accounted for 10 per cent; about 1910 these proportions had risen to 85 per cent and 44 per cent respectively. It is understandable that governments could only carry out an effective financial policy in collaboration with the banks.

The deposits of small savers collected in this way provided the basis for industrial investment. In Belgium the most important joint stock bank, the Société Générale, set up by King William I in 1822, after secession from the Netherlands in 1830 became the first bank to participate substantially in industry. This step was taken under the pressure of the political revolution to safeguard the bank's

assets, particularly in the mines and metal industries established in Hainault. In this way the Société Générale became the most important holding company of the young industrial state. After 1870 the large German banks were systematically to play a similar role in financing the heavily concentrated large-scale industries.

Prussia, ruled by the monarchy and the *Junkers,* up to about 1870 was still dominated by an aversion to joint stock banks, and this innovation took place in other centres such as Frankfurt, Darmstadt, Hamburg and Hesse. The founding of the Second *Reich* in 1871 made Berlin the centre of the German financial system. Only then was the setting up of joint stock companies liberalized, leading to the establishment of well-known banks such as the

Deutsche Bank in Berlin, the Commerz-und-Disconto-Bank in Hamburg and the Dresdner Bank. They accepted deposits and participated directly in industrial enterprises, which they controlled through their representatives on the boards. A famous example of the complex weave of interests was the support of the Deutsche Bank, led by Georg von Siemens, for the electro-technical business started in Berlin in 1847 by his cousin, the engineer Werner von Siemens. The Dresdner Bank had links with the textile industry in Saxony and the mines and metal industries of the Rhineland. The banks supported the tendency to concentrate shown by German industry from the end of the nineteenth century. They took over the handling of state loans from the earlier private banks, and also the financing of the railway companies in Germany and abroad. The capital and reserves of the four great D-banks (Deutsche Bank, Dresdner Bank, Darmstädter Bank and Diskontobank) and the Berliner Handelsgesellschaft grew spectacularly: from 125.5 million marks between them in 1877 to 5,089 million in 1913.

In countries where economic development came late, the state through the big banks stimulated the enormous investments required for plant and machinery, which by that time had grown larger and more complex. This was particularly the case in Germany, Austria, Italy and Russia. By profiting from the inventions of the first phase of industrialization, everything went much faster, and was on a larger scale and therefore more efficient in the second half of the nineteenth century. Especially the states – and particularly the empires – on the European periphery recognized the need to adopt a policy of controlled industrialization based on the necessity to keep themselves adequately equipped for military competition. For instance, the Russian defeat in the Crimean War (1854–1856) opened the eyes of the tsarist regime and was a turning point. The conflict had begun as a struggle with the Ottoman empire about hegemony over the Balkans and the Black Sea narrows. By themselves both empires were fairly evenly equipped militarily. When, however, British and French troops and naval units, and later also an Austrian army, came to the aid of the Turks, it was clear that Russia could no longer match the new military resources. The defeat led to great tensions in Russia and increased unrest among the peasants. The tsar reacted with reforms, including in 1861 the abolition of serfdom, the introduction of compulsory military service, making officer training more professional, and opening the country to foreign trade and industrial

investment. In the 1890s the state played a protective and also a guiding role for the joint stock banks in St Petersburg. Foreign investors were directed to those industries the state thought were of strategic importance: railways, shipyards, metal industry and armaments. When there was an economic recession the state bank supported the joint stock banks by loans, purchases on the market and treasury deposits. This enabled partial modernization to start, whose limitations were, however, exposed by each new international conflict, and particularly by the First World War. International competition placed increasing pressure on states industrializing late, because their military technology fell still further behind and they were therefore not only vulnerable, but dependent upon supplies of arms or transfers of capital and know-how from their rivals.

Alliances with, and investments from, western countries seemed to offer a solution, but this did not mean the end of the dependence on foreign political decisions. For instance, in 1887 Bismarck, the German chancellor, following an alteration in international exchange rates, forbade the Reichsbank to accept any more Russian government stocks as security for loans. Thereupon French banks took the lead in the Russian money market, and sold massive quantities of Russian valuta to small savers. In 1913, 23 per cent of the capital of the ten largest Russian joint stock banks was in the hands of French banks, and 53 per cent of the capital of five of them. The Franco-Russian Treaty of Alliance of 1893 expanded and strengthened this collaboration. In 1906 a loan on the Paris stock exchange, supported by the French government, saved the tsar from bankruptcy after his defeat by Japan. In the context of the Triple Alliance a consortium of German banks controlled the Italian credit system after 1890. French and German banks generally controlled the money markets of southern and eastern Europe, particularly by supplying capital, technical supervision and links with the international capital markets.

Although the world of high finance, by its international organization, maintained an indisputable autonomy from governments, some forms of collaboration could not be avoided. The international influence of capital formed an important element in the strategies of the great powers for gaining supremacy, even if politics could influence high finance only to a limited extent. In spite of their great rivalry it seemed possible for French banks to do business in Berlin after 1871, and they collaborated with German colleagues at an international level. On the other hand in 1903 the French government was unsuccessful in its efforts to prevent the Deutsche Bank acquiring a majority share in the Istanbul–Baghdad railway company, a dependant of the imperial Ottoman Bank in which the French banks held a major share.[5] Diplomacy and high finance were closely interconnected – as they were with military General Staffs – but they did not overlap.

The industrialization process caused a radical shift in power relationships within Europe. In the class structure the owners of industrial capital gained supremacy over the large landowners who for some fifteen centuries had run the show. For the Catholic Church, which after the confiscations during the Reformation had regained its economic position in the countries of the Counter Reformation, this meant a definitive loss of ground. There was large-scale confiscation of monastic property in countries where the French revolution exercised authority, but also, for example, in Portugal after the liberal victory in 1834. Two routes stood open for the nobility to retain their incomes, their authority and their respect: accepting state office, as they had for a long time in the army and in diplomacy, but now increasingly also in political representation, was one; in addition many aristocrats found their way onto the boards of large financial institutions and businesses. None the less, both routes were an acknowledgement of the weakening of their traditional power base, the ownership of land with the seigneurial rights associated with it before the revolution.

Government expenditure, expressed per head of population, tripled in Europe as a whole between 1830 and 1880. Between 1830 and 1913 the gross national product in the whole of Europe is estimated to have grown by an average of 1.8 per cent per year. At the state level, however, there were great differences in the rate of industrialization as a result of the great contrasts in its timing and intensity. Spain and Portugal reached only half the average rate of growth, France achieved only 1.4 per cent and Austro-Hungary with 1.6 was below the average. Until 1830 the gross national product of France was only exceeded in Europe by that of Russia, which had twice as great a population, even without its Asian territories. In 1860 Germany's economic potential already equalled that of France, while both of them were far below the United Kingdom and Russia. In 1913 Russia's supremacy had shrunk severely, and it was only just ahead of Germany, who had meanwhile overtaken the United Kingdom and left France far behind. Per head of population Russia remained steadily in the rear and the United Kingdom far ahead, but that hardly counted

in terms of competitive state power. Obviously these data must be interpreted in the context of the economic structure and geopolitical position of the state. It is certainly clear that by 1913 industrialization had appreciably enlarged differences in development in Europe. For instance, the British GNP in 1830 was 9.6 times as large as the Portuguese, but by 1913 it was 24.5 times as large. This led to shifts in power to the disadvantage of France and to the advantage of Britain, and particularly to that of Germany and Austro-Hungary.[6]

The reality is that states could create conditions within their frontiers, causing their influence on economic life to increase steadily. Meanwhile production rose enormously, markets became increasingly more integrated, also on an intercontinental scale, and regional differences within the states levelled out. Between parts of the European continent the differences in phase and intensity, however, effectively continued. About 1910 the United Kingdom was still able to maintain its policy of free trade, but as countries were farther removed from the centre, so they had to raise higher tariff barriers. Germany, Belgium and Switzerland then charged about 10 per cent import duties; France, Italy, Austro-Hungary and Sweden about 20 per cent, Spain and Russia about 40 per cent.[7] These figures reflect the need felt by most agricultural countries to protect their markets against the import of cheap American grain, which since the advent of steam had flooded the European markets. This was fine for industrial entrepreneurs in the west, because it lowered the cost of living of industrial workers, so that labour costs could fall or the purchasing power of the workers could rise. Both possibilities offered favourable opportunities, the second particularly because it increased the demand for consumer goods and so stimulated the whole economic cycle. In the still preponderantly agricultural countries in south, central and eastern Europe, the politically influential large landowners needed high import duties to protect their domestic markets. This, however, increased production costs to such an extent that they were forced to introduce higher duties on industrial products too.

Capital was protected against political interference by its international organization. Foreign investments were encouraged, to avoid customs duties and spread the entrepreneurs' risks. British entrepreneurs led the market in all aspects when it came to establishing business abroad, particularly in the transport, mining and manufacturing industries. The formation of cartels and concentrations continued intermittently, with accelerations in the two world wars and the Great Depression of the 1930s. Entrepreneurs tried by mutual agreements to make their market shares secure against a fall in demand during the great economic fluctuations in the period after 1870. In Germany there were almost 400 such agreements in 1906. In 1932 that had become 3,200, which between them regulated the sale of more than 50,000 products. At an international level before 1914 there were about 100 cartels, and 180 in 1939.

Well before 1914 there already existed a series of large industrial undertakings in Europe, which had been created by vertical and horizontal integration into giants consisting of multiple units, engaged in various activities, and established multinationally. The German metal industry was the most obvious example. Economies of scale enabled it to raise its production between 1900 and 1914 from 6.6 to 14.9 million tons while British production in the same period grew from 5 to 8 million. The chemical and pharmaceutical giants, Bayer, BASF and Hoechst were the most competitive on a world scale, and about the turn of the century already had world-wide marketing organizations. They invested systematically in research into the most efficient methods of management and product development. About 1900 the leading industries – still now the most capital-intensive ones – were machine construction, metal working, processed foods, oil, rubber, chemicals, pharmaceuticals and electrical appliances. Even before 1914 British businessmen showed less interest than their American and continental competitors in investing in expensive new and possibly still risky technology.[8] Since the late nineteenth century orientation towards research into more efficient technologies can therefore be seen as the most telling indicator of economic leadership.

The strong increase in population, and from the mid-nineteenth century also in purchasing power, offered the basis for an enormous increase in industrial production. The revolutions in the field of transport – making transport of mass-produced goods ever cheaper – and in communications (telegraph and telephone) lowered the costs of commercial traffic immensely. In countries where entrepreneurs and bankers exercised great influence on the political apparatus, the state acted mainly to encourage the functioning of the free market. Defensive reflexes in those countries which had remained more agricultural resulted, however, in government intervention increasing their economic and technological disadvantages.

Dying for one's country

If the fundamental economic innovations of the eighteenth century started in England, the epicentre of the political earthquake was in France. It is true that the French revolution was preceded by the American one, which provided an inspiring model for the intelligentsia. It is equally true that the American War of Independence was fought out with the ideological weapons forged during the English Civil War of the seventeenth century, in which the concepts of the rule of law – evoking the provisions of Magna Carta in 1215 – and of the sovereignty of the people were in practice taken to their ultimate conclusion: deposing and even executing despotic kings. These events were not entirely new, since as early as the fourteenth century English kings had been removed on similar grounds, and in 1581 the States General in the Netherlands had deposed King Philip II of Spain in their territories, on the basis of laws by which they considered the ruler was also bound.

Yet the effect of the revolutionary breakthrough in France was noticeably more profound for the continent of Europe than any of these precedents, for three reasons. First of all the revolutionary changes about 1800 went much further than the relationships between king and Parliament, as in 1648 or 1688. They involved a thorough modernization of the economic order, of social and political relationships, and they aimed at complete secularization. Secondly, the revolutionary and Napoleonic armies had since 1793 spread their revolutionary ideas over large parts of Europe. They sometimes led to changes as radical as they were in France itself: for instance, in Belgium and to a lesser degree in the Netherlands. Elsewhere they only had a superficial impact on the existing power relationships, and their reforms could not be maintained because of lack of support for them in society: this applied to the Empire, Spain and Italy. This did not prevent the French invasions bringing about enormous consequences in each of these areas, by arousing anti-French national feeling, and by driving home the realization that adjustments were inevitable. These would have to be moves towards the state becoming one which, like France, could make an emotive call on the militancy of its subjects and their willingness to make sacrifices. This was inevitable if they were to be able to mobilize mass armies.

During the French occupation the Iberian countries lost control of their colonies in Latin-America. The effects of the French invasions of

The share of women in bringing about the eighteenth-century French *salon* was decisive and unique in European intellectual history.
Every Wednesday Madame Geoffrin used to invite a group of philosophers to her town house in the Rue Saint-Honoré in Paris.
During and after dinner there were readings and discussions.
In Lemonnier's painting Madame Geoffrin is seated next to the Prince de Conti during a reading from a text by Voltaire.
Paris, Musée de Malmaison

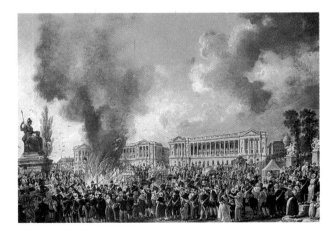

Public burning of royalist symbols and banners on 10 August 1793
on the 'Place de la Révolution', now the Place de la Concorde,
under the watchful eyes of soldiers of the revolutionary army.
This bonfire took place eight months after the execution of Louis XVI
on the same spot. Paris, Musée Carnavalet

After the proclamation of the republic in France (1792)
tens of thousands of volunteers enlisted as soldiers.
Here *Tirailleurs* accept a volunteer into their company.
Late eighteenth-century watercolour by Benjamin Zix.
Strasbourg, Bibliothèque des Musées de la ville, Estampes

Around 1858 the Viennese romantic painter Ferdinand Georg Waldmüller illustrated the emotions of a peasant family
when one of them left as a recruit. For a farmer each son in the army meant a tangible loss of income.
Vienna, Historisches Museum der Stadt Wien

central and eastern Europe were much less obtrusive because feudal domination had not yet been threatened there as such by the modernization of society. In Russia, for example, the war meant no more than an extra spur to the course of reform on which the enlightened Tsar Alexander I had already embarked. The departure of the French offered the Russians the opportunity of expanding further their hegemony over eastern Europe by the annexation of Finland and Poland.

Thirdly, the actions of the French revolutionaries were based on much more systematic and comprehensive theoretical thought than those of their predecessors. The Age of Reason had in the second half of the seventeenth century been given shape in the

United Provinces by scholars from a variety of countries – such as Descartes, Spinoza and Bayle. During the eighteenth century the philosophers of the Enlightenment, particularly in France, sought the rational foundations of political and social order.

Montesquieu, the one-time president of the *parlement* of Bordeaux, in his comparative political study *De l'Esprit des Lois* of 1748 distinguished three powers of the state which ideally ought to operate independently of each other: the legislative, the judicial and the executive. Although not yet worked out to its logical conclusions, this idea laid the foundation for the modern study of politics. It implied a fundamental break with the tradition in which all forms of power together were derived

Utterly demoralized and exhausted, the Napoleonic army retreated from Russia.
In 1836 Nicolas Toussaint Charlet depicted sympathetically this aura of misery. Lyons, Musée des Beaux-Arts

from the king, which had led to their being linked together in local governments.

The philosophers extended the logical and positivist thinking that had achieved demonstrable successes in science and technology increasingly to a view of the world as a whole and to political and social relationships, which they examined in various countries. The new thinking took all the gloss off the official values associated with the traditional legitimization of the monarchic order by reference to the delegation of divine power and its mythical origins. Enlightened opinions spread in sophisticated writings such as those of Voltaire, who exposed them in novels, pamphlets, letters and plays, or in the six hundred articles of his *Dictionnaire philosophique* of 1764 and the *Traité sur la Tolérance* published a year earlier. The works of various encyclopedists also reached a varied public who discussed the new views in the foyers of theatres, masonic lodges and literary salons. This lively movement gave birth both among enlightened aristocrats and intellectuals of bourgeois origin to a new ideology which was to form a blueprint for a new society. As these far from needy salon revolutionaries gave no thought to the strategy of any change of regime, this was accomplished chaotically, paying a high social price, and producing less permanent results than might have been possible.

The essential points of this revolutionary programme included constitutional restrictions on the ruler's powers, the abolition of feudal and clerical privileges, legislation by a representative assembly, with bourgeois participation, and rationalization of the economic system. These ideas were held in France by a minority of progressive aristocrats and educated bourgeois. Elsewhere in Europe these groups represented even less power, with no political effectiveness. In France this was only possible because the *ancien régime* was snared in its own internal contradictions. Tax reforms, proposed to liquidate the immense burden of debt which had accumulated during the wars waged against England between 1755 and 1783, came up against the inflexible resistance of the privileged aristocracy. From 1774 financial policy demonstrated only the desperation of the regime: French support for the

Satirical print by Josef Zutz on the greediness of the European monarchs at the Congress of Vienna in 1815.
Frontiers of European countries were redrawn drastically here from the point of view of the *raisons d'état* of the victors.
Vienna, Historisches Museum der Stadt Wien

American War of Independence (1778–1783) not only cost a great deal of money, but stirred up anti-monarchic feeling at home. It was, after all, illogical to understand why the king who in France excluded the bourgeoisie from any participation in government and protected the tax privileges of the first two Estates, should in America support a bourgeois rebellion over taxes against their king. Economic policy dominated by the interests of the large landowners led in 1786 to an industrial crisis as a result of opening the frontiers to English manufactures, and in 1788 to a food crisis, because the market regulations obstructed the grain trade. The entrepreneurial bourgeoisie felt themselves generally frustrated by the physiocratic policy, and found no more satisfying compensation in government offices in which the aristocracy saw that their precedence was respected.

When these tensions converged – causing popular risings against the high cost of living – and the government could offer no solutions, successive and ever more radical revolutionary waves broke through. Simple slogans like 'Equality' and 'Liberty' transmitted the theories of the new political dogma to the rebellious masses of peasants and artisans. The Reign of Terror under Robespierre

(1793–1794) went to extremes in democratizing judicial and political power and in the state control of economic life. Confronted with the counter-revolutionary war launched by the European monarchies in 1792, led by Austria and Prussia, the National Convention in August 1793 called for a *levée en masse*, general conscription, to protect the mother country threatened by all its neighbours.

This was an important turning point in European history: for the first time a popular army was mobilized on the grounds of an ideology which was soon to be concealed under the cloak of patriotism. For Europe this resulted in a deep polarization against the revolutionary programme, which since 1790 was also anti-clerical and by the execution of Louis XVI and Marie Antoinette in 1793 had become openly anti-royalist. Facing this, the monarchic regimes tightened their obsolescent positions, which they were able to maintain, particularly in Austria, Prussia and Russia, into about the middle of the nineteenth century. In France itself the foreign invasion to restore an almost universally hated *ancien régime* forged a divided population into the unified nation which it had never been so genuinely before. By fighting together to protect the prospect of a somewhat freer existence the regionally recruited regiments became well aware of their new national solidarity. The survival of France hung on the question of whether the high level of internal violence in the various risings and counter-revolutionary movements could be converted into the defence of the country and into victory. For this the state assumed the monopoly of the legitimate exercise of force both within and outside its frontiers. From this last the revolutionary leaders hoped for benefits which would eventually help the French state on to its feet again.

The French people's army produced no innovations in military techniques; they simply lacked the time and the resources. It was less professional than the traditional mercenary armies, but won by its massive numbers, which were twice those of its opponents. In 1814 Napoleon dragged 400,000 French along to Russia; the previous year he had put 350,000 in the field at Leipzig, who had, however, been defeated by 175,000 well-drilled Prussian soldiers. After their defeat at Jena in 1806 the Prussians had also introduced conscription. Between April 1792 and March 1795, 1.2 million soldiers were enrolled, of whom 550,000 died. Up to 1802 the revolutionary wars cost 950,000 lives. Napoleon's wars were to add a further 1,380,000.[9] In one generation the revolutionary and Napoleonic wars cost Europe 1.25 per cent of its total population in military casualties alone. The ideological and national bias of the conflict gave it a more ruthless character than the wars of the professional soldiers. The larger the armies, the more disastrous their passage was for the country which they devoured like termites. There are no estimates available of this damage in human or material terms.

The French population recovered noticeably more slowly from this blood-letting than the German one, which grew much faster during the nineteenth century. It is tempting to interpret German aggression towards Denmark, Austria and France, and most of all, of course, after 1900 against Russia and the west, in the light of population pressure, coupled with the strong economic growth after 1870. It is necessary, however, also to account for the substantial colonial expansion which the other western states went through in this period, and which was accompanied by large settlements of population and substantial investment. Germany took almost no part in this movement, which to some extent explains its aggressiveness within Europe.

The revolutionary and Napoleonic wars familiarized Europe with military conscription, although this in fact only became general towards the end of the century. Britain, which before 1750 had had no standing army on land of any significance, about 1850 kept about 1.1 per cent of its population under arms, as did the other western states. Russia then exceeded the average, with 1.5 per cent (850,000 men) as did Sweden, which in 1700 was the most militarized state in Europe, but in 1850, with 1.8 per cent of its population, could scarcely put 63,000 men in the field.[10] The Swedish defeat by Russia in 1809, which resulted in the loss of Finland, showed how far the potential of a population for recruiting had begun to become a decisive factor. In 1815 Swedish self-assurance was appeased by the occupation, without bloodshed, of Norway, at Denmark's expense. On the other hand, between 1780 and 1900 Russia used its military might six times in massive attacks against the Ottoman empire, five times against the Persians, twice against the Chinese and once against Afghanistan. Territorial gains were its harvest. At that time states saw wars as an obvious means of achieving their expansionary ends – 'the continuation of politics by other means', in the famous phrase of Clausewitz, the Prussian strategist.

On the whole the Congress of Vienna in 1815 ushered in a century of remarkably little warfare between the large European states. It drastically redrew the map, forming the German Federation, made up of thirty-five sovereign princes and four free cities. The Kingdom of the Netherlands and that of Lombardy-Venice should with other neighbours of France form solid buffers against any possible renewed drive for expansion from that quarter – as we now know a superfluous precaution. The British empire was substantially enlarged. Napoleon's conquerors tried to ensure that good conservative monarchies would remain in control everywhere. The 'Holy Alliance' of monarchs assumed to itself the right of intervention against any renewed revolutionary movements. France made use of this between 1820 and 1823 in Spain, and Austria in 1820 and 1821 in the Kingdom of the Two Sicilies, and in Piedmont. The Holy Alliance found itself in a moral dilemma over the equally liberal-inspired Greek War of Independence (should Christians support the Grand Turk against other Christians?) and Britain very soon appeared keen to reject the restoration policy which was the hobby-horse of the Austrian chancellor, Metternich.

The Franco-Prussian War of 1870–1871 was a sad exception to the predominantly peaceful nineteenth century in the heart of Europe. A total of 950,000 troops were engaged, with a quarter of a million dead. It demonstrated the recovery of

In the Crimean War Britain, France and Austria fought on the side of the Turks against Russia.
The British lost about half their strength in casualties. The survivors returned from the front weakened by sickness and privation.
Elizabeth Thompson, Lady Butler, pictured the infernal conditions of this war in several paintings.
Here the Scots Guards defend the Colours at the Alma (c. 1877). London, Chelsea Barracks

German strength after its defeat by the Napoleonic armies. Universal conscription made the united German army under officers trained in the strict Prussian regime a much stronger power than the French one. Moreover, the aggressor proved to be able to make excellent use of the railways, which had been laid out with a strategic aim, for moving troops and supplies. It is hardly possible to think of a more hurtful revenge than the proclamation, on 18 January 1871, of King Wilhelm I of Prussia as emperor of Germany – *in the Hall of Mirrors in Versailles*. The French would get their revenge in the same place in the much bleaker circumstances – for them – of the 1919 Peace Treaty. Apart from the war of 1870–1871, intended to be highly symbolical, there were a few instrumental wars, starting with Prussia against Austria, between Austria and Piedmont, and some limited conflicts during the unification of Italy. Otherwise the larger armed confrontations mainly involved revolts of the Balkan peoples against their Turkish occupiers (300,000 dead in Herzegovina and Bulgaria in 1875–1878) and the titanic struggle already mentioned between the

aggressive Russian and the ailing Ottoman empire. Because the Austrian empire, too, involved itself in this after 1908 by the annexation of Bosnia-Herzegovina, it set a spark to the powder barrel of ethnic and religious diversity of this region. This problem, a relic of the great shifts in domination of the Balkans over the centuries by the Greek Orthodox, Serbian Orthodox, Austrian Catholic and Islamic empires, produced grim conflicts during and after the Second World War, and again in the 1990s.

By 1914 there were various tensions in Europe. All the states had become much more powerful: since 1760 their budgets had increased eightfold in France and Britain, and by a multiple of forty in Prussia/Germany and in Austria. The European economies had experienced a dizzying growth and the population had risen steeply. The armed forces represented substantial proportions of the population: in 1900 as a proportion of males aged between 20 and 44 France had 8.8 per cent under arms, Austria 6.9 per cent, Britain 6.6 per cent and Germany 6.3 per cent.[11] To maintain the level of her numerical strength with a slower growth in population,

This intriguing painting by Christiaan van Couwenberg, depicting *The rape of the negress* by white men, expresses the imperialist arrogance of the European in Africa. Strasbourg, Musée des Beaux-Arts

France therefore had to withdraw more manpower from industry than her competitors, so that the state reined back the economy. In 1910 the German state devoted 52 per cent of its budget to military expenditure, the British 40 per cent, the French 37 per cent.[12] After the rush into Africa from 1884 onwards, most western European states had built up a colonial empire, dividing the whole world into spheres of influence. In Germany there was a movement which regarded the limited colonial possessions of the *Reich* as an invitation to an aggressive foreign policy. It was suggested that the prosperity of German workers depended on dominion over colonies. After 1900 it seemed as if the shift of competition between the European states and economies into expansion overseas had come to an end. Africa was finally completely shared out among the states of western Europe, and in the rest of the world the imperialist spheres of influence were equally no longer a matter of renewed discussion. Western competition gradually had to devote itself again to the position in Europe itself.

The relatively autonomous and vigorous growth of the various power systems – industrial capitalism, the state apparatus and particularly its armed forces, and the mass media (still to be discussed) – caused a dangerously uncoordinated situation to arise in the early twentieth century. All spheres of power had experienced an unprecedented expansion of their potentialities, without the limits of these ever being tested. Industrialization strongly forced up competition for raw materials, in production techniques and for markets. Business therefore called on their states for protection and conquest, both at home

When Austria annexed Bosnia-Herzegovina in 1908 the ethnic and religious diversity of the region posed a great problem for maintaining peace.
The Muslim quarter and bazaar in Sarajevo. Watercolour of 1851 by the Austrian Alois Schönn.
Vienna, Graphische Sammlung Albertina

and in the colonies. In international relationships people still thought as they did throughout the nineteenth century – which was mostly peaceful within Europe – in terms of military alliances, in which waging war became a real option for the continuation of diplomacy. If the Holy Alliance sealed in 1815 should still be seen as a guarantee of the maintenance of international peace, the pacts which came into existence later acquired an increasingly more aggressive character. The Triple Alliance, agreed secretly in 1882, assured Germany, Austro-Hungary and Italy of mutual support in the event of an attack by France. Five years later the members of the alliance widened the provisions bilaterally in an aggressive sense: Italy and Austro-Hungary by promising each other compensation for any expansion of territory in the Balkans, and Germany by promising Italy support in the case of any conflict with France over North Africa. The young Italian state sought

protection in this way, while the German and Austrian empires saw Italy as a strategically located partner. Then in 1892 France and Russia agreed on an alliance by which they promised to support each other against a German attack. This dual system of alliances remained in force and came into effect in 1914 because for Pan-Slavic and strategic considerations Russia chose the side of Serbian nationalism, which was opposed to Austrian dominion over Bosnia.

All these diplomatic agreements were designed some twenty or thirty years before 1914, at a time which from the point of view of military technology still looked much less dangerous. After 1871 the great powers had fought no wars against opponents of equal status. The Austrians and Russians had adventured in the Balkans and against the out-of-date Turkish army, the colonial powers had fought against heavily out-weaponed native peoples. General staffs had based their strategies on these small

The First World War is impressed in the collective memory as the most gruesome of all wars. Life in the trenches which stank of excrement, the loneliness and vulgarity from the enforced close quarters, with the constant fear of death, left deep traces in the front-line soldiers.
Otto Dix, *Flanders*, 1936. Berlin, Gemäldegalerie

wars, as they did their expectations of quick and easy victories. However, after 1850 there had been some breakthroughs in military technology. Smooth barrels had been replaced by the rifled barrel which made the projectile rotate on its axis; from now on loading was breech-loading, and this meant that the force and accuracy of ordnance greatly increased. In the late nineteenth century several new inventions were added to this new technology: heavily armed steel warships, submarines, guns with adjustable cradles and range-finders, reinforced concrete, flame throwers, poison gas, dynamite, aircraft, and above all machine guns. Industrialization penetrated into warfare and raised its destructive power immensely. However, strategic thinking hardly adapted itself at all to these new resources, and not a single power had ever tested them against an equally matched opponent. A tragic experience awaited the troops who were mobilized to man the fronts in 1914: four years of trench warfare in which no side could force a breakthrough, not even at the cost of sometimes hundreds of thousands of deaths within a few days. Sixty-five million soldiers were mobilized and 8.5 million of them died, because nobody had previously realized that the network of alliances and ultimatums would bring into action a destructive power which was unprecedented for all those involved, and uncontrollable.

Poor emigrants lingered on in the edges of the large towns and lapsed into beggary.

The most harrowing scenes occurred in winter.

In 1874 Samuel Luke Fildes showed in this picture the atmosphere outside the London refuge for the homeless.

London, Royal Holloway College

Bureaucratization

To cope with local particularisms and counter-revolutionary opposition, the French revolutionaries centralized power as much as possible in Paris, where they could manipulate the rebellious mob. In the *ancien régime* the state power was represented at local level by individuals enjoying a wide autonomy. Aristocrats and clergy enjoyed their own juridical status and applied administrative and judicial powers within their territory. Bourgeois officials had often purchased their offices, from which it was almost impossible to dismiss them. France was therefore administered indirectly, through a wide and varied layer of middlemen who did not stint themselves. Naturally they did not welcome the revolution, which drove the Jacobins in Paris to replace them in 1793 with reliable representatives of the central authority. Radical and permanent reorganization was forced through at high speed. The feudal divisions were replaced by eighty-six departments, with capitals which were generally – from the economic and demographic point of view – the most important towns in the region. Municipalities were combined,

the law courts were given a uniform hierarchy for the whole state, all private privileges – including those of the guilds – were abolished, taxation and tariffs were reformed, there were no more church tithes and feudal rights, monastic orders were dissolved and their property confiscated. To make all this possible against the resistance of the more rural districts, a hierarchical and centralized bureaucracy was formed which could break local resistance, if necessary by the threat of force from Paris. For this the machinery of a national police force was also set up, with officers who could take preventive action against any threat of opposition. The state of emergency in France caused by the attack of the conservative monarchies made it much easier to impose a strict authoritarian regime that would henceforth be administered directly from Paris.

It may be considered to be a general pattern for state apparatus to grow strongly in size and functions during phases of revolutionary change. This observation also applies to the Soviet Union, and for the same reasons: in the face of internal and external assault the new rulers had to try and achieve improvements in the lot of the masses and

The firm of Krupp was already producing heavy guns in the second half of the nineteenth century.
During the Second World War they also manufactured long-distance guns which could hit a target up to 100 km away.
Adolf Menzel, *The rolling mill in the Krupp steel works in 1875*.
Berlin, Gemäldegalerie

fundamental reforms in all fields in the middle of the total chaos they had inherited from the old regime.[13] In addition, even without a revolution, modernizing the economy and society increased the demand for services on the part of the government. In spite of liberal administrators preferring in principle maximum freedom of action for individuals and private organizations, in the face of the established aristocratic interests they only succeeded in making their objectives recognized by means of the power of the state. Once they were in power, as after 1830 in France, Belgium, England and Portugal, they were faced with situations which made government intervention unavoidable, because they resulted from the initiatives of many private bodies and individuals who could not be held reponsible for the consequences.

The effects of the great economic and social changes of the period are a case in point: should the expansion of new communications, ports, canals and railways be left entirely to private initiatives, or had the government, by its authority to grant concessions, also a guiding or even a co-ordinating task? The answer varied according to country, in which it is characteristic that the continental states were moved towards an active role by strategic interests. For instance, in 1910 building railways absorbed almost half of state expenditure in Prussia and at 29 per cent was the largest debit item in that of Austria. Norway and Belgium opted for railway companies under state control, while the French state only owned the rail network. In Britain, Germany and France central governments in 1910 devoted between 9 and 12 per cent of their budgets to transport infrastructure. Even in the United Kingdom, with its *laissez faire* policy, the government was already involved as part owner or subsidizer of the Cunard Steamship Company (1904), the Suez Canal, and shortly before the First World War the Anglo-Persian Oil Company and Marconi Radio Telegraph Company. In 1912 the Post Office bought up the largest telephone company, by which this service in effect became nationalized, though at the time they refused to call it that.[14]

It is almost impossible to overestimate the social consequences of the new transport networks. The mobility of the work force increased enormously with the building of the railways, so that the indus-

In wealthy families a great deal of attention was give to an engagement,
so that both families could reach agreement on the material side of the matter.
Breaking off an engagement could cause serious problems.
On 26 September 1792 the new code laid down the rules for marriages and divorce for everyone in France.
Michel Garnier (1753–1819), *Breaking off the marriage contract.* Paris, Musée Carnavalet

One more hour! on patrol is a caricature of a Parisian policeman of *c.*1850 by Honoré Daumier.
The middle classes were terrified of the mob in the large towns and built up the police apparatus to combat social unrest and petty crime.
Paris, Musée de la Préfecture de Police

At the end of the nineteenth century many European towns were decaying through the rapid growth of population and increasing industrialization. Johannes Hilverdink, *The Jewish quarter of Amsterdam*, 1889.
Amsterdam, Amsterdams Historisch Museum

trial towns expanded faster. For the state centralization became more achievable now that the speed, comfort and regularity of travel and information evolved to their advantage. Recruits could be sent from one side of the country to the other, accelerating the merging of regional cultures.

The rapid expansion of the towns created problems of public health and public order which even a *laissez faire* policy could not ignore, at the risk of widespread epidemics and disturbances. As in the Third World today, migrants from the impoverished and overpopulated rural areas hoped to find better opportunities of making a living in the towns. However, housing, and the urban infrastructure of streets, water supply and sewerage did not keep up with the rapid expansion, so that unhealthy slums grew up round the towns. For the civil population these marginal residents represented a double danger, because they easily fell into a life of crime, or joined protest movements. In addition infectious diseases such as cholera and typhus spread quickly in the thickly populated and unhygienic districts. In 1875 the first country-wide building and sanitary regulations came into force in the United Kingdom. In 1890 a law even allowed local authorities to engage in building houses.

Humanitarian care, but also sheer self-preservation, forced the urban authorities to improve medical services and to carry out large infrastructure projects to provide sanitation for the working-class districts and to expand traffic systems. Underground railways were built in capital cities; local authorities everywhere started to construct sewage systems, water supplies, gas works and schools. These kinds of local provisions anticipated the responsibilities which national governments were later to assume in these areas. Wide tree-lined avenues were not only airy, healthy and suitable for the citizens to promenade in, and to cope with the growing flow of traffic, they also made rapid intervention by the security forces possible if there were any signs of unrest. Similarly prostitution was regulated by a combination of medical controls and police repression. The urban authorities tried in these ways to discipline the heterogeneous masses assembled together in the megacities.

From this it is clear that local authorities, particularly in the large towns, started to take on important new public functions. With budgets rising fast everywhere, there was a relative increase in the contribution made by the decentralized authorities, showing that analysis of the expansion of public power should not be limited only to the level of the state. The measure of the relative increase in decentralized public budgets is an indication of how far the centralization achieved by the large states varied from one to another: France led the field here, while in 1910 Germany spent 44 per cent more money in its member states and towns than at the imperial level. In France the share of decentralized authorities grew from 35 per cent in 1870 to 45 per cent in 1910, while in Great Britain it grew from 37 per cent to 64 per cent.[15]

The social problems in the new industrial towns caused an intensification of intervention by the state. Particularly in the German empire, which industrialized late but very rapidly, industrial entrepreneurs pressed for state intervention. They had two reasons for this: they considered it to be in their interest to have social measures which would bind their workers to the factory, rather than seeing them take refuge in independent 'solidarity funds'; on the other hand they did not want any such measures to affect competition between businesses. To the conservative government social laws–which were combined with strong repression of any kind of propaganda for the ideas of social democracy–paradoxically also seemed a suitable means of taking the wind from the sails of both the liberals and the socialists. These circumstances explain why it was actually in Germany, controlled by the *Junkers*, that the first social laws were passed between 1881 and 1890. They set up a national system of insurance against sickness and industrial accidents and made workers and employers pay compulsory contributions to old-age pensions. For Chancellor Bismarck what mattered was 'to make the unpropertied classes, too, who are both the most numerous as well as the least educated, aware that the state is not only a necessary but a caring institution'.[16] Whatever the motivation, this legislation substantially broadened the state's field of operations.

In the other western European states there were already more legislative and practical provisions which made state intervention both less urgent and, in the view of the existing religious and secular charitable organizations, even less desirable. In the United Kingdom it was not until 1908 that a law gave the right to a state pension to everyone who had not 'enjoyed' relief under the old Poor Law. In 1911 the National Insurance Act brought in compulsory insurance against sickness and unemployment, which became the basis of the later welfare state. Unlike those in Germany, these allowances were not insurance payments financed by personal contributions, but were paid out by the state, and financed by taxation. One of the mainsprings for the recognition of the state's responsibility in these areas was the findings of research into recruits for the Boer War, that the physical condition of young working-class men left much to be desired, which threatened to weaken the fighting strength of the British army. If states began to accept social provisions as one of their packages of tasks, they had their own *raisons d'état* for doing so.

From the 1870s a debate arose in western Europe on the question of whether education was one of the areas in which the government should interest itself. Political liberals saw this as a task for the government because this would do justice to various differing philosophies, and could adequately prepare for the needs of a rapidly modernizing society. This was opposed by vested interests, particularly the churches, which since the Middle Ages had regarded the transmission of culture, including the provision of charity, as pre-eminently their business. A *Kulturkampf* broke out in Germany between 1872 and 1874 after the Prussian government passed a law taking upon itself the inspection of education, and began by publishing measures discriminating against the role in education of the Catholic priesthood. The problem also arose in other western countries, often in the form of a battle over schools which ended in giving the various governments the task of running non-denominational education themselves. Closely connected with this was the introduction of compulsory education. Eventually this ushered in a new phase in the centuries-long process of secularization which, however – in Spain for example – was only reached in the 1980s. The strength of liberal and socialist opinions and religious diversity strengthened the role of the government in education. On the other hand, the Church, particularly the Catholic Church, in practice retained its monopoly of education in southern and central Europe, which was still largely agricultural, until far into the twentieth century. Modernization and differentiation in society therefore invited increasing intervention by the authorities.

The First World War rapidly widened the role of the state. It also forced the British government to jettison its *laissez faire* principles. In practice it had to requisition the production of some factories, subject others to its requirements, and even take complete control of some for the war industry. Purchase of raw materials, movements of capital, and import and export trade became government business for reasons of security. Prices of consumer goods were fixed and their distribution controlled.

The import of various industrial products was from 1915 made subject to duties, bringing a formal end to the traditional policy of free trade. Although much of this state interference was repealed immediately after the war, a number of measures were retained, such as the import duty on cars. Above all the apparatus of state officials remained much larger than previously, and such questions as state intervention in the rationalization, mergers, or even nationalization of businesses could now also be discussed. The state had demonstrably been able to fulfil an essential role, and would go on to do so increasingly.

The mass society

Mass movements had gained the liberal breakthroughs of the French revolution and mass armies had spread them across Europe and consolidated most of them in France. During the nineteenth century the political significance of the masses was to increase constantly. The enormous concentrations of people in the megacities and in ever larger factories created the masses as a factor of power. In Great Britain and France liberals could at first base their political position on them, at least as long as they could and were prepared to meet the demands of the impoverished urban population. It was not until the last decades of the century that autonomous workers' parties were formed on a national basis, the last of them in Great Britain.

In industry, where tens of thousands of workers toiled together, class distinctions proved to be more irreconcilable. There, in vast numbers, they joined trade unions which protected their direct, and primarily material, interests. Around 1900 they had some 2 million members in Great Britain. In Germany their numbers grew from half a million in 1900 to 2.5 million in 1912; on top of that the Christian unions united another 750,000 workers. Meanwhile 15,000 salaried militants had found a career in the various workers' organizations, and 20,000 represented their interests as elected members of local councils or in parliament. They acquired a personal interest in the success of these large-scale organizations. France followed with half a million union members in 1900 and a million ten years later. These memberships were many times larger than those of political parties, an indication of the long-standing gap between the workers' movements and political power. Yet it was mainly through legislation and from political power that emancipation was to be won.

The socially committed German painter Köbler recorded a strike at a factory in 1886.

Angry workers express their dissatisfaction to the factory manager. Berlin, Archiv für Kunst und Geschichte

From 1890 workers over almost the whole of Europe celebrated Labour Day on 1 May with great demonstrations.

These boosted the collective consciousness and self-respect of the working class.

K. Cserna, *The May Day demonstration in Budapest in 1890.* Budapest, Magyar Nemzeti Muzeum

In the course of the nineteenth century there were riots and strikes in the industrialized regions of Catalonia and the Basque country.
Ramon Casas' *Charge of the Guardia Civil* happened in the neighbourhood of a factory in Gerona.
Gerona, Museo de Olot

LE GLOBE ILLUSTRÉ
JOURNAL DE LA FAMILLE

ABONNEMENTS: — PRIX DU NUMÉRO : 20 CENTIMES — VOLUME I — N° 48 — 29 août 1886 — BRUXELLES, 18, rue de la Madeleine, 18 — Directeur : THÉO SPÉE.

LA MANIFESTATION OUVRIÈRE SUR LE BOULEVARD ANSPACH
Dessin de M. Eschenbach

In Belgium universal plural suffrage was won after the general strikes of 1891 and 1893.
An illustrated account of the demonstration of August 1886 in *Le Globe Illustré* by M. Eschenbach.
Ghent, Archief en Museum van de Socialistische Arbeidersbeweging

Collective action was the main method by which a new identity based on class was formed. At least, this is how the impassioned leaders, who themselves usually came from the middle classes, saw it. Conflicts and strikes there were certainly, but also celebrations, such as the May Day festival widely introduced in 1890. In that year 70,000 to 80,000 workers demonstrated in Brussels, and 100,000 in Barcelona and Stockholm. What is most surprising is the incredible speed with which membership of workers' organizations grew at precisely the period around the turn of the century when the expansion of the franchise was achieved. This happened in stages: in the new German *Reich* of 1871 there was universal suffrage only for the *Reichstag;* in Great Britain almost all men had enjoyed it since 1884, provided they had resided long enough in the same place, which was unusual for workers. One interpretation of this evolution is that the material conditions in which the workers lived and worked were

Governments saw the establishment of state schools as a means of fighting poverty and overcoming the lack of education in the family.
The churches saw their monopoly of education threatened by this competition and started a battle of schooling.
Detail of a liberal print satirizing Catholic education in Belgium in 1912. Ghent, Liberaal Archief, Fonds Willemfonds

Progressive liberals and socialists campaigned for
non-denominational and free education.
J. Geoffroy *Class room,* 1889. Rouen, Musée national de l'Education

Coloured satirical print which appeared in the German satirical paper
Simplizissimus of 1899, in which Thomas Theodor Heine
sets out the worker's choice – factory or prison.

Evocative picture of Paris by Champin on the occasion
of the proclamation of the French Republic from the steps of the Parliament building.
This was the seventeenth-century Palais Bourbon to which a neo-classical peristyle had recently been added.
Paris, Musées de la Ville de Paris

the cause of the formation of workers' organizations and for the mounting of collective action. About 1870 the fight for shorter working hours and higher wages began to lead to a slow improvement of living standards.[17] This led to the masses as consumers also becoming an interesting target market for entrepreneurs.

When it transpired that only national legislation could eliminate some of the fundamental opposition of employers, activities were targeted on winning a majority in parliament. Strikes, originally a weapon used to improve working conditions, were now organized on a country-wide basis to add strength to political demands. In Belgium universal (if still plural) suffrage was won after general strikes in 1891 and 1893; in Sweden the successful general strike of 1902 led to the introduction of universal suffrage in 1909, making it the only country (then including Finland) where women, too, were included in the franchise. Before 1914 all European countries had introduced one form or another of universal male suffrage. After the war this became more general, even in eastern Europe, as a kind of compensation for the other forms of involvement which the states had by then imposed on their citizens.

The goal of winning political power implied a shift in objectives, away from the direct and unambiguous promotion of the interests of the workers. In spite of some brilliant electoral successes absolute majorities were still lacking. As the socialist movement increasingly aimed at winning political power, and visibly showed progress in doing so, they provoked more opposition. Having developed from the ideas and experiences of the Enlightenment and of the Jacobins, socialism was undoubtedly anchored on a solid ideological foundation.

The bourgeoisie who dominated the state in the nineteenth century assumed a pleasant life style reminiscent of the earlier court life.
Just as in the past kings built theatres, opera houses and art galleries, the bourgeoisie erected similar temples of culture
for their own enjoyment and glory. *The grand staircase of the Kunsthistorisches Museum in Vienna* dates from 1891.
Vienna, Graphische Sammlung Albertina

From the Utopian socialists of the early nineteenth century, through generations of theorists and pragmatists, a new and coherent framework of thought had emerged. So much so that its intellectual leaders have always expended a great deal of their energy on theoretical arguments. None the less the established rulers quite rightly saw in them a fundamental attack on their own norms and values. The Christian churches, in particular the Catholics, saw philosophical materialism as incompatible with their philosophy and tried to avert the 'Red Peril' by establishing their own workers' associations which would preserve the Christian community from disintegration. The papal encyclical *Rerum Novarum* in 1893 may have acknowledged the material and spiritual needs of the working classes, but aimed principally at containing the expansion of godless socialism within its own organizations.

The new emphasis on the organic unity of the Christian community denied the class warfare which was a reality to the socialists. Against the ideal image of international workers' solidarity the Church placed that of universal Christian charity. This was a clear challenge to the unity of the labour movement. The more conservative sections of the movement, which were still part of the denominational organizations, would, particularly in Catholic countries, form a counterweight to the rise of socialism. This also explains in part why the Protestant countries, Scandinavia and Britain, saw the first and strongest socialist majorities in parliament.

In their search for political power to achieve the emancipation of the workers, the socialists based their hopes on the state forcing their class enemies, the capitalist employers, to make concessions, or even eliminating them completely. The diversifica-

In 1877 Berlin decided to build a palatial university building in Strasburg
which would broadcast German scholarship over recently conquered Lorraine.
Otto Warth's design for a neo-Renaissance palace was chosen. On the pediment above the facade there still stand the figures
of prominent German scholars such as Luther, Kant and Leibniz. The building was part of a new quarter of the city with public buildings.

tion of the political spectrum resulting from the development of the socialist movement led to a heightening of the expectations they had of the state. The state was burdened with new functions: as mediator and to lay down the rules in industrial disputes, and with organizing various social security schemes. States and local authorities had concerned themselves with projects affecting the infrastructure. Partly under the pressure of the requirements of industry for a work force with at least some education, by the end of the nineteenth century all European states had introduced compulsory education, and themselves assumed part of the task of setting up that education. In Great Britain primary education became compulsory in 1870, so that illiteracy was reduced from 34 per cent in that year to 5 per cent in 1900; France continued the trend with a drop from 40 per cent to 15 per cent. Various sections of the community wanted active intervention by the state in specific fields, so that the package of government services was steadily enlarged. Education, however, meant power over the culture which it

transmitted, as was confirmed by the Church's resistance to state schools in the 1870s and 1880s.

Various research projects have shown that the civilizing role of the schoolteachers was particularly effective after 1870. Various subjects offered a clear opportunity for a civilizing offensive. Inevitably education in a single specific national language implied that dialects and regional languages were made subordinate to the language of the dominant group in the state. The role – or the absence – of religious teaching made it clear that the state schools, particularly in France, had a strong secularizing effect. The teaching of history postulated as self-evident that the French state, as it existed within its 1815 frontiers, had always been a logical development, and drop by drop imposed the evidence of a homogeneous French nation, the value of the establishment of the republican state, and the superiority of western civilization. The schoolmaster personified civic duty and republican nationalism. The informal curriculum, the values, attitudes and norms to which the children were continually exposed, taught

Between 1818 and 1828 this homogeneous Senate square with administrative and university buildings was built in Helsinki
in a severely classical style on the Berlin model. The whole is dominated by the Lutheran cathedral.
Helsinki, Helsingin Kaupungin Kuva-Arkisto

In 1896 the Hungarian nation celebrated the millennium
of its existence. This poster emphasized heroes from ancient
Hungarian history and the insignia of the kingdom.
Budapest, Orszagos Széchényi Könyvtar

The first monument erected
by the Third Republic in Paris
in 1874 was the equestrian statue of Joan of Arc,
in France the special symbol of hope and national unity.

As the number of daily and weekly newspapers increased, more people became informed about the political situation.
Newspapers, with their commentaries on events, became a formidable weapon for influencing public opinion.
Viennese print of 1837 by Johann Christian Schoeller.
Vienna, Historisches Museum der Stadt Wien

The Austrian language laws of 1897 which prescribed the equality
of German and local languages in non-German regions provoked
strong opposition from German speakers. Print after a sketch
by Franz Schlegel, detail. Vienna, Österreichische Nationalbibliothek

Garibaldi portrayed as an exhausted old lion.
Lithograph by Barousse
after a drawing by Faustin, 1871.
Rome, Museo centrale del Risorgimento

them respect for authority.[18] While on the political stage the fight was waged for the emancipation of the working class, their children were quietly being injected with bourgeois values in school.

Universal military conscription, introduced in the second half of the century, also gave the states a particularly effective medium of indoctrination, enabling them to reach the whole of their male population. The officer corps, a relic of the class society, still retained a strong aristocratic tinge and politically was extremely conservative.[19] Apart from the official language of the country, the recruits were taught discipline and submission to the authority and mystic presence of the state. Teachers and military instructors reached an almost complete cross-section of the rising generation.

In addition to this an increasing number of officials came in contact with the population through the various new government services. From the middle of the century striking newcomers among governmental officials were the police services at local, regional and national level. During the *ancien régime* there were very few forces responsible for public order, and when there were real disturbances the local citizen militias or the army were called out. Great Britain, up to the early 1990s, retained an unarmed police force under the control of the borough or county, with co-ordination by London only in emergencies. In France on the other hand, the Ministry of Home Affairs took control of the *Sûreté Nationale*, and the War Minister had the *Gendarmerie Nationale* under his command. The militarist Prussian police only came under civil control around 1900. In extreme cases on the continent the army was still employed, as against the Parisian 'revolutions' of 1830, 1848 and 1871, when there were at least 1,000 victims. Yet the introduction of three separate repression mechanisms, each designed to fight against a specific level of deviation or intensity of violence, on the one hand demonstrates the widening of the problem of law and order to one at the level of the state, and on the other a more effective control of everyday violence. Undoubtedly new forms of political and social action and arrangements for consultation absorbed a great deal of potential violence. Governments also learnt to cope with it in a more balanced way.[20]

In a strongly centralized state like France, which was a model for many others, all these new government officials, from schoolmasters to policemen, were trained in centrally planned institutes and each one promoted in his own field the image of a stronger and more homogeneous state. This was also the function of the many other institutions set up by the states, provinces and towns. As in earlier centuries, governments gave expression to their identity in monuments. Law courts and parliament buildings, ministries, town halls, barracks, schools and railway stations displayed, in a predominantly classical style, the weighty presence of government authority. Moreover, the choice of style evokes a well-defined automatic association. For instance, in 1836 there were fierce debates in Britain about the plans for the new Houses of Parliament. The Gothic Revival design won over the classical, because this style was thought to be more related to the British national character, and would evoke associations with the medieval origins of the constitutional liberties of the English.

New government institutions were an excuse for intense building activities, which offered the opportunity for the symbolic display of their ambitions for power. This was accompanied by a craze for putting up monuments. National heroes were deposited on every street corner, to imprint every citizen constantly with the renown of the people and the mother country. The bourgeoisie who dominated the nineteenth-century states created for their own satisfaction a variety of cultural institutions by which they could actually imitate the courtly life of the kings of bygone ages. Theatres, operas, concert halls and ballrooms, museums, libraries, parks, botanic and zoological gardens were established by states and local authorities to accommodate the cultural functions which the middle classes – following the example of the former princely courts – provided themselves with at public expense. These cultural activities also served political and social ends. Internally it was a matter of forging a tight cohesion based on a common cultural identity. The gradual opening up of the political system to the middle classes made it necessary for the newcomers to be 'socialized' in the dominant patterns of culture. Moreover, this cultural display was intended to exhibit the brilliance of the new elite to outsiders. Vienna and Berlin competed with each other in this monumentalism, and were imitated by each minor capital.

This exuberant self-portrayal by the state contained a cultural message which could not be misunderstood. It always propagated a well-defined view, that of the dominating bourgeois culture. National days of celebration, anthems, flags, and military parades transferred the earlier links of the subjects' dynastic loyalty to the abstract state and its national myth. In some countries such as Britain it succeeded

From 1831 onwards Honoré Daumier amused himself by modelling a number of caricature portraits in clay
of French parliamentarians which he later coloured in oils.
These representatives of the people are Antoine Odier, a banker, Alexandre Simon Pataille, a magistrate, and Pierre-Paul Royer Collard.
Paris, Musée d'Orsay

in getting both cultures to operate side by side, very much to the benefit of the cohesion of the people.

In a town like Strasburg, which in recent centuries had changed 'nationality' several times, this imposed identity was very clearly visible. After incorporation into the German *Reich* in 1871, an imposing urban complex was built in a new quarter of the town, with a theatre, library, university and provincial government buildings, which would express the glory of the new rulers beyond a shadow of doubt. Statues on the facade of the university represented great minds of the German people. In multinational states and empires the expression of identity was naturally an emotive issue. In Helsinki, the new capital of the grand duchy of Finland under the Russian empire, a remarkably homogeneous architectural symbolic centre arose in the years 1818 to 1828. Literally the highest point was formed by the Lutheran cathedral, while the three other sides of the square in front of it were taken up by the government building, the university and the town hall, all in a sober classical style of Berlin cut. Later the Orthodox cathedral rose as a symbolic counterpoint on a rise nearby. The Finns honoured the reform-minded Tsar Alexander II (1855–1881) with a statue in the middle of the square, by which they obviously emphasized their attachment to the Finnish autonomy which he tolerated. Not all peoples, however, could deal as sophisticatedly with

their rulers. In Warsaw the Polish theatre of the beginning of this century is a small building outside the centre, because the Russians dominated the historic heart of the town.

Empires by definition ruled over peoples with different cultures, languages and religions. As their control became more effective and more direct, the tensions between the dominant and the subordinate cultures heightened. For instance, in the Balkans the Ottoman empire, partly under pressure from Russian and Austrian challenges, had to cope with ever stronger movements for autonomy from its various peoples. In 1817 Serbia acquired the status of a tributary principality. The Greeks won their independence in 1829 with western support, which naturally infected their neighbours. The Russo-Turkish war of 1877–1878 led to the independence of Serbia, the establishment of an Austrian protectorate over Bosnia, the creation of an independent Romania, and the granting of the status of a dependent principality to Bulgaria. In this ethnic and religious patchwork quilt new states, whose leaders took great pains to provide them with a historical identity and legitimacy, appeared like magic. In 1881 Romania became an independent kingdom through the union of the Ottoman vassal principalities of Wallachia and Moldavia. By skilfully changing sides it doubled its territory after the First World War. Transylvania, one of the areas annexed, was inhabited mainly by Hungarians and Slavs, but the Romanian rulers went out of their way to create a national myth which made the population of the new state descend from the glorious Dacians who from 101 to 106 were incorporated into the Roman empire after heavy resistance. They therefore felt they had earlier valid 'claims' than the Slavs, Germans, Hungarians and Jews who shared the country with them. Until 1989 the Romanian state exercised a harsh cultural repression over them.

Nationalism often took the form of a secessionist movement, wanting to establish a separate state for their own people free from the ruling foreign imperium. However, it was not only multinational states and empires who had to face such counter-movements. The United Kingdom is still combating Scottish and Irish secessionist movements, and there are very active regional movements in Catalonia and the Basque country. It is the strengthening of the bourgeois states which caused the intensification of direct contacts between the administrative centre and the subjects. During the *ancien régime* state power was on the whole distant and fairly weak, being exercised indirectly by local potentates. However, the nineteenth-century state gradually demanded more involvement of its citizens and steadily penetrated further into their lives: it demanded more taxes, prescribed more laws, imposed compulsory education and military service, subjected them to statistical registration and forced a national culture on them ever more plainly. It also required their participation and loyalty. Rulers no longer owed their positions to their noble birth or inheritance, but had to prove their worth in elections. At first only the wealthiest enjoyed the franchise through some form of selective census, but gradually the body of electors became more massive. They therefore had to be addressed by the state as well as by the candidates wishing to represent them.

The greater intensity of its involvement enabled the state to display its cultural identity more emphatically. Since up to the eighteenth century monarchies had not really had to concern themselves with the homogeneity of their subjects, many very different cultural communities still existed within their political frontiers in the year 1800. The gradually more active intervention of the organs of state plainly benefited the subjects who shared the culture of the centre, and made the exercise of their civic rights by others appreciably more difficult. As the disadvantaged less dominant cultural communities became more clearly conscious of their posi-

tion, they became more susceptible to nationalist propaganda. Just as the rulers of most states thought in terms of the imposition of a single culture on all inhabitants of their territory, the nationalists demanded their own independent state as the best guarantee of the complete development of the cultural identity of their people.

There was much still to be discovered. In June 1848 the Pan-Slavic congress in Prague demanded the transformation of the Habsburg empire into 'a union of peoples with equal rights'. None the less this remained a bone of bitter contention until 1914. When in that year of revolutions of 1848 the Hungarians seized power in their ancestral kingdom, they did not in their turn think of granting equal rights to the Slavs. Besides, the Hungarian monarchy used no other administrative language except Latin; Hungarian, which was a minority language, could not be used in Croatia and Transylvania, and the vernacular languages had too limited a vocabulary for a modern bureaucracy. In the mid-nineteenth century nationalism was still an elitist movement of disadvantaged regional minorities. They created an image of a glorious national past which should give them the right, if not the noble mission, to embrace the language and culture of their ancestors. As state and culture were so interwoven, the nationalists thought that the emancipation of their people could only be achieved within their own state. The myth of their own national character was constructed on the basis of partly fictitious and certainly exalted historical romances and events, folk traditions, a mother tongue retrieved and added to by littérateurs and linguistic experts, and in some cases a specific type of religion. None of these elements formed – or forms now – an objective criterion of national identity: what people wanted to see in them was enough to distinguish them from the others and to provide them with a collective identity and dignity. The more the pressure of a state felt to be foreign made people realize that the dominant culture group put them at a disadvantage, the more massively they identified themselves with the premises of the nationalist movement. From being an elitist cultural trend it became a political power, particularly when the franchise was widened and minorities could make their votes count.

The demarcation of nationalities was a far from objective process: inclusion or exclusion was the consequence of the opinions of political rulers, coupled with the willingness or not – or the possibility – of assimilating sub-cultures. It is a pure figment of the imagination to suppose that ethnicity should

In his naive style Henri Rousseau glorified French national unity and to a certain degree also the republican feeling of superiority over other peoples. This picture, *Representatives of foreign powers welcome the Republic in the name of peace,* dates from 1907.
Paris, Musée du Louvre, Picasso Foundation

form an objective distinguishing criterion on which to base the identity of a people. People who after the many reversals of history lived in a particular district could have allowed themselves to be assimilated by foreign rulers, but could in a later generation under new rulers again find themselves counted among the oppressed. These drastic shifts in state frontiers in regions of great ethnic, linguistic and religious diversity such as the Balkans have still not yet banished the topicality of the question of nationality.

However, nationalism also acted as a force for political integration. The community to which a people felt it belonged, for whatever reason – and certainly under the influence of a propaganda campaign based on the preparatory work of the cultural protagonists – could be a motivation for the politi-

cal unification of states like Germany and Italy. In existing, still culturally heterogeneous large states, such as France, it supported the forging of the subjects into a solid nation. Established rulers also made intensive use of nationalism as an ideology which encouraged the cohesion of the population as well as their willingness for patriotic sacrifice, in good days as in bad. An extremely effective means of doing this was to evoke the image of an enemy. Since the Napoleonic wars Germans and Englishmen had a thorough distrust of France. The French, since their defeat in 1870, hated the Germans, who in their turn had a bone to pick with the Austrians, Poles and Russians. All the central-European peoples were against their powerful neighbours, both Germans and Russians. In the second half of the nineteenth century politicians played heavily on these antagonisms to increase the cohesion of their own countries and to justify their military expenditures. From the 1870s this was supplemented by European imperialist expansion, which went with conquests of colonies and trading posts. European states entered into a fierce competition for colonial conquests, which aroused their own self-satisfaction but also mutual opposition.

When around 1900 the rush for colonies came to an end, aggression turned back on Europe itself and its immediate periphery in North Africa and the Middle East. In some colonies where there had been European settlement, such as South Africa, the European states waged mutual wars with each other indirectly. In the home countries the reverberations of these were very great, a consequence of the new phenomena of the masses. Political decisions such as the committal of troops would from now on be discussed in elected parliaments and commented on in the mass media. This meant that public opinion became emotionally involved in the success of their national armies.

Inflamed nationalist feelings proved to be an unexpectedly effective weapon against socialism for conservative politicians. They evoked more elementary psychological feelings of association than the abstract concept of class. The collective ego of the glorious nation against the evil foreigners appealed strongly to mass emotions. Emphasizing national unity (meaning, of course, superiority) over other European peoples – which were presented as rival states – and less advanced civilizations drove the class struggle into the background for large sections of the population. So much so that in 1914 even the German social democrats, from fear of losing their adherents, did not dare to use their strong position in the *Reichstag* to speak – in accordance with their ideology – against imperialist domination or against voting credits for war. A long century of civilizing campaigns by bourgeois and conservative politicians had developed national identities so strongly that the western European states were made extremely antagonistic to each other, while the empires in eastern Europe were torn asunder by it internally. As well as the socialist ideology the churches too had lost ground: as institutional disseminators of values and norms their voice was now hardly heard in the midst of the secularized violence of the states.

The First World War was the unexpected paroxysm of the various nationalisms. However, their strength was in no way drained by it, but rather reinforced. When they achieved political participation, the peoples learnt to regard themselves as loyal subjects who loved their country as their mother. The idea of nation-states was so deeply ingrained that by the end of the twentieth century it is still extraordinarily difficult to rid oneself of the state mythology which has been imprinted in us for generations.

1 POLLARD 1994, 61–62.
2 KUZNETS 1959, 20–21.
3 POLLARD 1994, 60, 70–71.
4 O'BRIEN 1989, 345–377.
5 KURGAN-VAN HENTENRYK 1994, 285–315.
6 TILLY 1993, tab. 12–13.
7 POLLARD 1981b, 259.
8 CHANDLER 1994, 115–116.
9 BOUTHOUL & CARRÈRE 1976, 199–201.
10 TILLY 1990, 79.
11 TILLY 1990, 123.
12 MANN 1993, 363–373.
13 SKOCPOL 1978.
14 HOBSBAWM 1968, 241–242.
15 MANN 1993, 363.
16 THOMPSON 1968, 295.
17 HOBSBAWM 1968, 159–165.
18 WEBER 1976, 332–338.
19 MANN 1993, 426–438.
20 MANN 1993, 404–412.

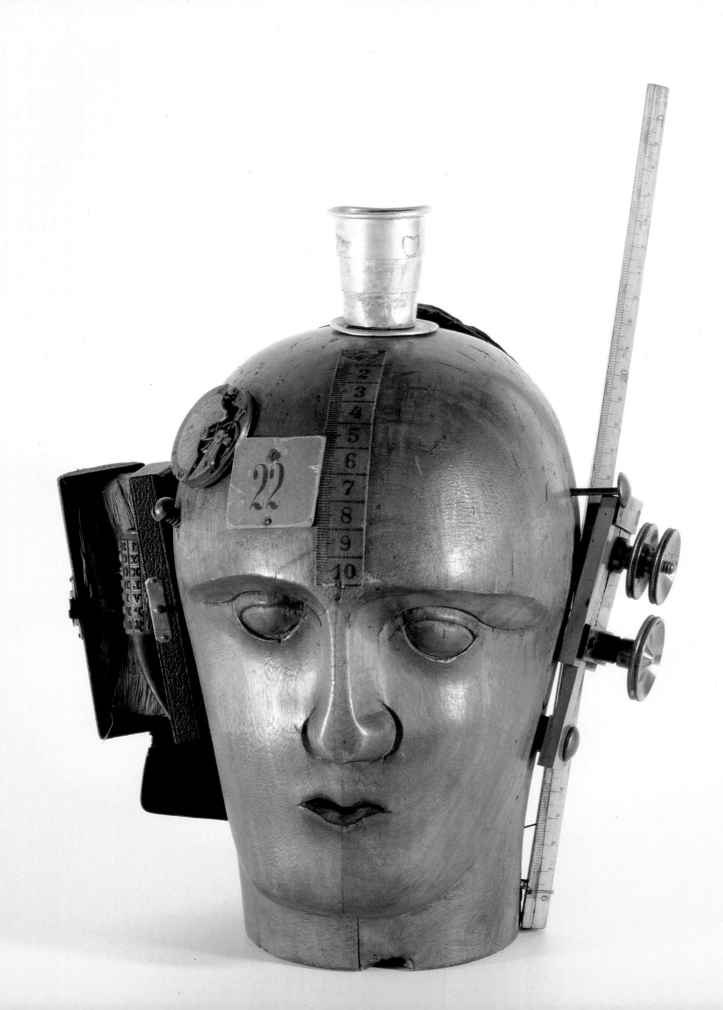

CHAPTER IX
Economics, Politics and Culture at Odds

During the nineteenth century the state developed into the decisive configuration of power. The increase in scale of economic production required integration of domestic markets, infrastructures, and legislation covering companies, banks and foreign trade. A few colonial conquests could improve the supply of raw materials and influence the balance of trade positively. The state acquired a steadily more effective hold on its subjects, to whom more individual and collective rights were gradually granted in exchange for much heavier obligations, and for being subjected to the dominant culture. By also embarking expressly on this last territory, the state further undermined the radius of action of the churches which had already seen their adherents decline steeply as a result of urbanization. In the early twentieth century nationalism appeared to have become the strongest single political and cultural movement, and was to remain so until the Second World War.

The first half of the century even saw the development of the totalitarian state which unashamedly concerned itself with the total encapsulation of society, the economy and culture, so that the individual was turned into a pawn in the deliberate manipulation of the masses. Expectations of the guiding powers of the state with regard to the economy were also pitched very high in countries under different ideological regimes. Communist and fascist regimes alike aspired to create a new culture from on high and with a prescribed ideological message. The unitary and authoritarian nature of these concentrations of power in the leadership (not chosen democratically) of states, meant a fundamental break with the cen-

turies-old European traditions of pluralism. To the extent that the totalitarian states can be considered responsible for the universal disaster which was the Second World War, totalitarianism must also be labelled a pernicious failure in European history. More than people are generally inclined to recognize, however, it was directly in line with ambitions fostered by all western European states about the turn of the century.

Global enterprise

The communist Soviet Union obviously banished free enterprise and the market economy, but in their ideological opponents of Nazi Germany, fascist Italy and falangist Spain state interventions also penetrated deep into social and economic relationships. These last two states nationalized the most important industries: in 1960 nine of the fifteen largest businesses in Spain still belonged to the state, and this included the four most important. Most of them had been established by the state, the others had been bought up. In Italy the state had financed the building of roads and railways and the development of the steel industry immediately after unification in 1861. In this tradition it retained, through the *Istituto di Ricostruzione Nazionale*, set up in 1933, large shareholdings in the steel, electro-mechanical and mechanical engineering industries. These took over weak businesses and directed investment more for political than economic reasons. In France governments with a socialist and communist character in 1936–1937 and between 1944 and 1948 started large-scale nationalization of business-

Mechanical mannequin's head with attachments, entitled *The spirit of our time*, an assemblage of 1919 by the Austrian artist Raoul Hausmann. Paris, Musée d'Art moderne, Centre Georges Pompidou

In 1917 the new government in Russia had posters printed such as this *Victorious peasant with a sheaf of corn,* to persuade women
to come forward and work in the newly established co-operative farms. Amsterdam, International Institute for Social History

Notes: see p. 387

es, as did the British Labour government after the Second World War.[1]

In the 1990s the enthusiasm for state industries in all these countries seems to have cooled considerably. It would not be correct in all cases to call their performance inadequate from a purely economic point of view; it was often a matter of political choices from the start, frequently with unprofitable businesses in a generally unfavourable business climate, and negative economic conditions internationally. What is certain is that no-one would now be anxious to define the responsibilities of the state as widely as they did both on the left and the right of the political spectrum during the first half of the twentieth century.

The First World War for the first time put the European countries in debt to the Americans on a large scale. Loans had supported their war efforts, new loans had to be incurred for reconstruction, for paying off the burden of interest, and to

In 1920, soon after the First World War, Pierre Bonnard painted the *Bernheim Brothers,* both bankers, in their office at Villers. Paris, Musée d'Orsay

settle the gigantic reparations payments which, in the nineteenth-century tradition, had in 1919 been imposed upon the defeated Germany. These were so clearly above the power of the crippled German economy to bear that they could not be paid in time or in full. This started a chain of indebtedness of Germany to the victorious states and of Europe to the United States, which after the crash of the New York stock exchange in October 1929 recoiled on the European economies like a boomerang.

It is revealing that less industrialized countries such as Denmark, Norway, Hungary and Greece suffered very little harm from this crisis. In western Europe on the other hand it showed not only the strong international integration of the capital market, but also the extent to which the western states were tightly woven into the world economy. The collapse of the market created massive unemployment, which produced a double problem for the states: falling revenues and a rising pressure on ex-

The Berlin *Börsen-Courier* rolling off the press. This expressive picture by Magnus Zeller
illustrates the nervous tension of business in Berlin between the wars.
Berlin, Axel Springer Verlag AG

Wählt Spartakus (Vote Spartacus) is a 1925 propaganda poster inviting German electors to vote for the Spartacists of the far left.
In 1919 they had unleashed a rising of revolutionary workers in Berlin,
which was savagely suppressed by the army with the support of the social democrats.
Amsterdam, International Institute for Social History

penditure. Confronted for the first time with an industrial crisis on a worldwide scale, governments reacted with the recipes for recovery with which they were familiar: sticking to the gold standard, restricting government expenditure, strict *laissez-faire*, protectionism and other deflationary measures. According to economists, led by J.M. Keynes, they only aggravated the negative consequences of the crisis and made them last longer. Only the Second World War absorbed – or rather swamped – these effects.

In the delicate relationship between politics and economics each was thoroughly at cross-purposes with the other during the first half of the century. Drastic disruption of normal political life, such as the two world wars, the profound political instability during the declining years of the Weimar regime, and the Spanish civil war, had clearly crippled economic activity. The origin of the international financial crisis of 1929 was as political as it was economic, just as it was the economic policy of governments which aggravated its negative effects and made them last longer. On the other hand governments were confronted with an international economic phenomenon on which they could not get a grip but which drastically upset their domestic policies and social relationships. Both spheres of power, the political and the economic, had before 1940 not yet found an adequate balance for their new relationship, now that both had developed so strongly. The problems of the First World War and its aftermath offered industries in the neutral countries, Sweden, Switzerland and the Netherlands, the opportunity to strengthen their international position. Precisely in the capital-intensive and technologically advanced sectors of processed food, chemicals, metals, mechanical engineering and electrical appliances, they developed strongly into international concerns. On the other hand the large German firms evolved after 1934 into tools of the Nazi regime, and so into links in their war machine.

Having learnt from the tragic social and political aftermath of the Versailles Peace Treaty and the Great Depression, democratic politicians – actually during the course of the Second World War – developed a new system that broke radically away from the tradition of *laissez-faire:* the welfare state. It was not, in fact, the western European democracies that had produced the model for economic success, but radical interventionist governments of various political colours: social democrats in Sweden, communists in the Soviet Union, the Democrats' New Deal policy in the United States, and even the National Socialists in Germany. They inspired a variant of democracy which aimed at linking economic and political stability with democracy, consultation, participation, welfare and prosperity. This would impose on the state a new and heavy task, but no longer that of undertaking comprehensive economic and cultural programmes itself. Politics in future would lay down rules and mediate, economics would independently supply the means. Both systems followed their own logic: businesses aimed rationally, often authoritatively and competitively for profit; politics pressed for compromises, and had to take proper account of the sometimes emotive effect on public opinion of blurred or even incorrect perceptions. Each in its own sphere and with its own methods would have to make the future captains of industry and politicians do business with each other by consultation. The consultative economy with a social dimension seemed to offer a solution for the pre-war dilemmas.

The welfare state put in place social legislation at the government's expense, so that every citizen should enjoy a secure existence from the cradle to the grave. Expansion of compulsory education and the associated governmental provisions supplied the growing need for a trained work force for industry, but put the cost of this training largely on the public sector. The post-war system guaranteed a fairly stable strong growth of prosperity until the mid-1970s, without serious economic fluctuations, and with compensating intervention by governments to maintain purchasing power and investment.

After the oil crises in the mid-1970s the costs of the welfare state outgrew its capacity because of over-consumption. As during the 1930s, the remedies of the previous crisis (deficit spending, thought up by Keynes) were again applied, and state debt was allowed to run up to 100 per cent, in Belgium in 1993 even to 146 per cent, of the gross national product. In the light of this problem the call for 'getting rid of the fat' of the state gradually gained more response.

The enormous weight with which the states in the course of the twentieth century had burdened the economy – as regulators in all kinds of directions, as the largest employers, levying taxes up to an average of seven-twelfths of individual incomes (the Netherlands, 1993) – explains why movements of the economy in the second half of the twentieth century are so evened out that it is primarily the state budgets which bear their traces. Through their international organization, however, the

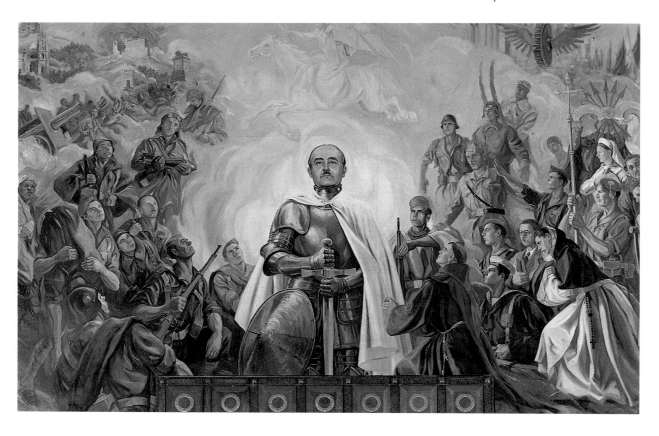

On 8 July 1936 in Morocco General Franco called for a rebellion against the Spanish Republic;
his declaration was followed by a bitter civil war. On a great mural fresco Franco had himself portrayed as St Iago,
the knightly patron saint, who had once liberated the Spaniards from the Muslims
and was therefore revered as the national saint.

Felix Nussbaum portrayed himself in 1943, confined by a concrete wall with a star of David and Jewish identity card.
He lived in hiding, in terror of the Nazis.
Osnabruck, Kulturgeschichtliches Museum

As industrial production increased,
the need also rose for advertising media
to sell the products to the maximum number of consumers.
Poster of 1911 by Ernst Deutsch for Mercedes typewriters
which would make a secretary's life
so much more pleasant …
Stuttgart, Staatsgalerie

Advertising introduced a more leisured and independent life style
for the individual. In this particular case, also greater mobility.
A 1932 poster for Fiat by Riccobaldi. Lucerne, Verkehrshaus

largest operators in the economy escape much of the oppressive taxation and social regulations of the western welfare states so that these fall mainly on the less mobile enterprises with less capital backing, and on individual citizens. Larger units therefore keep their advantage.

Export of productive investments and profits, and the practice of playing off states and trade unions against each other with employment as the stake, seem to be extremely effective means by which multinational enterprises can escape disadvantageous government interference. By its relative autonomy from the states, capitalism contributes strongly to the global integration of markets. This means that individual states can exercise hardly any influence on the economic processes taking place within their frontiers. The increase in scale of the political organization in Europe should offer a response to this challenge, but this was completely lacking before the 1950s, and even since then it has only so far developed on a very limited scale.

The alternative which up to the 1960s appeared to be offered by the Soviet Union finally fell by the wayside in the 1980s, just as happened earlier with the unprofitable government-owned businesses in Spain. Large companies did not operate as separate units, but were subordinated to the overall decision-making structure of the imperium, where planning and the flow of products were co-ordinated. Production units, in contrast to those in developed market economies, remained limited to one single function. They were not allowed to involve themselves in the distribution of their products, nor had they any contact with their suppliers of raw materials or components. The lack of direct and continuous contact with suppliers and customers restricted the strategic understanding of managers, so that they were not sufficiently aware of the possibilities for product innovation or technological improvement. The lack of competition on a domestic or international scale also deprived them of an additional opportunity of learning from

The *Kurfürstendamm* in (West) Berlin in 1951.

This elegant boulevard was laid out in 1870 on the initiative of Bismarck and was the entertainment and business centre of the city.

After the Second World War the *Kurfürstendamm* recovered its activity remarkably quickly.

Berlin, Archiv für Kunst und Geschichte

New processes and products led to a massive increase in patents for the protection of the owner or inventor.
Once a patent was granted, this was taxable by the government. A patent office near Paris, pictured in 1890 by Henri Rousseau,
who was an excise officer *(douanier)*.
London, The Courtauld Institute

the experiences of others. Particularly the separation of the three basic functions of a modern industrial company, development and commercialization, production, and distribution prevented Soviet businesses from carrying out innovations which made the large companies in market economies capable of becoming continually more productive, larger and more diversified.[2]

Quite against the expectations of the first half of the twentieth century, the great economic powers of the year 1997 have far outstripped the politicians. High in their skyscrapers they shift around amounts of money politicians can only dream about from one end of the world to the other. That this affects thousands of jobs, communities and the environment comes at the bottom of their lists. Politicians can still do business with smaller firms or specific industries, such as the armaments industry, and otherwise only tinker with the margins of strategies that have been outlined elsewhere. If on political grounds too many restrictions of, say, a social or ecological nature are put in the way, then capital removes itself as soon as it can find a more profitable combination of factors somewhere else.

The paradoxical – at first sight – success of mini-states fits into the logic of this. On a global scale their real gross domestic product per head of population has grown faster since 1950 than it has in larger countries. Small scale again offers various advantages, as it did in the time before industrialization. Since 1950 imports and exports have grown by 10 per cent per year in the world economy. Even during the difficult 1980s world trade still increased by 5 per cent per year. This meant that prosperity was determined less and less by the domestic economy. Large states, on the other hand, became increasingly more vulnerable through conflicts of interest about trade quotas and other international restrictions. The economies of small states suffered less from these because their small scale made them concentrate on a limited number of highly specialized products and services. The attraction of states such as Luxembourg – where one out of every three inhabitants is a foreigner, and in the capital as much as one in every two – and even more, that of Liechtenstein and Monaco, is based less on their position as historical anomalies than on their efficient capitalist functioning. They operate as the registered domiciles of specialized international trading organizations and wealthy individuals, who find a tax-free haven there. On 149 hectares Monaco crowds – in addition to 5,000 citizens – another 30,000 residents who make this fiscal miracle possible by driving land prices up to about six times their level in neighbouring places on French soil. The young Czech republic is also enjoying rapid economic growth from the re-orientation of its economy to its export industries. If in the nineteenth century large and powerful states and colonies were necessary for the protection of domestic markets, they have since then rather become hindrances for concerns operating on a global scale.[3]

It is important to realize that the capitalist entrepreneurial spirit has since the Middle Ages not only distanced itself from political rulers, but also from religious ethics. The value orientation of capitalism is simply determined by the logic of maximizing profit. It has no local loyalties but is global, and so can always play one state off against another, eastern Europe against the west, the Third World against the First World. By the unprecedented accumulation and concentration of capital in concerns which have branched out into quite dissimilar industries, their power is now substantially larger than that of most states. Against politicians the directors of concerns are always in an extremely strong negotiating position because they are not tied to a single locality, and are responsible to no-one except their anonymous and calculating shareholders. In this sense capitalist logic runs counter to democracy which fundamentally serves other values and interests.

Hollowing out the state

Compared with the advancing integration and globalization of the free market economy, the scope for political rulers has shrunk appreciably. Yet in an absolute sense their power has not diminished since they have the disposal of astronomically increased budgets, are the largest category of employers, and have wider powers than ever before. Through their financing of medical care states are now involved in ethical questions such as abortion and euthanasia; formerly the churches claimed to have the only voice about such problems. Secularization and the multicultural composition of western societies have meant that only the public governmental institutions can now be the forums in which publicly binding guidelines can be announced on questions such as these. In spite of all the rhetoric nobody is really pressing for a reduction of state activities to, for instance, the level of the 1930s. No-one wants to experience the disastrous social effects of the Great Depression again,

In 1913, after the second Balkan War, Macedonia was divided into three parts.
The old Greek name was used for the part allocated to Serbia. Print by Sir Bernard Partridge
conceived as a Greek vase painting entitled *The persuading of Tino*. It appeared in *Punch* on 24 November 1915,
and is a satire on the Greek king Constantine and the situation in the Balkans.
London, Victoria and Albert Museum

so everyone sticks to a social safety net for the unemployed and to social provisions for the sick, the aged and the handicapped. Moreover, everyone expects the state to intervene in the areas of public works, education, research and cultural policy.

And yet the prosperous 1960s have shown that the enormous growth of the state bureaucracy necessary to accomplish all these tasks alienated the citizen from the state. Politics became too complicated, too technocratic to release great visions and strong emotions. It was a time when in several prosperous countries of western Europe regional movements raised their heads with demands ranging from cultural rights to secession. The German-speaking inhabitants of south Tyrol, incorporated into Italy in 1919, the Bretons, Corsicans, Catalans, Basques, Flemings, Scots, Welshmen and, of course, the Catholic Northern Irish: they were not driven by

acute material needs but by dissatisfaction about discrimination against their culture, and therefore their community as a whole, in the bonds of the state in which through the course of history they now found themselves. The advancing bureaucratization of the welfare state had provoked this 'luxury problem'. The cultural needs of sections of the population were placed on the political agenda because the electorate began to think them important. The result was that regional authorities were recognized in Italy, France, Spain, Great Britain and Belgium, but for some of the conflicts which escalated into violence no peaceful solution has yet been found. Only the few relatively small European states, with no far-reaching cultural heterogeneity, such as Denmark or Portugal, or who had dealt with such matters tolerantly, such as the Netherlands, Norway and Finland, did not encounter this problem; nor did the

After the Second World War the state was seen as the body that stood guarantor
for the welfare and prosperity of every citizen from the cradle to the grave.
'The state guarantees all payments' and 'A nest egg' (*'n appeltje voor den dorst*). Dutch 1950 poster.
Amsterdam, International Institute for Social History

The terrorism of Catholic and Protestant extremists in the Northern Irish troubles led to a continual increase in violence.
In 1987 Christine Spengler photographed this mural painting in Londonderry (Bogside).
Lausanne, Musée de l'Elysée

federal states such as the German Federal Republic and Switzerland, simply because their political structure was more aligned on regional diversity. That is why in 1989 Germany was the only state in Europe which could expand massively by the incorporation of the former GDR, and is now, after Russia, the largest and unquestionably the strongest, as it has always wanted to be since the days of the Ottonian and Salian emperors.

That the same urge for regionalization manifested itself as soon as the pressure of the Soviet empire over central and eastern Europe diminished is only logical. In all those countries the state apparatus had been heavily enlarged out of all proportion and was extraordinarily irritating to the subject population, particularly where there were also garrisons of Russian troops. The whole conglomeration that had been assembled by the imperial powers, and which had been bound by the Yalta agreements in February 1945 – the Baltic states, Slovakia, Slovenia

and many other peoples – hankered after its own dignity again. Their efforts for their own state system were no different in essence from the trends for regionalization in the west. It took harsher forms there because these people have for centuries had little opportunity in their political culture of regulating affairs through negotiation. Every armed conflict caused new scars which would be torn open again in the next outburst. Their inland and mountainous locations isolated some peoples more than others and therefore made them less receptive to contact with cultural diversity. The armed racial conflicts of the late twentieth century are a reminder to Europe of the differences in its internal development.

European states in 1997 have become more numerous, smaller and less centralist than they were around 1960. More taxation is now collected and powers are now exercised at a regional level without control from the centre. With considerable

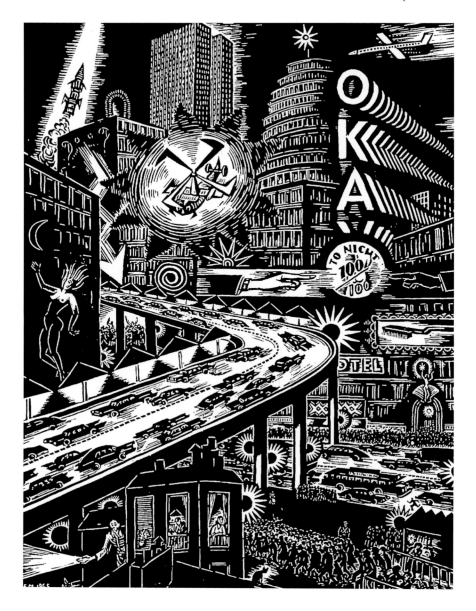

In 1965 Frans Masereel illustrated the advance of the American consumer society
in a series of woodcuts with the theme of 'the city'. This print is entitled *Okay*.
Antwerp, private collection

difficulty this has removed another offshoot of the nineteenth-century state: its unitarianism and its centralism. The most dangerous forms of nationalism arose in the first half of the twentieth century from just those large western European peoples who had been indoctrinated with the idea that outside their frontiers there were only savages. From their own experience they could know no better. The fear of such nationalisms being multiplied would seem to be misplaced because there are now more of them, and because they are smaller they are

also weaker. Moreover, people from small language areas, who are accessible to external contacts, show a tendency to multilingualism and cultural openness more quickly than do large nations. In the next few generations Europe will have to depend on just that pluralism if it wants to avoid the totalitarian forms of nationalism which it developed earlier.

Western states exercise a much more diffuse power now than they did a century ago, because they have built up a close-knit network of advisory and consultative structures in the framework of the consultative economy. Paralysis has become a greater danger than all the fuses blowing at once, as happened in the summer of 1914. Large parts of state budgets are allocated by consortia in which social organizations have a participatory voice. Unions of employers, employees, the self-employed, professional associations, health and life insurance institutions and many more, in effect help to sketch out government policy, and are sometimes responsible for the implementation of part of it. In this way the state avoids large public conflicts but contracts out a substantial proportion of its resources and its powers. Religious denominations, in reality private organizations, control many of the hospitals, welfare institutions and schools, by agreement with the government, using government resources but with a large degree of autonomy. The western welfare state is therefore deeply rooted in social organizations which in their turn are often linked to political parties. The concepts of pillarization and neo-corporatism are applied to this incorporation of interest groups. They perhaps deprive the state of more resources than strictly necessary, but the pluralism of interests at the same time builds in some mutual controls which again include more guarantees for efficient administration than a monolithic state bureaucracy. Moreover, the corporative organization reflects the process of organic growth in modern societies in which the affinity of segments of the population with a specific religion, ideology or other identity is acknowledged, which again underpins the stability of the welfare state.

By 1995 therefore governments manipulated substantially more resources than those of fifty or a hundred years earlier, but in practice the state shares its powers extensively with lesser authorities and with social organizations. This could be described as a more diffuse and more controlled form of exercising power. Strictly speaking the state has bought peace and quiet by relinquishing many of its responsibilities. The late-twentieth-century state has also lost much of its power in another direction: to supranational institutions. The policy of neutrality which countries such as Belgium and the Netherlands had still tried to follow in the 1930s was in 1940 shown to be as meaningless as bilateral military agreements between states. After 1945 only wider alliances with a superpower still offered real security. This process has been deployed in military pacts such as NATO in which in exchange for protection an originally fundamental aspect of state sovereignty is handed over to an intergovernmental institution. In a formal sense the member states retained their prerogatives, but the application of military policy would in future be determined by an international consultative body in which the United States enjoyed a great superiority.

From the 1950s other steps towards European integration followed: first came the joint restructuring of problem industries in the economy: mining, steel, agriculture, the control of atomic energy, so as gradually to achieve a unified market. This involved even the formal transfer of powers from the original six member states to supranational institutions. Certainly each state retained the right of veto, but none the less a supranational dynamic gradually came into being. Just as the German *Zollverein* in 1833 had created a wider market for expanding industry through clearing away political obstacles, so the European Economic Common Market achieved a further stage of integration of international markets. The multinational organization of production and distribution was only too anxious for the politicians to remove their hindrances to free trade in goods. Otherwise only American businesses, which had the advantage of their immense domestic market, would have retained substantial advantages of economies of scale. Since the integration of markets also made increased productivity possible and widened consumer choice, usually accompanied by lower prices, all parties could benefit from this operation. Unquestionably the desire for peace of idealist politicians and citizens contributed to the overruling of state sovereignty, but the decisive force was still that arising from the economies of scale which could be achieved by expanding businesses; they had, after all, long expanded across national frontiers.

For three decades the European Community functioned predominantly as an organ for regulating the market. Not until the Maastricht Treaty of 1992 did the effort for political co-ordination, with difficulty, gain ground, and it also began to be apparent that culture threatened to be debased into a product of the market mechanism. The multiplicity of European languages poses a real problem as the Union grows: in the fifteen member states of 1995 there are eleven official languages and for the sake of full equal rights every document and each meeting requires 110 combinations of translations; even then languages such as Scottish and Irish Gaelic are still disadvantaged. Should the smaller language areas accept second-class treatment, as has already been agreed for the establishment of the European Patent and Trade Mark Office in Madrid? This may seem an unimportant question of procedure, which goes on the political agenda mainly because of the high costs of translation. However, for the language community which can no longer be informed in its mother tongue of the activities of the higher institutions to which it is subject, or to which it can turn in that language, it means crossing an extremely emotive line. Insufficient sensitivity by the larger language communities could evoke the same reaction against the European institutions as nationalist or regional feelings do now against national states. Europe has always been a multicultural continent, and from that it has drawn its dynamic. Dealing rashly with this diversity would not only threaten to bring about homogeneity and impoverishment but also to provoke unsuspectedly strong crises of identity and opposition.

The benefits of culture

Freedom of the press was one of the basic rights liberals wrote into their nineteenth-century constitutions. By this they did away with the censorship applied by the authoritarian monarchies in the hope of preventing the spread of modern ideas. In Germany, where liberals never made any headway, Bismarck still used censorship in the 1880s against socialist propaganda – equally in vain. Just as the state had been unable to bring capital effectively under its control, it was equally unsuccessful with cultural products, and these were just what constituted Europe's strength. About the turn of the century liberal and conservative governments had to tolerate the fact that the press had begun to reach a mass audience, and was spreading other ideas than their own. Literacy had grown enormously and the new technology in printing, transport and communications media had made the rapid dissemination of information cheap. Newspapers were private businesses, most of which could be linked through personal networks and the relationships of their proprietors to political organizations, but not to the state.

States certainly laid their hands on new communications media which could be thought to have a specific use in the public domain. During the first decades of this century telephone and telegraph services, usually combined with postal and money order services, were set up as businesses with a state monopoly, and when in the 1920s radio networks were established the states pulled this function into their monopolies. After the war television was to be introduced within the same structures.

Because in the early stages it required large investments, private capital was not anxious to come forward, while politicians, immediately after the First World War, were very conscious of the strategic value of the new communications media. At the end of the century all these monopolies were breached because technology had flooded the market with a plethora of possibilities for transmitting and receiving all kinds of messages in sound, pictures or text. This made the monopolies as unrealistic as the independent foreign policy of small states had become.

States were selective in their methods of controlling the new media. For a correct understanding of government interference it is particularly necessary to take account of the circumstances of the time and the micro-economic factors affecting their introduction. At that time private enterprise in Europe showed more interest in the production and distribution of appliances than in the exploitation of cable companies or networks. Moreover, there was still very little expertise in this kind of cultural production. The different outcome of developments in the United States is probably connected with their larger, and linguistically more homogeneous, market. Just as the press remained formally independent and advertising took its free course, film also remained a purely private enterprise. Products were distributed by the large international, mainly American, companies. The state only concerned itself with the protection of public decency, particularly where minors were involved.

Much more care was displayed by the Catholic Church which, in those countries where it had traditionally enjoyed supremacy, saw its philosophy threatened by a more attractive medium than the priest in his pulpit. They set up their own film censorship, and tried to save what they could by at least keeping cinemas as much as possible out of the villages where time did not run so fast, and where they could no longer prevent them, by keeping them under their care and protection. Priests fully understood that films appealed to the general public much more directly and strongly than the written version of the same story. They were aware that the norms, values and images of society which were exposed more or less implicitly in films, penetrated to the hearts and souls of their audiences. Inevitably for many people this had to lead to alienation from the message which the Church itself propagated.

In the early days of silent films these did not affect the images of society to the same extent, because they were simply produced for amusement without much text. None the less it was at this stage

This 1927 poster for a cabaret performance in the Théatre des Champs Elysées
where the black American singing star Josephine Baker displayed her art with verve,
reflects the atmosphere of the frenetic 1920s in Europe.
Paris, Bibliothèque nationale de France, Estampes

The government, who paid for, and so had to watch over, public health care, finally realized the importance of imposing some restrictions on advertising. Alain Le Quernec's, *La Pub tue,* 1991. Paris, Bibliothèque nationale de France, Estampes

that the film became the main medium in international circulation where theatre was produced for the lower classes, who found tickets to the middle-class theatres too expensive. In the period between the two world wars the working classes had much more free time, and before the slump also a rather higher standard of living, so that they eagerly consumed what radio and particularly films had to offer. When the gramophone record industry also came along, a new international fashion sensitive to imagery, behaviour, dance and music emerged in the 1930s, which penetrated down to the working classes and so brought about a true cultural revolution. Advertising supplemented the imagery of film

to guide the mass consumers. The combination of a new stylized industrial supply of goods, advertising and entertainment ousted the traditional culture of the middle and lower classes, which they had already left behind with their grandparents on joining the urban masses. For the producers what mattered now was the large numbers of consumers, so that even the bourgeois culture of the *belle époque* began to look *passé.*

During the interwar years the totalitarian states tried to force through a culture policy of their own. In the first years after the revolution the Soviet state made a remarkably avant-garde art possible. However, Stalin's regime soon condemned it as

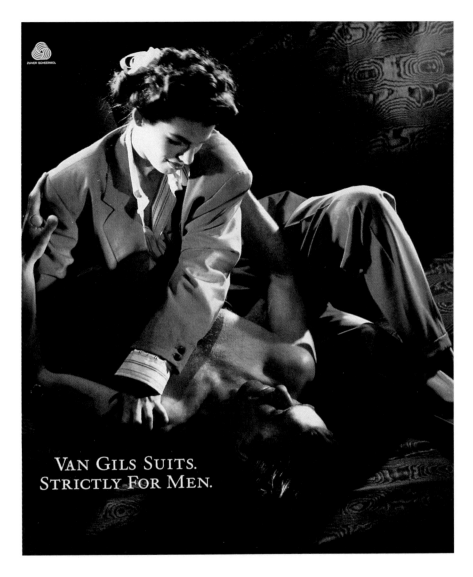

In this advertisement from the late 1980s the emancipation of the modern woman and the emergence of her role model
is shown as an attractive and positive fact. *Van Gils Suits. Strictly for men.*

esoteric and bourgeois, if not counter-revolutionary, and demanded realistic art which would represent the ideal socialist society in a way comprehensible to the proletariat. Prominent artists were harassed with regulations and sanctions and many fled the country. In view of the eventual functionality of the official art for its target audience, it was usually written off in western eyes as uninspired, crude and traditional in execution and deadly dull in its message. Only Eisenstein's films, such as his *Battleship Potemkin* in 1925 on the 1905 naval mutiny, and *Ten Days that Shook the World* in 1928 to commemorate the October revolution were, in spite of their plainly propagandist intent, highly praised for their innova-

tive use of the medium, and especially for their crowd scenes. Architecture had to have bulk and straight lines, and be heavily monumental. Statues unrelentingly displayed the triumphs of labour.

It is striking that at that time Italian fascism used almost the same artistic vocabulary to give shape to its message, and official buildings in Nazi Germany were also in the same style. There, too, any spark of creativity was stifled by labelling it 'degenerate art'. Yet remarkable innovations were still achieved in the cultural field, which must stand to the credit of some of the leaders. First of all the talent for theatrical rhetoric of both Mussolini and Hitler was a break from the dry-as-dust presentations of former

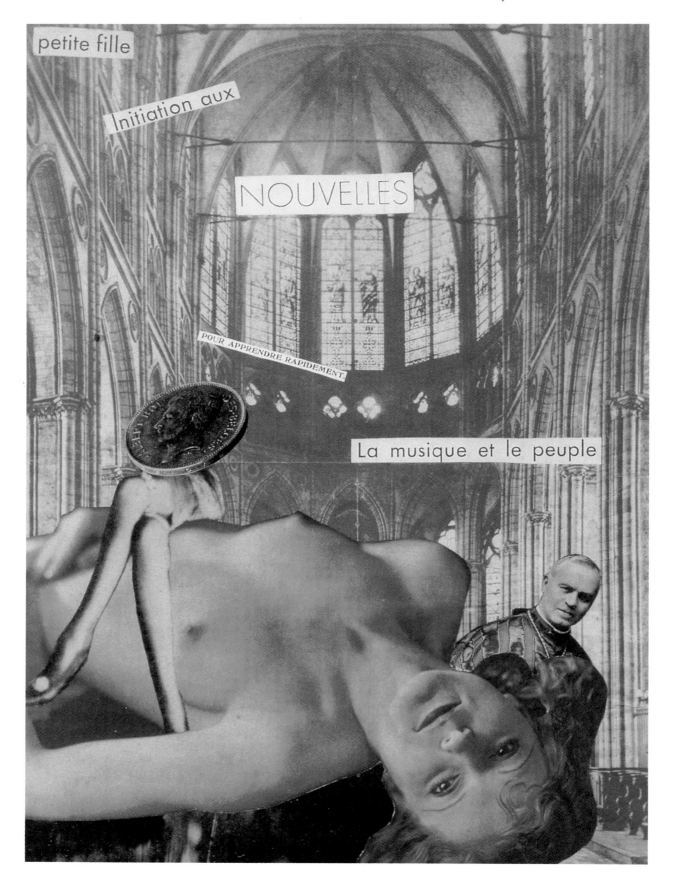

The totalitarian art of the Stalinist period used the same megalomaniac vocabulary as Nazi Germany. 1935 design for the Palace of the Soviets in Moscow. This was to be the largest building in the world, crowned by a sixty-metre high statue of Lenin. Design by V.G. Gelfreich, B.M. Jofan and V.A. Shtsuko. Moscow, Scusev Architecture Museum

Mitterand's socialist administration hoped to make their mark with a number of imposing building projects, particularly in Paris. Frédéric Cey's *Grande Arche* is a modern version of the traditional triumphal arch and stands exactly in the extension of the axis of the *Arc de Triomphe*.

German chancellors or of politicians elsewhere. They were the first to be able to manipulate the masses effectively by making use of the newly invented sound and lighting effects. Secondly, the mass spectacles produced by the Nazis were a remarkable innovation. At party rallies thousands of members of the movement were lined up in enormous stadiums and marched in parades, dressed up in colourful attire, in disciplined ranks. These exhibitions had no special content, other than a grandiose self-presentation which gave every insignificant participant the idea that they were contributing to something magnificent. Naturally the whole event built up to a climax with the entry of the Führer.

Thirdly, the Nazis, whose leaders were not burdened with middle-class culture, made full use of the new mass media for their propaganda, and especially of film. Leni Riefenstahl, the filmmaker, was given a free hand by the

The priesthood saw with envious eyes how through the images on film norms and values were propagated which alienated many people from the Catholic Church. The Church continually tried to counter this, often in a very reactionary way, so that it also antagonized well-meaning progressives among its members. Marcel Lefrancq, *Initiation or Open Letter to Mgr van Roey*, 1939. Brussels, Musées royaux des Beaux-Arts de Belgique

party leadership to make feature films of the Nuremberg rally in 1934 and the Munich Olympic games in 1936 *(Triumph of the Will)*. All resources were made available to her to produce imposing visual effects. She had a camera mounted in a lift on a flagpole behind the dais to take oblique shots of the massed crowds. Cameras mounted in traps on the startline filmed the athletes from the most unexpected angles to bring out to the full the beauty of their bodies. Her superior application of the new medium had a startling effect on her contemporaries, and undoubtedly reinforced Nazi propaganda. It is remarkable that both in the Soviet Union and in Nazi Germany the only artistic creativity showed itself in a medium for which no-one had yet laid down the rules. In all other genres they tried to derive their credibility from repeating classical models.

After 1945 the traumas caused by the totalitarian regimes took the inclination of western governments to involve themselves directly in the production of art to a new low. In 1992, the anniversary year of its first colonial discoveries in America, the Spanish state promoted its still new democratic image by adding architectural splendour to the Olympic Games in Barcelona and the World Exhibition at Seville. Presidents Pompidou and Mitterand emphatically left their traces on the Paris scene. Governments facilitate, even take occasional initiatives, but make no pronouncements themselves on design or context, and remain detached and remote where the symbolism of power is concerned.

States have discovered an indirect form of nationalist support through the identification of supporters in international sporting contests. Between the wars both playing and watching matches became the most popular mass leisure activities. This sector too became subjected to increases in scale, commercialization and becoming 'media events'. Even in front of the TV screen the audience identifies with national heroes. In the stands flags are waved enthusiastically, while no-one bothers about them at official ceremonies. Here nationalism has become the province of private enterprise, not through, or even for, the state, but as the collective ego that happens to be available to everyone.

By the end of the twentieth century the states therefore, having learnt the hard way, seem to have abandoned the ambition of themselves producing culture for all their subjects. Other traditional producers of culture have, reluctantly, also had to moderate their pretensions, particularly the churches, but also the educational establishments and even the political parties. The ideologies of the eighteenth and nineteenth centuries – except perhaps for nationalism? – appear to have passed their peak and apart from some specific fields, such as care for the environment, inspirational political and social programmes, are few and far between in western Europe. The dream of a European pacifist integration is laboriously dragging itself out of the quicksand on which its credibility for any sort of compelling action is built. The values by which the present-day West can really be recognized are materialism and competitiveness based on consumption. Naturally there is more, such as the belief in the rule of law and the peaceful resolution of problems, as Europe has learnt from its long and bloody history. But all this seems so much less credible and real than the cult of the consumer, the behaviour of the citizen who from being a subject is now primarily a consumer.

Who then lays down the norms and values in western European society? The state indisputably does this: it intervenes in increasing areas of private and public life, because public resources are devoted to them, and general principles of laws are at issue. However, the state only prescribes norms in the second instance, aiming to provide compromises between the differing points of view and interests of segments in society. The state therefore sets standards as a reaction and as a mediator. Rapid social change and the complexity of western societies release a great diversity of opinions from segments of the population. Moreover, the increased maturity and the abundant presence of the mass media mean that these opinions are expressed much more plainly than before. Hence the relative nature of each norm is more clearly brought into discussion than ever before, when norms were presented as being God-given, or at least as being from time immemorial and sacrosanct. For many people this new situation has produced intolerable uncertainty, which is aggressively projected on to scapegoats just as happened in the earlier critical phases of European awareness in the 1930s. It is not the state which is responsible for this: above all it should not be allowed to prescribe all values and norms anew, although the greater freedom to discuss them is indeed a result of the stronger dynamic, the greater openness and the more forceful exposure to the media of our societies.

In the multicultural societies which now populate Europe, several different systems of values live in close proximity to each other. Traditional religious views of Christian and Muslim homes are confronted with more or less consistently thought-through secular ideas. Unlike the situation in some other continents, nowhere does one single religious philosophy dominate a whole state. There is an accelerating tendency towards secularization, partly as a result of the more pronounced pluralism, but certainly also influenced by the manifest importance of science and technology in everyday life. The traditional monopolists of culture, the churches and states, who for centuries had tried to squeeze each other out, have both had their day.

This vacuum has been filled by the third major player, the capitalist entrepreneur. Unconstrained by church and state his kingdom is the whole world, without him being completely responsible anywhere. Elusive, mobile, flexible and all-pervasive; his make-up is essentially dynamic, such as that of the producer of culture, the artist or scholar. Every solution is always capable of revision. Innovation and change are constant driving forces. Their direction

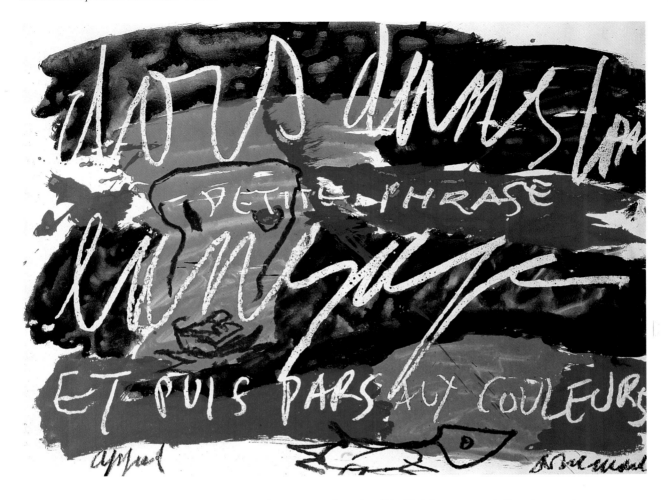

The maintenance of regional diversity and its accompanying cultural identity is for many people the only guarantee
of a well-functioning modern Europe. *Dors dans ton language – Slaap in je taal* (Sleep in your own language)
by Christian Dotremont and Karel Appel in 1962 can be interpreted against this background.
Gouache and pencil drawing on paper.
Silkeborg, Kunstmuseum

is as unpredictable as human creativity which is stimulated by complexity. The entrepreneur and the cultural creator differ in one essential point; the first strives for profit, the other for values.

As the audiovisual mass media became more general in the form of appliances which can be found in every house – indeed, are almost part of every individual – the producers began to see the value of getting more control of the messages which were sent out round the world in this way. They started buying in production companies into their business organizations or setting them up. This was, however, more than just standard vertical integration. The combination of form and content seemed a cast-iron opportunity to influence the mass audience. Early on the psychological and ide-

ological effects of sustained and abundant advertising messages were recognized. Film and video images perfected and varied the techniques of seduction still further. They absorbed more and more of the average consumer's time. The general privatization of the mass media which has been seen during the last decades of the twentieth century has enormously widened the audience that is exposed to an unprecedented campaign of indoctrination in the form of unrelentingly cute shows interspersed with news announcements and advertising spots. Thanks to the international scale of the media giants they are successful in offering technically more attractive programmes than the national networks, and can get very accurate information about their viewers' assessments of them, so that

Bob Geldof organized several Live-Aid pop concerts in Wembley Stadium in London in the late 1980s
to make people aware of the famine in the drought-afflicted Sahel region of Africa.
London, Redferns Music Picture Library

they can go on playing on their latest sensibilities. Since capitalist entrepreneurs are not interested in values, as long as their products bring in large returns, they can permit themselves a much more entertaining and so a more attractive offering than state producers could ever have imagined. They may also distribute politically and environmentally sensitive products. The degree of tolerance of their offerings is a characteristic for their innovative and creative adjustment, and ensures for their products a wide and stable market share in as many segments of the multicultural societies of the West as possible.

By the end of the twentieth century it therefore seems that the thousand-year-long titanic struggle between economic, cultural and political powers has been settled to the advantage of the first. Up to now the market economy seems indeed, thanks to its inherent capacity for creative adaptability, to be the most enduring form of power in European, and perhaps even in human history. The exercise of this power is as untransparent to the ordinary citizen as it is all-pervasive; it determines his activities, directs his purchases, and gives him his role models. Through the operations of the mass media, power is sublimated into inherent stimuli, transmitted through messages in the media. It is no longer church leaders or politicians who pull the strings, but entrepreneurs in diversified multinational organizations. Religious reformers and enlightened despots have pursued this goal for centuries, but it is modern technology which has dealt the effective means of achieving it into the hands of the captains of industry. These display a tendency to reduce culture into a mass market product whose production and distribution on a global scale can be calculated in the same way as for all their other products.

Popularity is now made or destroyed by the media. The scale of these operations reduces substantially the scope for action by politicians and church leaders. To get any hearing they have to be media-friendly and package their message into appetizing advertising spots. Coverage of hard reality can now hardly be distinguished from the everlasting shows. It is not the politicians who can now be considered the most effective interpreters of values and norms but the hidden persuaders of capitalism who in the form of entertainment play on the aesthetic and emotional dimensions of the public. In this they have reached a degree of technical perfection which makes the propaganda campaigns of preachers in the thirteenth century, Jesuits in the seventeenth, nationalists in 1900, and bolshevists and Nazis look paltry. What then is

their message? Materialism, individualism and competition, the core values of capitalism. Other values such as democracy, the rights of man and pacifism are put second by the capitalist entrepreneur and are in practice desecrated daily whenever that improves his profit.

The picture outlined above is as yet one-sided because it still operates side by side with the older established systems of values. By its continual innovation the network occasionally produces anti-heroes who break all the rules of presentation and surprise everyone with an intractable message. Moreover, it would be naive to present the economic power structures as purely rational and cohesive. It is certainly true that they are all accounted for every year on the basis of the same profit and loss balances, which gives a unique consistency to their actions. They form the most all-embracing and therefore the most expansive constellations of power of these and even of all times. The situation will only become truly dangerous when – as always in the past – a real monopoly should emerge that would include all dimensions of power on a global scale. In view of the complexity of global relationships this fear seems unfounded at present. Nevertheless, understanding of these tendencies towards concentrations of power remains essential, because every 'absolute power corrupts absolutely'.

1   CHANDLER 1994, 122, 135–136, 140–141.
2   CHANDLER 1994, 127–131.
3   GARY S. BECKER, 'Why so many mice are roaring', *Business Week*, 7 November 1994, 11.

Epilogue

The history of Europe has much to teach us about the reasons for the emergence of European construction, and the direction it has taken during the latter half of the twentieth century. However, we need to be clear about the events to which we are referring. The painful history of conflict in Europe which, between 1870 and 1945, devastated the continent in itself suffices to explain the setting up during the 1950s of structures which, in order to guarantee the peaceful coexistence of European states, established among the ashes of war the foundations of a future community – the Treaty of Rome created a community of interests interwoven with the economy.

Forty years later the gaping wounds of that period have healed, peace between France and Germany is no longer an ideal but a reality, the Treaty of Rome has been completed by the Single Act and the Maastricht Treaty; the European Community has become the European Union and it is both our privilege and duty to look deep into our history to find what it is that has united six, nine, ten, twelve and now fifteen Member States and what, tomorrow, could unite or divide some 400 million Europeans.

I should like to pay tribute here to this scholarly work by Professor Blockmans. In choosing to analyse the millennium now drawing to a close from the viewpoint of interaction between political, economic and cultural forces he has provided us with a rich key to understanding the dynamic which, with in one movement, has stimulated the construction of States, underpinned the power of the marketplace and fostered the identity of the nations of Europe.

More striking still is the iconography of this work, the images and symbols placed as landmarks along the historian's route and which touch both our heart and mind.

How can we make best use of this powerful account and assert Jacques Santer's correct affirmation that it is the politician's responsibility to offer a perspective on the future, except by using as a starting point the circumstances

which have accompanied the slow progress of the peoples of Europe
towards a common aspiration for democracy and by examining closely
the origins of this aspiration. It is this, more or less, which has given it meaning
for all citizens of Europe and which, in the future will either topple
or consolidate democracy as the principle of integration.

While the beginning of this millennium saw an end to the absolute power of the
Church – the Crusades being the swan song of theocracy – the early modern period
was characterised by the co-existence of political and religious power,
though in varying spheres of influence according to whether they were operating
within a system of empire or monarchy. The author points out that this distinction
is considerable and, from the outset, hinged on the fact that the East of Europe,
with the exception of Poland where a new type of monarchy developed,
would remain subjugated for most of the millennium by imperial States
which did not accede to the idea of the nation. The notion of empire relied on
a certain conception of the world, a politico-religious doctrine, universal in intention,
in which the emperor, though he remained distant, was the supreme guarantor of
the effective exercise of power. In the West, on the other hand, the monarchies
which became established created the basis of the nation-state as both guardians of
political power and guarantors of a specific cultural identity . Spiritual power,
which for a long period acted as the binding force of this cultural identity,
was generally distinct, operating as a counter-force. Economic power, based on
the ownership of limited resources, emerged separately as a third force with the industrial revolution. From the eighteenth century to the present day the debate between
political and economic power (public service, private property) has, to a large extent,
dominated the European scene from the Atlantic to the Urals with economic power
recently stealing the lead over an enfeebled political power.

At the same time cultural power has gradually diminished, after reaching its height during the period of the Enlightenment. The influence of culture – torn between
lay values and those of a moral and religious nature and marginalised by philosophers
of a Marxist, Freudian, structuralist tendency, who questioned the liberty of
the subject – is now confined to the private sphere, to family life and leisure.
European construction taking place today can itself be seen as a form of creative tension
mobilising, in the first place, political and economic power. Is it not the case
that political power seeks to retain control of our collective destiny? Is the great
internal market not an illustration of the desire of nation-states to respond
to market globalization? And, leaving aside for one moment the complexities of
its creation, was not political union in fact foreseeable back in the 1950s?
As we reach the end of the century has political union not become the unavoidable
and necessary counterbalance to the power of a world market made accessible

through the progress of technology? The question that remains is on what terms this counterbalance will be sufficient to meet the challenge of market globalization.

It is clear today that the main challenge for Europe and democracy, in both East and West, is no longer, as it was for Montesquieu, a matter of ensuring balance between the executive, legislative and judicial spheres within the nation-state, but of giving political power in Europe sufficient strength to restabilise the power of the economy. In a conclusion which might appear Manichean in some respects Wim Blockmans appeals for vigilance regarding values, the ultimate test of balance between the three powers of an integrated Europe – the political, the economic and the cultural.

He tells us that, due to the absence of any tangible counterforce, economic power has already, via the media, impregnated cultural power with its materialist, competitive and individualist values. Equally, a rather shaky European Union finds itself stumbling over the defence of peace, is questioned by its electorate regarding its democratic credibility and fails to respond strongly enough to violations of basic respect for the rights of its citizens taking place within the Union itself. Democracy, pacifism and respect for human rights would be under threat if not sustained by a power sufficiently politically inspired to be make it truly legitimate.

Without seeking a return to a cultural power that would dominate politics, as it did in the Middle Ages, is this not time for European culture – for all that heritage built on both diversity and unity and on the conviction of the fundamental dignity of man – again to become an integral part of our system? Has the time not come to re-establish this conviction in our worn-out democracies, to take advantage of aspirations for a democracy based on participation, in which citizens recognize not only rights but also duties – inspired by the progress of knowledge and education and by the entry of women into public life? Perhaps we may find deep within our cultures the inspiration to give meaning to the political unity of the citizens of Europe.

This outstanding work has strengthened my conviction of the urgent need for us to pursue, alongside intellectuals, the cultural, religious and humanist traditions and the democratic movements of civil society and to update the sources of our ethics and culture – the very inspirations that give direction to the adventure that is Europe.

Marcelino Oreja Aguirre
Member of the European Commission

Photographic credits

Bibliography

Aho, J.A., *Religious Mythology and the Art of War.* London 1981

Alderman, G., ed., *Governments, Ethnic Groups and Political Representations.* New York 1992

Anderson, B., *Imagined Communities. Reflections on the origin and spread of nationalism.* London 1991[2]

Anderson, P., *Lineages of the absolutist state.* London 1974

Bak, J.M., ed., *Coronations. Medieval and Early Modern Monarchic Ritual.* Berkeley 1990

Barret-Kriegel, B., 'La politique juridique de la monarchie française', Coulet, N. & Genet, J.-Ph., eds., *L'Etat Moderne.* Paris 1990

Barthélemy, D., *La société dans le comté de Vendôme, de l'an mil au XIVe siècle.* Paris 1993

Bartlett, R., *The Making of Europe. Conquest, Colonization and Cultural Change 950–1350.* London 1993

Beaune, C., *Naissance de la nation France.* Paris 1985

Bernal, A.M., *Economia y historia de los latifundios.* Madrid 1988

Bertelli, S., ed., *Lo Stato e il Potere nel Rinascimento.* Perugia 1981

Bisson, T.N., *The Medieval Crown of Aragon.* Oxford 1986

Black, A., *Political Thought in Europe 1250–1450.* Cambridge 1992

Black, J., *Convergence and Divergence, Britain and the Continent.* London 1994

Blickle, P., *Landschaften im alten Reich. Die staatliche Funktion des gemeinen Mannes in Oberdeutschland.* München 1973

Blickle, P., *Deutsche Untertanen. Ein Widerspruch.* München 1981

Blickle, P., 'Kommunalismus, Parlamentarismus, Republikanismus', *Historische Zeitschrift,* 242, 1986

Blickle, P., ed., *Resistance, Representation and the Sense of Community.* Oxford 1997

Blockmans, W. & J.-Ph. Genet, eds., *Visions sur le développement des états européens. Théories et historiographies de l'état moderne.* Rome 1993

Blockmans, W.P., 'Le dialogue imaginaire entre princes et sujets: les Joyeuses Entrées en Brabant en 1494 et en 1496', *Publication du centre européen d'études Bourguignonnes (XIVe–XVIe siècle).* 34, 1994

Bogaert, R., Kurgan-Van Hentenryk, G. & Van der Wee, H., *A History of European Banking.* Antwerp 1994

Bonney, R., *The European Dynastic States 1494–1660.* Oxford 1991

Bonney, R., ed., *Economic Systems and State Finance.* Oxford 1995

Bouthoul, G. & Carrère, R., *Le défi de la guerre (1740–1974).* Paris 1976

Braudel, F., *La Méditerranée et le Monde Méditerranéen à l'époque de Philippe II.* Paris 1966[2]; transl. London 1972

Braudel, F., *Civilisation matérielle, Economie et Capitalisme.* 3 vols., Paris 1979

Brewer, J., *The Sinews of Power.* London 1989

Brulez, W., 'Het gewicht van de oorlog in de nieuwe tijden. Enkele aspecten', in *Tijdschrift voor Geschiedenis.* 90, 1978

Brulez, W., *Cultuur en getal. Aspecten van de relatie tussen economie – maatschappij – cultuur in Europa tussen 1400 en 1800.* Amsterdam 1986

Bryant, L.M., 'The Medieval Entry Ceremonial at Paris' in J.M. Bak, ed., *Coronations. Medieval and Early Modern Monarchic Ritual.* Berkeley 1990

Bulst, N. & Genet, J.-P., eds., *La Ville, la Bourgeoisie et la Genèse de l'Etat Moderne (XIIe–XVIIe siècles).* Paris 1988

Bulst, N., Descimon, R. & Guerreau, A., eds., *L'Etat ou le Roi. Les fondations de la modernité en France (XIVe–XVIIe siècles).* Paris 1996

Caenegem, R.C. van & Milis, L., eds., 'Kritische uitgave van de "Grote Keure" van Filips van de Elzas, graaf van Vlaanderen, voor Gent en Brugge (1165–1177)', *Bulletin Commission royale d'Histoire,* 143, 1977

The New Cambridge Modern History. vol. VI, Cambridge 1970

Cerboni, G., e.a., eds., *Federico di Montefeltro. Lo Stato.* Roma 1986

Chandaman, C.D., *The English Public Revenue 1660–1688.* Oxford 1975

Chandler, A.D. Jr., ed., 'Global Enterprise': big business and the wealth of nations in the past century, 1880s–1980s, *Debates and controversies in economic history.* Eleventh International Economic History Congress Milan 1994

Coleman, J., ed., *The Individual in Political Theory and Practice.* Oxford 1996

Colley, L., *Britons. Forging the Nation 1707–1837.* New Haven 1992

Contamine, Ph., 'Mourir pour la Patrie', *La Nation,* II, 1986

Contamine, Ph., ed., *L'Etat et les Aristocraties, XIIe–XVIIe siècle (France, Angleterre, Ecosse).* Paris 1989

Contamine, Ph., ed., *War and the Competition between States.* Oxford 1998

Corbin A., e.a., eds., *Les usages politiques des fêtes aux XIXe–XXe siècles.* Paris 1994

Corvisier, A., *Armées et Sociétés en Europe de 1494 à 1789.* Paris 1976

Coulet, N. & Genet, J.P., eds., *L'Etat Moderne: le droit, l'espace et les formes de l'état.* Paris 1990

Culture et Idéologie dans la Genèse de l'Etat Moderne. Rome 1985

Dhondt, J., *Etudes sur la naissance des principautés territoriales en France (IXe–Xe siècle).* Bruges 1948

Downing, B.M., *The Military Revolution and Political Change.* Princeton 1992

Duby, G., *Guerriers et paysans. VIIe–XIIe siècle. Premier essor de l'économie européenne.* Paris 1973

Duby, G., *Le Chevalier, la Femme et le Prêtre. Le mariage dans la France féodale.* Paris 1981

Duby, G., *Guillaume le Maréchal ou le meilleur chevalier du monde.* Paris 1984

Dunk, Th.H. von der, *Das deutsche Denkmal. Ein Abriss in Stein.*

Die politische Bedeutung des Denkmalkults im deutschen Kulturbereich. Doct. diss. Leiden 1994

ELIAS, N., *Über den Prozess der Zivilisation.* Bern 1969²

ELIAS, N., *Die höfische Gesellschaft.* Darmstadt 1981⁵

ELLENIUS, A., ed., *Iconography, Propaganda, and Legitimation.* Oxford 1998

ELLENIUS, A., 'Visual Culture in Seventheenth-Century Sweden. Images of Power and Knowledge', *The Age of New Sweden.* Stockholm 1988

ELLIOTT, J.H., *Imperial Spain, 1469–1716.* London 1965

ESTEPA DIEZ, C., 'La Curia de León en 1188 y los origines de las Cortes', *Las Cortes de Castilla y León 1188–1988.* 2 vols., Valladolid 1990

EVANS, P.B., RUESCHEMEYER, D., SKOCPOL, TH., eds., *Bringing the State Back In.* Cambridge 1985

FERNANDEZ-ARMESTO, F., *Millennium.* London 1995.

FOLZ, R., *La Naissance du Saint Empire.* Paris 1967

Galbert of Bruges, *The murder of Charles the Good count of Flanders.* ed. J.B. Ross, New York 1967²

GALLETTI, A.I., 'La Città come universo culturale e simbolico', *Società e Istitutioni dell' Italia Communale: l'esempio di Perugia (secoli XII–XIV).* II, Perugia 1988.

GELDEREN, M. VAN, *The Political Thought of the Dutch Revolt 1555–1590.* Cambridge 1992

GELLNER, E., *Nations and Nationalism.* Oxford 1983

GENET, J.-PH. & VINCENT, B., eds., *Etat et Eglise dans la Genèse de l'Etat Moderne.* Madrid 1986

GENET, J.-P. & LE MENÉE, M., eds., *Genèse de l'Etat Moderne. Prélèvement et Redistribution.* Paris 1987

GENET, J.-PH., ed., *Etat Moderne: Genèse. Bilans et perspectives.* Paris 1990

GIDDENS, A., *The Nation-State and Violence.* Cambridge 1985

GLETE, J., *Navies and Nations.* Stockholm 1993

GOUBERT, P., *L'Ancien Régime. La société. Les pouvoirs.* 2 vols., Paris 1969–73

GOURON, A. & RIGAUDIÈRE, A., eds., *Renaissance du pouvoir législatif et genèse de l'état.* Montpellier 1988

GREENFELD, L., *Nationalism. Five roads to modernity.* Harvard 1992

GUENÉE, B., *L'Occident aux XIVᵉ et XVᵉ siècles. Les Etats.* Paris 1971

GUENÉE B. & LEHOUX, FR., *Les Entrées royales françaises de 1328 à 1515.* Paris 1968

HALE, J.R., *War and Society.* Leicester 1985

HALL, J.A., ed., *States in History.* Oxford 1986

HART, M.C. 'T, *The making of a bourgeois state. War, politics and finance during the Dutch Revolt.* Manchester 1993

HAVERKAMP, A., *Aufbruch und Gestaltung. Deutschland 1056–1273.* München 1993²

HEERS, J., *Parties and political life in the medieval West.* Amsterdam 1977

HELLIE, R., *Enserfment and Military Change in Muscovy.* Chicago 1992

HILLENBRAND, E., ed., *Vita Caroli Quarti. Die Autobiographie Karels IV.* Stuttgart 1979

HINTZE, O., *Feudalismus – Kapitalismus.* G. Oestreich, ed., Göttingen 1970

HOBSBAWM, E.J., *The Age of Revolution. Europe 1789–1848.* Harmondsworth 1962

HOBSBAWM, E.J., *Industry and Empire.* Harmondsworth 1968

HOBSBAWM, E.J., *Nations and Nationalism since 1780: programme, myth, reality.* Cambridge 1990

HOBSBAWM, E.J., *The Age of Extremes. The short twentieth century 1914–1991* London 1995

HOCQUET, J.-C., *Le sel de la terre.* Paris 1989

HOLENSTEIN, A., *Die Huldigung der Untertanen. Rechtskultur und Herrschaftsordnung (800–1800).* Stuttgart 1991

HOUSLEY, N., *The Later Crusades from Lyons to Alcazar 1274–1580.* Oxford 1992

HOWARD, M., *War in European History.* Oxford 1976

HROCH, M., *Social preconditions of national revival in Europe: a comparative analysis of the social composition of patriotic groups among smaller European nations.* Cambridge 1985

KAEUPER, R.W., *War, Justice and Public Order.* Oxford 1988

KANTOROWICZ, E., *The King's Two Bodies: a Study in Mediaeval Political Theology.* Princeton 1957

KEMPERS, B., *Kunst, Macht und Mäzenatentum: der Beruf des Malers in der italienischen Renaissance.* München 1989

KENNEDY, P., *The Rise and Fall of the Great Powers. Economic Change and Military Conflict from 1500 to 2000.* New York 1987

KERR, D.A., ed., *Religion, State and Ethnic Groups.* New York 1992

KURGAN-VAN HENTENRYK, G., see BOGAERT, R. & VAN DER WEE, H., *A History of European Banking.* Antwerp 1994

KUZNETS, S.S., *Economic growth of nations: total output and production structure.* Cambridge 1971

KRYNEN, J., *L'Empire du roi. Idées et croyances politiques en France, XIIIᵉ–XVᵉ siècle.* Paris 1993

LADERO QUESADA, M.-A., 'Aristocratie et régime seigneurial dans l'Andalousie du XVᵉ siècle', *Annales. Economies, Sociétés, Civilisations,* 38, 1983

La Lana come materia prima. Firenze 1974

LE GOFF, J., 'A coronation Program for the Age of Saint Louis: the Ordo of 1250' in J.M. BAK, ed., *Coronations. Medieval and Early Modern Monarchic Ritual.* Berkeley 1990

LE ROY LADURIE, E., *L'Etat royal 1460–1610.* Paris 1987

LIS, C., SOLY, H., DAMME, D. VAN, *Op vrije voeten? Sociale politiek in West-Europa (1450–1914).* Leuven 1985

LLOBERA, J.R., *The God of Modernity. The development of nationalism in Western Europe.* Oxford 1994

LOMBARD-JOURDAN, A., *Fleur de lis et Oriflamme. Signes célestes du Royaume de France.* Paris 1991

MACFARLANE, A., *The Origins of English Individualism: the Family, Property and Social Transition.* Oxford 1978

MANN, M., *States, War and Capitalism.* Oxford 1988

MANN, M., *The Sources of Social Power,* 2 vols. Cambridge 1986–93

MCNEILL, W.H., *The Pursuit of Power. Technology, Armed Force and Society since A.D. 1000.* Chicago 1982

MCNEILL, W.H., *The Global Condition. Conquerors, Catastrophes and Community.* Princeton, New York 1992

MOLHO, A., *Florentine Public Finances in the Early Renaissance, 1400–1433.* Cambridge Mass. 1971

MOORE, R.I., *The Formation of a Persecuting Society. Power and Deviance in Western Europe, 950–1250.* Oxford 1987

MORAND, S.J., *Histoire de la Sainte-Chapelle du Palais.* Paris 1790

MORAW, P., *Von offener Verfassung zu gestalteter Verdichtung. Das Reich im späten Mittelalter, 1250 bis 1490.* Berlin 1985

MORAW, P., *Wahlreich und Territorien. Deutschland 1273–1500.* München 1993

MÖRKE, O., '"Konfessionalisierung" als politisch-soziales Strukturprinzip?', *Tijdschrift voor Sociale Geschiedenis,* 16, 1990

MUCHEMBLED, R., *L'invention de l'homme moderne. Sensibilités en France du XVᵉ au XVIIIᵉ siècle.* Paris 1994².

MUCHEMBLED, R., *Le Temps des supplices.* Paris 1992

NICOLAS, J., 'Pouvoir et contestation populaire à l'époque du second absolutisme', GENET, J.-PH., ed., *L'Etat Moderne: Genèse.* Paris 1990

O'BRIEN, P.K., *Power with Profit: The State and the Economy 1688–1815.* London 1991

O'BRIEN, P.K., 'The impact of the Revolutionary and Napoleonic wars, 1793–1815, on the Long-Run Growth of the British Economy', *Review,* 12, 1989

O'CALLAGHAN, J.F., *The Cortes of Castile-León 1188–1350.* Philadelphia 1989

ORMROD, W.M., 'The Crown and the English Economy, 1290–1348', CAMPBELL, B.M.S., ed., *Before the Black Death.* Machester 1991

PADOA SCHIOPPA, A., ed., *Legislation and Justice. Legal Instruments of Power.* Oxford 1997

PADOA SCHIOPPA, A., *Il diritto nella storia d'Europa. Il medioevo.* 1, Padova 1995

PARKER, G., *The Army of Flanders and the Spanish Road 1567–1659.* Cambridge 1972

PARKER, G., *The Military Revolution. Military Innovation and the Rise of the West, 1500–1800.* Cambridge 1988

PAVIOT, 'La Mappemonde attribuée à Jan van Eyck par Fàcio: une pièce à retirer du catalogue de son oeuvre', *Revue des Archéologues et Historiens d'Art de Louvain,* XXIV, 1991

PENNINGTON, K., *The Prince and the Law, 1200–1600. Sovereignty and Rights in the Western Legal Tradition.* Berkeley 1993

POLLARD, S., *The Integration of the European Economy since 1815.* London 1981 (1981a)

POLLARD, S., *Peaceful Conquest. The Industrialisation of Europe 1760–1970.* Oxford 1981 (1981b)

POLLARD, S., 'Regional and inter-regional economic development in Europe in the eighteenth and nineteenth centuries', *Debates and controversies in economic history.* Eleventh International Economic History Congress Milan 1994

PORTER, B.D., *War and the Rise of the State: the military Foundations of Modern Politics.* New York 1994

PRESS, V., 'Die Niederlande und das Reich in der frühen Neuzeit', BLOCKMANS, W.P. & VAN NUFFEL, H., eds., *Etat et Religion aux XVe et XVIe siècles.* Bruxelles 1986

PRESS, V., *Kriege und Krisen. Deutschland 1600–1715.* München 1991

PRINZ, F., *Grundlagen und Anfänge. Deutschland bis 1056.* München 1985

PRINZ, F., ed., *Deutsche Geschichte im Osten Europas. Böhmen und Mähren.* Berlin 1993

RACINE, P., 'Fêtes à la cour de Ludovic le More', *Publication du centre européen d'études Bourguignonnes (XIVe–XVIe siècle).* 34, 1994

REINHARD, W., ed., *Power Elites and State Building in Europe (13th–18th centuries).* Oxford 1996

RILEY-SMITH, L. & J., *The Crusades, idea and reality 1095–1274.* London 1981

The Rise of the State, Historical Research, 65, no. 157, 1992

ROSENBERG, H., *Bureaucracy, aristocracy and autocracy. The Prussian experience 1660–1815.* Boston 1958

RUCQUOI, A., ed., *Genèse médiévale de l'état moderne: la Castille et la Navarre (1250–1370).* Valladolid 1987

RYSTAD, G., ed., *Europe and Scandinavia.* Lund 1983

SAHLINS, P., *Boundaries. The Making of France and Spain in the Pyrenees.* Berkeley 1989

SAUERLÄNDER, W., 'Die Sainte-Chapelle du Palais Ludwigs der Heiligen', *Jahrbuch der Bayerischen Akademie der Wissenschaften,* 1977

SCHELLER, R.W., 'Imperial themes in art and literature of the early French renaissance: the period of Charles VIII', *Simiolus,* 12, 1981–82

SCHELLER, R.W., 'Gallia cisalpina: Louis XII and Italy 1499–1508', *Simiolus,* 15, 1985

SCHILLING, H., 'Nation und Konfession in der frühneuzeitlichen Geschichte', GARBER, K., ed., *Nation und Literatur im Europa der Frühen Neuzeit.* Tübingen 1987

SKINNER, Q., *The Foundations of Modern Political Thought.* 2 vols., Cambridge 1978

SKINNER, Q., 'Ambrogio Lorenzetti: the Artist as Political Philosopher', in H. BELLING & D. BLUME, ed., *Malerei und Stadtkultur in der Dantezeit.* München 1989

SKOCPOL, TH., *States & Social Revolutions.* Cambrige 1979

SOLY, H., 'Plechtige intochten in de steden van de Zuidelijke Nederlanden tijdens de overgang van Middeleeuwen naar Nieuwe Tijd: communicatie, propaganda, spektakel', *Tijdschrift voor Geschiedenis,* 97, 1984

SPRUYT, H., *The Sovereign State and its Competitors.* Princeton 1994

STEGMANN, A., ed., *Pouvoir et institutions en Europe au XVIeme siècle.* Paris 1987

STRAYER, J.R., *On the Medieval Origins of the Modern State.* Princeton 1970

STUURMAN, S., 'Duizend jaar staatsvorming in Europa', *Amsterdams Sociologisch Tijdschrift,* 20, 1993

STUURMAN, S., *Staatsvorming en politieke theorie.* Amsterdam 1995

THOMPSON, E.P., *The Making of the English Working Class.* Harmondsworth 1968

THOMPSON, I.A.A., *War and government in Habsburg Spain 1560–1620.* London 1976

TIERNEY, B., *Religion, Law, and the Growth of Constitutional Thought, 1150–1650.* Cambridge 1982

TILLY, C., ed., *The Formation of National States in Western Europe.* Princeton 1975

TILLY, C., *Coercion, Capital and European States, AD 990–1990.* Cambridge Mass. 1990

TILLY, C., *European Revolutions, 1492–1992.* Oxford 1993

TILLY, C. & BLOCKMANS, W.P., eds., *Cities and the Rise of States in Europe, A.D. 1000 to 1800.* Boulder 1994

TOPOLSKI, J., *An Outline History of Poland.* Warsaw 1986

TREXLER, R.C., *Public Life in Renaissance Florence.* New York 1980

ULLMANN, W., *A History of Political Thought: The Middle Ages.* London 1965

VILFAN, S., ed., *Ethnic Groups and Language Rights.* New York 1992

VRIES, J. DE, *European Urbanization 1500–1800.* Cambridge 1984

WAALE, M.J., *De Arkelse oorlog 1401–1412.* Hilversum 1990

WEBER, E., *Peasants into Frenchmen. The modernization of rural France 1870–1914.* Stanford 1976

WEE, H. VAN DER, see BOGAERT, R., KURGAN-VAN HENTENRYK, G., *A History of European Banking.* Antwerp 1994

WEISS, L. & HOBSON, J.M., *States and Economic Development. A Comparative Historical Analysis.* Cambridge 1995

WOOD, I., *The Merovingian Kingdoms 450–751.* London 1994

Index

A History of Power in Europe by Wim Blockmans
was published by Fonds Mercator of the Banque Paribas
in the Spring of nineteen hundred ninety seven
on the occasion of the 40th anniversary of the Treaty of Rome.
French, German, Dutch, Spanish and Italian editions were published simultaneously.

The texts were typeset in Linotype Didot and Stone Sans
by De Diamant Pers in Zandhoven (Belgium)
following a book design by Antoon De Vylder, who also designed the binding and jacket.

The colour separation was carried out by Photogravure De Schutter in Antwerp,
and the book was printed on Arjo-Wiggins' Satimat Club 150 g
by Gráficas Santamaría s.a. in Vitoria (Spain).
The book was bound by Atanes Lainez s.a. in Madrid
in Brillianta from Van Heek Textiles, Losser (The Netherlands).